The Basics of Financial Econometrics

The Basics of Financial Econometrics

Tools, Concepts, and Asset Management Applications

FRANK J. FABOZZI
SERGIO M. FOCARDI
SVETLOZAR T. RACHEV
BALA G. ARSHANAPALLI
WITH THE ASSISTANCE OF
MARKUS HÖCHSTÖTTER

WILEY

Library of Congress Cataloging-in-Publication Data:
ISBN 978-1-118-57320-4 (Hardcover)
ISBN 978-1-118-72743-0 (ePDF)
ISBN 978-1-118-72723-2 (ePub)

Typeset in 10/12 pt Sabon LT Std by Aptara

Printed in the United States of America.
10 9 8 7 6 5 4 3 2 1

FJF
To my son, Francesco, who I hope will read this book

SMF
To my family

STR
To my grandchildren Iliana, Zoya, and Svetlozar

BGA
To my wife Vidya and my children Priyanka and Ashish

Contents

Preface

Econometrics is the branch of economics that draws heavily on statistics for testing and analyzing economic relationships. Within econometrics, there are theoretical econometricians who analyze statistical properties of estimators of models. Several recipients of the Nobel Prize in Economic Sciences received the award as a result of their lifetime contribution to this branch of economics. To appreciate the importance of econometrics to the discipline of economics, when the first Nobel Prize in Economic Sciences was awarded in 1969, the co-recipients were two econometricians, Jan Tinbergen and Ragnar Frisch (the latter credited for first using the term econometrics in the sense that it is known today). The co-recipient of the 2013 Nobel Prize was Lars Peter Hansen who had made major contributions to the field of econometrics.

Further specialization within econometrics, and the area that directly relates to this book, is *financial econometrics*. As Jianqing Fan writes, the field of financial econometrics

> *uses statistical techniques and economic theory to address a variety of problems from finance. These include building financial models, estimation and inferences of financial models, volatility estimation, risk management, testing financial economics theory, capital asset pricing, derivative pricing, portfolio allocation, risk-adjusted returns, simulating financial systems, hedging strategies, among others.*[1]

Robert Engle and Clive Granger, two econometricians who shared the 2003 Nobel Prize in Economics Sciences, have contributed greatly to the field of financial econometrics.

Why this book? There is growing demand for learning and teaching implementation issues related to the deployment of financial econometrics in finance. The unique feature of this book is the focus on applications and implementation issues of financial econometrics to the testing of theories and development of investment strategies in asset management. The key messages expressed in this book come from our years of experience in

---

[1]"An Introduction to Financial Econometrics," Unpublished paper, Department of Operations Research and Financial Engineering, Princeton University, 2004.

designing, developing, testing, and operating financial econometric applications in asset management.

In this book we explain and illustrate the basic tools that are needed to implement financial econometric models. While many books describe the abstract mathematics of asset management, the unique feature of this book is to address the question of how to construct asset management strategies using financial econometric tools. We discuss all aspects of this process, including model risk, limits to the applicability of models, and the economic intuition behind models. We describe the critical issues using real life examples.

We start by discussing the process of applying financial econometrics to asset management. The three basic steps of model selection, estimation, and testing are discussed at length. We emphasize how in this phase economic intuition plays an important role. Before designing models we have to decide what phenomena we want to exploit in managing assets.

We then discuss the most fundamental financial econometric technique: regression analysis. Despite its apparent simplicity, regression analysis is a powerful tool the application of which requires careful consideration. We describe different types of regression analysis, including quantile regressions and regressions with categorical variables, their applicability, and the conditions under which regression fails. We discuss the robustness of regression analysis, introducing the concept and technique of robust regression. All concepts are illustrated with real-life examples.

Next, we analyze the dynamic behavior of time series, introducing vector and scalar autoregressive models. We formalize mean-reversion, introducing the concept of cointegration, and describe the heteroscedastic behavior of financial time series. We discuss the economic intuition behind each model, their estimation, and methods for parameter testing. We also analyze the limits of the applicability of autoregressive techniques, the advantage of exploiting mean reversion when feasible, and the model risk associated with autoregressive models. We again use real-life examples to illustrate.

Subsequently, we move to consider large portfolios and discuss the techniques used to model large numbers of simultaneous time series, in particular factor models and principal components analysis. The issues associated with the estimation and testing of large models and techniques to separate information from noise in large sets of mutually interacting time series are discussed.

Finally, we discuss the specific process of implementing a financial econometric model for asset management. We describe the various steps of this process and the techniques involved in making modeling decisions.

One important characteristic of model development today is the availability of good econometric software. Many building blocks of the process of implementing a financial econometric application are available as off-the-shelf software. Most technical tasks, from optimization to the estimation of regression and autoregressive models, are performed are performed by econometric software. Using these software tools has become common practice among those who develop financial applications. For this reason we do spend much time discussing computational issues. These are highly technical subjects that are handled by specialists. The general user and/or developer of econometric applications do not spend time in rewriting applications that are commercially available. For this reason we focus on the process of designing financial econometric models and we do not handle the computational aspects behind basic techniques.

Frank J. Fabozzi
Sergio M. Focardi
Svetlozar T. Rachev
Bala G. Arshanapalli

Acknowledgments

We are grateful to Markus Höchstötter for his assistance in the preparation of several chapters and Appendices A, B, and C. His contribution was of such significance that he is identified on the cover and title pages of this book.

Chapter 15 is coauthored with Dr. K. C. Ma of KCM Asset Management, and Professor of Finance and Director of the George Investments Institute and Roland George Investments Program at Stetson University.

We also thank a number of doctoral students in the Department of Applied Mathematics and Statistics at Stony Brook University, SUNY, for taking time from their studies to review and provide feedback for various chapters and appendices in this book. Below we have listed each student and the chapters/appendices reviewed:

Fangfei (Sophia) Dong	Chapters 2, 3, and 12
Tetsuo Kurosaki	Chapters 8, 9, 11, and 12
Tiantian Li	Chapter 13
Barret Shao	Chapters 7 and 12
Naoshi Tsuchida	Chapters 8, 9, and 12
Yuzhong (Marco) Zhang	Chapters 2, 3, and 12

About the Authors

Frank J. Fabozzi is Professor of Finance at EDHEC Business School and a member of the EDHEC Risk Institute. He has held various professorial positions at Yale and MIT. In the 2013–2014 academic year, he was appointed the James Wei Visiting Professor in Entrepreneurship at Princeton University and since 2011 has been a Research Fellow in the Department of Operations Research and Financial Engineering at the same institution. The editor of the *Journal of Portfolio Management* since 1986, Professor Fabozzi has authored and edited many books in asset management and quantitative finance. He serves on the advisory board of The Wharton School's Jacobs Levy Equity Management Center for Quantitative Financial Research, the Q Group Selection Committee, and from 2003 to 2011 on the Council for the Department of Operations Research and Financial Engineering at Princeton University. He is a Fellow of the International Center for Finance at Yale University. He is a trustee for the BlackRock family of closed-end funds. He is the CFA Institute's 2007 recipient of the C. Stewart Sheppard Award and an inductee into the Fixed Income Analysts Society Hall of Fame. Professor Fabozzi earned a PhD in Economics in September 1972 from the City University of New York and holds the professional designations of Chartered Financial Analyst (1977) and Certified Public Accountant (1982).

Sergio M. Focardi is a Visiting Professor at Stony Brook University, SUNY, where he holds a joint appointment in the College of Business and the Department of Applied Mathematics and Statistics. Prior to that, he was a Professor of Finance at the EDHEC Business School in Nice. Professor Focardi is a founding partner of the Paris-based consulting firm The Intertek Group. A member of the editorial board of the *Journal of Portfolio Management*, he has authored numerous articles and books on financial modeling and risk management including the following Wiley books: *Mathematical Methods in Finance* (2013), *Probability and Statistics for Finance* (2010), *Quantitative Equity Investing: Techniques and Strategies* (2010), *Robust Portfolio Optimization and Management* (2007), *Financial Econometrics* (2007), *Financial Modeling of the Equity Market* (2006), *The Mathematics of Financial Modeling and Investment Management* (2004), *Risk Management: Framework,*

Methods, and Practice (1998), and *Modeling the Markets: New Theories and Techniques* (1997). He also coauthored three monographs published by the Research Foundation of the CFA Institute: *Challenges in Quantitative Equity Management* (2008), *The Impact of the Financial Crisis on the Asset Management Industry* (2010), *Trends in Quantitative Finance* (2006). Professor Focardi holds a degree in Electronic Engineering from the University of Genoa and a PhD in Mathematical Finance and Financial Econometrics from the University of Karlsruhe.

Svetlozar (Zari) T. Rachev is holds a joint appointment at Stony Brook University, SUNY, as a professor in the Department of Applied Mathematics and Statistics and the College of Business. Previously he was Chair-Professor in Statistics, Econometrics, and Mathematical Finance at the Karlsruhe Institute of Technology (KIT) in the School of Economics and Business Engineering, and is now Professor Emeritus at the University of California, Santa Barbara in the Department of Statistics and Applied Probability. Professor Rachev has published 14 monographs, 10 handbooks, and special edited volumes, and over 300 research articles. His recently coauthored books published by Wiley in mathematical finance and financial econometrics include *Financial Models with Lèvy Processes and Volatility Clustering* (2011), *A Probability Metrics Approach to Financial Risk Measures* (2011), *Financial Econometrics: From Basics to Advanced Modeling Techniques* (2007), and *Bayesian Methods in Finance* (2008). He is cofounder of Bravo Risk Management Group specializing in financial risk-management software. Bravo Group was acquired by FinAnalytica for which he currently serves as Chief Scientist. Professor Rachev completed his PhD in 1979 from Moscow State (Lomonosov) University, and his Doctor of Science degree in 1986 from Steklov Mathematical Institute in Moscow.

Bala G. Arshanapalli is professor and Gallagher-Mills Chair of Business and Economics at Indiana University Northwest. Before joining Indiana University, Professor Arshanapalli was the Virginia and Harvey Hubbell Professor of Business and Finance at University of Bridgeport. He also held visiting appointments at Concordia University and Purdue University. He served on the board of Legacy Foundation. He serves on the editorial board of *International Journal of Bonds and Currency Derivatives* and *International Journal of Economics and Finance*. Professor Arshanapalli also served on the editorial board of *European Financial Management* and *International Journal of Operations and Quantitative Management*. His current research interests include asset allocation, retirement planning, and empirical methods in financial time series modeling. Professor Arshanapalli has published over 45 articles and his work has appeared in the *Journal of Risk and Uncertainty*, *Journal of Banking and Finance*, *International Journal of Money and Finance*, *Journal of Portfolio Management*, and *Industrial and Labor Relations Review*. He has consulted and taught executive development classes for nationally recognized companies. Professor Arshanapalli earned a PhD in Finance in 1988 from Northern Illinois University.

CHAPTER 1

Introduction

After reading this chapter you will understand:

- What the field of financial econometrics covers.
- The three steps in applying financial econometrics: model selection, model estimation, and model testing.
- What is meant by the data generating process.
- How financial econometrics is used in the various phases of investment management.

Financial econometrics is the science of modeling and forecasting financial data such as asset prices, asset returns, interest rates, financial ratios, defaults and recovery rates on debt obligations, and risk exposure. Some have described financial econometrics as the econometrics of financial markets. The development of financial econometrics was made possible by three fundamental enabling factors: (1) the availability of data at any desired frequency, including at the transaction level; (2) the availability of powerful desktop computers at an affordable cost; and (3) the availability of off-the-shelf econometric software. The combination of these three factors put advanced econometrics within the reach of most financial firms such as banks and asset management firms.

In this chapter, we describe the process and the application of financial econometrics. Financial econometrics is applied to either time series data, such as the returns of a stock, or cross-sectional data such as the market capitalization[1] of all stocks in a given universe at a given moment. With the progressive diffusion of high-frequency financial data and ultra high-frequency financial data, financial econometrics can now be applied to

---

[1] A firm's market capitalization, popularly referred to as "market cap," is a measure of the firm's size in terms of the total market value of its common stock. This is found by multiplying the number of common stock shares outstanding by the price per share of common stock.

larger databases making statistical analysis more accurate as well as providing the opportunity to investigate a wider range of issues regarding financial markets and investment strategies.[2]

FINANCIAL ECONOMETRICS AT WORK

Applying financial econometrics involves three key steps:

  Step 1. Model selection
  Step 2. Model estimation
  Step 3. Model testing

For asset managers, traders, and analysts, the above three steps should lead to results that can be used in formulating investment strategies. Formulating and implementing strategies using financial econometrics is the subject of the final chapter of this book, Chapter 15.

Below we provide a brief description of these three steps. More details are provided in later chapters. Model selection is the subject of Chapter 14 and model estimation is covered in Chapter 13.

Step 1: Model Selection

In the first step, model selection, the modeler chooses a family of models with given statistical properties. This entails the mathematical analysis of the model properties as well as financial economic theory to justify the model choice. It is in this step that the modeler decides to use, for example, an econometric tool such as regression analysis to forecast stock returns based on fundamental corporate financial data and macroeconomic variables.

In general, it is believed that one needs a strong economic intuition to choose models. For example, it is economic intuition that might suggest what factors are likely to produce good forecasting results, or under what conditions we can expect to find processes that tend to revert to some long-run mean. We can think of model selection as an adaptive process where

---

[2] Engle provides the following distinction between high-frequency financial data and ultra high-frequency data. Observations on financial variables such as prices that are taken daily or at a finer time scale are referred to as high-frequency financial data. Typically, such observations are regularly spaced over time. Ultra high-frequency financial data refers to time stamped transaction-by-transaction or tick-by-tick data which are irregularly spaced. See Robert F. Engle, "The Econometrics of Ultra-High Frequency Data," *Econometrica* 69, no. 1 (2000), 1–22.

economic intuition suggests some family of models which need, however, to pass rigorous statistical testing.

On the other hand, financial econometrics might also use an approach purely based on data. "Let the data speak" is the mantra of this approach. An approach purely based on data is called *data mining*. This approach might be useful but must be used with great care. Data mining is based on using very flexible models that adapt to any type of data and letting statistics make the selection. The risk is that one might capture special characteristics of the sample which will not repeat in the future. Stated differently, the risk is that one is merely "fitting noise." The usual approach to data mining is to constrain models to be simple, forcing models to capture the most general characteristics of the sample.

Hence, data mining has to be considered a medicine which is useful but which has many side effects and which should be administered only under strict supervision by highly skilled doctors. Imprudent use of data mining might lead to serious misrepresentations of risk and opportunities. On the other hand, a judicious use of data mining might suggest true relationships that might be buried in the data.

Step 2: Model Estimation

In general, models are embodied in mathematical expressions that include a number of parameters that have to be estimated from sample data, the second step in applying financial econometrics. Suppose that we have decided to model returns on a major stock market index such as the Standard & Poor's 500 (S&P 500) with a regression model, a technique that we discuss in later chapters. This requires the estimation of the regression coefficients, performed using historical data. Estimation provides the link between reality and models. We choose a family of models in the model selection phase and then determine the optimal model in the estimation phase.

There are two main aspects in estimation: finding estimators and understanding the behavior of estimators. Let's explain. In many situations we simply directly observe the magnitude of some quantity. For example, the market capitalization of firms is easily observed. Of course there are computations involved, such as multiplying the value of a stock by the number of outstanding stocks, but the process of computing market capitalization is essentially a process of direct observation.

When we model data, however, we cannot directly observe the parameters that appear in the model. For example, consider a very simple model of trying to estimate a linear relationship between the weekly return on General Electric (GE) stock and the return on the S&P 500. When we discuss the econometric technique known as simple linear regression analysis in Chapter 2, we will see the relationship of interest to use would be[3]

Return on GE stock = $\alpha + \beta$ (Return on S&P 500) + Error term

The two parameters in the above relationship are α and β and are referred to as regression coefficients. We can directly observe from trading data the information necessary to compute the return on both the GE stock and the S&P 500. However, we cannot directly observe the two parameters. Moreover, we cannot observe the error term for each week. The process of estimation involves finding estimators. Estimators are numbers computed from the data that approximate the parameter to be estimated.

Estimators are never really equal to the theoretical values of the parameters whose estimate we seek. Estimators depend on the sample and only approximate the theoretical values. The key problem in financial econometrics is that samples are generally small and estimators change significantly from sample to sample. This is a major characteristic of financial econometrics: samples are small, noise is very large, and estimates are therefore very uncertain. Financial econometricians are always confronted with the problem of extracting a small amount of information from a large amount of noise. This is one of the reasons why it is important to support econometric estimates with financial economic theory.

Step 3: Model Testing

As mentioned earlier, model selection and model estimation are performed on historical data. As models are adapted (or fitted) to historical data there is always the risk that the fitting process captures characteristics that are specific to the sample data but are not general and will not reappear in future samples. For example, a model estimated in a period of particularly high returns for stocks might give erroneous indications about the true average returns. Thus there is the need to test models on data different from the data on which the model was estimated. This is the third step in applying financial econometrics, model testing. We assess the performance of models on fresh data. This is popularly referred to as "backtesting."

A popular way of backtesting models is the use of moving windows. Suppose we have 30 years of past weekly return data for some stock and we want to test a model that forecasts one week ahead. We could estimate the model on the past 30 years minus one week and test its forecasting

---

[3] As explained in Chapter 2, this relationship for a stock is referred to as its characteristic line.

abilities on the last week. This method would have two major drawbacks. First, we would have only one forecast as a test; second, the model would be estimated on data that do not reflect the market situation today.

A sensible way to solve the problem of backtesting is to use samples formed from a shorter series of data (say, three or four years), estimate the model on the sample data, and then test the forecast on the week immediately following the sample data. We then move the window forward one week and we repeat the process. In this way, we can form a long series of test forecasts. Note two things about this procedure. First, for each window there is a strict separation of sample and testing data. Second, we do not test a single model, but a family of models that are reestimated in each window.

The choice of the length of the estimation window is a critical step. One must choose a window sufficiently long to ensure a reasonable estimation of the model. At the same time, the window must be sufficiently short so that the parameters don't change too much within the window.

THE DATA GENERATING PROCESS

The basic principles for formulating quantitative laws in financial econometrics are the same as those that have characterized the development of quantitative science over the last four centuries. We write mathematical models—relationships between different variables and/or variables in different moments and different places. The basic tenet of quantitative science is that there are relationships that do not change regardless of the moment or the place under consideration. For example, while sea waves might look like an almost random movement, in every moment and location the basic laws of hydrodynamics hold without change. Similarly, in financial markets, asset price behavior might appear to be random, but financial econometric laws should hold in every moment and for every asset class.[4]

There are similarities between financial econometric models and models of the physical sciences but there are also important differences. The physical sciences aim at finding immutable laws of nature; financial econometric

---

[4]In most developed countries, the four major asset classes are (1) common stocks, (2) bonds, (3) cash equivalents, and (4) real estate. Typically, an asset class is defined in terms of the following three investment characteristics that the members of an asset class have in common: (1) the major economic factors that influence the value of the asset class and, as a result, correlate highly with the returns of each member included in the asset class, (2) a similar risk and return characteristic, and (3) a common legal or regulatory structure. Based on this way of defining an asset class, the correlation between the returns of different asset classes would be low.

models model the economy or financial markets—artifacts subject to change. For example, U.S. financial markets in the form of stock exchanges have been in operation since May 1792 (the origin of the New York Stock Exchange). Since that time, stock exchanges in the United States—as well as throughout the world—have changed significantly both in the number of stocks listed and the type of trading. And the information available on transactions has also changed. Consider that in the 1950s, market participants had access only to daily closing prices and this typically was available the next day rather than at the close of the trading day; now we have instantaneous information on every single transaction. Because the economy and financial markets are artifacts subject to change, financial econometric models are not unique representations valid throughout time; they must adapt to the changing environment.

We refer to the mathematical model that represents future data in function of past and present data as the *data generating process* (DGP). If we know the DGP, we can generate data with the same statistical characteristics as our empirical data. If we know a DGP as a mathematical expression, we can implement computer programs that simulate data. These simulated data can be used to compute statistical quantities that would be difficult or even impossible to compute mathematically. Methods based on simulation techniques are generally called *Monte Carlo methods*.

APPLICATIONS OF FINANCIAL ECONOMETRICS TO INVESTMENT MANAGEMENT

Researchers investigating important issues in finance employ financial econometrics in their empirical analysis. The issues that they have tackled in finance cover critical issues in the fields of financial markets, corporate finance, and investment management. Many of the studies on financial markets have helped either formulate or discredit policies used by investors and regulators. Empirical studies of the impact of capital structure (i.e., the mix of debt and equity in the financing of a firm) decision, the dividend decision, and the stock-buyback decision using financial econometrics have provided a useful guide to senior corporate management and boards of directors in formulating corporate financial policy.

The most significant use of financial econometrics since the early 1990s has been in the field of investment management. It is an important part of the arsenal of tools used by quantitative asset management firms. Within the real world of investment management, financial econometrics has been used in the following tasks: asset allocation, portfolio construction, and portfolio risk management. Since the key real-world use of financial econometrics has been in investment management and many of the illustrations in this book are from this field, we conclude this chapter with a brief explanation of asset allocation, portfolio construction, and portfolio risk management.

Asset Allocation

A major activity in the investment management process is establishing policy guidelines to satisfy a client's investment objectives. Setting policy begins with the asset allocation decision. That is, a decision must be made as to how the funds to be invested should be distributed among the major asset classes.

The term "asset allocation" means different things to different people in different contexts. One can divide asset allocation into three types: (1) policy asset allocation, (2) dynamic asset allocation, and (3) tactical asset allocation.[5] The policy asset allocation decision can loosely be characterized as a long-term asset allocation decision, in which the investor seeks to assess an appropriate long-term "normal" asset mix that represents an ideal blend of controlled risk and enhanced return. In dynamic asset allocation, the asset mix is mechanistically shifted in response to changing market conditions. Once the policy asset allocation has been established, the investor can turn attention to the possibility of active departures from the normal asset mix established by policy. That is, suppose that the long-run asset mix is established as 40% stocks and 60% bonds. A departure from this mix under certain circumstances may be permitted. If a decision to deviate from this mix is based upon rigorous objective measures of value, it is often called tactical asset allocation. Tactical asset allocation broadly refers to active strategies that seek to enhance performance by opportunistically shifting the asset mix of a portfolio in response to the changing patterns of reward available in the capital markets. Notably, tactical asset allocation tends to refer to disciplined processes for evaluating prospective rates of return on various asset classes and establishing an asset allocation response intended to capture higher rewards.

Models used in each type of asset allocation described above rely on the forecasting of returns for the major asset classes and the expected future relationship among the asset classes. Broad-based market indexes are used to represent major asset classes. For U.S. common stock, this would typically mean forecasting returns for the S&P 500 index, and for bonds, the returns for the Barclays U.S. Aggregate Bond index.

---

[5] Robert D. Arnott and Frank J. Fabozzi, "The Many Dimensions of the Asset Allocation Decision," in *Active Asset Allocation*, ed. Robert D. Arnott and Frank J. Fabozzi (Chicago: Probus Publishing, 1992).

Forecasting for asset allocation goes beyond just forecasting returns. A fundamental principle of finance is that investors must accept a trade-off between risk and returns. Hence in asset allocation modeling, one must forecast risk and not only returns. The most fundamental ingredient to forecast risk is the covariance matrix. Hence, a fundamental component of portfolio formation is the estimation of the covariance matrix between the major asset classes.

Portfolio Construction

Selecting a portfolio strategy that is consistent with the investment objectives and investment policy guidelines of a client or an institution is a major activity in the investment management process. Portfolio strategies can be classified as either active or passive.

An *active portfolio strategy* uses available information and forecasting techniques to seek a better performance than a portfolio that is simply diversified broadly. Essential to all active strategies are expectations about the factors that have been found to influence the performance of an asset class. For example, with active common stock strategies this may include forecasts of future earnings, dividends, or price-earnings ratios. With bond portfolios that are actively managed, expectations may involve forecasts of future interest rates and sector spreads. Active portfolio strategies involving foreign securities may require forecasts of local interest rates and exchange rates.

Portfolio construction and optimization in active portfolio strategies require models for forecasting returns: There is no way to escape the need to predict future returns. In stock portfolios, we would need a forecast of the return for every candidate stock that a portfolio manager wants to consider for inclusion into the portfolio. Moreover, as explained in our discussion of asset allocation, risk must be forecasted in constructing a portfolio. The covariance matrix for the candidate assets must therefore be estimated.

A *passive portfolio strategy* involves minimal expectational input, and instead relies on diversification to match the performance of some market index. In effect, a passive strategy assumes that the marketplace will efficiently reflect all available information in the price paid for all assets.[6] Passive strategies eschew the need to forecast future returns of individual asset classes by investing in broad indexes. These strategies effectively shift the need to forecast to a higher level of analysis and to longer time horizons. Active strategies, however, form portfolios based on forecasts of future returns.

---

[6]Between these extremes of active and passive strategies, several strategies have sprung up that have elements of both. For example, the core of a portfolio may be passively managed while the balance is actively managed.

The most sophisticated models used in portfolio construction are factor risk models (or simply factor models) using the financial econometric tools of factor analysis and principal components analysis described in Chapter 12.

Portfolio Risk Management

Portfolio risk management can be broadly defined as a set of methods and techniques to set portfolio risk objectives, estimate the risk of a portfolio strategy, and take appropriate corrective measures if necessary. Portfolio risk itself can be defined in many different ways but essentially is a measurement of the uncertainty related to future returns. There is risk when there is the possibility that future returns, and therefore the value of future wealth, will deviate from expectations.

Portfolio management is essentially the management of the trade-off between risk and return. There are various analytical measures that can be used to identify the various risks of a portfolio such as standard deviation, value-at-risk, or conditional value-at-risk, tracking error, to name just a few. (These measures are described later in this book.) Often these measures must be estimated using the financial econometrics tools described in the chapters to follow. The larger asset management firms have an in-house risk group that monitors portfolio risk and provides at least daily the portfolio's risk exposure.

In portfolio management, the key risk is that the performance of the portfolio manager is below the return earned on a client-approved benchmark after adjusting for management fees. The benchmark could be any index such as the S&P 500 index or the Barclays Capital U.S. Aggregate Bond index. The key measure used in controlling a portfolio's risk is *tracking error*. Tracking error measures the dispersion of a portfolio's returns relative to the returns of its benchmark. That is, tracking error is the standard deviation of the portfolio's *active return*, where active return is defined as:

Active return = Portfolio's actual return – Benchmark's actual return

A portfolio created to match the benchmark (referred to as an index fund) that regularly has zero active returns (i.e., always matches its benchmark's actual return) would have a tracking error of zero. But an actively managed portfolio that takes positions substantially different from the benchmark would likely have large active returns, both positive and negative, and thus would have an annual tracking error of, say, 5% to 10%. By taking positions that differ from the benchmark is where the portfolio manager is making bets. For example, in common stock portfolio management this could involve one or more of the following factors: portfolio sensitivity to the benchmark (referred to as the portfolio beta), sector allocations that differ from the benchmark, style tilt (i.e., value versus growth stocks) that differs from the benchmark, and individual stock selections whose weight in the portfolio differs from that of the benchmark.

There are two types of tracking error: backward-looking tracking error and forward-looking tracking error. The former is obtained from a straightforward calculation based on the historical returns of a portfolio over some period of time. For example, suppose 52 weeks are computed for a portfolio return and the benchmark. An active return can then be calculated for each week and the annualized standard deviation can be calculated. The result is the backwark-looking tracking error. This tracking error, also referred to as an ex-post tracking error, is the result of the portfolio manager's decisions during those 52 weeks with respect to portfolio positioning issues.

One problem with a backward-looking tracking error is that it does not reflect the effect of current decisions by the portfolio manager on the future active returns and hence the future tracking error that may be realized. If, for example, the portfolio manager significantly changes the portfolio beta or sector allocations today, then the backward-looking tracking error that is calculated using data from prior periods would not accurately reflect the current portfolio risks going forward. That is, the backward-looking tracking error will have little predictive value and can be misleading regarding the portfolio's risks going forward.

The portfolio manager needs a forward-looking estimate of tracking error to more accurately reflect the portfolio risk going forward. The way this is done in practice is by using factor risk models, discussed in Chapter 12, that have defined the risks associated with a benchmark. Financial econometric tools analyzing the historical return data of the stocks in the benchmark index are used to obtain the factors and quantify their risks. Using the portfolio manager's current portfolio holdings, the portfolio's current exposure to the various factors can be calculated and compared to the benchmark's exposures to the same factors. Using the differential factor exposures and the risks of the factors, a forward-looking tracking error for the portfolio can be computed. This tracking error is also referred to as the predicted tracking error or ex-ante tracking error.

KEY POINTS

- Financial econometrics is the science of modeling and forecasting financial data.
- The three steps in applying financial econometrics are model selection, model estimation, and model testing.

- In model selection, the modeler chooses a family of models with given statistical properties. Financial economic theory is used to justify the model choice. The financial econometric tool used is determined in this step.
- Data mining is an approach to model selection based solely on the data and, although useful, must be used with great care because the risk is that the model selected might capture special characteristics of the sample which will not repeat in the future.
- In general, models are embodied in mathematical expressions that include a number of parameters that have to be estimated from sample data. Model estimation involves finding estimators and understanding the behavior of estimators.
- Model testing is needed because model selection and model estimation are performed on historical data and, as a result, there is the risk that the estimation process captures characteristics that are specific to the sample data used but are not general and will not necessarily reappear in future samples.
- Model testing involves assessing the model's performance using fresh data. The procedure for doing so is called backtesting and the most popular way of doing so is using a moving window.
- The data generating process refers to the mathematical model that represents future data in function of past and present data. By knowing the data generating process as a mathematical expression, computer programs that simulate data using Monte Carlo methods can be implemented and the data generated can be used to compute statistical quantities that would be difficult or even impossible to compute mathematically.
- Financial econometric techniques have been used in the investment management process for making decisions regarding asset allocation (i.e., allocation of funds among the major asset classes) and portfolio construction (i.e., selection of individual assets within an asset class). In addition, the measurement of portfolio risk with respect to risk factors that are expected to impact the performance of a portfolio relative to a benchmark are estimated using financial econometric techniques.

CHAPTER 2

Simple Linear Regression

After reading this chapter you will understand:

- How to estimate a simple linear regression.
- What is meant by the residual or error of a regression model.
- The distributional assumptions of a regression model.
- The assumptions about mean and variance of the error term in a regression model.
- How to measure the goodness-of-fit of a regression model.
- How to estimate a linear regression for a nonlinear relationship.

In this chapter, we introduce methods to express joint behavior of two variables. It is assumed that, at least to some extent, the behavior of one variable is the result of a functional relationship between the two variables. In this chapter, we introduce the linear regression model including its ordinary least squares estimation, and the goodness-of-fit measure for a regression. Although in future chapters covering econometric tools we will not focus on estimating parameters, we will do so here in order to see how some of the basic measures are calculated. We devote Chapter 13 to explaining the various methods for estimating parameters.

Before advancing into the theory of regression, we note the basic idea behind a regression. The essential relationship between the variables is expressed by the measure of scaled linear dependence, that is, correlation.

THE ROLE OF CORRELATION

In many applications, how two entities behave together is of interest. Hence, we need to analyze their joint distribution. In particular, we are interested in the joint behavior of those two entities, say x and y, linearly. The appropriate tool is given by the covariance of x and y. More exactly, we are interested in their correlation expressed by the correlation coefficient explained in Appendix A. Generally, we know that correlation assumes values between

–1 and 1 where the sign indicates the direction of the linear dependence. So, for example, a correlation coefficient of –1 implies that all pairs (x,y) are located perfectly on a line with negative slope. This is important for modeling the regression of one variable on the other. The strength of the intensity of dependence, however, is unaffected by the sign. For a general consideration, only the absolute value of the correlation is of importance. This is essential in assessing the extent of usefulness of assuming a linear relationship between the two variables.

When dealing with regression analysis, a problem may arise from data that seemingly are correlated, but actually are not. This is expressed by accidental comovements of components of the observations. This effect is referred to as a *spurious regression* and is discussed further in Chapter 10.

Stock Return Example

As an example, we consider monthly returns of the S&P 500 stock index for the period January 31, 1996, through December 31, 2003. The data are provided in Table 2.1. This time span includes 96 observations. To illustrate the linear dependence between the index and individual stocks, we take the monthly stock returns of an individual stock, General Electric (GE), covering the same period. The data are also given in Table 2.1. The correlation coefficient of the two series is $r^{monthly}_{S\&P500,GE} = 0.7125$ using the formula shown in Appendix A. This indicates a fairly strong correlation in the same direction between the stock index and GE. So, we can expect with some certainty that GE's stock moves in the same direction as the index. Typically, there is a positive correlation between stock price movement and a stock index.

For comparison, we also compute the correlation between these two series using weekly as well as daily returns from the same period. (The data are not shown here.) In the first case, we have $r^{weekly}_{S\&P500,GE} = 0.7616$ while in the latter, we have $r^{daily}_{S\&P500,GE} = 0.7660$. This difference in value is due to the fact that while the true correlation is some value unknown to us, the correlation coefficient as a statistic depends on the sample data.

REGRESSION MODEL: LINEAR FUNCTIONAL RELATIONSHIP BETWEEN TWO VARIABLES

So far, we have dealt with cross-sectional bivariate data understood as being coequal variables, x and y. Now we will present the idea of treating one variable as a reaction to the other where the other variable is considered to be exogenously given. That is, y as the *dependent variable* depends on the realization of the *explanatory variable*, x, also referred to as the *independent*

TABLE 2.1   Monthly Returns of the S&P 500 Stock Index and General Electric during the Period January 31, 1996, through December 31, 2003

	S&P 500	GE		S&P 500	GE		S&P 500	GE
Jan 31, '96	0.0321	0.0656	Sep 30, '98	0.0605	0.0077	May 31, '01	0.0050	0.0124
Feb 29, '96	0.0069	–0.015	Oct 30, '98	0.0772	0.1019	Jun 29, '01	–0.025	–0.002
Mar 29, '96	0.0078	0.0391	Nov 30, '98	0.0574	0.0343	Jul 31, '01	–0.010	–0.105
Apr 30, '96	0.0133	–0.006	Dec 31, '98	0.0548	0.1296	Aug 31, '01	–0.066	–0.056
May 31, '96	0.0225	0.0709	Jan 29, '99	0.0401	0.0307	Sep 28, '01	–0.085	–0.073
Jun 28, '96	0.0022	0.0480	Feb 26, '99	–0.032	–0.041	Oct 31, '01	0.0179	–0.017
Jul 31, '96	–0.046	–0.045	Mar 31, '99	0.0380	0.1050	Nov 30, '01	0.0724	0.0603
Aug 30, '96	0.0186	0.0121	Apr 30, '99	0.0372	–0.042	Dec 31, '01	0.0075	0.0474
Sep 30, '96	0.0527	0.0968	May 28, '99	–0.025	–0.032	Jan 31, '02	–0.015	–0.072
Oct 31, '96	0.0257	0.0622	Jun 30, '99	0.0530	0.1084	Feb 28, '02	–0.020	0.0443
Nov 29, '96	0.0708	0.0738	Jul 30, '99	–0.032	–0.030	Mar 28, '02	0.0360	–0.024
Dec 31, '96	–0.021	–0.042	Aug 31, '99	–0.006	0.0330	Apr 30, '02	–0.063	–0.163
Jan 31, '97	0.0595	0.0489	Sep 30, '99	–0.028	0.0597	May 31, '02	–0.009	–0.005
Feb 28, '97	0.0059	–0.004	Oct 29, '99	0.0606	0.1373	Jun 28, '02	–0.075	–0.058
Mar 31, '97	–0.043	–0.028	Nov 30, '99	0.0188	–0.037	Jul 31, '02	–0.082	0.1194
Apr 30, '97	0.0567	0.1154	Dec 31, '99	0.0562	0.1786	Aug 30, '02	0.0048	–0.056
May 30, '97	0.0569	0.0867	Jan 31, '00	–0.052	–0.141	Sep 30, '02	–0.116	–0.185
Jun 30, '97	0.0425	0.0757	Feb 29, '00	–0.020	–0.003	Oct 31, '02	0.0829	0.0390
Jul 31, '97	0.0752	0.0822	Mar 31, '00	0.0923	0.1754	Nov 29, '02	0.0555	0.0791
Aug 29, '97	–0.059	–0.109	Apr 28, '00	–0.031	0.0160	Dec 31, '02	–0.062	–0.097
Sep 30, '97	0.0517	0.0918	May 31, '00	–0.022	0.0099	Jan 31, '03	–0.027	–0.046
Oct 31, '97	–0.035	–0.044	Jun 30, '00	0.0236	0.0108	Feb 28, '03	–0.017	0.0488
Nov 28, '97	0.0436	0.1373	Jul 31, '00	–0.016	–0.023	Mar 31, '03	0.0083	0.0645
Dec 31, '97	0.0156	0.0002	Aug 31, '00	0.0589	0.1354	Apr 30, '03	0.0779	0.1469
Jan 30, '98	0.0100	0.0569	Sep 29, '00	–0.054	–0.012	May 30, '03	0.0496	–0.024
Feb 27, '98	0.0680	0.0038	Oct 31, '00	–0.004	–0.041	Jun 30, '03	0.0112	0.0077
Mar 31, '98	0.0487	0.1087	Nov 30, '00	–0.083	–0.096	Jul 31, '03	0.0160	–0.006
Apr 30, '98	0.0090	–0.010	Dec 29, '00	0.0040	–0.023	Aug 29, '03	0.0177	0.0407
May 29, '98	–0.019	–0.019	Jan 31, '01	0.0340	–0.028	Sep 30, '03	–0.012	0.0164
Jun 30, '98	0.0386	0.0881	Feb 28, '01	–0.096	0.0159	Oct 31, '03	0.0535	–0.025
Jul 31, '98	–0.011	–0.010	Mar 30, '01	–0.066	–0.087	Nov 28, '03	0.0071	–0.010
Aug 31, '98	–0.157	–0.105	Apr 30, '01	0.0740	0.1569	Dec 31, '03	0.0495	0.0848

variable or the *regressor*. In this context, the joint behavior described in the previous section is now thought of as y being some function of x and possibly some additional quantity. In other words, we assume a functional relationship between the two variables given by the equation

$$y = f(x) \tag{2.1}$$

which is an exact deterministic relationship.

However, we admit that the variation of y will be influenced by other quantities. Thus, we allow for some additional quantity representing a *residual term* that is uncorrelated with x, which is assumed to account for any movement of y unexplained by equation (2.1). Since it is commonly assumed that these residuals are normally distributed, and that x and the residuals are jointly normally distributed, assuming that residuals are uncorrelated is equivalent to assuming that the residuals are independent of x. (Note that x and the residuals are defined as joint normal when any linear combination of x and residuals has a normal distribution.) Hence, we obtain a relationship as modeled by the following equation

$$y = f(x) + \varepsilon \tag{2.2}$$

where the residual or error is given by ε.

In addition to being independent of anything else, the residual is modeled as having zero mean and some constant variance denoted by σ_e^2. A disturbance of this sort is considered to be some unforeseen information or shock. Assume a linear functional relationship,

$$f(x) = \alpha + \beta x \tag{2.3}$$

where the population parameters α and β are the vertical axis intercept and slope, respectively. With this assumption, equation (2.2) is called a *simple linear regression* or a *univariate regression*. We refer to the simple linear regression as a univariate regression because there is only one independent variable whereas a multiple linear regression (the subject of later chapters) is a regression with more than one independent variable. In the regression literature, however, a simple linear regression is sometimes referred to as a *bivariate regression* because there are two variables, one dependent and one independent.

The parameter β determines how much y changes with each unit change in x. It is the average change in y dependent on the average change in x one can expect. This is not the case when the relationship between x and y is not linear.

DISTRIBUTIONAL ASSUMPTIONS OF THE REGRESSION MODEL

The independent variable can be a deterministic quantity or a random variable. The first case is typical of an experimental setting where variables are controlled. The second case is typical in finance where we regress quantities over which we do not have any direct control, for example the returns of an individual stock or of some stock index.

The error terms (or residuals) in equation (2.2) are assumed to be independently and identically distributed (denoted by i.i.d.). The concept of independent and identical distribution means the following: First, independence guarantees that each error assumes a value that is unaffected by any of the other errors. So, each error is absolutely unpredictable from knowledge of the other errors. Second, the distributions of all errors are the same. Consequently, for each pair (x,y), an error or residual term assumes some value independently of the other residuals in a fashion common to all the other errors, under equivalent circumstances. The i.i.d. assumption is important if we want to claim that all information is contained in equation (2.1) and deviations from equation (2.1) are purely random. In other words, the residuals are *statistical noise* such that they cannot be predicted from other quantities. If the errors do not seem to comply with the i.i.d. requirement, then something would appear to be wrong with the model. Moreover, in that case, a lot of estimation results would be faulty.

The distribution identical to all residuals is assumed to have zero mean and constant variance, such that the mean and variance of y conditional on x are, respectively,

$$\mu_{y|x} = f(x) = \alpha + \beta x$$
$$\sigma^2_{y|x} = \sigma^2_e$$

$$(2.4)$$

In words, once a value of x is given, we assume that, on average, y will be exactly equal to the functional relationship. The only variation in equation (2.4) stems from the residual term. This is demonstrated in Figure 2.1. We can see the ideal line given by the linear function. Additionally, the disturbance terms are shown taking on values along the dash-dotted lines for each pair x and y. For each value of x, ε has the mean of its distribution located on the line $\alpha + \beta \cdot x$ above x. This means that, on average, the error term will have no influence on the value of y, $\bar{y} = \bar{f}(x)$ where the bar above a term denotes the average. The x is either exogenous and, hence, known such that $\bar{f}(x) = f(x)$ or x is some endogenous variable and thus $\bar{f}(x)$ is the expected value of $f(x)$.[1]

---

[1] Exogenous and endogenous variables are classified relative to a specific causal model. In regression analysis, a variable is said to be endogenous when it is correlated with the error term. An exogenous variable is a variable whose value is determined by states of other variables.

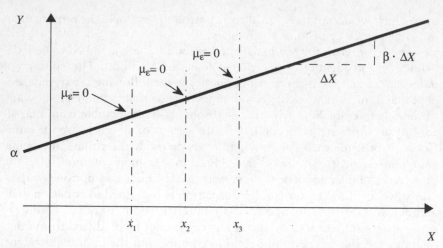

FIGURE 2.1   Linear Functional Relationship between x and y with Distribution of Disturbance Term

The distributions of all ε are identical. Typically, these distributions are assumed to follow *normal distributions*.[2] Consequently, the error terms are continuous variables that are normally distributed with zero mean and constant variance.[3]

ESTIMATING THE REGRESSION MODEL

Even if we assume that the linear assumption in equation (2.2) is plausible, in most cases we will not know the population parameters. We have to estimate the population parameters to obtain the sample regression parameters. An initial approach might be to look at the scatter plot of x and y and iteratively draw a line through the points until one believes the best line has been found. This approach is demonstrated in Figure 2.2. We have five pairs of bivariate data. While at first glance both lines appear reasonable, we do not know which one is optimal.

There might very well exist many additional lines that will look equally suited if not better. The intuition behind retrieving the best line is to balance

---

[2] See Appendix B for a discussion of the normal distribution.
[3] Formally, this is indicated by

$$\varepsilon \overset{iid}{\sim} N(0, \sigma^2)$$

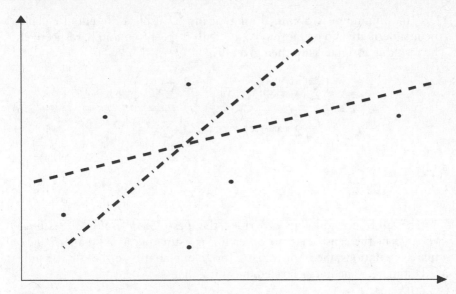

FIGURE 2.2   Scatter Plot of Data with Two Different Lines as Linear Fits

it such that the sum of the vertical distances of the y-values from the line is minimized. However, the problem is that in the scatter plot, positive errors will cancel out negative errors. To address this, one could just look at the absolute value of the error terms (i.e., ignore the negative sign). An alternative, and the method used here, is to square the error terms to avoid positive and negative values from canceling out.

What we need is a formal criterion that determines optimality of some linear fit. Measuring the errors in terms of the squared errors, we want to minimize the total sum of the squared errors. Mathematically, we have to solve

$$\min_{a,b} \sum_{i=1}^{n} (y_i - a - bx_i)^2 \tag{2.5}$$

That is, we need to find the estimates a and b of the parameters α and β, respectively, that minimize the total of the squared errors. Here, the error is given by the disturbance between the line and the true observation y. By taking the square, not only do we avoid having positive and negative errors from canceling out, but we also penalize larger disturbances more strongly than smaller ones.

The estimation approach given by equation (2.5) is the *ordinary least squares* (OLS) methodology, which we describe in more detail in Chapter 13.

Here, the minimum is obtained analytically by using differential calculus (the first derivative to be more specific) with respect to α and β, respectively. The resulting estimates are then given by

$$b = \frac{\frac{1}{n}\sum_{i=1}^{n}(x_i - \bar{x})(y_i - \bar{y})}{\frac{1}{n}\sum_{i=1}^{n}(x_i - \bar{x})^2} = \frac{\left(\frac{1}{n}\sum_{i=1}^{n}x_i y_i\right) - \overline{xy}}{\left(\frac{1}{n}\sum_{i=1}^{n}x_i^2\right) - \bar{x}^2} \tag{2.6}$$

and

$$a = \bar{y} - b\bar{x} \tag{2.7}$$

The OLS methodology provides the *best linear unbiased estimate approach* in the sense that no other linear estimate has a smaller sum of squared deviations. (See Appendix C for an explanation of best linear unbiased estimate.) The line is leveled, meaning that

$$\sum_{i=1}^{n} e_i = 0$$

That is, the disturbances cancel each other out. The line is balanced on a pivot point $(\bar{x}, \bar{y})$ like a scale.

If x and y were uncorrelated, b would be zero. Since there is no correlation between the dependent variable, y, and the independent variable, x, all variations in y would be purely random, that is, driven by the residuals, ε. The corresponding scatter plot would then look something like Figure 2.3 with the regression line extending horizontally. This is in agreement with a regression coefficient $\beta = 0$.

Application to Stock Returns

As an example, consider again the monthly returns from the S&P 500 index (indicated by x) and the GE stock (indicated by y) from the period between January 31, 1996, and December 31, 2003. We list the intermediate results of regressing the index returns on the stock returns as follows:

$$\bar{x} = 0.0062$$
$$\bar{y} = 0.0159$$
$$\frac{1}{96}\sum_{i=1}^{96} x_i y_i = 0.0027$$

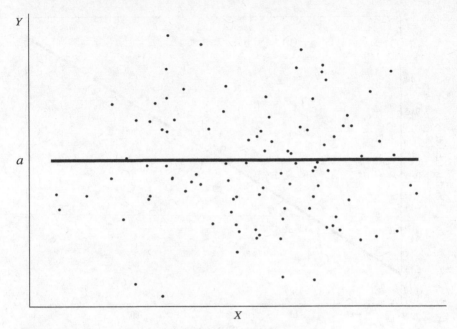

FIGURE 2.3   Regression of Uncorrelated Variables x and y

$$\frac{1}{96}\sum_{i=1}^{96} x_i^2 = 0.0025$$

$$\bar{x}^2 = 0.00004$$

(Here, we chose to present $\bar{x}^2$ with the more precise five digits since the rounded number of 0.0000 would lead to quite different results in the subsequent calculations.) Putting this into equations (2.6) and (2.7), we obtain

$$b = \frac{0.0027 - 0.0062 \cdot 0.0159}{0.0025 - 0.00004} = 1.0575$$
$$a = 0.0159 - 1.0575 \cdot 0.0062 = 0.0093$$

The estimated regression equation is then

$$\hat{y} = 0.0093 + 1.0575x$$

The scatter plot of the observation pairs and the resulting least squares regression line are shown in Figure 2.4.

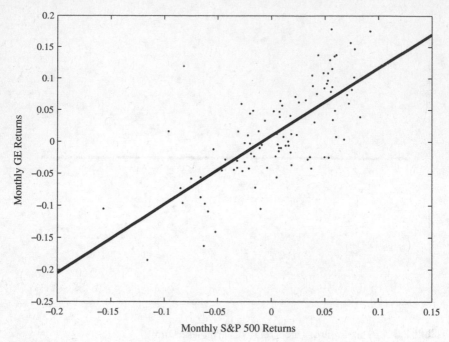

FIGURE 2.4 Scatter Plot of Observations and Resulting Least Squares Regression Line

From both the regression parameter b as well as the graphic, we see that the two variables tend to move in the same direction. This supports the previous finding of a positive correlation coefficient. This can be interpreted as follows. For each unit return in the S&P 500 index value, one can expect to encounter about 1.06 times per unit return in the GE stock return. The equivalent values for the parameters using weekly and daily returns are $b = 1.2421$ and $a = 0.0003$ and $b = 1.2482$ and $a = 0.0004$, respectively.

GOODNESS-OF-FIT OF THE MODEL

As explained in Appendix A, the correlation coefficient, denoted by $r_{x,y}$, is a measure of the linear association between x and y. We need to find a related measure to evaluate the suitability of the regression line that has been derived from the OLS estimation. For this task, the *coefficient of determination*, commonly denoted by R^2, is introduced. This goodness-of-fit measure calculates how much of the variation in y is caused or explained by the variation in x. If the percentage explained by the coefficient of determination is small, the fit might not be a too overwhelming one. Before introducing this measure formally, we present some initial considerations.

Consider the variance of the observations y by analyzing the *total sum of squares* of y around its means as given by

$$\text{SST} = \sum_{i=1}^{n} (y_i - \bar{y})^2 \tag{2.8}$$

The total sum of squares (denoted by SST) can be decomposed into the *sum of squares explained by the regression* (denoted by SSR) and the *sum of squared errors* (denoted by SSE). That is,[4]

$$\text{SST} = \text{SSR} + \text{SSE} \tag{2.9}$$

with

$$\text{SSR} = \sum_{i=1}^{n} (\hat{y}_i - \bar{y})^2 \tag{2.10}$$

and

$$\text{SSE} = \sum_{i}^{n} (y_i - \hat{y}_i)^2 = \sum_{i=1}^{n} e_i^2 = \sum_{i=1}^{n} y_i^2 - a\sum_{i=1}^{n} y_i - b\sum_{i=1}^{n} x_i y_i$$

where $\hat{y}$ is the estimated value for y from the regression.

The SSR is that part of the total sum of squares that is explained by the regression term $f(x)$. The SSE is the part of the total sum of squares that is unexplained or equivalently the sum of squares of the errors. Now, the coefficient of determination is defined by[5]

$$R^2 = \frac{\text{var}(f(x))}{s_y^2} = \frac{\frac{1}{n}\sum_{i=1}^{n}(a+bx_i-\bar{y})^2}{s_y^2} = \frac{\frac{1}{n}\sum_{i=1}^{n}(\hat{y}_i-\bar{y})^2}{\frac{1}{n}\sum_{i=1}^{n}(y_i-\bar{y})^2}$$

$$= \frac{\text{SSR}}{\text{SST}} = \frac{\text{SST}-\text{SSE}}{\text{SST}} = 1 - \frac{\text{SSE}}{\text{SST}}$$

---

[4]The notation explaining the R^2 differs. In some books, SSR denotes sum of squares of the residuals (where R represents residuals, i.e., the errors) and SSE denotes sum of squares explained by the regression (where E stands for explained). Notice that the notation is just the opposite of what we used.

[5]Note that the average means of y and $\hat{y}$ are the same (i.e., they are both equal to $\bar{y}$).

R^2 takes on values in the interval $[0,1]$. The meaning of $R^2 = 0$ is that there is no discernable linear relationship between x and y. No variation in y is explained by the variation in x. Thus, the linear regression makes little sense. If $R^2 = 1$, the fit of the line is perfect. All of the variation in y is explained by the variation in x. In this case, the line can have either a positive or negative slope and, in either instance, expresses the linear relationship between x and y equally well.[6] Then, all points (x_i, y_i) are located exactly on the line.[7]

As an example, we use the monthly return data from the previous example. Employing the parameters $b = 1.0575$ and $a = 0.0093$ for the regression $\hat{y}_t$ estimates, we obtain SST = 0.5259, SSR = 0.2670, and SSE = 0.2590. The $R^2 = 0.5076$ (0.2670/0.5259). For the weekly fit, we obtain, SST = 0.7620, SSR = 0.4420, and SSE = 0.3200 while got daily fit we have SST= 0.8305, SSR = 0.4873, and SSE = 0.3432. The coefficient of determination is $R^2 = 0.5800$ for weekly and $R^2 = 0.5867$ for daily.

Relationship between Coefficient of Determination and Correlation Coefficient

Further analysis of the R^2 reveals that the coefficient of determination is just the squared correlation coefficient, $r_{x,y}$, of x and y. The consequence of this equality is that the correlation between x and y is reflected by the goodness-of-fit of the linear regression. Since any positive real number has a positive and a negative root with the same absolute value, so does R^2. Hence, the extreme case of $R^2 = 1$ is the result of either $r_{x,y} = -1$ or $r_{x,y} = 1$. This is repeating the fact mentioned earlier that the linear model can be increasing or decreasing in x. The extent of the dependence of y on x is not influenced by the sign. As stated earlier, the examination of the absolute value of $r_{x,y}$ is important to assess the usefulness of a linear model.

With our previous example, we would have a perfect linear relationship between the monthly S&P 500 (i.e., x) and the monthly GE stock returns (i.e., y), if say, the GE returns were $y = 0.0085 + 1.1567x$. Then $R^2 = 1$ since all residuals would be zero and, hence, the variation in them (i.e., SSE would be zero, as well).

---

[6] The slope has to be different from zero, however, since in that case, there would be no variation in the y-values. As a consequence, any change in value in x would have no implication on y.

[7] In the next chapter we introduce another measure of goodness-of-fit called the adjusted $R2$. This measure takes into account not only the number of observations used to estimate the regression but also the number of independent variables.

TWO APPLICATIONS IN FINANCE

In this section, we provide two applications of simple linear regression analysis to finance.

Estimating the Characteristic Line of a Mutual Fund

We discuss now a model for security returns. This model suggests that security returns are decomposable into three parts. The first part is the return of a risk-free asset. The second is a security-specific component. And finally, the third is the return of the market in excess of the risk-free asset (i.e., *excess return*) which is then weighted by the individual security's covariance with the market relative to the market's variance. Formally, this is

$$R_S = R_f + \alpha_S + \beta_{S,M}\left(R_M - R_f\right) \tag{2.11}$$

where
R_S = the individual security's return
R_f = the risk-free return
α_S = the security-specific term
$\beta_{S,M} = \text{cov}(R_S, R_M) / \text{var}(R_M)$ = the so-called beta factor

The beta factor measures the sensitivity of the security's return to the market. Subtracting the risk-free interest rate R_f from both sides of equation (2.11) we obtain the expression for excess returns:

$$R_S - R_f = \alpha_S + \beta_{S,M}\left(R_M - R_f\right)$$

or equivalently

$$r_S = \alpha_S + \beta_{S,M} r_M \tag{2.12}$$

which is called the *characteristic line* where $r_S = R_S - R_f$ and $r_M = R_M - R_f$ denote the respective excess returns of the security and the market.

This form provides for a version similar to equation (2.3). The model given by equation (2.12) implies that at each time t, the observed excess return of some security $r_{S,t}$ is the result of the functional relationship

$$r_{S,t} = \alpha_S + \beta_{S,M} r_{M,t} + \varepsilon_{S,t} \tag{2.13}$$

So, equation (2.13) states that the actual excess return of some security S is composed of its specific return and the relationship with the market excess return, that is, $\alpha_s + \beta_{s,M} r_{M,t}$, and some error $\varepsilon_{S,t}$ from the exact model at time t. The term α_S is commonly interpreted as a measure of performance of the security above or below its performance that is attributed to the market performance. It is often referred to as the average abnormal performance of the stock.

While we have described the characteristic line for a stock, it also applies to any portfolio or funds. To illustrate, we use the monthly returns between January 1995 and December 2004, shown in Table 2.2, for two actual mutual funds which we refer to as fund A and fund B. Both are large capitalization stock funds. As a proxy for the market, we use the S&P 500 stock index.[8] For the estimation of the characteristic line in excess return form given by equation (2.12), we use the excess return data in Table 2.2. We employ the estimators in equations (2.6) and (2.7). For fund A, the estimated regression coefficients are $a_A = -0.21$ and $b_{A,S\&P500} = 0.84$, and therefore $r_A = -0.21 + 0.84 \cdot r_{S\&P500}$. For fund B we have $a_B = 0.01$ and $b_{B,S\&P500} = 0.82$, and therefore $r_B = 0.01 + 0.82 \cdot r_{S\&P500}$.

Interpreting the results of the performance measure estimates of a, we see that for fund A there is a negative performance relative to the market while it appears that fund B outperformed the market. For the estimated betas (i.e., b) for fund A, we determine that with each expected unit return of the S&P 500 index, fund A yields, on average, a return of 84% of that unit. This is roughly equal for fund B where for each unit return to be expected for the index, fund B earns a return of 82% that of the index. So, both funds are, as expected, positively related to the performance of the market.

The goodness-of-fit measure (R^2) is 0.92 for the characteristic line for fund A and 0.86 for fund B. So, we see that the characteristic lines for both mutual funds provide good fits.

Controlling the Risk of a Stock Portfolio

An asset manager who wishes to alter exposure to the market can do so by revising the portfolio's beta. This can be done by rebalancing the portfolio with stocks that will produce the target beta, but there are transaction costs associated with rebalancing a portfolio. Because of the leverage inherent in futures contracts, asset managers can use stock index futures to achieve a target beta at a considerably lower cost. Buying stock index futures will increase a portfolio's beta, and selling will reduce it.

The major economic function of futures markets is to transfer price risk from hedgers to speculators. *Hedging* is the employment of futures contracts as a substitute for a transaction to be made in the cash market. If the cash

---

[8]The data were provided by Raman Vardharaj. The true fund names cannot be revealed.

TABLE 2.2 Data to Estimate the Characteristic Line of Two Large-Cap Mutual Funds

Month	Market Excess Return	Excess Return for Fund A	Excess Return for Fund B
01/31/1995	2.18	0.23	0.86
02/28/1995	3.48	3.04	2.76
03/31/1995	2.50	2.43	2.12
04/30/1995	2.47	1.21	1.37
05/31/1995	3.41	2.12	2.42
06/30/1995	1.88	1.65	1.71
07/31/1995	2.88	3.19	2.83
08/31/1995	−0.20	−0.87	0.51
09/30/1995	3.76	2.63	3.04
10/31/1995	−0.82	−2.24	−1.10
11/30/1995	3.98	3.59	3.50
12/31/1995	1.36	0.80	1.24
01/31/1996	3.01	2.93	1.71
02/29/1996	0.57	1.14	1.49
03/31/1996	0.57	0.20	1.26
04/30/1996	1.01	1.00	1.37
05/31/1996	2.16	1.75	1.78
06/30/1996	0.01	−1.03	−0.40
07/31/1996	−4.90	−4.75	−4.18
08/31/1996	1.71	2.32	1.83
09/30/1996	5.18	4.87	4.05
10/31/1996	2.32	1.00	0.92
11/30/1996	.7.18	5.68	4.89
12/31/1996	−2.42	−1.84	−1.36
01/31/1997	5.76	3.70	5.28
02/28/1997	0.42	1.26	−1.75
03/31/1997	−4.59	−4.99	−4.18
04/30/1997	5.54	4.20	2.95
05/31/1997	5.65	4.76	5.56
06/30/1997	4.09	2.61	2.53
07/31/1997	7.51	5.57	7.49
08/31/1997	−5.97	−4.81	−3.70
09/30/1997	5.04	5.26	4.53
10/31/1997	−3.76	−3.18	−3.00
11/30/1997	4.24	2.81	2.52
12/31/1997	1.24	1.23	1.93
01/31/1998	0.68	−0.44	−0.70
02/28/1998	6.82	5.11	6.45
03/31/1998	4.73	5.06	3.45
04/30/1998	0.58	−0.95	0.64

(continued)

TABLE 2.2　(*continued*)

Month	Market Excess Return	Excess Return for Fund A	Excess Return for Fund B
05/31/1998	−2.12	−1.65	−1.70
06/30/1998	3.65	2.96	3.65
07/31/1998	−1.46	−0.30	−2.15
08/31/1998	−14.89	−16.22	−13.87
09/30/1998	5.95	4.54	4.40
10/31/1998	7.81	5.09	4.24
11/30/1998	5.75	4.88	5.25
12/31/1998	5.38	7.21	6.80
01/31/1999	3.83	2.25	2.76
02/28/1999	−3.46	−4.48	−3.36
03/31/1999	3.57	2.66	2.84
04/30/1999	3.50	1.89	1.85
05/31/1999	−2.70	−2.46	−1.66
06/30/1999	5.15	4.03	4.96
07/31/1999	−3.50	−3.53	−2.10
08/31/1999	−0.89	−1.44	−2.45
09/30/1999	−3.13	−3.25	−1.72
10/31/1999	5.94	5.16	1.90
11/30/1999	1.67	2.87	3.27
12/31/1999	5.45	8.04	6.65
01/31/2000	−5.43	−4.50	−1.24
02/29/2000	−2.32	1.00	2.54
03/31/2000	9.31	6.37	5.39
04/30/2000	−3.47	−4.50	−5.01
05/31/2000	−2.55	−3.37	−4.97
06/30/2000	2.06	0.14	5.66
07/31/2000	−2.04	−1.41	1.41
08/31/2000	5.71	6.80	5.51
09/30/2000	−5.79	−5.24	−5.32
10/31/2000	−0.98	−2.48	−5.40
11/30/2000	−8.39	−7.24	−11.51
12/31/2000	−0.01	2.11	3.19
01/31/2001	3.01	−0.18	4.47
02/28/2001	−9.50	−5.79	−8.54
03/31/2001	−6.75	−5.56	−6.23
04/30/2001	7.38	4.86	4.28
05/31/2001	0.35	0.15	0.13
06/30/2001	−2.71	−3.76	−1.61
07/31/2001	−1.28	−2.54	−2.10
08/31/2001	−6.57	−5.09	−5.72

TABLE 2.2 (*continued*)

Month	Market Excess Return	Excess Return for Fund A	Excess Return for Fund B
09/30/2001	−8.36	−6.74	−7.55
10/31/2001	1.69	0.79	2.08
11/30/2001	7.50	4.32	5.45
12/31/2001	0.73	1.78	1.99
01/31/2002	−1.60	−1.13	−3.41
02/28/2002	−2.06	−0.97	−2.81
03/31/2002	3.63	3.25	4.57
04/30/2002	−6.21	−4.53	−3.47
05/31/2002	−0.88	−1.92	−0.95
06/30/2002	−7.25	−6.05	−5.42
07/31/2002	−7.95	−6.52	−7.67
08/31/2002	0.52	−0.20	1.72
09/30/2002	−11.01	−9.52	−6.18
10/31/2002	8.66	3.32	4.96
11/30/2002	5.77	3.69	1.61
12/31/2002	−5.99	−4.88	−3.07
01/31/2003	−2.72	−1.73	−2.44
02/28/2003	−1.59	−0.57	−2.37
03/31/2003	0.87	1.01	1.50
04/30/2003	8.14	6.57	5.34
05/31/2003	5.18	4.87	6.56
06/30/2003	1.18	0.59	1.08
07/31/2003	1.69	1.64	3.54
08/31/2003	1.88	1.25	1.06
09/30/2003	−1.14	−1.42	−1.20
10/31/2003	5.59	5.23	4.14
11/30/2003	0.81	0.67	1.11
12/31/2003	5.16	4.79	4.69
01/31/2004	1.77	0.80	2.44
02/29/2004	1.33	0.91	1.12
03/31/2004	−1.60	−0.98	−1.88
04/30/2004	−1.65	−2.67	−1.81
05/31/2004	1.31	0.60	0.77
06/30/2004	1.86	1.58	1.48
07/31/2004	−3.41	−2.92	−4.36
08/31/2004	0.29	−0.44	−0.11
09/30/2004	0.97	1.09	1.88
10/31/2004	1.42	0.22	1.10
11/30/2004	3.90	4.72	5.53
12/31/2004	3.24	2.46	3.27

and futures markets move together, any loss realized by the hedger on one position (whether cash or futures) will be offset by a profit on the other position. When the profit and loss are equal, the hedge is called a *perfect hedge*.

A *short hedge* is used to protect against a decline in the future cash price of the underlying. To execute a short hedge, the hedger sells a futures contract. Consequently, a short hedge is also referred to as a *sell hedge*. By establishing a short hedge, the hedger has fixed the future cash price and transferred the price risk of ownership to the buyer of the contract.

As an example of an asset manager who would use a short hedge, consider a pension fund manager who knows that the beneficiaries of the fund must be paid a total of $30 million four months from now. This will necessitate liquidating a portion of the fund's common stock portfolio. If the value of the shares that she intends to liquidate in order to satisfy the payments to be made decline in value four months from now, a larger portion of the portfolio will have to be liquidated. The easiest way to handle this situation is for the asset manager to sell the needed amount of stocks and invest the proceeds in a Treasury bill that matures in four months. However, suppose that for some reason, the asset manager is constrained from making the sale today. She can use a short hedge to lock in the value of the stocks that will be liquidated.

A *long hedge* is undertaken to protect against rising prices of future intended purchases. In a long hedge, the hedger buys a futures contract, so this hedge is also referred to as a *buy hedge*. As an example, consider once again a pension fund manager. This time, suppose that the manager expects a substantial contribution from the plan sponsor four months from now, and that the contributions will be invested in the common stock of various companies. The pension fund manager expects the market price of the stocks in which she will invest the contributions to be higher in four months and, therefore, takes the risk that she will have to pay a higher price for the stocks. The manager can use a long hedge to effectively lock in a futwure price for these stocks now.

Hedging is a special case of controlling a stock portfolio's exposure to adverse price changes. In a hedge, the objective is to alter a current or anticipated stock portfolio position so that its beta is zero. A portfolio with a beta of zero should generate a risk-free interest rate. Thus, in a perfect hedge, the return will be equal to the risk-free interest rate. More specifically, it will be the risk-free interest rate corresponding to a maturity equal to the number of days until settlement of the futures contract.

Therefore, a portfolio that is identical to the S&P 500 (i.e., an S&P 500 index fund) is fully hedged by selling an S&P 500 futures contract with 60 days to settlement that is priced at its theoretical futures price. The return on this hedged position will be the 60-day, risk-free return. Notice what has been done. If a portfolio manager wanted to temporarily eliminate all exposure to the S&P 500, she could sell all the stocks and, with the funds received, invest in a Treasury bill. By using a stock index futures contract, the manager can eliminate exposure to the S&P 500 by hedging, and the hedged position will earn the same return as that on a Treasury bill. The manager thereby saves on the transaction costs associated with selling a stock portfolio. Moreover, when the manager wants to get back into the stock market, rather than having to incur the transaction costs associated with buying stocks, she simply removes the hedge by buying an identical number of stock index futures contracts.

In practice, hedging is not a simple exercise. When hedging with stock index futures, a perfect hedge can be obtained only if the return on the portfolio being hedged is identical to the return on the futures contract.

The effectiveness of a hedged stock portfolio is determined by:

- The relationship between the cash portfolio and the index underlying the futures contract.
- The relationship between the cash price and futures price when a hedge is placed and when it is lifted (liquidated).

The difference between the cash price and the futures price is called the *basis*. It is only at the settlement date that the basis is known with certainty. At the settlement date, the basis is zero. If a hedge is lifted at the settlement date, the basis is therefore known. However, if the hedge is lifted at any other time, the basis is not known in advance. The uncertainty about the basis at the time a hedge is to be lifted is called *basis risk*. Consequently, hedging involves the substitution of basis risk for price risk.

A stock index futures contract has a stock index as its underlying. Since the portfolio that an asset manager seeks to hedge will typically have different characteristics from the underlying stock index, there will be a difference in return pattern of the portfolio being hedged and the futures contract. This practice—hedging with a futures contract that is different from the underlying being hedged—is called *cross hedging*. In the commodity futures markets, this occurs, for example, when a farmer who grows okra hedges that crop by using corn futures contracts, because there are no exchange-traded futures contracts in which okra is the underlying. In the stock market, an asset manager who wishes to hedge a stock portfolio must choose the stock index, or combination of stock indexes, that best (but imperfectly) tracks the portfolio.

Consequently, cross hedging adds another dimension to basis risk, because the portfolio does not track the return on the stock index perfectly. Mispricing of a stock index futures contract is a major portion of basis risk and is largely random.

The foregoing points about hedging will be made clearer in the next illustrations.

Hedge Ratio   To implement a hedging strategy, it is necessary to determine not only which stock index futures contract to use, but also how many of the contracts to take a position in (i.e., how many to sell in a short hedge and buy in a long hedge). The number of contracts depends on the relative return volatility of the portfolio to be hedged and the return volatility of the futures contract. The *hedge ratio* is the ratio of volatility of the portfolio to be hedged and the return volatility of the futures contract.

It is tempting to use the portfolio's beta as a hedge ratio because it is an indicator of the sensitivity of a portfolio's return to the stock index return. It appears, then, to be an ideal way to adjust for the sensitivity of the return of the portfolio to be hedged. However, applying beta relative to a stock index as a sensitivity adjustment to a stock index futures contract assumes that the index and the futures contract have the same volatility. If futures were always to sell at their theoretical price, this would be a reasonable assumption. However, mispricing is an extra element of volatility in a stock index futures contract. Since the futures contract is more volatile than the underlying index, using a portfolio beta as a sensitivity adjustment would result in a portfolio being overhedged.

The most accurate sensitivity adjustment would be the beta of a portfolio relative to the futures contract. It can be shown that the beta of a portfolio relative to a futures contract is equivalent to the product of the portfolio relative to the underlying index and the beta of the index relative to the futures contract.[9] The beta in each case is estimated using regression analysis in which the data are historical returns for the portfolio to be hedged, the stock index, and the stock index futures contract.

The regression to be estimated is

$$r_P = a_P + B_{PI} r_I + e_P$$

where
r_P = the return on the portfolio to be hedged
r_I = the return on the stock index
B_{PI} = the beta of the portfolio relative to the stock index
a_P = the intercept of the relationship
e_P = the error term

---

[9] See Edgar E. Peters, "Hedged Equity Portfolios: Components of Risk and Return," *Advances in Futures and Options Research* 1, part B (1987): 75–92.

and

$$r_I = a_I + B_{IF}\, r_F + e_I$$

where r_F = the return on the stock index futures contract

B_{IF} = the beta of the stock index relative to the stock index futures contract

a_I = the intercept of the relationship

e_I = the error term

Given B_{PI} and B_{IF}, the minimum risk hedge ratio can then be expressed as

$$\text{Hedge ratio} = B_{PI} \times B_{IF}$$

The R^2 of the regression will indicate how good the estimated relationship is, and thereby allow the asset manager to assess the likelihood of success of the proposed hedge.

The number of contracts needed can be calculated using the following three steps after B_{PI} and B_{IF} are estimated:

Step 1. Determine the equivalent market index units of the market by dividing the market value of the portfolio to be hedged by the current index price of the futures contract:

$$\text{Equivalent market index units} = \frac{\text{Market value of the protfolio to be hedged}}{\text{Current index value of the futures contract}}$$

Step 2. Multiply the equivalent market index units by the hedge ratio to obtain the beta-adjusted equivalent market index units:

Beta-adjusted equivalent market index units
= Hedge ratio × Equivalent market index units

or

Beta-adjusted equivalent market index units
= $B_{PI} \times B_{IF} \times$ Equiv5alent market index units

Step 3. Divide the beta-adjusted equivalent units by the multiple specified by the stock index futures contract:

$$\text{Number of contracts} = \frac{\text{Beta-adjusted equivalent market index units}}{\text{Multiple of the contract}}$$

We will use two examples to illustrate the implementation of a hedge and the risks associated with hedging.

Illustration 1 Consider a portfolio manager on January 30, 2009, who is managing a $100 million portfolio that is identical to the S&P 500. The manager wants to hedge against a possible market decline. More specifically, the manager wants to hedge the portfolio until February 27, 2009. To hedge against an adverse market move during the period January 30, 2009, to February 27, 2009, the portfolio manager decides to enter into a short hedge by selling the S&P 500 futures contracts that settled in March 2009. On January 30, 2009, the March 2009 futures contract was selling for 822.5.

Since the portfolio to be hedged is identical to the S&P 500, the beta of the portfolio relative to the index (B_{PI}) is, of course, 1. The beta relative to the futures contract (B_{IF}) was estimated to be 0.745. Therefore, the number of contracts needed to hedge the $100 million portfolio is computed as follows:

Step 1.

$$\text{Equivalent market index units} = \frac{\$100,000,000}{822.5} = \$121,581$$

Step 2.

$$\text{Beta-adjusted equivalent market index units} = 1 \times 0.745 \times \$121,581$$
$$= \$90,578$$

Step 3. The multiple for the S&P 500 contract is 250. Therefore,

$$\text{Number of contracts to be sold} = \frac{\$90,578}{\$250} = 362$$

This means that the futures position was equal to $74,500,000 (362 × $250 × 822.5). On February 27, 2009, the hedge was removed. The portfolio that mirrored the S&P 500 had lost $10,993,122. At the time the hedge was lifted, the March 2009 S&P 500 contract was selling at 734.2. Since the contract was sold on January 30, 2009, for 822.5 and bought back on February 27, 2009, for 734.2, there was a gain of 88.3 index units per contract. For the 362 contracts, the gain was $7,997,994 (88.3 × $250 × 362). This results in a smaller loss of $2,995,129 ($7,997,994 gain on the futures position and $10,993,122 loss on the portfolio). The total transaction costs for the futures position would have been less than $8,000. Remember, had the asset manager not hedged the position, the loss would have been $10,993,122.

Let's analyze this hedge to see not only why it was successful, but also why it was not a perfect hedge. As explained earlier, in hedging, basis risk is substituted for price risk. Consider the basis risk in this hedge. At the time the hedge was placed, the cash index was at 825.88, and the futures contract was selling at 822.5. The basis was equal to 3.38 index units (the cash index of 825.88 minus the futures price of 822.5). At the same time, it was calculated that, based on the cost of carry, the theoretical basis was 1.45 index units. That is, the theoretical futures price at the time the hedge was placed should have been 824.42. Thus, according to the pricing model, the futures contract was mispriced by 1.92 index units.

When the hedge was removed at the close of February 27, 2009, the cash index stood at 735.09, and the futures contract at 734.2. Thus, the basis changed from 3.38 index units at the time the hedge was initiated to 0.89 index units (735.09 − 734.2) when the hedge was lifted. The basis had changed by 2.49 index units (3.38 − 0.89) alone, or $622.5 per contract (2.49 times the multiple of $250). This means that the basis alone cost $225,538 for the 362 contracts ($622.5 × 362). The index dropped 90.79 index units, for a gain of $22,698 per contract, or $8,223,532. Thus, the futures position cost $225,538 due to the change in the basis risk, and $8,223,532 due to the change in the index. Combined, this comes out to be the $7,997,994 gain in the futures position.

Illustration 2   We examined basis risk in the first illustration. Because we were hedging a portfolio that was constructed to replicate the S&P 500 index using the S&P 500 futures contract, there was no cross-hedging risk. However, most portfolios are not matched to the S&P 500. Consequently, cross-hedging risk results because the estimated beta for the price behavior of the portfolio may not behave as predicted by B_{PI}. To illustrate this situation, suppose that an asset manager owned all the stocks in the Dow Jones Industrial Average (DJIA) on January 30, 2009. The market value of the portfolio held was $100 million. Also assume that the portfolio manager wanted to hedge the position against a decline in stock prices from January 30, 2009, to February 27, 2009, using the March 2009 S&P 500 futures contract. Since the S&P 500 futures September contract is used here to hedge a portfolio of DJIA to February 27, 2009, this is a cross hedge.

Information about the S&P 500 cash index and futures contract when the hedge was placed on January 30, 2009, and when it was removed on February 27, 2009, was given in the previous illustration. The beta of the index relative to the futures contract (B_{IF}) was 0.745. The DJIA in a regression analysis was found to have a beta relative to the S&P 500 of 1.05 (with an R-squared of 93%). We follow the three steps enumerated above to obtain the number of contracts to sell:

Step 1.

$$\text{Equivalent market index units} = \frac{\$100,000,000}{822.5} = \$121,581$$

Step 2.

Beta-adjusted equivalent market index units $= 1.05 \times 0.745 \times \$121,581$
$$= \$95,106$$

Step 3. The multiple for the S&P 500 contract is 250. Therefore,

$$\text{Number of contracts to be sold} = \frac{\$95,106}{250} = 380$$

During the period of the hedge, the DJIA actually lost \$11,720,000. This meant a loss of 11.72% on the portfolio consisting of the component stocks of the DJIA. Since 380 S&P 500 futures contracts were sold and the gain per contract was 88.3 points, the gain from the futures position was \$8,388,500 (\$88.3 × 380 × 250). This means that the hedged position resulted in a loss of \$3,331,500, or equivalently, a return of −3.31%.

We already analyzed why this was not a perfect hedge. In the previous illustration, we explained how changes in the basis affected the outcome. Let's look at how the relationship between the DJIA and the S&P 500 Index affected the outcome. As stated in the previous illustration, the S&P 500 over this same period declined in value by 10.99%. With the beta of the portfolio relative to the S&P 500 Index (1.05), the expected decline in the value of the portfolio based on the movement in the S&P 500 was 11.54% (1.05 × 10.99%). Had this actually occurred, the DJIA portfolio would have lost only \$10,990,000 rather than \$11,720,000, and the net loss from the hedge would have been \$2,601,500, or −2.6%. Thus, there is a difference of a \$730,000 loss due to the DJIA performing differently than predicted by beta.

LINEAR REGRESSION OF A NONLINEAR RELATIONSHIP

Sometimes, the original variables do not allow for the concept of a linear relationship. However, the assumed functional relationship is such that a transformation $h(y)$ of the dependent variable y might lead to a linear function between x and the transform, h. This is demonstrated by hypothetical data in Figure 2.5, where the y-values appear to be the result of some exponential function of the x-values. The original data pairs in Table 2.3 are indicated by the $\bigcirc$ symbols in Figure 2.5.

We assume that the functional relationship is of the form

$$y = \alpha e^{\beta x} \tag{2.14}$$

TABLE 2.3 Values of Exponential Relationship between x and y Including Least Squares Regression Fit, $\hat{y}$

x	y	$\hat{y}$
0.3577	1.5256	1.4900
1.0211	2.8585	2.8792
3.8935	49.1511	49.8755
4.3369	76.5314	77.4574
4.6251	102.0694	103.1211
5.7976	329.5516	330.3149
5.9306	376.3908	376.9731
7.1745	1305.7005	1296.2346
7.1917	1328.3200	1318.5152
7.5089	1824.2675	1806.7285

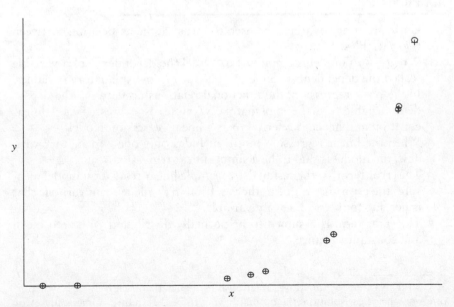

FIGURE 2.5 Least Squares Regression Fit for Exponential Functional Relationship

To linearize equation (2.14), we have the following natural logarithm transformation of the y-values to perform:

$$\ln y = \ln \alpha + \beta x \qquad (2.15)$$

Linear Regression of Exponential Data

We estimate using OLS the $\ln y$ on the x-values to obtain $\ln a = 0.044$ and $b = 0.993$. Retransformation yields the following functional equation:

$$\hat{y} = a \cdot e^{b \cdot x} = 1.045 \cdot e^{0.993 \cdot x} \qquad (2.16)$$

The estimated $\hat{y}$-values from equation (2.16) are represented by the + symbol in Figure 2.5 and in most cases lie exactly on top of the original data points. The coefficient of determination of the linearized regression is given by approximately $R^2 = 1$ which indicates a perfect fit. Note that this is the least squares solution to the linearized problem in equation (2.15) and not the originally assumed functional relationship. The regression parameters for the original problem obtained in some fashion other than via linearization may provide an even tighter fit with an R^2 even closer to one.[10]

KEY POINTS

- Correlation or covariance is used to measure the association between two variables.
- A regression model is employed to model the dependence of a variable (called the dependent variable) on one (or more) explanatory variables.
- In the basic regression, the functional relationship between the dependent variable and the explanatory variables is expressed as a linear equation and hence is referred to as a linear regression model.
- When the linear regression model includes only one explanatory variable, the model is said to be a simple linear regression.
- The error term, or the residual, in a simple linear regression model measures the error that is due to the variation in the dependent variable that is not due to the explanatory variable.
- The error term is assumed to be normally distributed with zero mean and constant variance.

---

[10]As noted earlier, for functional relationships higher than of linear order, there is often no analytical solution, the optima having to be determined numerically or by some trial-and-error algorithms.

- The parameters of a simple linear regression model are estimated using the method of ordinary least squares and provides a best linear unbiased estimate of the parameter.
- The coefficient of determination, denoted by R^2, is a measure of the goodness-of-fit of the regression line. This measure, which has a value that ranges from 0 to 1, indicates the percentage of the total sum of squares explained by the explanatory variable in a simple linear regression.

CHAPTER 3

Multiple Linear Regression

After reading this chapter you will understand:

- What a multiple linear regression model is.
- The assumptions about the error terms in a multiple linear regression model.
- How the regression coefficients of the model are estimated.
- The three steps necessary in designing a regression model: specification, fitting/estimating, and diagnosis.
- The tests used for determining the significance of the model and each independent variable.

It is often the case in finance that it is necessary to analyze more than one variable simultaneously. In Chapter 2, we explained how to estimate a linear dependence between two variables using the linear regression method. When there is only one independent variable, the regression model is said to be a simple linear regression or a univariate regression.

Univariate modeling in many cases is not sufficient to deal with real problems in finance. The behavior of a certain variable of interest sometimes needs to be explained by two or more variables. For example, suppose that we want to determine the financial or macroeconomic variables that affect the monthly return on the Standard & Poor's 500 (S&P 500) index. Let's suppose that economic and financial theory suggest that there are 10 such explanatory variables. Thus we have a setting of 11 dimensions—the return on the S&P 500 and the 10 explanatory variables.

In this chapter and in the next, we explain the multiple linear regression model to explain the linear relationship between several independent variables and some dependent variable we observe. As in the univariate case (i.e., simple linear regression) discussed in Chapter 2, the relationship between the variables of interest may not be linear. However, that can be handled by a suitable transformation of the variables.

THE MULTIPLE LINEAR REGRESSION MODEL

The *multiple linear regression model* for the population is of the form

$$y = \beta_0 + \beta_1 x_1 + \beta_2 x_2 + \ldots + \beta_k x_k + \varepsilon \tag{3.1}$$

where we have β_0 = constant intercept

$\beta_1, \ldots, \beta_k$ = regression coefficients of k explanatory or independent variables

β = model error

In vector notation, given samples of dependent and explanatory or independent variables, we can represent equation (3.1) as

$$y = X\beta + \varepsilon \tag{3.2}$$

where y is an $n \times 1$ column vector consisting of the n observations of the dependent variable, that is,

$$y = \begin{pmatrix} y_1 \\ \vdots \\ y_n \end{pmatrix} \tag{3.3}$$

where X is a $n \times (k + 1)$ matrix consisting of n observations of each of the k independent variables and a column of ones to account for the vertical intercepts β_0 such that

$$X = \begin{pmatrix} 1 & x_{11} & \ldots & x_{1k} \\ 1 & x_{21} & & x_{2k} \\ \vdots & \vdots & & \vdots \\ 1 & x_{n1} & \ldots & x_{nk} \end{pmatrix} \tag{3.4}$$

The $(k+1)$ regression coefficients including intercept are given by the $k+1$ column vector:

$$\beta = \begin{pmatrix} \beta_0 \\ \vdots \\ \beta_k \end{pmatrix} \tag{3.5}$$

Each observation's residual is represented in the column vector ε:

$$\varepsilon = \begin{pmatrix} \varepsilon_1 \\ \vdots \\ \varepsilon_n \end{pmatrix} \tag{3.6}$$

The regression coefficient of each independent variable given in equation (3.5) represents the average change in the dependent variable per unit change in the independent variable with the other independent variables held constant.

ASSUMPTIONS OF THE MULTIPLE LINEAR REGRESSION MODEL

For the multiple linear regression model, we make the following three assumptions about the error terms:

Assumption 1. The regression errors are normally distributed with zero mean.

Assumption 2. The variance of the regression errors (σ_ε^2) is constant.

Assumption 3. The error terms from different points in time are independent such that $\varepsilon_t \neq \varepsilon_{t+d}$ for any $d \neq 0$ are independent for all t.

Formally, we can restate the above assumptions in a concise way as

$$\varepsilon_i \overset{i.i.d.}{\sim} N\left(0, \sigma^2\right)$$

Furthermore, the residuals are assumed to be uncorrelated with the independent variables. In the next chapter, we describe how to deal with situations when these assumptions are violated.

ESTIMATION OF THE MODEL PARAMETERS

Since the model is not generally known for the population, we need to estimate it from some sample. Thus, the estimated regression is

$$\hat{y} = b_0 + b_1 x_1 + b_2 x_2 + \cdots + b_k x_k \tag{3.7}$$

The matrix notation analogue of equation (3.7) is

$$y = \hat{y} + e = Xb + e \tag{3.8}$$

which is similar to equation (3.2) except the model's parameters and error terms are replaced by their corresponding estimates, b and e.

The independent variables $x_1, \ldots, x_k$ are thought to form a space of dimension k. Then, with the y-values, we have an additional dimension such that our total dimensionality is $k + 1$. The estimated model generates values on a k-multidimensional *hyperplane*, which expresses the functional linear relationship between the dependent and independent variables. The estimated hyperplane is called a *regression hyperplane*. In the univariate case, this is simply the regression line of the $\hat{y}$ estimates stemming from the one single independent variable x.[1]

Each of the k coefficients determines the slope in the direction of the corresponding independent variable. In the direction of the $k + 1$st dimension of the y-values, we extend the estimated errors, $e = y - \hat{y}$. At each y-value, these errors denote the distance between the hyperplane and the observation of the corresponding y-value.

To demonstrate this, we consider some variable y. Suppose, we also have a two-dimensional variable x with independent components x_1 and x_2. Hence, we have a three-dimensional space as shown in Figure 3.1. For y, we have three observations, y_1, y_2, and y_3. The hyperplane for equation (3.7) formed

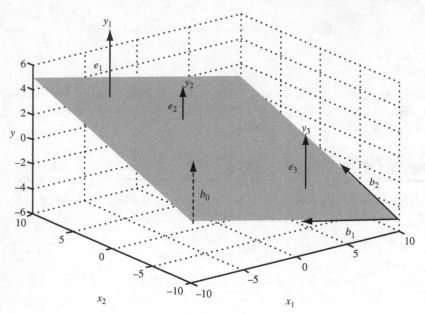

FIGURE 3.1 Vector Hyperplane and Residuals

---

[1]In general, the hyperplane formed by the linear combination of the x-values is always one dimension less than the overall dimensionality.

by the regression is indicated by the gray plane. The intercept b_0 is indicated by the dashed arrow while the slopes in the directions of x_1 and x_2 are indicated by the arrows b_1 and b_2, respectively.[2] Now, we extend vertical lines between the hyperplane and the observations, e_1, e_2, and e_3, to show by how much we have missed approximating the observations with the hyperplane.

Generally, with the ordinary least squares regression method described in Chapter 2, the estimates are, again, such that $\Sigma(y - \hat{y})^2$ is minimized with respect to the regression coefficients. For the computation of the regression estimates, we need to indulge somewhat in matrix computation. If we write the minimization problem in matrix notation, finding the vector β that minimizes the squared errors looks like[3]

$$\sum_{i=1}^{n}(y_i - \hat{y})^2 = (y - X\beta)^T(y - X\beta) \tag{3.9}$$

Differential calculus and matrix algebra lead to the optimal regression coefficient estimates and estimated residuals given by

$$b = \left(X^T X\right)^{-1} X^T y \tag{3.10}$$

and

$$e = y - X^T b = y - \hat{y} \tag{3.11}$$

where b in equation (3.10) and e in equation (3.11) are $(k + 1) \times 1$ and $n \times 1$ column vectors, respectively. One should not worry however if this appears rather complicated and very theoretical. Most statistical software have these computations implemented and one has to just insert the data for the variables and select some least squares regression routine to produce the desired estimates according to equation (3.10).

DESIGNING THE MODEL

Although in the previous chapter we introduced the simple linear regression model, we did not detail the general steps necessary for the design of

---

[2]The arrow b_0 is dashed to indicate that it extends from our point of view vertically from the point (0,0,0) behind the hyperplane.

[3]The transpose and matrix inverse are explained in Appendix D. When we use the matrix inverse, we implicitly assume the matrix of interest to be full rank, a requirement for the inversion of a matrix.

the regression and its evaluation. This building process consists of three steps:

1. Specification
2. Fitting/estimating
3. Diagnosis

In the specification step, we need to determine the dependent and independent variables. We have to make sure that we do not include independent variables that seem to have nothing to do with the dependent variable. More than likely, in dealing with a dependent variable that is a financial variable, financial and economic theory will provide a guide to what the relevant independent variables might be. Then, after the variables have been identified, we have to gather data for all the variables. Thus, we obtain the vector y and the matrix X. Without defending it theoretically here, it is true that the larger the sample, the better the quality of the estimation. Theoretically, the sample size n should at least be one larger than the number of independent variables k. A rule of thumb is, at least, four times k.

The fitting or estimation step consists of constructing the functional linear relationship expressed by the model. That is, we need to compute the correlation coefficients for the regression coefficients. We perform this even for the independent variables to test for possible interaction between them as explained in the next chapter. The estimation, then, yields so-called point estimates of the dependent variable for given values of the independent variables.[4]

Once we have obtained the estimates for equation (3.10), we can move on to evaluating the quality of the regression with respect to the given data. This is the diagnosis step.

DIAGNOSTIC CHECK AND MODEL SIGNIFICANCE

As just explained, diagnosing the quality of some model is essential in the building process. Thus we need to set forth criteria for determining model quality. If, according to some criteria, the fit is determined to be insufficient, we might have to redesign the model by including different independent variables.

We know from the previous chapter the goodness-of-fit measure is the coefficient of determination (denoted by R^2). We will use that measure here as well. As with the univariate regression, the coefficient of determination measures the percentage of variation in the dependent variable explained by all of the independent variables employed in the regression. The R^2 of the

---

[4]This is in contrast to a range or interval of values as given by a confidence interval. Appendix C explains what a confidence interval is.

multiple linear regression is referred to as the *multiple coefficient of determination*. We reproduce its definition from Chapter 2 here:

$$R^2 = \frac{\text{SSR}}{\text{SST}}$$ (3.12)

where   SSR = sum of squares explained by the regression model
       SST = total sum of squares

Following the initial assessment, one needs to verify the model by determining its statistical significance. To do so, we compute the overall model's significance and also the significance of the individual regression coefficients. The estimated regression errors play an important role as well. If the standard deviation of the regression errors is found to be too large, the fit could be improved by an alternative. The reason is that too much of the variance of the dependent y is put into the residual variance s^2. Some of this residual variance may, in fact, be the result of variation in some independent variable not considered in the model so far. And a final aspect is testing for the interaction of the independent variables that we discuss in the next chapter.

Testing for the Significance of the Model

To test whether the entire model is significant, we consider two alternative hypotheses. The first, our null hypothesis H_0, states that all regression coefficients are equal to zero, which means that none of the independent variables play any role. The alternative hypothesis H_1, states that at least one coefficient is different from zero. More formally,

$H_0 : \beta_0 = \beta_1 = \ldots = \beta_k = 0$

$H_1 : \beta_j \neq 0$ for at least one $j \in \{1, 2, \ldots, k\}$

In the case of a true null hypothesis, the linear model with the independent variables we have chosen does not describe the behavior of the dependent variable. To perform the test, we carry out an *analysis of variance* (ANOVA) *test*. In this context, we compute the F-statistic defined by

$$F = \frac{\dfrac{\text{SSR}}{k}}{\dfrac{\text{SSE}}{n-k-1}} = \frac{\text{MSR}}{\text{MSE}}$$ (3.13)

where SSE = unexplained sum of squares

TABLE 3.1 ANOVA Component Pattern

	df	SS	MS	F	p-Value of F
Regression	k	SSR	$MSR = \dfrac{SSR}{k}$	$\dfrac{MSR}{MSE}$	
Residual	$n - k - 1$	SSE	$MSE = \dfrac{SSE}{n-k-1}$		
Total	$n - 1$	SST			

SSE was defined in the previous chapter but in the multiple linear regression case $\hat{y}$ is given by equation (3.7) and the error terms by equation (3.11).

The degrees of freedom of the SSR equal the number of independent variables, $d_n = k$, while the degrees of freedom of the SSE are $d_d = n - k - 1$.[5] The MSR and MSE are the *mean squares of regression* and *mean squared errors*, respectively, obtained by dividing the sum of squared deviations by their respective degrees of freedom. All results necessary for the ANOVA are shown in Table 3.1.

If the statistic is found significant at some predetermined level (i.e., $p_F < \alpha$), the model does explain some variation of the dependent variable y.[6]

We ought to be careful not to overdo it; that is, we should not create a model more complicated than necessary. A good guideline is to use the simplest model suitable. Complicated and refined models tend to be inflexible and fail to work with different samples. In most cases, they are poor models for forecasting purposes. So, the best R^2 is not necessarily an indicator of the most useful model. The reason is that one can artificially increase R^2 by including additional independent variables into the regression. But the resulting seemingly better fit may be misleading. One will not know the true quality of the model if one evaluates it by applying it to the same data used for the fit. However, often if one uses the fitted model for a different set of data, the weakness of the overfitted model becomes obvious.

---

[5] In total, the SST is chi-square distributed with $n - 1$ degrees of freedom. See Appendix B for an explanation of the chi-square test.

[6] Alternatively, one can check whether the test statistic is greater than the critical value, that is, $F > F_\alpha$.

It is for this reason that a redefined version of the coefficient of determination is needed and is called the *adjusted R-squared* (or *adjusted* R^2) given by

$$R^2_{adj} = 1 - \left(1 - R^2\right)\left(\frac{n-1}{n-k-1}\right) \tag{3.14}$$

This adjusted goodness-of-fit measure incorporates the number of observations, n, as well as the number of independent variables, k, plus the constant term in the denominator $(n - k - 1)$. For as long as the number of observations is very large compared to k, R^2 and R^2_{adj} are approximately the same.[7] However, if the number k of independent variables included increases, the R^2_{adj} drops noticeably compared to the original R^2. One can interpret this new measure of fit as penalizing excessive use of independent variables. Instead, one should set up the model as parsimoniously as possible. To take most advantage of the set of possible independent variables, one should consider those that contribute a maximum of explanatory variation to the regression. That is, one has to balance the cost of additional independent variables and reduction in the adjusted R^2.

Testing for the Significance of the Independent Variables

Suppose we have found that the model is significant. Now, we turn to the test of significance for individual independent variables. Formally, for each of the k independent variables, we test

$$H_0 : \beta_j = 0 \qquad H_1 : \beta_j \neq 0$$

conditional on the other independent variables already included in the regression model.

The appropriate test would be the t-test, given by

$$t_j = \frac{b_j - 0}{s_{b_j}} \tag{3.15}$$

---

[7]For instance, inserting $k = 1$ into equation (3.14) we obtain

$$R^2_{adj} = \frac{(n-2)R^2 + R^2 - 1}{n-2} = R^2 - \frac{1 - R^2}{n-2}$$

which, for large n, is only slightly less than R^2.

with $n - k - 1$ degrees of freedom. The value b_j is the sample estimate of the jth regression coefficient and s_{b_j} is the *standard error of the coefficient estimate*.

The standard error of each coefficient is determined by the estimate of the variance matrix of the entire vector β, given by

$$s^2 \left(X^T X \right)^{-1} \tag{3.16}$$

which is a matrix multiplied by the univariate *standard error of the regression*, s^2. The latter is given by

$$s^2 = \frac{e^T e}{n-k-1} = \frac{\text{SSE}}{n-k-1} \tag{3.17}$$

SSE was previously defined and the degrees of freedom are determined by the number of observations, n, minus the number of independent parameters, k, and minus one degree of freedom lost on the constant term. Hence, we obtain $n - k - 1$ degrees of freedom. The jth diagonal element of equation (3.16), then, is the standard error of the jth regression coefficient used in equation (3.15).[8] This test statistic in equation (3.15) needs to be compared to the critical values of the tabulated t-distribution with $n - k - 1$ degrees of freedom at some particular significance level α, say 0.05. So, if the test statistic should exceed the critical value then the independent variable is said to be statistically significant. Equivalently, the p-value of equation (3.15) would then be less than α.

The *F*-Test for Inclusion of Additional Variables

Suppose we have $k - 1$ independent variables in the regression. The goodness-of-fit is given by R_1^2. If we want to check whether it is appropriate to add another independent variable to the regression model, we need a test statistic measuring the improvement in the goodness-of-fit due to the additional variable. Let R^2 denote the goodness-of-fit of the regression after the additional independent variable has been included into the regression. Then the improvement in the explanatory power is given by $R^2 - R_1^2$, which is chi-square distributed with one degree of freedom. Because $1 - R^2$ is chi-square distributed with $n - k - 1$ degrees of freedom, the statistic

$$F_1 = \frac{R^2 - R_1^2}{\dfrac{1 - R^2}{n-k-1}} \tag{3.18}$$

---

[8]Typically one does not have to worry about all these rather mathematical steps because statistical software performs these calculations. The interpretation of that output must be understood.

is F-distributed with 1 and $n - k - 1$ degrees of freedom under the null hypothesis that the true model consists of $k - 1$ independent variables only.[9]

APPLICATIONS TO FINANCE

We conclude this chapter with several applications of multiple linear regression analysis to various areas in finance.

Estimation of Empirical Duration

A commonly used measure of the interest-rate sensitivity of a financial asset's value is its *duration*. For example, if a financial asset has a duration of 5, this means that the financial asset's value or price will change by roughly 5% for a 100 basis point change in interest rates. The direction of the change is determined by the sign of the duration. Specifically, if the duration is positive, the price will decline when the relevant interest rate increases but will increase if the relevant interest rate declines. If the duration is negative, the price will increase if the relevant interest rate increases and fall if the relevant interest rate decreases.

So suppose that a common stock selling at a price of $80 has a duration of +5 and that the relevant interest rate that affects the value of the common stock is currently 6%. This means that if that relevant interest rate increases by 100 basis points (from 6% to 7%), the price of the financial asset will decrease by 5%. Since the current price is $80, the price will decline by about $4. On the other hand, if the relevant interest rate decreases from 6% to 5% (a decline of 100 basis points), the price will increase by roughly 5% to $84.

Duration can be estimated by using a valuation model or empirically by estimating from historical returns the sensitivity of the asset's value to changes in interest rates. When duration is measured in the latter way, it is referred to as *empirical duration*. Since it is estimated using regression analysis, it is sometimes referred to as *regression-based duration*.

The dependent variable in the regression model is the percentage change in the value of the asset. We will not use individual assets in our illustration. Rather we will use sectors of the financial market and refer to them as assets. Effectively, these sectors can be viewed as portfolios that are comprised of the components of the index representing the sector. The assets we will estimate the duration for are (1) the electric utility sector of the S&P 500 index, (2) the commercial bank sector of the S&P 500 index, and (3) Lehman U.S.

---

[9]The chi-square and the F-distribution are covered in Appendix A and Appendix B, respectively.

Aggregate Bond Index.[10] For each of these indexes the dependent variable is the monthly return in the value of the index. The time period covered is from October 1989 to November 2003 (170 observations) and the monthly return observations are given in the last three columns of Table 3.2.[11]

Let's begin with just one independent variable, an interest rate index. We will use the monthly change in the U.S. Treasury yield index as measured by the Lehman Treasury Index as the relevant interest rate variable. The monthly values are given in the second column of Table 3.2. Notice that the data are reported as the percentage difference between two months. So, if in one month the value of the Treasury yield index is 7.20% and in the next month it is 7.70%, the value for the observation is 0.50%. In finance, a basis point is equal to 0.0001 or 0.01% so that 0.50% is equal to 50 basis points. A 100 basis point change in interest rates is 1% or 1.00. We'll need to understand this in order to interpret the regression results.

The simple linear regression model (i.e., the univariate case) is

$$y = b_0 + b_1 x_1 + e$$

where y = the monthly return of an index
          x_1 = the monthly change in the Treasury yield

The estimated regression coefficient b_1 is the empirical duration. To understand why, if we substitute 100 basis points in the above equation for the monthly change in the Treasury yield, the regression coefficient b_1 tells us that the estimated change in the monthly return of an index will be b_1. This is precisely the definition of empirical duration: the approximate change in the value of an asset for a 100 basis point change in interest rates.

The estimated regression coefficient and other diagnostic values are reported in Table 3.3. Notice that negative values for the estimated empirical duration are reported. In practice, however, the duration is quoted as a positive value. Let's look at the results for all three assets.

For the electric utility sector, the estimated regression coefficient for b_1 is −4.5329, suggesting that for a 100 basis point change in Treasury yields, the percentage change in the value of the stocks comprising this sector will

---

[10]The Lehman U.S. Aggregate Bond Index is now the Barclays Capital U.S. Aggregate Bond Index.

[11]The data for this illustration were supplied by David Wright of Northern Illinois University.

TABLE 3.2   Data for Empirical Duration Illustration

Month	Change in Lehman Bros Treasury Yield	S&P 500 Return	Monthly Returns for		
			Electric Utility Sector	Commercial Bank Sector	Lehman U.S. Aggregate Bond Index
Oct-1989	−0.46	−2.33	2.350	−11.043	2.4600
Nov-1989	−0.10	2.08	2.236	−3.187	0.9500
Dec-1989	0.12	2.36	3.794	−1.887	0.2700
Jan-1990	0.43	−6.71	−4.641	−10.795	−1.1900
Feb-1990	0.09	1.29	0.193	4.782	0.3200
Mar-1990	0.20	2.63	−1.406	−4.419	0.0700
Apr-1990	0.34	−2.47	−5.175	−4.265	−0.9200
May-1990	−0.46	9.75	5.455	12.209	2.9600
Jun-1990	−0.20	−0.70	0.966	−5.399	1.6100
Jul-1990	−0.21	−0.32	1.351	−8.328	1.3800
Aug-1990	0.37	−9.03	−7.644	−10.943	−1.3400
Sep-1990	−0.06	−4.92	0.435	−15.039	0.8300
Oct-1990	−0.23	−0.37	10.704	−10.666	1.2700
Nov-1990	−0.28	6.44	2.006	18.892	2.1500
Dec-1990	−0.23	2.74	1.643	6.620	1.5600
Jan-1991	−0.13	4.42	−1.401	8.018	1.2400
Feb-1991	0.01	7.16	4.468	12.568	0.8500
Mar-1991	0.03	2.38	2.445	5.004	0.6900
Apr-1991	−0.15	0.28	−0.140	7.226	1.0800
May-1991	0.06	4.28	−0.609	7.501	0.5800
Jun-1991	0.15	−4.57	−0.615	−7.865	−0.0500
Jul-1991	−0.13	4.68	4.743	7.983	1.3900
Aug-1991	−0.37	2.35	3.226	9.058	2.1600
Sep-1991	−0.33	−1.64	4.736	−2.033	2.0300
Oct-1991	−0.17	1.34	1.455	0.638	1.1100
Nov-1991	−0.15	−4.04	2.960	−9.814	0.9200
Dec-1991	−0.59	11.43	5.821	14.773	2.9700
Jan-1992	0.42	−1.86	−5.515	2.843	−1.3600
Feb-1992	0.10	1.28	−1.684	8.834	0.6506
Mar-1992	0.27	−1.96	−0.296	−3.244	−0.5634
Apr-1992	−0.10	2.91	3.058	4.273	0.7215
May-1992	−0.23	0.54	2.405	2.483	1.8871
Jun-1992	−0.26	−1.45	0.492	1.221	1.3760
Jul-1992	−0.41	4.03	6.394	−0.540	2.0411
Aug-1992	−0.13	−2.02	−1.746	−5.407	1.0122
Sep-1992	−0.26	1.15	0.718	1.960	1.1864
Oct-1992	0.49	0.36	−0.778	2.631	−1.3266
Nov-1992	0.26	3.37	−0.025	7.539	0.0228
Dec-1992	−0.24	1.31	3.247	5.010	1.5903
Jan-1993	−0.36	0.73	3.096	4.203	1.9177
Feb-1993	−0.29	1.35	6.000	3.406	1.7492
Mar-1993	0.02	2.15	0.622	3.586	0.4183
Apr-1993	−0.10	−2.45	−0.026	−5.441	0.6955

(continued)

TABLE 3.2   *(continued)*

Month	Change in Lehman Bros Treasury Yield	S&P 500 Return	Monthly Returns for		
			Electric Utility Sector	Commercial Bank Sector	Lehman U.S. Aggregate Bond Index
May-1993	0.25	2.70	−0.607	−0.647	0.1268
Jun-1993	−0.30	0.33	2.708	4.991	1.8121
Jul-1993	0.05	−0.47	2.921	0.741	0.5655
Aug-1993	−0.31	3.81	3.354	0.851	1.7539
Sep-1993	0.00	−0.74	−1.099	3.790	0.2746
Oct-1993	0.05	2.03	−1.499	−7.411	0.3732
Nov-1993	0.26	−0.94	−5.091	−1.396	−0.8502
Dec-1993	0.01	1.23	2.073	3.828	0.5420
Jan-1994	−0.17	3.35	−2.577	4.376	1.3502
Feb-1994	0.55	−2.70	−5.683	−4.369	−1.7374
Mar-1994	0.55	−4.35	−4.656	−3.031	−2.4657
Apr-1994	0.37	1.30	0.890	3.970	−0.7985
May-1994	0.18	1.63	−5.675	6.419	−0.0138
Jun-1994	0.16	−2.47	−3.989	−2.662	−0.2213
Jul-1994	−0.23	3.31	5.555	2.010	1.9868
Aug-1994	0.12	4.07	0.851	3.783	0.1234
Sep-1994	0.43	−2.41	−2.388	−7.625	−1.4717
Oct-1994	0.18	2.29	1.753	1.235	−0.0896
Nov-1994	0.37	−3.67	2.454	−7.595	−0.2217
Dec-1994	0.11	1.46	0.209	−0.866	0.6915
Jan-1995	−0.33	2.60	7.749	6.861	1.9791
Feb-1995	−0.41	3.88	−0.750	6.814	2.3773
Mar-1995	0.01	2.96	−2.556	−1.434	0.6131
Apr-1995	−0.18	2.91	3.038	4.485	1.3974
May-1995	−0.72	3.95	7.590	9.981	3.8697
Jun-1995	−0.05	2.35	−0.707	0.258	0.7329
Jul-1995	0.14	3.33	−0.395	4.129	−0.2231
Aug-1995	−0.10	0.27	−0.632	5.731	1.2056
Sep-1995	−0.05	4.19	6.987	5.491	0.9735
Oct-1995	−0.21	−0.35	2.215	−1.906	1.3002
Nov-1995	−0.23	4.40	−0.627	7.664	1.4982
Dec-1995	−0.18	1.85	6.333	0.387	1.4040
Jan-1996	−0.13	3.44	2.420	3.361	0.6633
Feb-1996	0.49	0.96	−3.590	4.673	−1.7378
Mar-1996	0.31	0.96	−1.697	2.346	−0.6954
Apr-1996	0.25	1.47	−4.304	−1.292	−0.5621
May-1996	0.18	2.58	1.864	2.529	−0.2025
Jun-1996	−0.14	0.41	5.991	−0.859	1.3433
Jul-1996	0.08	−4.45	−7.150	0.466	0.2736
Aug-1996	0.15	2.12	1.154	4.880	−0.1675
Sep-1996	−0.23	5.62	0.682	6.415	1.7414
Oct-1996	−0.35	2.74	4.356	8.004	2.2162
Nov-1996	−0.21	7.59	1.196	10.097	1.7129

TABLE 3.2 (*continued*)

Month	Change in Lehman Bros Treasury Yield	S&P 500 Return	Monthly Returns for		
			Electric Utility Sector	Commercial Bank Sector	Lehman U.S. Aggregate Bond Index
Dec-1996	0.30	−1.96	−0.323	−4.887	−0.9299
Jan-1997	0.06	6.21	0.443	8.392	0.3058
Feb-1997	0.11	0.81	0.235	5.151	0.2485
Mar-1997	0.36	−4.16	−4.216	−7.291	−1.1083
Apr-1997	−0.18	5.97	−2.698	5.477	1.4980
May-1997	−0.07	6.14	4.240	3.067	0.9451
Jun-1997	−0.11	4.46	3.795	4.834	1.1873
Jul-1997	−0.43	7.94	2.627	12.946	2.6954
Aug-1997	0.30	−5.56	−2.423	−6.205	−0.8521
Sep-1997	−0.19	5.48	5.010	7.956	1.4752
Oct-1997	−0.21	−3.34	1.244	−2.105	1.4506
Nov-1997	0.06	4.63	8.323	3.580	0.4603
Dec-1997	−0.11	1.72	7.902	3.991	1.0063
Jan-1998	−0.25	1.11	−4.273	−4.404	1.2837
Feb-1998	0.17	7.21	2.338	9.763	−0.0753
Mar-1998	0.05	5.12	7.850	7.205	0.3441
Apr-1998	0.00	1.01	−3.234	2.135	0.5223
May-1998	−0.08	−1.72	−0.442	−3.200	0.9481
Jun-1998	−0.09	4.06	3.717	2.444	0.8483
Jul-1998	0.03	−1.06	−4.566	0.918	0.2122
Aug-1998	−0.46	−14.46	7.149	−24.907	1.6277
Sep-1998	−0.53	6.41	5.613	2.718	2.3412
Oct-1998	0.05	8.13	−2.061	9.999	−0.5276
Nov-1998	0.17	6.06	1.631	5.981	0.5664
Dec-1998	0.02	5.76	2.608	2.567	0.3007
Jan-1999	−0.01	4.18	−6.072	−0.798	0.7143
Feb-1999	0.55	−3.11	−5.263	0.524	−1.7460
Mar-1999	−0.05	4.00	−2.183	1.370	0.5548
Apr-1999	0.05	3.87	6.668	7.407	0.3170
May-1999	0.31	−2.36	7.613	−6.782	−0.8763
Jun-1999	0.11	5.55	−4.911	5.544	−0.3194
Jul-1999	0.11	−3.12	−2.061	−7.351	−0.4248
Aug-1999	0.10	−0.50	1.508	−4.507	−0.0508
Sep-1999	−0.08	−2.74	−5.267	−6.093	1.1604
Oct-1999	0.11	6.33	1.800	15.752	0.3689
Nov-1999	0.16	2.03	−8.050	−7.634	−0.0069
Dec-1999	0.24	5.89	−0.187	−9.158	−0.4822
Jan-2000	0.19	−5.02	5.112	−2.293	−0.3272
Feb-2000	−0.13	−1.89	−10.030	−12.114	1.2092
Mar-2000	−0.20	9.78	1.671	18.770	1.3166
Apr-2000	0.17	−3.01	14.456	−5.885	−0.2854
May-2000	0.07	−2.05	2.985	11.064	−0.0459
Jun-2000	−0.26	2.47	−5.594	−14.389	2.0803
Jul-2000	−0.08	−1.56	6.937	6.953	0.9077

(*continued*)

TABLE 3.2   (*continued*)

Month	Change in Lehman Bros Treasury Yield	S&P 500 Return	Monthly Returns for		
			Electric Utility Sector	Commercial Bank Sector	Lehman U.S. Aggregate Bond Index
Aug-2000	−0.17	6.21	13.842	12.309	1.4497
Sep-2000	−0.03	−5.28	12.413	1.812	0.6286
Oct-2000	−0.06	−0.42	−3.386	−1.380	0.6608
Nov-2000	−0.31	−7.88	3.957	−3.582	1.6355
Dec-2000	−0.33	0.49	4.607	12.182	1.8554
Jan-2001	−0.22	3.55	−11.234	3.169	1.6346
Feb-2001	−0.16	−9.12	6.747	−3.740	0.8713
Mar-2001	−0.08	−6.33	1.769	0.017	0.5018
Apr-2001	0.22	7.77	5.025	−1.538	−0.4151
May-2001	0.00	0.67	0.205	5.934	0.6041
Jun-2001	0.01	−2.43	−7.248	0.004	0.3773
Jul-2001	−0.40	−0.98	−5.092	2.065	2.2357
Aug-2001	−0.14	−6.26	−0.149	−3.940	1.1458
Sep-2001	−0.41	−8.08	−10.275	−4.425	1.1647
Oct-2001	−0.39	1.91	1.479	−7.773	2.0930
Nov-2001	0.41	7.67	−0.833	7.946	−1.3789
Dec-2001	0.21	0.88	3.328	3.483	−0.6357
Jan-2002	0.00	−1.46	−3.673	1.407	0.8096
Feb-2002	−0.08	−1.93	−2.214	−0.096	0.9690
Mar-2002	0.56	3.76	10.623	7.374	−1.6632
Apr-2002	−0.44	−6.06	1.652	2.035	1.9393
May-2002	−0.06	−0.74	−3.988	1.247	0.8495
Jun-2002	−0.23	−7.12	−4.194	−3.767	0.8651
Jul-2002	−0.50	−7.80	−10.827	−4.957	1.2062
Aug-2002	−0.17	0.66	2.792	3.628	1.6882
Sep-2002	−0.45	−10.87	−8.677	−10.142	1.6199
Oct-2002	0.11	8.80	−2.802	5.143	−0.4559
Nov-2002	0.34	5.89	1.620	0.827	−0.0264
Dec-2002	−0.45	−5.88	5.434	−2.454	2.0654
Jan-2003	0.11	−2.62	−3.395	−0.111	0.0855
Feb-2003	−0.21	−1.50	−2.712	−1.514	1.3843
Mar-2003	0.05	0.97	4.150	−3.296	−0.0773
Apr-2003	−0.03	8.24	5.438	9.806	0.8254
May-2003	−0.33	5.27	10.519	5.271	1.8645
Jun-2003	0.08	1.28	1.470	1.988	−0.1986
Jul-2003	0.66	1.76	−5.649	3.331	−3.3620
Aug-2003	0.05	1.95	1.342	−1.218	0.6637
Sep-2003	−0.46	−1.06	4.993	−0.567	2.6469
Oct-2003	0.33	5.66	0.620	8.717	−0.9320
Nov-2003	0.13	0.88	0.136	1.428	0.2391

TABLE 3.3 Estimation of Regression Parameters for Empirical Duration—Simple Linear Regression

	Electric Utility Sector	Commercial Bank Sector	Lehman U.S. Aggregate Bond Index
Intercept			
b_0	0.6376	1.1925	0.5308
t-statistic	1.8251	2.3347	21.1592
p-value	0.0698	0.0207	0.0000
Change in the Treasury Yield			
b_1	−4.5329	−2.5269	−4.1062
t-statistic	−3.4310	−1.3083	−43.2873
p-value	0.0008	0.1926	0.0000
Goodness-of-Fit			
R^2	0.0655	0.0101	0.9177
F-value	11.7717	1.7116	1873.8000
p-value	0.0007	0.1926	0.0000

be roughly 4.53%. Moreover, as expected, the change will be in the opposite direction to the change in interest rates—when interest rates increase (decrease) the value of this sector decreases (increases). The regression coefficient is statistically significant at the 1% level as can be seen from the t-statistic and p-value. The R^2 for this regression is 6.5%. Thus although statistically significant, this regression only explains 6.5% of the variation is the movement of the electric utility sector, suggesting that there are other variables that have not been considered.

Moving on to the commercial bank sector, the estimated regression coefficient is not statistically significant at any reasonable level of significance. The regression explains only 1% of the variation in the movement of the stocks in this sector.

Finally, the Lehman U.S. Aggregate Bond Index is, not unexpectedly, highly statistically significant, explaining almost 92% of the movement in this index. The reason is obvious. This is a bond index that includes all bonds including Treasury securities.

Now let's move on to add another independent variable that moves us from the univariate case to the multiple linear regression case. The new independent variable we shall add is the return on the Standard & Poor's 500 (S&P 500 hereafter). The observations are given in Table 3.2.

So, in this instance we have $k = 2$. The multiple linear regression to be estimated is

$$y = b_0 + b_1 x_1 + b_2 x_2 + e$$

where y = the monthly return of an index
x_1 = the monthly change in the Treasury yield
x_2 = the monthly return on the S&P 500

In a simple linear regression involving only x_2 and y, the estimated regression coefficient b_2 would be the beta of the asset. In the multiple linear regression model above, b_2 is the asset beta taking into account changes in the Treasury yield.

The regression results including the diagnostic statistics are shown in Table 3.4. Looking first at the independent variable x_1, we reach the same conclusion as to its significance for all three assets as in the univariate

TABLE 3.4 Estimation of Regression Parameters for Empirical Duration—Multiple Linear Regression

	Electric Utility Sector	Commercial Bank Sector	Lehman U.S. Aggregate Bond Index
Intercept			
b_0	0.3937	0.2199	0.5029
t-statistic	1.1365	0.5835	21.3885
p-value	0.2574	0.5604	0.0000
Change in the Treasury Yield			
b_1	−4.3780	−1.9096	−4.0885
t-statistic	−3.4143	−1.3686	−46.9711
p-value	0.0008	0.1730	0.0000
Return on the S&P 500			
b_2	0.2664	1.0620	0.0304
t-statistic	3.4020	12.4631	5.7252
p-value	0.0008	0.0000	0.0000
Goodness-of-Fit			
R_2	0.1260	0.4871	0.9312
F-value	12.0430	79.3060	1130.5000
p-value	0.00001	0.00000	0.00000

case. Note also that the estimated value of the regression coefficients are not much different than in the univariate case. As for our new independent variable, x_2, we see that it is statistically significant at the 1% level of significance for all three asset indexes. While we can perform statistical tests discussed earlier for the contribution of adding the new independent variable, the contribution of the two stock sectors to explaining the movement in the return in the sector indexes is clearly significant. The R^2 for the electric utility sector increased from around 7% in the univariate case to 13% in the multiple linear regression case. The increase was obviously more dramatic for the commercial bank sector, the R^2 increasing from 1% to 49%.

Next we analyze the regression of the Lehman U.S. Aggregate Bond Index. Using only one independent variable, we have $R_1^2 = 91.77\%$. If we include the additional independent variable, we obtain the improved $R^2 = 93.12\%$. For the augmented regression, we compute with $n = 170$ and $k = 2$ the adjusted R^2 as

$$
\begin{aligned}
R_{adj}^2 &= 1 - \left(1 - R^2\right)\left(\frac{n-1}{n-k-1}\right) \\
&= 1 - (1 - 0.9312)\left(\frac{170-1}{170-2-1}\right) \\
&= 0.9304
\end{aligned}
$$

Let's apply the F-test to the Lehman U.S. Aggregate Bond Index to see if the addition of the new independent variable increasing the R^2 from 91.77% to 93.12% is statistically significant.

From equation (3.18), we have

$$
F_1 = \frac{R^2 - R_1^2}{\dfrac{1-R^2}{n-k-1}} = \frac{0.9312 - 0.9177}{\dfrac{1-0.9312}{170-2-1}} = 32.7689
$$

This value is highly significant with a p-value of virtually zero. Hence, the inclusion of the additional variable is statistically reasonable.

Predicting the 10-Year Treasury Yield[12]

The U.S. Treasury securities market is the world's most liquid bond market. The U.S. Department of the Treasury issues two types of securities:

---

[12]We are grateful to Robert Scott of the Bank for International Settlements for suggesting this example and for providing the data.

zero-coupon securities and coupon securities. Securities issued with one year or less to maturity are called Treasury bills; they are issued as zero-coupon instruments. Treasury securities with more than one year to maturity are issued as coupon-bearing securities. Treasury securities from more than one year up to 10 years of maturity are called Treasury notes; Treasury securities with a maturity in excess of 10 years are called Treasury bonds. The U.S. Treasury auctions securities of specified maturities on a regular calendar basis. The Treasury currently issues 30-year Treasury bonds but had stopped issuance of them from October 2001 to January 2006.

An important Treasury note is the 10-year Treasury note. In this illustration, we try to forecast this rate based on two independent variables suggested by economic theory. A well-known theory of interest rates, known as the Fisher equation, is that the interest rate in any economy consists of two components. The first is the expected rate of inflation. The second is the real rate of interest. We use regression analysis to produce a model to forecast the yield on the 10-year Treasury note (simply, the 10-year Treasury yield)— the dependent variable—and the expected rate of inflation (simply, expected inflation) and the real rate of interest (simply, real rate).

The 10-year Treasury yield is observable, but we need a proxy for the two independent variables (i.e., the expected rate of inflation and the real rate of interest) because they are not observable at the time of the forecast. Keep in mind that since we are forecasting, we do not use as our independent variable information that is unavailable at the time of the forecast. Consequently, we need a proxy available at the time of the forecast.

The inflation rate is available from the U.S. Department of Commerce. However, we need a proxy for expected inflation. We can use some type of average of past inflation as a proxy. In our model, we use a five-year moving average. There are more sophisticated methodologies for calculating expected inflation, but the five-year moving average is sufficient for our illustration.[13] For the real rate, we use the rate on three-month certificates of deposit (CDs). Again, we use a five-year moving average.

The monthly data for the three variables from November 1965 to December 2005 (482 observations) are provided in Table 3.5. The regression results are reported in Table 3.6. As can be seen, the regression coefficients of both independent variables are positive (as would be predicted by economic theory) and highly significant. The R^2 and adjusted R^2 are 0.90 and 0.83, respectively. The ANOVA table is also shown as part of Table 3.6. The results suggest a good fit for forecasting the 10-year rate.

---

[13]For example, one can use an exponential smoothing of actual inflation, a methodology used by the Organisation for Economic Co-operation and Development (OECD).

TABLE 3.5 Monthly Data for 10-Year Treasury Yield, Expected Inflation (%), and Real Rate (%), November 1965–December 2005

Date	10-Yr. Treas. Yield	Exp. Infl.	Real Rate	Date	10-Yr. Treas. Yield	Exp. Infl.	Real Rate	Date	10-Yr. Treas. Yield	Exp. Infl.	Real Rate
1965											
Nov	4.45	1.326	2.739								
Dec	4.62	1.330	2.757								
1966				**1969**				**1972**			
Jan	4.61	1.334	2.780	Jan	6.04	2.745	2.811	Jan	5.95	4.959	2.401
Feb	4.83	1.348	2.794	Feb	6.19	2.802	2.826	Feb	6.08	4.959	2.389
Mar	4.87	1.358	2.820	Mar	6.3	2.869	2.830	Mar	6.07	4.953	2.397
Apr	4.75	1.372	2.842	Apr	6.17	2.945	2.827	Apr	6.19	4.953	2.403
May	4.78	1.391	2.861	May	6.32	3.016	2.862	May	6.13	4.949	2.398
June	4.81	1.416	2.883	June	6.57	3.086	2.895	June	6.11	4.941	2.405
July	5.02	1.440	2.910	July	6.72	3.156	2.929	July	6.11	4.933	2.422
Aug	5.22	1.464	2.945	Aug	6.69	3.236	2.967	Aug	6.21	4.924	2.439
Sept	5.18	1.487	2.982	Sept	7.16	3.315	3.001	Sept	6.55	4.916	2.450
Oct	5.01	1.532	2.997	Oct	7.1	3.393	3.014	Oct	6.48	4.912	2.458
Nov	5.16	1.566	3.022	Nov	7.14	3.461	3.045	Nov	6.28	4.899	2.461
Dec	4.84	1.594	3.050	Dec	7.65	3.539	3.059	Dec	6.36	4.886	2.468
1967				**1970**				**1973**			
Jan	4.58	1.633	3.047	Jan	7.80	3.621	3.061	Jan	6.46	4.865	2.509
Feb	4.63	1.667	3.050	Feb	7.24	3.698	3.064	Feb	6.64	4.838	2.583
Mar	4.54	1.706	3.039	Mar	7.07	3.779	3.046	Mar	6.71	4.818	2.641
Apr	4.59	1.739	3.027	Apr	7.39	3.854	3.035	Apr	6.67	4.795	2.690
May	4.85	1.767	3.021	May	7.91	3.933	3.021	May	6.85	4.776	2.734
June	5.02	1.801	3.015	June	7.84	4.021	3.001	June	6.90	4.752	2.795
July	5.16	1.834	3.004	July	7.46	4.104	2.981	July	7.13	4.723	2.909
Aug	5.28	1.871	2.987	Aug	7.53	4.187	2.956	Aug	7.40	4.699	3.023
Sept	5.3	1.909	2.980	Sept	7.39	4.264	2.938	Sept	7.09	4.682	3.110
Oct	5.48	1.942	2.975	Oct	7.33	4.345	2.901	Oct	6.79	4.668	3.185
Nov	5.75	1.985	2.974	Nov	6.84	4.436	2.843	Nov	6.73	4.657	3.254
Dec	5.7	2.027	2.972	Dec	6.39	4.520	2.780	Dec	6.74	4.651	3.312
1968				**1971**				**1974**			
Jan	5.53	2.074	2.959	Jan	6.24	4.605	2.703	Jan	6.99	4.652	3.330
Feb	5.56	2.126	2.943	Feb	6.11	4.680	2.627	Feb	6.96	4.653	3.332
Mar	5.74	2.177	2.937	Mar	5.70	4.741	2.565	Mar	7.21	4.656	3.353
Apr	5.64	2.229	2.935	Apr	5.83	4.793	2.522	Apr	7.51	4.657	3.404
May	5.87	2.285	2.934	May	6.39	4.844	2.501	May	7.58	4.678	3.405
June	5.72	2.341	2.928	June	6.52	4.885	2.467	June	7.54	4.713	3.419
July	5.5	2.402	2.906	July	6.73	4.921	2.436	July	7.81	4.763	3.421
Aug	5.42	2.457	2.887	Aug	6.58	4.947	2.450	Aug	8.04	4.827	3.401
Sept	5.46	2.517	2.862	Sept	6.14	4.964	2.442	Sept	8.04	4.898	3.346
Oct	5.58	2.576	2.827	Oct	5.93	4.968	2.422	Oct	7.9	4.975	3.271
Nov	5.7	2.639	2.808	Nov	5.81	4.968	2.411	Nov	7.68	5.063	3.176
Dec	6.03	2.697	2.798	Dec	5.93	4.964	2.404	Dec	7.43	5.154	3.086

(continued)

TABLE 3.5 (*continued*)

Date	10-Yr. Treas. Yield	Exp. Infl.	Real Rate	Date	10-Yr. Treas. Yield	Exp. Infl.	Real Rate	Date	10-Yr. Treas. Yield	Exp. Infl.	Real Rate
1975				1978				1981			
Jan	7.5	5.243	2.962	Jan	7.96	6.832	1.068	Jan	12.57	8.520	1.132
Feb	7.39	5.343	2.827	Feb	8.03	6.890	0.995	Feb	13.19	8.594	1.242
Mar	7.73	5.431	2.710	Mar	8.04	6.942	0.923	Mar	13.12	8.649	1.336
Apr	8.23	5.518	2.595	Apr	8.15	7.003	0.854	Apr	13.68	8.700	1.477
May	8.06	5.585	2.477	May	8.35	7.063	0.784	May	14.1	8.751	1.619
June	7.86	5.639	2.384	June	8.46	7.124	0.716	June	13.47	8.802	1.755
July	8.06	5.687	2.311	July	8.64	7.191	0.598	July	14.28	8.877	1.897
Aug	8.4	5.716	2.271	Aug	8.41	7.263	0.482	Aug	14.94	8.956	2.037
Sept	8.43	5.738	2.241	Sept	8.42	7.331	0.397	Sept	15.32	9.039	2.155
Oct	8.15	5.753	2.210	Oct	8.64	7.400	0.365	Oct	15.15	9.110	2.256
Nov	8.05	5.759	2.200	Nov	8.81	7.463	0.322	Nov	13.39	9.175	2.305
Dec	8	5.761	2.186	Dec	9.01	7.525	0.284	Dec	13.72	9.232	2.392
1976				1979				1982			
Jan	7.74	5.771	2.166	Jan	9.1	7.582	0.254	Jan	14.59	9.285	2.497
Feb	7.79	5.777	2.164	Feb	9.1	7.645	0.224	Feb	14.43	9.334	2.612
Mar	7.73	5.800	2.138	Mar	9.12	7.706	0.174	Mar	13.86	9.375	2.741
Apr	7.56	5.824	2.101	Apr	9.18	7.758	0.108	Apr	13.87	9.417	2.860
May	7.9	5.847	2.060	May	9.25	7.797	0.047	May	13.62	9.456	2.958
June	7.86	5.870	2.034	June	8.91	7.821	−0.025	June	14.3	9.487	3.095
July	7.83	5.900	1.988	July	8.95	7.834	−0.075	July	13.95	9.510	3.183
Aug	7.77	5.937	1.889	Aug	9.03	7.837	−0.101	Aug	13.06	9.524	3.259
Sept	7.59	5.981	1.813	Sept	9.33	7.831	−0.085	Sept	12.34	9.519	3.321
Oct	7.41	6.029	1.753	Oct	10.3	7.823	0.011	Oct	10.91	9.517	3.363
Nov	7.29	6.079	1.681	Nov	10.65	7.818	0.079	Nov	10.55	9.502	3.427
Dec	6.87	6.130	1.615	Dec	10.39	7.818	0.154	Dec	10.54	9.469	3.492
1977				1980				1983			
Jan	7.21	6.176	1.573	Jan	10.8	7.825	0.261	Jan	10.46	9.439	3.553
Feb	7.39	6.224	1.527	Feb	12.41	7.828	0.418	Feb	10.72	9.411	3.604
Mar	7.46	6.272	1.474	Mar	12.75	7.849	0.615	Mar	10.51	9.381	3.670
Apr	7.37	6.323	1.427	Apr	11.47	7.879	0.701	Apr	10.4	9.340	3.730
May	7.46	6.377	1.397	May	10.18	7.926	0.716	May	10.38	9.288	3.806
June	7.28	6.441	1.340	June	9.78	7.989	0.702	June	10.85	9.227	3.883
July	7.33	6.499	1.293	July	10.25	8.044	0.695	July	11.38	9.161	3.981
Aug	7.4	6.552	1.252	Aug	11.1	8.109	0.716	Aug	11.85	9.087	4.076
Sept	7.34	6.605	1.217	Sept	11.51	8.184	0.740	Sept	11.65	9.012	4.152
Oct	7.52	6.654	1.193	Oct	11.75	8.269	0.795	Oct	11.54	8.932	4.204
Nov	7.58	6.710	1.154	Nov	12.68	8.356	0.895	Nov	11.69	8.862	4.243
Dec	7.69	6.768	1.119	Dec	12.84	8.446	1.004	Dec	11.83	8.800	4.276

TABLE 3.5 (*continued*)

Date	10-Yr. Treas. Yield	Exp. Infl.	Real Rate	Date	10-Yr. Treas. Yield	Exp. Infl.	Real Rate	Date	10-Yr. Treas. Yield	Exp. Infl.	Real Rate
1984				1987				1990			
Jan	11.67	8.741	4.324	Jan	7.08	4.887	4.607	Jan	8.418	4.257	3.610
Feb	11.84	8.670	4.386	Feb	7.25	4.793	4.558	Feb	8.515	4.254	3.595
Mar	12.32	8.598	4.459	Mar	7.25	4.710	4.493	Mar	8.628	4.254	3.585
Apr	12.63	8.529	4.530	Apr	8.02	4.627	4.445	Apr	9.022	4.260	3.580
May	13.41	8.460	4.620	May	8.61	4.551	4.404	May	8.599	4.264	3.586
June	13.56	8.393	4.713	June	8.4	4.476	4.335	June	8.412	4.272	3.589
July	13.36	8.319	4.793	July	8.45	4.413	4.296	July	8.341	4.287	3.568
Aug	12.72	8.241	4.862	Aug	8.76	4.361	4.273	Aug	8.846	4.309	3.546
Sept	12.52	8.164	4.915	Sept	9.42	4.330	4.269	Sept	8.795	4.335	3.523
Oct	12.16	8.081	4.908	Oct	9.52	4.302	4.259	Oct	8.617	4.357	3.503
Nov	11.57	7.984	4.919	Nov	8.86	4.285	4.243	Nov	8.252	4.371	3.493
Dec	12.5	7.877	4.928	Dec	8.99	4.279	4.218	Dec	8.067	4.388	3.471
1985				1988				1991			
Jan	11.38	7.753	4.955	Jan	8.67	4.274	4.180	Jan	8.007	4.407	3.436
Feb	11.51	7.632	4.950	Feb	8.21	4.271	4.149	Feb	8.033	4.431	3.396
Mar	11.86	7.501	4.900	Mar	8.37	4.268	4.104	Mar	8.061	4.451	3.360
Apr	11.43	7.359	4.954	Apr	8.72	4.270	4.075	Apr	8.013	4.467	3.331
May	10.85	7.215	5.063	May	9.09	4.280	4.036	May	8.059	4.487	3.294
June	10.16	7.062	5.183	June	8.92	4.301	3.985	June	8.227	4.504	3.267
July	10.31	6.925	5.293	July	9.06	4.322	3.931	July	8.147	4.517	3.247
Aug	10.33	6.798	5.346	Aug	9.26	4.345	3.879	Aug	7.816	4.527	3.237
Sept	10.37	6.664	5.383	Sept	8.98	4.365	3.844	Sept	7.445	4.534	3.223
Oct	10.24	6.528	5.399	Oct	8.8	4.381	3.810	Oct	7.46	4.540	3.207
Nov	9.78	6.399	5.360	Nov	8.96	4.385	3.797	Nov	7.376	4.552	3.177
Dec	9.26	6.269	5.326	Dec	9.11	4.384	3.787	Dec	6.699	4.562	3.133
1986				1989				1992			
Jan	9.19	6.154	5.284	Jan	9.09	4.377	3.786	Jan	7.274	4.569	3.092
Feb	8.7	6.043	5.249	Feb	9.17	4.374	3.792	Feb	7.25	4.572	3.054
Mar	7.78	5.946	5.225	Mar	9.36	4.367	3.791	Mar	7.528	4.575	3.014
Apr	7.3	5.858	5.143	Apr	9.18	4.356	3.784	Apr	7.583	4.574	2.965
May	7.71	5.763	5.055	May	8.86	4.344	3.758	May	7.318	4.571	2.913
June	7.8	5.673	4.965	June	8.28	4.331	3.723	June	7.121	4.567	2.864
July	7.3	5.554	4.878	July	8.02	4.320	3.679	July	6.709	4.563	2.810
Aug	7.17	5.428	4.789	Aug	8.11	4.306	3.644	Aug	6.604	4.556	2.757
Sept	7.45	5.301	4.719	Sept	8.19	4.287	3.623	Sept	6.354	4.544	2.682
Oct	7.43	5.186	4.671	Oct	8.01	4.273	3.614	Oct	6.789	4.533	2.624
Nov	7.25	5.078	4.680	Nov	7.87	4.266	3.609	Nov	6.937	4.522	2.571
Dec	7.11	4.982	4.655	Dec	7.84	4.258	3.611	Dec	6.686	4.509	2.518

(*continued*)

TABLE 3.5   (*continued*)

Date	10-Yr. Treas. Yield	Exp. Infl.	Real Rate	Date	10-Yr. Treas. Yield	Exp. Infl.	Real Rate	Date	10-Yr. Treas. Yield	Exp. Infl.	Real Rate
1993				**1996**				**1999**			
Jan	6.359	4.495	2.474	Jan	5.58	3.505	1.250	Jan	4.651	2.631	2.933
Feb	6.02	4.482	2.427	Feb	6.098	3.458	1.270	Feb	5.287	2.621	2.964
Mar	6.024	4.466	2.385	Mar	6.327	3.418	1.295	Mar	5.242	2.605	2.998
Apr	6.009	4.453	2.330	Apr	6.67	3.376	1.328	Apr	5.348	2.596	3.018
May	6.149	4.439	2.272	May	6.852	3.335	1.359	May	5.622	2.586	3.035
June	5.776	4.420	2.214	June	6.711	3.297	1.387	June	5.78	2.572	3.058
July	5.807	4.399	2.152	July	6.794	3.261	1.417	July	5.903	2.558	3.079
Aug	5.448	4.380	2.084	Aug	6.943	3.228	1.449	Aug	5.97	2.543	3.103
Sept	5.382	4.357	2.020	Sept	6.703	3.195	1.481	Sept	5.877	2.527	3.129
Oct	5.427	4.333	1.958	Oct	6.339	3.163	1.516	Oct	6.024	2.515	3.150
Nov	5.819	4.309	1.885	Nov	6.044	3.131	1.558	Nov	6.191	2.502	3.161
Dec	5.794	4.284	1.812	Dec	6.418	3.102	1.608	Dec	6.442	2.490	3.165
1994				**1997**				**2000**			
Jan	5.642	4.256	1.739	Jan	6.494	3.077	1.656	Jan	6.665	2.477	3.175
Feb	6.129	4.224	1.663	Feb	6.552	3.057	1.698	Feb	6.409	2.464	3.186
Mar	6.738	4.195	1.586	Mar	6.903	3.033	1.746	Mar	6.004	2.455	3.195
Apr	7.042	4.166	1.523	Apr	6.718	3.013	1.795	Apr	6.212	2.440	3.215
May	7.147	4.135	1.473	May	6.659	2.990	1.847	May	6.272	2.429	3.240
June	7.32	4.106	1.427	June	6.5	2.968	1.899	June	6.031	2.421	3.259
July	7.111	4.079	1.394	July	6.011	2.947	1.959	July	6.031	2.412	3.282
Aug	7.173	4.052	1.356	Aug	6.339	2.926	2.016	Aug	5.725	2.406	3.302
Sept	7.603	4.032	1.315	Sept	6.103	2.909	2.078	Sept	5.802	2.398	3.324
Oct	7.807	4.008	1.289	Oct	5.831	2.888	2.136	Oct	5.751	2.389	3.347
Nov	7.906	3.982	1.278	Nov	5.874	2.866	2.189	Nov	5.468	2.382	3.368
Dec	7.822	3.951	1.278	Dec	5.742	2.847	2.247	Dec	5.112	2.374	3.388
1995				**1998**				**2001**			
Jan	7.581	3.926	1.269	Jan	5.505	2.828	2.306	Jan	5.114	2.368	3.396
Feb	7.201	3.899	1.261	Feb	5.622	2.806	2.369	Feb	4.896	2.366	3.393
Mar	7.196	3.869	1.253	Mar	5.654	2.787	2.428	Mar	4.917	2.364	3.386
Apr	7.055	3.840	1.240	Apr	5.671	2.765	2.493	Apr	5.338	2.364	3.366
May	6.284	3.812	1.230	May	5.552	2.744	2.552	May	5.381	2.362	3.343
June	6.203	3.781	1.222	June	5.446	2.725	2.611	June	5.412	2.363	3.313
July	6.426	3.746	1.223	July	5.494	2.709	2.666	July	5.054	2.363	3.279
Aug	6.284	3.704	1.228	Aug	4.976	2.695	2.720	Aug	4.832	2.365	3.242
Sept	6.182	3.662	1.232	Sept	4.42	2.680	2.767	Sept	4.588	2.365	3.192
Oct	6.02	3.624	1.234	Oct	4.605	2.666	2.811	Oct	4.232	2.366	3.136
Nov	5.741	3.587	1.229	Nov	4.714	2.653	2.854	Nov	4.752	2.368	3.076
Dec	5.572	3.549	1.234	Dec	4.648	2.641	2.894	Dec	5.051	2.370	3.013

TABLE 3.5 *(continued)*

Date	10-Yr. Treas. Yield	Exp. Infl.	Real Rate	Date	10-Yr. Treas. Yield	Exp. Infl.	Real Rate
2002				2004			
Jan	5.033	2.372	2.950	Jan	4.134	2.172	1.492
Feb	4.877	2.372	2.888	Feb	3.973	2.157	1.442
Mar	5.396	2.371	2.827	Mar	3.837	2.149	1.385
Apr	5.087	2.369	2.764	Apr	4.507	2.142	1.329
May	5.045	2.369	2.699	May	4.649	2.136	1.273
June	4.799	2.367	2.636	June	4.583	2.134	1.212
July	4.461	2.363	2.575	July	4.477	2.129	1.156
Aug	4.143	2.364	2.509	Aug	4.119	2.126	1.097
Sept	3.596	2.365	2.441	Sept	4.121	2.124	1.031
Oct	3.894	2.365	2.374	Oct	4.025	2.122	0.966
Nov	4.207	2.362	2.302	Nov	4.351	2.124	0.903
Dec	3.816	2.357	2.234	Dec	4.22	2.129	0.840
2003				2005			
Jan	3.964	2.351	2.168	Jan	4.13	2.131	0.783
Feb	3.692	2.343	2.104	Feb	4.379	2.133	0.727
Mar	3.798	2.334	2.038	Mar	4.483	2.132	0.676
Apr	3.838	2.323	1.976	Apr	4.2	2.131	0.622
May	3.372	2.312	1.913	May	3.983	2.127	0.567
June	3.515	2.300	1.850	June	3.915	2.120	0.520
July	4.408	2.288	1.786	July	4.278	2.114	0.476
Aug	4.466	2.267	1.731	Aug	4.016	2.107	0.436
Sept	3.939	2.248	1.681	Sept	4.326	2.098	0.399
Oct	4.295	2.233	1.629	Oct	4.553	2.089	0.366
Nov	4.334	2.213	1.581	Nov	4.486	2.081	0.336
Dec	4.248	2.191	1.537	Dec	4.393	2.075	0.311

Note:
Exp. Infl. (%) = Expected rate of inflation as proxied by the five-year moving average of the actual inflation rate.
Real Rate (%) = Real rate of interest as proxied by the five-year moving average of the interest rate on three-month certificates of deposit.

Benchmark Selection: Sharpe Benchmarks

Because of the difficulty of classifying an asset manager into any one of the generic investment styles used in the investment industry in order to evaluate performance, William Sharpe suggested that a benchmark can be constructed using multiple regression analysis from various specialized market

TABLE 3.6 Results of Regression for Forecasting 10-Year Treasury Yield

Regression Statistics				
Multiple R^2		0.9083		
R^2		0.8250		
Adjusted R^2		0.8243		
Standard Error		1.033764		
Observations		482		

Analysis of Variance				
	df	SS	MS	F	Significance F
Regression	2	2413.914	1206.957	1129.404	4.8E-182
Residual	479	511.8918	1.068668		
Total	481	2925.806			

	Coefficients	Standard Error	t	Statistics p-value
Intercept	1.89674	0.147593	12.85	1.1E-32
Expected Inflation	0.996937	0.021558	46.24	9.1E-179
Real Rate	0.352416	0.039058	9.02	4.45E-18

indexes.[14] The rationale is that potential clients can buy a combination of specialized index funds to replicate a style of investing. A benchmark can be created using regression analysis that adjusts for a manager's index-like tendencies. Such a benchmark is called a *Sharpe benchmark*.

The 10 mutually exclusive indexes suggested by Sharpe to provide asset class diversification are (1) the Russell Price-Drive Stock Index (an index of large value stocks), (2) the Russell Earnings-Growth Stock Index (an index of large growth stocks), (3) the Russell 2000 Small Stock Index, (4) a 90-Day Bill Index, (5) the Lehman Intermediate Government Bond Index, (6) the Lehman Long-Term Government Bond Index, (7) the Lehman Corporate Bond Index, (8) the Lehman Mortgage-Backed Securities Index, (9) the Salomon Smith Barney Non-U.S. Government Bond Index, and (10) the Financial Times Actuaries Euro-Pacific Index.[15]

---

[14] William F. Sharpe, "Determining a Fund's Effective Asset Mix," *Investment Management Review* 9 (September–October 1988): 16–29.

[15] At the time that Sharpe introduced his model, the bond indexes were published by the investment banking firms of Shearson-Lehman and Salomon Brothers.

Sharpe benchmarks are determined by regressing periodic returns (e.g., monthly returns) on various market indexes. The Sharpe benchmark was reported for one portfolio management firm based on performance from the period January 1981 through July 1988 using monthly returns.[16] The resulting Sharpe benchmark based on monthly observations was

Sharpe benchmark = 0.43 × (FRC Price-Driven Index)
$\qquad$ + 0.13 × (FRC Earnings-Growth Index)
$\qquad$ + 0.44 × (FRC 2000 Index)

where FRC is an index produced by the Frank Russell Company.

The three indexes were selected because they were the only indexes of the 10 that were statistically significant. Notice that the sum of the three coefficients is equal to one. This is done by estimating a constrained regression, a topic we do not cover in this book. The R^2 for this regression is 97.6%. The intercept term for this regression is 0.365%, which represents the average excess monthly return.

By subtracting the style benchmark's monthly return from the manager's monthly portfolio return, performance can be measured. This difference, which we refer to as "added value residuals," is what the manager added over the return from three "index funds" in the appropriate proportions. For example, suppose that in some month the return realized by this manager is 1.75%. In the same month, the return for the three indexes were as follows: 0.7% for the FRC Price-Driven Index, 1.4% for the FRC Earnings-Growth Index, and 2.2% for the FRC 2000 Index. The added value residual for this month would be calculated as follows. First, calculate the value of the Sharpe benchmark:

Sharpe benchmark = 0.43 × (0.7%) + 0.13 × (1.4%) + 0.44 × (2.2%)
$\qquad$ = 1.45%

The added value residual is then:

Added value residual = Actual return − Sharpe benchmark return

Since the actual return for the month is 1.75%,

Added value residual = 1.75% − 1.45% = 0.3%

Notice that if this manager had been benchmarked against a single investment style index such as the FRC Price-Driven Index, the manager

[16] See H. Russell Fogler, "Normal Style Indexes—An Alternative to Manager Universes?" in *Performance Measurement: Setting the Standards, Interpreting the Numbers* (ICFA, 1989), 102.

would have outperformed the benchmark by a wide margin (1.05%). In contrast, if the FRC 2000 Index is used as the benchmark, the manager would have underperformed by 0.45%.

One interpretation of the results of a Sharpe benchmark that has arisen in practice is that if the R^2 is low, this is an indication that the portfolio is actively managed because it is not associated with any particular style. However, this need not be the case as pointed out by Dor and Jagannathan.[17] One of the reasons could be due to inadequate asset class indexes. Dor and Jagannathan illustrate the importance of including adequate asset class indexes using the Putnam Utilities Growth and Income, a mutual fund. Table 3.7 reports the Sharpe benchmark based on regression analysis of returns from January 1992 through August 2001.

TABLE 3.7 Sharpe Benchmark for Putnam Utilities Growth and Income, January 1992 through August 2001

Asset Class	Basic Model	Extended Model
Bills	0	3.4%
Treasury 1–10 yrs	11.9%	0
Treasury 10+ yrs	20.5%	0
Corporate Bonds	0	0
Large-Cap Value	56.8%	14.7%
Large-Cap Growth	0	0
Small-Cap Value	0	4.4%
Small-Cap Growth	0	0
Developed Countries	0	0
Japan	0	0
Emerging Markets	0	0
Foreign Bonds	10.8%	10.6%
Dow Jones Utilities	—	44.6%
Dow Jones Communications	—	16.5%
Dow Jones Energy	—	5.9%
R^2	0.669	0.929

Source: Exhibit 1.10 in Arik Ben Dor and Ravi Jagannathan, "Style Analysis: Asset Allocation and Performance Evaluation," in *The Handbook of Equity Style Management*, 3rd ed., ed. T. Daniel Coggin and Frank J. Fabozzi (Hoboken, NJ: John Wiley & Sons, 2003).

---

[17] Arik Ben Dor and Ravi Jagannathan, "Style Analysis: Asset Allocation and Performance Evaluation," in *The Handbook of Equity Style Management*, 3rd ed., ed. T. Daniel Coggin and Frank J. Fabozzi (Hoboken, NJ: John Wiley & Sons, 2003).

There are two models reported. The first, denoted "Basic Model," uses 12 asset class indexes selected by Dor and Jagannathan. As can be seen, the R^2 is 66.9%. However, Putnam Utilities Growth and Income is a sector-oriented fund. In creating a Sharpe benchmark for sector-oriented funds, it is important to use relevant sector indexes. The "Extended Model" reported in Table 3.7 includes three sector indexes: Dow Jones Utilities, Dow Jones Communications, and Dow Jones Energy. Notice that not only does the R^2 increase from 66.9%, the weights (regression coefficients) change dramatically. For example, a 56.8% weight in the basic model is assigned to Large-Cap Value but only 14.7% in the extended model. Look also at the Treasury 10+-year asset class index. This is the second largest weight in the basic model; however, in the extended model it has no weight assigned to it.

Return-Based Style Analysis for Hedge Funds

The use of the Sharpe benchmark is typical for evaluating non-hedge fund managers. The difficulty with employing the Sharpe benchmark for hedge funds is attributable to the wide range of assets in which they are free to invest and the dynamic nature of their trading strategy (i.e., flexibility of shifting among asset classes, the higher leverage permitted, and the ability to short sell).

Dor and Jagannathan illustrate this difficulty using four hedge funds.[18] Two of the hedge funds are directional funds and two are nondirectional funds. The former employ strategies seeking to benefit from broad market movements and the latter employ strategies seeking to exploit short-term pricing discrepancies between related securities but at the same time maintain market exposure to a minimum. Nondirectional funds are referred to as *market-neutral funds*. The directional funds are Hillsdale U.S. Market Neutral Fund (Hillside fund) and The Nippon Performance Fund (Nippon fund); the nondirectional funds are Axiom Balanced Growth Fund (Axiom fund) and John W. Henry & Company—Financial and Metals Portfolio (CTA fund).

Table 3.8 reports two regression results for the four hedge funds. The first regression (referred to as the "Basic Model" in the table) uses 12 asset classes. The R^2 is lower for these hedge funds than for mutual funds for the reason cited earlier regarding the wide range of strategies available to hedge funds. Note, however, that the R^2 of the nondirectional funds (i.e., market-neutral funds) is higher than that of the directional funds.

Theory and empirical evidence can help us identify factors to improve upon the explanatory power of hedge fund returns. Several researchers

---

[18] Dor and Jagannathan, "Style Analysis: Asset Allocation and Performance Evaluation."

TABLE 3.8 Hedge Funds Style Analysis (I)

	Basic Model				Basic Model + Options Strategy			
	Hillsdale	Nippon	Axiom	CTA	Hillsdale	Nippon	Axiom	CTA
Bills	161.9	219.0	257.5	9.2	137.7	295.7	393.7	-432.0
Treasury 1–10 yrs	-161.4	-281.6	-324.8	676.0	-223.1	-404.0	-450.0	698.5
Treasury 10+ yrs	44.0	-6.6	-21.9	85.3	32.4	8.8	-35.5	-4.5
Corporate Bonds	22.9	177.6	216.8	-297.0	79.8	215.1	240.1	-166.1
Large Value	27.4	-22.3	-24.8	14.0	40.6	-33.5	-44.4	7.6
Large Growth	21.1	10.0	-5.0	-32.6	48.9	-12.3	-23.0	-7.0
Small Value	-3.4	28.3	50.1	24.4	2.2	20.8	89.0	19.5
Small Growth	7.7	-11.3	-23.9	-9.8	0.3	-4.8	-38.2	-12.5
Developed Countries	-14.8	2.4	14.3	0.2	-8.9	4.3	19.5	8.8
Japan	6.7	25.8	25.5	-30.4	10.2	19.7	38.9	-53.3
Emerging Markets	-36.7	-16.7	37.9	30.8	-38.4	-15.5	21.8	28.7
Foreign Bonds	27.4	-24.7	-94.4	-15.0	16.7	4.4	-107.2	8.5
Cat	—	—	—	—	0.1	3.3	-0.1	5.9
Pat	—	—	—	—	-2.0	2.9	-12.7	11.2
Cout	—	—	—	—	-0.8	-1.7	-0.8	-4.3
Pout	—	—	—	—	4.1	-3.3	9.0	-9.1
R^2	28.3	29.6	55.4	37.5	32.2	39.8	77.3	55.4

Note: This exhibit reports the results of style analysis for three hedge funds and a CTA during March 1997 to November 2001. The coefficients are not constrained to be nonnegative due to the use of leverage and short-sales, but the sum of the coefficients is constrained to one. All figures in the table are in percents. The columns titled "Basic Model" report the results for the set of 12 asset classes. The next four columns show the results of reestimating the coefficients for each fund using the 12 asset classes and returns on four S&P 500 options strategies. At-the-money call (put) options are denoted as Cat (Pat) and out-of-the-money call (put) option as Cout (Pout).
Source: Exhibit 1.11 in Arik Ben Dor and Ravi Jagannathan, "Style Analysis: Asset Allocation and Performance Evaluation," in *The Handbook of Equity Style Management*. 3rd ed., ed. T. Daniel Coggin and Frank J. Fabozzi (Hoboken, NJ: John Wiley & Sons, 2003).

have argued that hedge funds pursue strategies that have option-like (non-linear) payoffs and this occurs even if an option strategy is not pursued.[19] Consequently, Dor and Jagannathan add four S&P 500 index strategies to the 12 asset classes. This second regression, referred to as the "Basic Model + Options Strategy," shows that by adding the four option indexes, the R^2 increases significantly for each hedge fund.

Rich/Cheap Analysis for the Mortgage Market

Regression analysis has long been used to attempt to identify rich and cheap sectors of the bond market. Here we will use a relative value regression model developed by the Mortgage Strategy Group of UBS. The dependent variable is the mortgage spread, a variable measured as the difference between the current coupon mortgage[20] and the average swap rate. The average swap rate is measured by the average of the 5-year swap rate and 10-year swap rate.

There are three explanatory variables in the model that have historically been found to affect mortgage pricing:

1. The level of interest rates
2. The shape of the yield curve
3. The volatility of interest rates

The level of interest rates is measured by the average of the 5-year swap rate and 10-year swap rate. The shape of the yield curve is measured by the spread between the 10-year swap rate and 2-year swap rate. The volatility measure is obtained from swaption prices.

---

[19] See Lawrence A. Glosten and Ravi Jagannathan, "A Contingent Claim Approach to Performance Evaluation," *Journal of Empirical Finance* 1 (1994): 133–160; Mark Mitchell and Todd Pulvino, "Characteristics of Risk in Risk Arbitrage," *Journal of Finance* 56 (December 2001): 2135–2175; and William Fung and David A. Hsieh, "The Risks in Hedge Fund Strategies: Theory and Evidence from Trend Followers," *Review of Financial Studies* 14 (2001): 313–341; Philip H. Dybvig and Stephen A. Ross, "Differential Information and Performance Measurement using a Security Market Line," *Journal of Finance* 40 (1985): 383–399; and Robert C. Merton, "On Market Timing and Investment Performance I: An Equilibrium Theory of Values for Markets Forecasts," *Journal of Business* 54 (1981): 363–406.

[20] More specifically, it is what UBS calls the "perfect current coupon mortgage," which is a proxy for the current coupon mortgage.

The multiple regression model is[21]

$$\text{Mortgage spread} = \alpha + \beta_1(\text{Average swap rate})$$
$$+ \beta_2(\text{10-year/2-year swap spread})$$
$$+ \beta_3(\text{10-year/2-year swap spread})^2$$
$$+ \beta_4(\text{Swaption volatility}) + e$$

Two years of data were used to estimate the regression model. While the R^2 for the estimated model is not reported, Figure 3.2 shows the actual mortgage spread versus the spread projected by the regression model for the Fannie Mae 30-year mortgage passthrough security, one type of *mortgage-backed security* (MBS).

Let's see how the model is used. The analysis was performed in early March 2004 to assess the relative value of the MBS market.

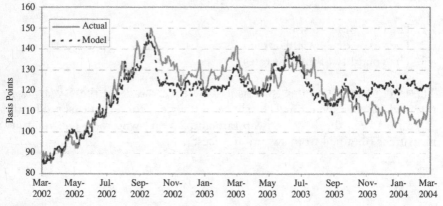

FIGURE 3.2   Mortgage Spreads: Actual versus Model
Source: Figure 4 in "Mortgages—Hold Your Nose and Buy," *UBS Mortgage Strategist*, 9 (March 2004): 19. Reprinted with permission.

---

[21] See "Mortgages—Hold Your Nose and Buy," *UBS Mortgage Strategist*, 9 (March 2004): 15–26. UBS has argued in other issues of its publication that with this particular regression model the richness of mortgages may be overstated because the model does not recognize the reshaping of the mortgage market. Alternative regression models that do take this into account are analyzed by UBS but the results are not reported here.

If the spread predicted by the model (i.e., model spread) exceeds the actual spread, the market is viewed as rich; it is viewed as cheap if the model spread is less than actual spread. The market is fairly priced if the two spreads are equal. The predicted and actual spreads for March 2004 are the last ones shown in Figure 3.2. While the model suggests that the market is rich, it is less rich in comparison to the prior months. In fact, at the close of March 9, 2004, when the article was written, it was only 5 basis points.

Testing for Strong-Form Pricing Efficiency

At the heart of the debate as to whether investors should pursue an active or passive equity strategy is the pricing efficiency of the market. The pricing efficiency of a market can be classified into three forms: (1) weak form, (2) semistrong form, and (3) strong form. The distinction among these forms lies in the relevant information that is hypothesized to be locked into the price of the security. Weak efficiency means that the price of the security reflects the past price and trading history of the security. Semistrong efficiency means that the price of the security fully reflects all public information (which, of course, includes but is not limited to historical price and trading patterns). Strong efficiency exists in a market where the price of a security reflects all information, whether or not it is publicly available.

Multiple linear regression analysis is used in most tests of the pricing efficiency of the market. These tests examine whether it is possible to generate abnormal returns from an investment strategy. An abnormal return is defined as the difference between the actual return and the expected return from an investment strategy. The expected return used in empirical tests is the return predicted from a pricing model. The pricing model itself adjusts for risk. Because the testing relies on the pricing model used, tests of market pricing efficiency are joint tests of both the efficiency of the market and the validity of the pricing model employed in the study.

Let's illustrate a test for strong-form pricing efficiency using multiple linear regression analysis. This will be done by comparing the performance of equity mutual fund managers against a suitable stock market index to assess the performance of fund managers in general. For example, it is common to compare the average large-cap mutual fund's performance to that of the S&P 500 Index. But this is not a fair comparison because it ignores risk. Specifically, the risk parameters of the average mutual fund may be different than that of the benchmark, making a simple direct comparison of the mutual fund's performance and that of the benchmark inappropriate.

Robert Jones analyzed the performance of the average large-cap mutual fund adjusted for risk.[22] As noted earlier, tests of market efficiency are joint tests of the assumed asset pricing model. Jones used a model similar to the three-factor model proposed by Eugene Fama and Kenneth French that we will describe later in this chapter. The variables in his regression model are

Y_t = the difference between the returns on a composite mutual fund index and the S&P 500 in month t

$X_{1,t}$ = the difference between the S&P 500 return and the 90-day Treasury rate for month t

$X_{2,t}$ = the difference between the returns on the Russell 3000 Value Index and the Russell 3000 Growth Index for month t

$X_{3,t}$ = the difference between the returns on the Russell 1000 Index (large-cap stocks) and the Russell 2000 Index (small-cap stocks) for month t

The dependent variable, (Y_t), is obtained from indexes published by Lipper, a firm that constructs performance indexes for mutual funds classified by investment category. Specifically, the dependent variable in the study was the average of the return on the Lipper Growth Index and the Lipper Growth and Income Index each month minus the return on the S&P 500. Y_t is the active return.

The first independent variable $(X_{1,t})$ is a measure of the return of the market over the risk-free rate and is therefore the excess return on the market in general. The second independent variable $(X_{2,t})$ is a proxy for the difference in performance of two "styles" that have been found to be important in explaining stock returns: value and growth. (We describe this further later in this chapter.) In the regression, the independent variable $X_{2,t}$ is the excess return of value style over growth style. Market capitalization is another style factor. The last independent variable $(X_{3,t})$ is the difference in size between large-cap and small-cap stocks and therefore reflects size.

The regression was run over 219 months from January 1979 through March 1997. The results are reported below with the t-statistic for each parameter shown in parentheses:

$$\hat{Y}_t = -0.007 - 0.083X_{1,t} - 0.071X_{2,t} - 0.244X_{3,t}$$
$$\phantom{\hat{Y}_t =} (-0.192) \quad (-8.771) \quad\quad (-3.628) \quad\quad (-17.380)$$

---

[22] Robert C. Jones, "The Active versus Passive Debate: Perspectives of an Active Quant," in *Active Equity Portfolio Management*, ed. Frank J. Fabozzi (New York: John Wiley & Sons, 1998).

Let's interpret the results. The *t*-statistics of the betas are statistically significant for all levels of significance. The regression results suggest that relative to the S&P 500, the average large-cap mutual fund makes statistically significant bets against the market, against value, and against size. The adjusted R^2 is 0.63. This means that 63% of the variation in the average large-cap mutual fund's returns is explained by the regression model. The intercept term, *a*, is −0.007 (−7 basis points) and is interpreted as the average active return after controlling for risk (i.e., net of market, value, and size). Statistically, the intercept term is not significant. So, the average active return is indistinguishable from zero. Given that the return indexes constructed by Lipper are net of fees and expenses, the conclusion of this simple regression model is that the average large-cap mutual funds covers its costs on a risk-adjusted basis.

Tests of the Capital Asset Pricing Model

The Capital Asset Pricing Model (CAPM) is an equilibrium model of asset pricing. While portfolio managers do not devote time to testing the validity of this model since few have to be convinced of its limitation, there has been more than 40 years of empirical testing of the validity of this model and the primary tool that has been used is regression analysis. While there have been extensions of the CAPM first developed by William Sharpe in 1964, we will only discuss the tests of the original model.

Based on the above assumptions, the CAPM is

$$E(R_i) - R_f = \beta_i[E(R_M) - R_f] \tag{3.19}$$

where $E(R_i)$ = expected return for asset *i*
        R_f = risk-free rate
    $E(R_M)$ = expected return for the market portfolio
        β_i = the index of systematic risk of asset *i*

The index of systematic risk of asset *i*, β_i, popularly referred to as *beta*, is the degree to which an asset covaries with the market portfolio and for this reason is referred to as the asset's *systematic risk*. More specifically, systematic risk is the portion of an asset's variability that can be attributed to a common factor. Systematic risk is the risk that results from general market and economic conditions that cannot be diversified away. The portion of an asset's variability that can be diversified away is the risk that is unique to an asset. This risk is called *nonsystematic risk*, *diversifiable risk*, *unique risk*, *residual risk*, or *company-specific risk*. We calculated the beta for individual securities in the previous chapter.

The CAPM states that, given the assumptions, the expected return on asset is a positive linear function of its index of systematic risk as measured by beta. The higher the β_i or beta is, the higher the expected return. There are no other factors that should significantly affect an asset's expected return other than the index of systematic risk. A stock's beta is estimated from the characteristic line that we described and illustrated in the previous chapter.

The beta for an asset can be estimated using the following simple linear regression:

$$r_{it} - r_{ft} = \alpha_i + \beta_i[r_{Mt} - r_{ft}] + \varepsilon_{it}$$

where r_{it} = observed return on asset i for time t
         r_{ft} = observed return on the risk-free asset for time t
         r_{Mt} = observed return on the market portfolio for time t
         ε_{it} = error term for time t

The above regression equation is called the *characteristic line*. Since there is only one independent variable, $r_{Mt} - r_{ft}$, there is a simple linear regression.
    If

$$x_t = r_{Mt} - r_{ft}$$

and

$$y_t = r_{it} - r_{ft}$$

then the characteristic line can be rewritten as

$$y_t = \alpha_i + \beta_i x_t + \varepsilon_{it}$$

The parameters to be estimated are the coefficients α_i and β_i and the standard deviation of the error term, ε_i. The parameter β_i is the focus of interest in this section. Later in this chapter, when we provide an illustration of how regression analysis is used in performance measurement, we will see the economic meaning of the intercept term, α_i.

To estimate the characteristic line for an asset using regression analysis, we consider three time series of returns for (1) the asset, (2) the market index, and (3) the risk-free rate. The beta estimates will vary with the particular market index selected as well as with the sample period and frequency used.

Typically, a methodology referred to as a *two-pass regression* is used to test the CAPM. The first pass involves the estimation of beta for each security from its characteristic line. The betas from the first-pass regression are then used to form portfolios of securities ranked by portfolio beta.

The portfolio returns, the return on the risk-free asset, and the portfolio betas (denoted by β_p) are then used to estimate the second-pass regression. Then the following second-pass regression which is the empirical analogue of the CAPM is estimated:

$$R_p - R_F = b_0 + b_1\beta_p + \varepsilon_p \tag{3.20}$$

where the parameters to be estimated are b_0 and b_1, and ε_p is the error term for the regression.

Unlike the estimation of the characteristic line which uses time series data, the second-pass regression is a cross-sectional regression. The return data are frequently aggregated into five-year periods for this regression.

According to the CAPM, the following should be found:

1. b_0 should not be significantly different from zero. This can be seen by comparing equations (3.19) and (3.20).
2. b_1 should equal the observed risk premium $(R_M - R_F)$ over which the second-pass regression is estimated. Once again, this can be seen by comparing equations (3.19) and (3.20).
3. The relationship between beta and return should be linear. That is, if, for example, the following multiple regression is estimated,

$$R_p - R_F = b_0 + b_1\beta_p + b_2(\beta_p)^2 + \varepsilon_p$$

   the parameters b_0 and b_2 should not be significantly different from zero.
4. Beta should be the only factor that is priced by the market. That is, other factors such as the variance or standard deviation of the returns, and variables such as the price-earnings ratio, dividend yield, and firm size, should not add any significant explanatory power to the equation.

The general results of the empirical tests of the CAPM are as follows:

1. The estimated intercept term b_0, is significantly different from zero and consequently different from what is hypothesized for this value.
2. The estimated coefficient for beta, b_1, has been found to be less than the observed risk premium $(R_M - R_F)$. The combination of this and the previous finding suggests that low-beta stocks have higher returns than the CAPM predicts and high-beta stocks have lower returns than the CAPM predicts.
3. The relationship between beta and return appears to be linear; hence the functional form of the CAPM is supported.

4. Beta is not the only factor priced by the market. Several studies have discovered other factors that explain stock returns. These include a price-earnings factor, a dividend factor, a firm-size factor, and both a firm-size factor and a book-market factor.

It is the last of these findings that has fostered the empirical search for other factors using the financial econometric models.[23]

Evidence for Multifactor Models

Regression-based tests seeking to dispute the CAPM have helped identify factors that have been found to be statistically significant in explaining the variation in asset returns. Employing regression analysis, Robert Jones of Goldman Sachs Asset Management at the time reported factors he found in the U.S. stock market.[24] For the period 1979 through 1996, he regressed monthly stock returns against the following factors: "value" factors, "momentum" factors, and risk factors. The value factors included four ratios: book/market ratio, earnings/price ratio, sales/price ratio, and cash flow/price ratio. The three momentum factors included estimate revisions for earnings, revisions ratio, and price momentum. Three risk factors were used. The first is the systematic risk or beta from the CAPM.[25] The second is the residual risk from the CAPM; this is the risk not explained by the CAPM. The third risk is an uncertainty estimate measure. The factors are beginning-of-month values that are properly lagged where necessary.[26]

Jones calculated the average monthly regression coefficient and t-statistic for the series. Table 3.9 shows the estimated coefficient for each factor and the t-statistic. All of the factors are highly significant. The lowest t-statistic is

---

[23] It should be noted that in 1977 Richard Roll criticized the published tests of the CAPM. He argued that while the CAPM is testable in principle, no correct test of the theory had yet been presented. He also argued that there was practically no possibility that a correct empirical test would ever be accomplished in the future. See Richard R. Roll, "A Critique of the Asset Pricing Theory: Part I. On the Past and Potential Testability of the Theory," *Journal of Financial Economics* 5 (March 1977): 129–176.

[24] Jones, "The Active versus Passive Debate: Perspectives on an Active Quant."

[25] In the calculation of the CAPM a proxy for the market portfolio is needed. Jones used the Russell 1000 Index. This index includes large-cap stocks.

[26] Lagging is required because certain financial information is reported with lag. For example, year-end income and balance sheet information for a given year is not reported until three months after the corporation's year-end.

TABLE 3.9 Factors Found for U.S. Equity Market: Regression Results

	U.S. Results (1979–1996)	
	Coefficient	*t*-Statistic
Value Factors		
Book/market	0.24	2.96
Earnings/price	0.40	5.46
Sales/price	0.28	4.25
Cash flow/price	0.38	5.28
Momentum Factors		
Estimate revisions	0.56	13.22
Revisions ratio	0.55	14.72
Price momentum	0.61	7.17
Risk Factors		
CAPM beta	−0.17	−1.83
Residual risk	−0.42	−4.05
Estimate uncertainty	−0.33	−6.39

Source: Adapted from Exhibit 5 in Robert C. Jones, "The Active versus Passive Debate: Perspectives on an Active Quant," in *Active Equity Portfolio Management*, ed. Frank J. Fabozzi (Hoboken, NJ: John Wiley & Sons, 1998), Chapter 3.

that of the CAPM beta. The conclusion from the regression results reported in Table 3.9 is that there are factors other than the CAPM beta that explain returns.

KEY POINTS

- A multiple linear regression is a linear regression that has more than one independent or explanatory variable.
- There are three assumptions regarding the error terms in a multiple linear regression: (1) they are normally distributed with zero mean, (2) the variance is constant, and (3) they are independent.
- The ordinary least squares method is used to estimate the parameters of a multiple linear regression model.
- The three steps involved in designing a multiple linear regression model are (1) specification of the dependent and independent variables to be included in the model, (2) fitting/estimating the model, and (3) evaluating

the quality of the model with respect to the given data (diagnosis of the model).

- There are criteria for diagnosing the quality of a model. The tests used involve statistical tools from inferential statistics. The estimated regression errors play an important role in these tests and the tests accordingly are based on the three assumptions about the error terms.

- The first test is for the statistical significance of the multiple coefficient of determination, which is the ratio of the sum of squares explained by the regression and the total sum of squares.

- If the standard deviation of the regression errors from a proposed model is found to be too large, the fit could be improved by an alternative specification. Some of the variance of the errors may be attributable to the variation in some independent variable not considered in the model.

- An analysis of variance test is used to test for the statistical significance of the entire model.

- Because one can artificially increase the original R^2 by including additional independent variables into the regression, one will not know the true quality of the model by evaluating the model using the same data. To deal with this problem, the adjusted goodness-of-fit measure or adjusted R^2 is used. This measure takes into account the number of observations as well as the number of independent variables.

- To test for the statistical significance of individual independent variables, a t-test is used.

- To test for the statistical significance of a set or group of independent variables, an F-test is used.

CHAPTER 4

Building and Testing a Multiple Linear Regression Model

After reading this chapter you will understand:

- What is meant by multicollinearity in a multiple linear regression model.
- How to detect multicollinearity and mitigate the problem caused by it.
- The model building process in the sense of ascertaining the independent variables that best explain the variable of interest.
- How stepwise regression analysis is used in model building and the different stepwise regression methods.
- How to test for the various assumptions of the multiple linear regression model and correct the model when violations are found.

In this chapter we continue with our coverage of multiple linear regression analysis. The topics covered in this chapter are the problem of multicollinearity, model building techniques using stepwise regression analysis, and testing the assumptions of the models that were described in Chapter 3.

THE PROBLEM OF MULTICOLLINEARITY

When discussing the suitability of a model, an important issue is the structure or interaction of the independent variables. The statistical term used for the problem that arises from the high correlations among the independent variables used in a multiple regression model is *multicollinearity* or, simply, *collinearity*. Tests for the presence of multicollinearity must be performed after the model's significance has been determined and all significant independent variables to be used in the final regression have been determined.

A good deal of intuition is helpful in assessing if the regression coefficients make any sense. For example, one by one, select each independent variable and let all other independent variables be equal to zero. Now, estimate a regression merely with this particular independent variable and see if the regression coefficient of this variable seems unreasonable because if its sign is counterintuitive or its value appears too small or large, one may want to consider removing that independent variable from the regression. The reason may very well be attributable to multicollinearity. Technically, multicollinearity is caused by independent variables in the regression model that contain common information. The independent variables are highly intercorrelated; that is, they have too much linear dependence. Hence the presence of multicollinear independent variables prevents us from obtaining insight into the true contribution to the regression from each independent variable.

Formally, the notion of perfect collinearity, which means that one or more independent variables are a linear combination of the other independent variables, can be expressed by the following relationship:

$$\text{rank of } (X^T X) < k + 1 \tag{4.1}$$

where the matrix X was defined in equation (3.4) in Chapter 3. Equation (4.1) can be interpreted as X now consisting of vectors X_i, $i = 1, \ldots, k + 1$.

In a very extreme case, two or more variables may be perfectly correlated (i.e., their pairwise correlations are equal to one), which would imply that some vectors of observations of these variables are merely linear combinations of others. The result of this would be that some variables are fully explained by others and, thus, provide no additional information. This is a very extreme case, however. In most problems in finance, the independent data vectors are not perfectly correlated but may be correlated to a high degree. In any case, the result is that, roughly speaking, the regression estimation procedure is confused by this ambiguity of data information such that it cannot produce distinct regression coefficients for the variables involved. The β_i, $i = 1, \ldots, k$ cannot be identified; hence, an infinite number of possible values for the regression coefficients can serve as a solution. This can be very frustrating in building a reliable regression model.

We can demonstrate the problem with an example. Consider a regression model with three independent variables—X_1, X_2, and X_3. Also assume the following regarding these three independent variables:

$$X_1 = 2X_2 = 4X_3$$

such that there is, effectively, just one independent variable, either X_1, X_2, or X_3. Now, suppose all three independent variables are erroneously used to model the following regression

$$y = \beta_1 X_1 + \beta_2 X_2 + \beta_3 X_3$$
$$= 4\beta_1 X_3 + 2\beta_2 X_3 + \beta_3 X_3$$

Just to pick one possibility of ambiguity, the same effect is achieved by either increasing β_1 by, for example, 0.25 or by increasing β_3 by 1, and so forth. In this example, the rank would just be 1. This is also intuitive since, generally, the rank of $(X^TX)^{-1}$ indicates the number of truly independent sources.[1]

Procedures for Mitigating Multicollinearity

While it is quite impossible to provide a general rule to eliminate the problem of multicollinearity, there are some techniques that can be employed to mitigate the problem.

Multicollinearity might be present if there appears to be a mismatch between the sign of the correlation coefficient and the regression coefficient of that particular independent variable. So, the first place to always check is the correlation coefficient for each independent variable and the dependent variable.

Three other indicators of multicollinearity are:

1. The sensitivity of regression coefficients to the inclusion of additional independent variables.
2. Changes from significance to insignificance of already included independent variables after new ones have been added.
3. An increase in the model's standard error of the regression.

A consequence of the above is that the regression coefficient estimates vary dramatically as a result of only minor changes in the data X.

A remedy most commonly suggested is to try to single out independent variables that are likely to cause the problems. This can be done by excluding those independent variables so identified from the regression model. It may be possible to include other independent variables, instead, that provide additional information.

In general, due to multicollinearity, the standard error of the regression increases, rendering the t-ratios of many independent variables too small to indicate significance despite the fact that the regression model, itself is highly significant.

To find out whether the variance error of the regession is too large, we present a commonly employed tool. We measure multicollinearity by computing the impact of the correlation between some independent variables and the

---

[1] One speaks of "near collinearity" when the determinant of X^TX is very small so that matrix inversion is unstable and the estimation of the regression parameters is unstable.

jth independent variable. Therefore, we need to regress the jth variable on the remaining $k - 1$ variables. The resulting regression would look like

$$x_j = c + b_1^{(j)} x_1 + \ldots + b_{j-1}^{(j)} x_{j-1} + b_{j+1}^{(j)} x_{j+1} + \ldots + b_k^{(j)} x_k \quad j = 1, 2, \ldots, k$$

Then we obtain the coefficient of determination of this regression, R_j^2. This, again, is used to divide the original variance of the jth regression coefficient estimate by a correction term. This correction term is called the *variance inflation factor* (VIF) and is expressed as

$$\text{VIF} = \frac{1}{(1 - R_j^2)} \tag{4.2}$$

So, if there is no correlation present between independent variable j and the other independent variables, the variance of b_j will remain the same and the t-test results will be unchanged. On the contrary, in the case of more intense correlation, the variance will increase and most likely reject variable x_j as significant for the overall regression.

Consequently, prediction for the jth regression coefficient becomes less precise since its confidence interval increases due to equation (4.2).[2] The confidence interval for the regression coefficient at the level α is given by

$$\left[b_j - t_{\alpha/2} \cdot s_{b_j}, b_j + t_{\alpha/2} \cdot s_{b_j} \right] \tag{4.3}$$

where $t_{\alpha/2}$ is the critical value at level α of the t-distribution with $n - k$ degrees of freedom. This means that with probability $1-\alpha$, the true coefficient is inside of this interval.[3] Naturally, the result of some VIF > 1 leads to a widening of the confidence interval given by equation (4.3).

As a rule of thumb, a benchmark for the VIF is often given as 10. A VIF that exceeds 10 indicates a severe impact due to multicollinearity and the independent variable is best removed from the regression.

MODEL BUILDING TECHNIQUES

We now turn our attention to the model building process in the sense that we attempt to find the independent variables that best explain the variation in the dependent variable y. At the outset, we do not know how many and

---

[2] The confidence level is often chosen as $1 - \alpha = 0.99$ or $1 - \alpha = 0.95$ such that the parameter is inside of the interval with 0.95 or 0.99 probability, respectively.
[3] This is based on the assumptions stated in the context of estimation.

which independent variables to use. Increasing the number of independent variables does not always improve regressions. The econometric theorem known as *Pyrrho's lemma* relates to the number of independent variables.[4] Pyrrho's lemma states that by adding one special independent variable to a linear regression, it is possible to arbitrarily change the size and sign of regression coefficients as well as to obtain an arbitrary goodness-of-fit. This tells us that if we add independent variables without a proper design and testing methodology, we risk obtaining spurious results.

The implications are especially important for those financial models that seek to forecast prices, returns, or rates based on regressions over economic or fundamental variables. With modern computers, by trial and error, one might find a complex structure of regressions that give very good results in-sample but have no real forecasting power.

There are three methods that are used for the purpose of determining the suitable independent variables to be included in a final regression model. They are:

1. Stepwise inclusion regression method
2. Stepwise exclusion regression method
3. Standard stepwise regression method

We explain each next.

Stepwise Inclusion Regression Method

In the *stepwise inclusion regression method* we begin by selecting a single independent variable. It should be the one most highly correlated (positive or negative) with the dependent variable.[5] After inclusion of this independent variable, we perform an *F*-test to determine whether this independent variable is significant for the regression. If not, then there will be no independent variable from the set of possible choices that will significantly explain the variation in the dependent variable y. Thus, we will have to look for a different set of variables.

If, on the other hand, this independent variable, say x_1, is significant, we retain x_1 and consider the next independent variable that best explains the remaining variation in y. We require that this additional independent variable, say x_2, be the one with the highest *coefficient of partial determination*. This is a measure of the goodness-of-fit given that the first x_1 is already in the regression. It is defined to be the ratio of the remaining variation

---

[4]T. K. Dijkstra, "Pyrrho's Lemma, or Have it Your Way," *Metrica* 42 (1995): 119–225.
[5]The absolute value of the correlation coefficient should be used since we are only interested in the extent of linear dependence, not the direction.

explained by the second independent variable to the total of unexplained variation before x_2 was included. Formally, we have

$$\frac{\text{SSE}_1 - \text{SSE}_2}{\text{SSE}_1} \tag{4.4}$$

where SSE_1 = the variation left unexplained by x_1
   SSE_2 = the variation left unexplained after both x_1 and x_2 have been included

This is equivalent to requiring that the additional variable is to be the one that provides the largest coefficient of determination once included in the regression. After the inclusion, an F-test with

$$F = \frac{\text{SSE}_1 - \text{SSE}_2}{\dfrac{\text{SSE}_1}{n-2}} \tag{4.5}$$

is conducted to determine the significance of the additional variable.

The addition of independent variables included in some set of candidate independent variables is continued until either all independent variables are in the regression or the additional contribution to explain the remaining variation in y is not significant anymore. Hence, as a generalization to equation (4.5), we compute

$$F = \left(\text{SSE}_i - \text{SSE}_{i+1}\right) / \left(\text{SSE}_i\right) \times \left(n - i - 1\right)$$

after the inclusion of the $i + 1$st variable and keep it included only if F is found to be significant. Accordingly, SSE_i denotes the sum of square residuals with i variables included while SSE_{i+1} is the corresponding quantity for $i + 1$ included variables.

Stepwise Exclusion Regression Method

The *stepwise exclusion regression method* mechanically is basically the opposite of the stepwise inclusion method. That is, one includes all independent variables at the beginning. One after another of the insignificant variables are eliminated until all insignificant independent variables have been removed. The result constitutes the final regression model. In other words, we include all k independent variables into the regression at first. Then we consider all variables for exclusion on a step-wise removal basis.

For each independent variable, we compute

$$F = \left(SSE_{k-1} - SSE_k\right) / \left(SSE_{k-1}\right) \times \left(n - k\right) \tag{4.6}$$

to find the ones where F is insignificant. The one that yields the least significant value F is discarded. We proceed stepwise by alternatively considering all remaining variables for exclusion and, likewise, compute the F-test statistic given by equation (4.7) for the new change in the coefficient of partial determination.

In general, at each step i, we compute

$$F = \left(SSE_{k-i} - SSE_{k-i+1}\right) / \left(SSE_{k-i}\right) \times \left(n - k + i - 1\right) \tag{4.7}$$

to evaluate the coefficient of partial determination lost due to discarding the ith independent variable.[6] If no variable with an insignificant F-test statistic can be found, we terminate the elimination process.

Standard Stepwise Regression Method

The *standard stepwise regression method* involves introducing independent variables based on significance and explanatory power and possibly eliminating some that have been included at previous steps. The reason for elimination of any such independent variables is that they have now become insignificant after the new independent variables have entered the model. Therefore, we check the significance of all coefficient statistics according to equation (3.16) in Chapter 3. This methodology provides a good means for eliminating the influence from possible multicollinearity discussed earlier.

Application of the Stepwise Regression Method   In the previous chapter, we used an illustration to show how multiple linear regression analysis can be used for hedge fund style analysis. We first explained the use of the Sharpe benchmark for this purpose and then explained using an illustration by Dor and Jagannathan the issues with using the Sharpe benchmark for hedge fund style analysis.[7] We will continue with that illustration here

---

[6]The SSE_{k-i+1} is the sum of square residuals before independent variable i is discarded. After the ith independent variable has been removed, the sum of square residuals of the regression with the remaining $k - i$ variables is given by SSE_{k-i}.

[7]Arik Ben Dor and Ravi Jagannathan, "Style Analysis: Asset Allocation and Performance Evaluation," in *The Handbook of Equity Style Management*, 3rd ed., ed. T. Daniel Coggin and Frank J. Fabozzi (Hoboken, NJ: John Wiley & Sons, 2003).

because Dor and Jagannathan use a stepwise regression to further illustrate their point.

Dor and Jagannathan show how the style analysis can be further improved by including peer-group performance as measured by hedge fund indexes created by several organizations. Three examples of such organizations are Hedge Fund Research Company (HFR), CSFB/Tremont (TRE), and MAR Futures (MAR). The five hedge fund indexes that are used by Dor and Jagannathan in their illustration are (1) Market Neutral, (2) Emerging Markets, (3) Managed Futures, (4) Fixed Income, and (5) Event Driven. A total of 21 explanatory variables then can be used in the style analysis: twelve asset classes, five hedge fund indexes, and four of the S&P 500 option strategies. Because of the large number of variables and their high correlations, Dor and Jagannathan employ stepwise regression analysis. The results are shown in Table 4.1. In implementing the stepwise regression, Dor and Jagannathan specify a 10% significance level for deleting or adding an explanatory variable in the stepwise regression procedure. The results of the stepwise regression results show a higher ability to track the returns of the two directional funds relative to the two nondirectional funds by including the five hedge fund indexes (i.e., peer groups).

TESTING THE ASSUMPTIONS OF THE MULTIPLE LINEAR REGRESSION MODEL

After we have come up with some regression model, we have to perform a diagnosis check. The question that must be asked is: How well does the model fit the data? This is addressed using diagnosis checks that include the coefficient of determination, R^2 as well as R^2_{adj}, and the standard error or square root of the mean squared error (MSE) of the regression. In particular, the diagnosis checks analyze whether the linear relationship between the dependent and independent variables is justifiable from a statistical perspective.

As we also explained in the previous chapter, there are several assumptions that are made when using the general multiple linear regression model. The first assumption is the independence of the independent variables used in the regression model. This is the problem of multicollinearity that we discussed earlier where we briefly described how to test and correct for this problem. The second assumption is that the model is in fact linear. The third assumption has to do with assumptions about the statistical properties of the error term for the general multiple linear regression model. Furthermore, we assumed that the residuals are uncorrelated with the independent variables. Here we look at the assumptions regarding the linearity of the model

TABLE 4.1 Hedge Funds Style Analysis Using Stepwise Regression

This exhibit reports for each fund the results of a stepwise estimation using 12 asset classes, five hedge funds indexes, and four option strategies. The analysis is repeated separately for each hedge fund database. Stepwise regression involves adding and/or deleting variables sequentially depending on the F value. We specify a 10% significance level for deleting a variable in the stepwise regression procedure. The single (*) and double (**) asterisks denote significantly different than zero at the 5% and 1% level, respectively.

	Hillsdale Market Neutral			Nippon Market Neutral			Axiom Emerging Markets			CTA		
	HFR	TRE	MAR	HFR	TRE	MAR	HFR	TRE	MAR	HFR	TRE	MAR
Bills	−23.36*						31.9**		23.36			
Treasury 1–10 yrs							−7.32**	−4.58**	−6.07**			
Treasury 10+ yrs												
Corporate Bonds							3.11**	1.75*	2.62**	2.86**		−0.37
Large-Cap Value				−0.21	−0.24*	−0.37**						
Large-Cap Growth		0.38**	0.35**			−0.29						
Small-Cap Value							−0.39**	−0.18**	−0.26**		0.47**	0.52**
Small-Cap Growth											−0.17	−0.23*
Developed Countries											−0.29	
Japan							0.23**		0.15	−0.23	−0.33**	−0.19**
Emerging Markets		−0.33**	−0.33**				0.36**					
Foreign Bonds							−0.58**			0.60	0.49**	0.72**
Market Neutral	1.86**				0.98*	2.49**	1.89**	1.44**	3.01**			
Emerging Markets	−0.51**								0.81**			−0.17
Managed Futures		0.32						0.32**		1.28**	1.28**	1.51**
Fixed Income				0.81*	0.85**							
Event Driven							1.47**	1.82**				
At-the-money call	−0.10*			0.014*	0.012*	0.02**				0.02**	0.02**	
At-the-money put	0.08*								−0.12		0.08	−0.10**
Out-of-the-money put						−0.02				0.2**	−0.08	0.09**
R^2	0.46	0.27	0.22	0.21	0.33	0.29	0.82	0.82	0.80	0.19	0.68	0.77

Source: Exhibit 1.13 in Arik Ben Dor and Ravi Jagannathan, "Style Analysis: Asset Allocation and Performance Evaluation," in *The Handbook of Equity Style Management*, 3rd ed., ed. T. Daniel Coggin and Frank J. Fabozzi (Hoboken, NJ: John Wiley & Sons, 2003).

and the assumptions about the error term. We discuss the implications of the violation of these assumptions, some tests used to detect violations, and provide a brief explanation of how to deal with any violations. In some cases, we discuss these violations in more detail in later chapters.

Tests for Linearity

To test for linearity, a common approach is to plot the regression residuals on the vertical axis and values of the independent variable on the horizontal axis. This graphical analysis is performed for each independent variable. What we are looking for is a random scattering of the residuals around zero. If this should be the case, the model assumption with respect to the residuals is correct. If not, however, there seems to be some systematic behavior in the residuals that depends on the values of the independent variables. The explanation is that the relationship between the independent and dependent variables is not linear.

The problem of a nonlinear functional form can be dealt with by transforming the independent variables or making some other adjustment to the variables. For example, suppose that we are trying to estimate the relationship between a stock's return as a function of the return on a broad-based stock market index such as the S&P 500. Letting y denote the return on the stock and x the return on the S&P 500 we might assume the following bivariate regression model:

$$y = b_0 + b_1 x + \varepsilon \tag{4.8}$$

where ε is the error term.

We have made the assumption that the functional form of the relationship is linear. Suppose that we find that a better fit appears to be that the return on the stock is related to the return on the broad-based market index as

$$y = b_0 + b_1 x + b_2 x^2 + \varepsilon \tag{4.9}$$

If we let $x = x_1$ and $x^2 = x_2$ and we adjust our table of observations accordingly, then we can rewrite equation (4.9) as

$$y = b_0 + b_1 x_1 + b_2 x_2 + \varepsilon \tag{4.10}$$

The model given by equation (4.10) is now a linear regression model despite the fact that the functional form of the relationship between y and x is nonlinear. That is, we are able to modify the functional form to create a linear regression model.

Let's see how a simple transformation can work as explained in Chapter 2. Suppose that the true relationship of interest is exponential, that is,

$$y = \beta \varepsilon^{\alpha x} \tag{4.11}$$

Taking the natural logarithms of both sides of equation (4.11) will result in

$$\ln y = \ln \beta + \alpha x \tag{4.12}$$

which is again linear.

Now consider that the fit in equation (4.12) is not exact; that is, there is some random deviation by some residual. Then we obtain

$$\ln y = \ln \beta + \alpha x + \varepsilon \tag{4.13}$$

If we let $z = \ln y$ and adjust the table of observations for y accordingly and let $\lambda = \ln \beta$, we can then rewrite equation (4.13) as

$$z = \lambda + \alpha x + \varepsilon \tag{4.14}$$

This regression model is now linear with the parameters to be estimated being λ and α.

Now we transform equation (4.14) back into the shape of equation (4.11) ending up with

$$y = \beta \varepsilon^{\alpha x} \cdot \varepsilon^{\varepsilon} = \beta \varepsilon^{\alpha x} \cdot \xi \tag{4.15}$$

where in equation (4.15) the deviation is multiplicative rather than additive as would be the case in a linear model. This would be a possible explanation of the nonlinear function relationship observed for the residuals.

However, not every functional form that one might be interested in estimating can be transformed or modified so as to create a linear regression. For example, consider the following relationship:

$$y = (b_1 x)/(b_2 + x) + \varepsilon \tag{4.16}$$

Admittedly, this is an odd looking functional form. What is important here is that the regression parameters to be estimated (b_1 and b_2) cannot be transformed to create a linear regression model. A regression such as equation (4.16) is referred to as a *nonlinear regression* and the estimation of nonlinear regressions is far more complex than that of a linear regression because they have no closed-form formulas for the parameters to be estimated. Instead, nonlinear regression estimation techniques require the use of optimization techniques to identify the parameters that best fit the model. Researchers in disciplines such as biology and physics often have to deal with nonlinear regressions.

Assumed Statistical Properties about the Error Term

The third assumption about the general linear model concerns the three assumptions about the error term that we listed in Chapter 3 and repeat below:

> *Assumption 1.* The regression errors are normally distributed with zero mean.
>
> *Assumption 2.* The variance of the regression errors (σ_ε^2) is constant.
>
> *Assumption 3.* The error terms from different points in time are independent such that ε_t are independent variables for all t.

Assumption 1 states that the probability distribution for the error term is that it is normally distributed. Assumption 2 says that the variance of the probability distribution for the error term does not depend on the level of any of the independent variables. That is, the variance of the error term is constant regardless of the level of the independent variable. If this assumption holds, the error terms are said to be *homoscedastic* (also spelled *homoskedastic*). If this assumption is violated, the variance of the error term is said to be *heteroscedastic* (also spelled *heteroskedastic*). Assumption 3 says that there should not be any statistically significant correlation between adjacent residuals. The correlation between error terms is referred to as *autocorrelation*. Recall that we also assume that the residuals are uncorrelated with the independent variables.

Tests for the Residuals Being Normally Distributed

An assumption of the general linear regression model is that the residuals are normally distributed. The implications of the violation of this assumption are:

- The regression model is misspecified.
- The estimates of the regression coefficients are also not normally distributed.
- The estimates of the regression coefficients, although still the best linear unbiased estimators, are no longer efficient estimators.

From the second implication above we can see that violation of the normality assumption makes hypothesis testing suspect. More specifically, if the assumption is violated, the *t*-tests explained in Chapter 3 will not be applicable.

Typically the following three methodologies are used to test for normality of the error terms (1) chi-square statistic, (2) Jarque-Bera test statistic, and (3) analysis of standardized residuals.

Chi-Square Statistic The *chi-square statistic* is defined as

$$\chi^2 = \sum_{i=1}^{k} \frac{\left(n_i - n \cdot p_i\right)^2}{n \cdot p_i} \tag{4.17}$$

where some interval along the real numbers is divided into k segments of possibly equal size. The p_i indicate which percentage of all n values of the sample should fall into the ith segment if the data were truly normally distributed. Hence, the theoretical number of values that should be inside of segment i is $n \cdot p_i$. The n_i are the values of the sample that actually fall into that segment i. The test statistic given by equation (4.17) is approximately chi-square distributed with $k - 1$ degrees of freedom. As such, it can be compared to the critical values of the chi-square distribution at arbitrary α-levels. If the critical values are surpassed or, equivalently, the *p*-value of the statistic is less than α, then the normal distribution has to be rejected for the residuals.

Jarque-Bera Test Statistic The *Jarque-Bera test statistic* is not simple to calculate manually, but most computer software packages have it installed. Formally, it is

$$JB = \frac{n}{6}\left(S^2 + \frac{(K-3)^2}{4}\right) \tag{4.18}$$

with

$$S = \frac{\frac{1}{n}\sum_{i=1}^{n}(x - \bar{x})^3}{\left(\frac{1}{n}\sum_{i=1}^{n}(x - \bar{x})^2\right)^{\frac{3}{2}}} \tag{4.19}$$

$$K = \frac{\dfrac{1}{n}\sum_{i=1}^{n}(x - \overline{x})^4}{\left(\dfrac{1}{n}\sum_{i=1}^{n}(x - \overline{x})^2\right)^2} \tag{4.20}$$

for a sample of size n.

The expression in equation (4.19) is the skewness statistic of some distribution, and equation (4.20) is the kurtosis. Kurtosis measures the peakedness of the probability density function of some distribution around the median compared to the normal distribution. Also, kurtosis estimates, relative to the normal distribution, the behavior in the extreme parts of the distribution (i.e., the tails of the distribution). For a normal distribution, $K = 3$. A value for K that is less than 3 indicates a so-called *light-tailed distribution* in that it assigns less weight to the tails. The opposite is a value for K that exceeds 3 and is referred to as a *heavy-tailed distribution*. The test statistics given by equation (4.18) are approximately distributed chi-square with two degrees of freedom.

Analysis of Standardized Residuals   Another means of determining the appropriateness of the normal distribution are the standardized residuals. Once computed, they can be graphically analyzed in histograms. Formally, each standardized residual at the ith observation is computed according to

$$\tilde{e}_i = n \cdot \frac{e_i}{s_e\sqrt{(n+1) + \dfrac{(x_i - \overline{x})^2}{s_x^2}}} \tag{4.21}$$

where s_e is the estimated standard error (as defined in Chapter 3) and n is the sample size. This can be done with most statistical software.

If the histogram appears skewed or simply not similar to a normal distribution, the linearity assumption is very likely to be incorrect. Additionally, one might compare these standardized residuals with the normal distribution by plotting them against their theoretical normal counterparts in a normal probability plot. There is a standard routine in most statistical software that performs this analysis. If the pairs lie along the line running through the sample quartiles, the regression residuals seem to follow a normal distribution and, thus, the assumptions of the regression model stated in Chapter 3 are met.

Tests For Constant Variance of the Error Term (Homoscedasticity)

The second test regarding the residuals in a linear regression analysis is that the variance of all squared error terms is the same. As we noted earlier, this assumption of constant variance is referred to as homoscedasticity. However, many time series data exhibit heteroscedasticity, where the error terms may be expected to be larger for some observations or periods of the data than for others.

There are several tests that have been used to detect the presence of heteroscedasticity. These include the

- White's generalized heteroscedasticity test
- Park test
- Glejser Test
- Goldfeld-Quandt test
- Breusch-Pagan-Godfrey Test (Lagrangian multiplier test)

These tests will not be described here.

If heteroscedasticity is detected, the issue then is how to construct models that accommodate this feature of the residual variance so that valid regression coefficient estimates and models are obtained for the variance of the error term. There are two methodologies used for dealing with heteroscedasticity: weighted least squares estimation technique and autoregressive conditional heteroscedastic (ARCH) models. We describe the first method here. We devote an entire chapter, Chapter 11, to the second methodology because of its importance for not just testing for heteroscedasticity but in forecasting volatility.

Weighted Least Squares Estimation Technique   A potential solution for correcting the problem of heteroscedasticity is to give less weight to the observations coming from the population with larger variances and more weight to the observations coming from observations with higher variance. This is the basic notion of the *weighted least squares* (WLS) *technique*.

To see how the WLS technique can be used, let's consider the case of the bivariate regression given by

$$y_t = \beta_0 + \beta_1 x_t + \varepsilon_t \tag{4.22}$$

Let's now make the somewhat bold assumption that the variance of the error term for each time period is known. Denoting this variance by σ_t^2

(dropping the subscript ε for the error term), we can then deflate the terms in the bivariate linear regression given by equation (4.22) by the assumed known standard deviation of the error term as follows:

$$\left(\frac{y_t}{\sigma_t}\right) = \beta_0\left(\frac{1}{\sigma_t}\right) + \beta_1\left(\frac{x_t}{\sigma_t}\right) + \left(\frac{\varepsilon_t}{\sigma_t}\right) \tag{4.23}$$

We have transformed all the variables in the bivariate regression, including the original error term. It can be demonstrated that the regression with the transformed variables as shown in equation (4.23) no longer has heteroscedasticity. That is, the variance of the error term in equation (4.23), ε_t/σ_t, is homoscedastic.

Equation (4.23) can be estimated using ordinary least squares by simply adjusting the table of observations so that the variables are deflated by the known σ_t. When this is done, the estimates are referred to as *weighted least squares estimators*.

We simplified the illustration by assuming that the variance of the error term is known. Obviously, this is an extremely aggressive assumption. In practice, the true value for the variance of the error term is unknown. Other less aggressive assumptions are made but nonetheless are still assumptions. For example, the variance of the error term can be assumed to be proportional to one of the values of the independent variables. In any case, the WLS estimator requires that we make some assumption about the variance of the error term and then transform the value of the variables accordingly in order to apply the WLS technique.

Absence of Autocorrelation of the Residuals

Assumption 3 is that there is no correlation between the residual terms. Simply put, this means that there should not be any statistically significant correlation between adjacent residuals. In time series analysis, this means no significant correlation between two consecutive time periods.

The correlation of the residuals is critical from the point of view of estimation. Autocorrelation of residuals is quite common in financial data where there are quantities that are time series. A time series is said to be autocorrelated if each term is correlated with its predecessor so that the variance of each term is partially explained by regressing each term on its predecessor.

Autocorrelation, which is also referred to as *serial correlation* and *lagged correlation* in time series analysis, like any correlation, can range from –1 to +1. Its computation is straightforward since it is simply a correlation using the residual pairs e_t and e_{t-1} as the observations. The formula is

$$\rho_{auto} = \frac{\sum_{t=2}^{n} e_t e_{t-1}}{\sum_{t=1}^{n} e_t^2} \qquad (4.24)$$

where ρ_{auto} means the estimated autocorrelation and e_t is the computed residual or error term for the tth observation.

A *positive autocorrelation* means that if a residual t is positive (negative), then the residual that follows, $t + 1$, tends to be positive (negative). Positive autocorrelation is said to exhibit persistence. A *negative autocorrelation* means that a positive (negative) residual t tends to be followed by a negative (positive) residual $t + 1$.

The presence of significant autocorrelation in a time series means that, in a probabilistic sense, the series is predictable because future values are correlated with current and past values. From an estimation perspective, the existence of autocorrelation complicates hypothesis testing of the regression coefficients. This is because although the regression coefficient estimates are unbiased, they are not best linear unbiased estimates. Hence, the variances may be significantly underestimated and the resulting hypothesis test questionable.

Detecting Autocorrelation How do we detect the autocorrelation of residuals? Suppose that we believe that there is a reasonable linear relationship between two variables, for instance stock returns and some fundamental variable. We then perform a linear regression between the two variables and estimate regression parameters using the OLS method. After estimating the regression parameters, we can compute the sequence of residuals. At this point, we can apply statistical tests. There are several tests for autocorrelation of residuals that can be used. Two such tests are the Durbin-Watson test and the Dickey-Fuller test. We discuss only the first below.

The most popular test is the Durbin-Watson test, or more specifically, the *Durbin-Watson d-statistic,* computed as

$$d = \frac{\sum_{t=2}^{n} (e_t - e_{t-1})^2}{\sum_{t=1}^{n} e_t^2} \qquad (4.25)$$

The denominator of the test is simply the sum of the squares of the error terms; the numerator is the squared difference of the successive residuals.

It can be shown that if the sample size is large, then the Durbin-Watson d test statistic given by equation (4.25) is approximately related to the autocorrelation given by equation (4.24) as

$$d \approx 2\left(1 - \rho_{auto}\right) \qquad (4.26)$$

Since ρ_{auto} can vary between -1 and 1, this means that d can vary from 0 to 4 as shown:

Value of ρ_{auto}	Interpretation of ρ_{auto}	Approximate Value of d
-1	Perfect negative autocorrelation	4
0	No autocorrelation	2
1	Perfect positive autocorrelation	0

From the above table we see that if d is close to 2 there is no autocorrelation. A d value less than 2 means there is potentially positive autocorrelation; the closer the value to 0 the greater the likelihood of positive autocorrelation. There is potentially negative autocorrelation if the computed d exceeds 2 and the closer the value is to 4, the greater the likelihood of negative autocorrelation.

In previous hypothesis tests discussed in this book, we stated that there is a critical value that a test statistic had to exceed in order to reject the null hypothesis. In the case of the Durbin-Watson d statistic, there is not a single critical value but two critical values, which are denoted by d_L and d_U. Moreover, there are ranges for the value of d where no decision can be made about the presence of autocorrelation. The general decision rule given the null hypothesis and the computed value for d is summarized in the following table:

Null Hypothesis	Range for Computed d	Decision Rule
No positive autocorrelation	$0 < d < d_L$	Reject the null hypothesis
No positive autocorrelation	$d_L \leq d \leq d_U$	No decision
No negative autocorrelation	$4 - d_L < d < 4$	Reject the null hypothesis
No negative autocorrelation	$4 - d_U \leq d \leq 4 - d_L$	No decision
No autocorrelation	$d_U < d < 4 - d_U$	Accept the null hypothesis

Where does one obtain the critical values d_L and d_U? There are tables that report those values for the 5% and 1% levels of significance. The critical values also depend on the sample size and the number of independent variables in the multiple regression.[8]

For example, suppose that there are 12 independent variables in a regression, there are 200 observations, and that the significance level selected is 5%. Then according to the Durbin-Watson critical value table, the critical values are

$$d_L = 1.643 \text{ and } d_U = 1.896$$

Then the tests in the previous table can be written as:

Null Hypothesis	Range for Computed d	Decision Rule
No positive autocorrelation	$0 < d < 1.643$	Reject the null hypothesis
No positive autocorrelation	$1.643 \leq d \leq 1.896$	No decision
No negative autocorrelation	$2.357 < d < 4$	Reject the null hypothesis
No negative autocorrelation	$2.104 \leq d \leq 2.357$	No decision
No autocorrelation	$1.896 < d < 2.104$	Accept the null hypothesis

Modeling in the Presence of Autocorrelation   If residuals are autocorrelated, the regression coefficient can still be estimated without bias using the formula given by equation (3.10) in Chapter 3. However, this estimate will not be optimal in the sense that there are other estimators with lower variance of the sampling distribution. Fortunately, there is a way to deal with this problem. An optimal linear unbiased estimator called the *Aitken's generalized least squares* (GLS) *estimator* can be used. The discussion about this estimator is beyond the scope of this chapter.

The principle underlying the use of such estimators is that in the presence of correlation of residuals, it is common practice to replace the standard regression models with models that explicitly capture autocorrelations and produce uncorrelated residuals. The key idea here is that autocorrelated residuals signal that the modeling exercise has not been completed. That is, if residuals are autocorrelated, this signifies that the residuals at a generic time t can be predicted from residuals at an earlier time.

Autoregressive Moving Average Models   There are models for dealing with the problem of autocorrelation in time series data. These models are called *autoregressive moving average* (ARMA) *models*. Although financial time

---

[8] See N. Eugene Savin and Kenneth J. White, "The Durbin-Watson Test for Serial Correlation with Extreme Sample Sizes or Many Regressors," *Econometrica* 45 (1977): 1989–1996.

series typically exhibit structures that are more complex than those provided by ARMA models, these models are a starting point and often serve as a benchmark to compare more complex approaches. There are two components to an ARMA model: (1) autoregressive process and (2) moving average process. We discuss these in Chapter 9.

KEY POINTS

- The structure or interaction of the independent variables is an important issue in a multiple linear regression model and is referred to as the multicollinearity problem. Investigation for the presence of multicollinearity involves the correlation between the independent variables and the dependent variable.
- Tests for the presence of multicollinearity must be performed after the model's significance has been determined and all significant independent variables to be used in the final regression have been determined.
- The process of building a multiple linear regression model involves identifying the independent variables that best explain the variation in the dependent variable.
- In the initial development of a model, how many and which independent variables to include in the model are unknown. Increasing the number of independent variables does not always improve regressions.
- Pyrrho's lemma states that by adding one special independent variable to a linear regression model, it is possible to arbitrarily change the sign and magnitude of the regression coefficients as well as to obtain an arbitrary goodness-of-fit.
- Without a proper design and testing methodology, the adding of independent variables to a regression model runs the risk of obtaining spurious results.
- Stepwise regression analysis is a statistical tool employed for determining the suitable independent variables to be included in a final regression model. The three stepwise regression methodologies are the stepwise inclusion method, the stepwise exclusion method, and the standard stepwise regression method.
- The process of building a model also calls for testing the assumptions of the multiple linear regression model (i.e., performing diagnosis checks).
- The diagnosis checks analyze whether the linear relationship between the dependent and independent variables is justifiable from a statistical perspective.
- These tests also involve testing for the several assumptions that are made when using the general multiple linear regression model: (1) independence

of the independent variables used in the regression model (e.g., the problem of multicollinearity), (2) the linearity of the model, and (3) whether the assumptions about the statistical properties of the error term are warranted.

- Visual inspection of a scatter diagram of each independent variable and the regression residuals is a common approach for checking for linearity. The presence of some systematic behavior in the residuals that depends on the values of the independent variables might suggest that the relationship between the independent variable investigated and dependent variable is not linear.
- The problem of a nonlinear functional form can be dealt with by transforming the independent variables or making some other adjustment to the variables.
- Testing for the assumptions about the error terms involves testing if (1) they are normally distribution with zero mean, (2) the variance is constant, and (3) they are independent.
- The implications of the violation of the normality assumption of the error terms are threefold: (1) the regression model is misspecified, (2) the estimates of the regression coefficients are not normally distributed, and (3) although still best linear unbiased estimators, the estimates of the regression coefficients are no longer efficient estimators.
- Three methodologies used to test for normality of the error terms are the chi-square statistic, the Jarque-Bera test statistic, and analysis of standardized residuals.
- In a linear regression model the variance of all squared error terms is assumed to be constant, an assumption referred to as homoscedasticity.
- When the homoscedasticity assumption is violated, the variance of the error terms is said to exhibit heteroscedasticity. Many time series data exhibit heteroscedasticity, where the error terms may be expected to be larger for some observations or periods of the data than for others.
- There are several tests that have been used to detect for the presence of heteroscedasticity and there are several methodologies for constructing models to accommodate this feature. Two of the most common methodologies are the weighted least squares estimation technique and the autoregressive conditional heteroscedasticity model (ARCH).
- The multiple linear regression model assumes that there is no statistically significant correlation between adjacent residuals. This means that there is no statistically significant autocorrelation between residuals.
- A time series is said to be autocorrelated if each term is correlated with its predecessor so that the variance of each term is partially explained by regressing each term on its predecessor. In time series analysis, this means no significant autocorrelation between two consecutive time periods.

- Autocorrelation of residuals is quite common in time series financial data. In time series analysis, autocorrelation is also referred to as serial correlation and lagged correlation.
- If a residual t is positive (negative) and the residual that follows, $t + 1$, tends to be positive (negative), this behavior is said to be persistent and is referred to as positive autocorrelation. If, instead, a positive (negative) residual t tends to be followed by a negative (positive) residual $t + 1$, this is referred to as negative autocorrelation.
- Significant autocorrelation in a time series means that, in a probabilistic sense, the series is predictable because future values are correlated with current and past values.
- The presence of autocorrelation complicates hypothesis testing of the regression coefficients. This is because although the regression coefficient estimates are unbiased, they are not best linear unbiased estimates so that the variances may be significantly underestimated and the resulting hypothesis tests questionable. When significant autocorrelation is present, the Aitken's generalized least squares (GLS) estimator, which is an optimal linear unbiased estimated, can be employed.
- The most popular test for the presence of autocorrelation of the residuals is the Durbin-Watson test, or more specifically, the Durbin-Watson d-statistic.
- Autoregressive moving average (ARMA) models are used for dealing with the problem of autocorrelation in time series data.

CHAPTER 5

Introduction to
Time Series Analysis

After reading this chapter you will understand:

- What is meant by time series data.
- What is meant by trend and seasonal terms in a time series.
- What is meant by autoregressive of order one and autocorrelation.
- The moving average method for estimating a time series model.
- How time series can be represented with difference equations.
- What is meant by a random walk and error corrections price processes.

In this chapter, we introduce the element of time as an index of a series of univariate observations. Thus, we treat observations as being obtained successively rather than simultaneously. We present a simple time series model and its components. In particular, we focus on the trend, the cyclical, and seasonal terms, as well as the error or disturbance of the model. Furthermore, we introduce the random walk and error correction models as candidates for modeling security price movements. Here the notion of innovation appears. Time series are significant in modeling price processes as well as the dynamics of economic quantities. In this chapter, we assume that trends are deterministic. In Chapter 10, we take a closer look at stochastic components of trends.

WHAT IS A TIME SERIES?

So far, we have either considered two-component variables cross-sectionally coequal, which was the case in correlation analysis, or we have considered one variable to be, at least partially, the functional result of some other quantity. The intent of this section is to analyze variables that change in time, in other words, the objects of the analysis are *time series*. The observations are conceived as compositions of functions of time and other exogenous and endogenous

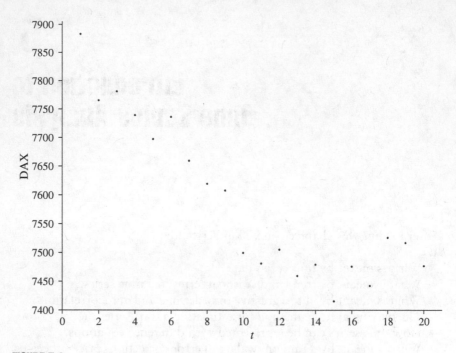

FIGURE 5.1   DAX Index Values: May 3 to May 31, 2007

variables as well as lagged values of the series itself or other quantities. These latter quantities may be given exogenously or also depend on time.

To visualize this, we plot the graph of 20 daily closing values of the German stock market index, the DAX (Deutscher Aktien IndeX), in Figure 5.1. The values are listed in Table 5.1. The time points of observation t with equidistant increments are represented by the horizontal axis while the DAX index values are represented by the vertical axis.

DECOMPOSITION OF TIME SERIES

Each point in Figure 5.1 is a pair of the components, time and value. In this section, the focus is on the dynamics of the observations; that is, one wants to know what the values are decomposable into at each point in time. A time series with observations x_t, $t = 1, 2, \ldots, n$ is usually denoted by $\{x\}_t$.[1] In the context of time series analysis, for any value x_t, the series is thought of as a composition of several quantities. The most traditional decomposition is of the form

TABLE 5.1 DAX Values of the Period May 3 to May 31, 2007

Date	t	Level
5/3/2007	1	7883.04
5/4/2007	2	7764.97
5/7/2007	3	7781.04
5/8/2007	4	7739.20
5/9/2007	5	7697.38
5/10/2007	6	7735.88
5/11/2007	7	7659.39
5/14/2007	8	7619.31
5/15/2007	9	7607.54
5/16/2007	10	7499.50
5/17/2007	11	7481.25
5/18/2007	12	7505.35
5/21/2007	13	7459.61
5/22/2007	14	7479.34
5/23/2007	15	7415.33
5/24/2007	16	7475.99
5/25/2007	17	7442.20
5/29/2007	18	7525.69
5/30/2007	19	7516.76
5/31/2007	20	7476.69

Source: Deutsche Börse, http://deutsche-boerse.com/.

$$x_t = T_t + Z_t + S_t + U_t \qquad (5.1)$$

where T_t = trend
Z_t = cyclical term
S_t = seasonal term
U_t = disturbance (or error)

While the trend and seasonal terms are assumed to be deterministic functions of time (i.e., their respective values at some future time t are known at any lagged time $t - d$, which is d units of time prior to t), the cyclical and disturbance terms are random. One also says that the last two terms are

---

[1]The number of dates n may theoretically be infinite. We will restrict ourselves to finite lengths.

stochastic.[2] Instead of the cyclical term Z_t and the disturbance U_t, one sometimes incorporates the so-called *irregular term* of the form $I_t = \phi \cdot I_{t-1} + U_t$ with $0 < \phi \leq 1$. That is, instead of equation (5.1), we now have

$$x_t = T_t + S_t + I_t \tag{5.2}$$

With the coefficient ϕ, we control how much of the previous time's irregular value is lingering in the present. If ϕ is close to zero, the prior value is less significant than if ϕ were close to one or even equal to one.

Note that U_t and I_{t-1} are independent. Since I_t depends on the prior value I_{t-1} scaled by ϕ and disturbed only by U_t, this evolution of I_t is referred to as *autoregressive of order one*.[3] As a consequence, there is some relation between the present and the previous level of I. Thus, these two are correlated to an extent depending on ϕ. This type of correlation between levels at time t and different times from the same variable is referred to as *autocorrelation*.

In Figure 5.2, we present the decomposition of some hypothetical time series. The straight solid line T is the linear trend. The irregular component I is represented by the dashed line and the seasonal component S are the two dash-dotted lines at the bottom of the figure. The resulting thick dash-dotted line is the time series $\{x\}_t$ obtained by adding all components.

Application to S&P 500 Index Returns

As an example, we use the daily S&P 500 returns from January 2, 1996, to December 31, 2003. To obtain an initial impression of the data, we plot them in the scatter plot in Figure 5.3. At first glance, it is kind of difficult to detect any structure within the data. However, we will decompose the returns according to equation (5.2). A possible question might be, is there a difference in the price changes depending on the day of the week? For the seasonality, we consider a period of length five since there are five trading days within a week. The seasonal components, $S_t(weekday)$, for each weekday (i.e., Monday through Friday) are given below:

Monday	−0.4555
Tuesday	0.3814
Wednesday	0.3356
Thursday	−0.4723
Friday	0.1759

---

[2]The case where all four components of the time series are modeled as stochastic quantities is not considered here.

[3]Order one indicates that the value of the immediately prior period is incorporated into the present period's value.

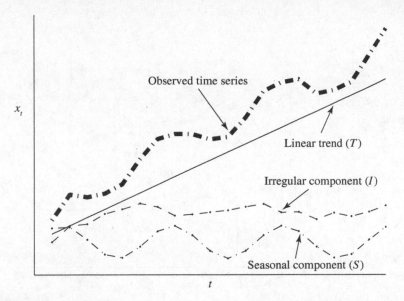

FIGURE 5.2 Decomposition of Time Series into Trend *T*, Seasonal Component *S*, and Irregular Component *I*

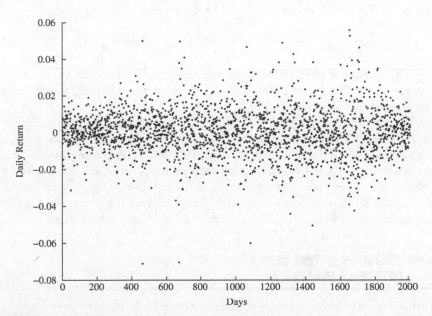

FIGURE 5.3 Daily Returns of S&P 500 Stock Index between January 2, 1996, and December 31, 2003

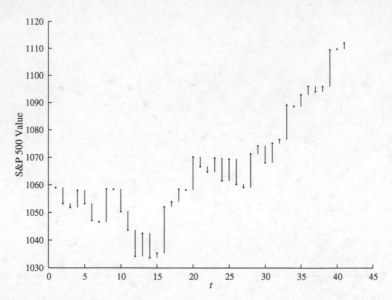

FIGURE 5.4 Daily S&P 500 Stock Index Prices with Daily Changes Extending Vertically

The coefficient of the irregular term is $\phi = 0.2850$ indicating that the previous period's value is weighted by about one third in the computation of this period's value. The overall model of the returns, then, looks like

$$y_t = T_t + S_t + I_t = T_t + S_t\,(weekday) - 0.2850I_{t-1} + U_t$$

The technique used to estimate the times series model is the *moving average method*. Since it is beyond the scope of this chapter, we will not discuss it here.

As can be seen by Figure 5.4, it might appear difficult to detect a linear trend, at least when one does not exclude the first 15 observations. If there really is no trend, most of the price is contained in the other components rather than any deterministic term. Efficient market theory that is central in financial theory does not permit any price trend since this would indicate that today's price does not contain all information available. By knowing that the price grows deterministically, this would have to be already embodied into today's price.

REPRESENTATION OF TIME SERIES
WITH DIFFERENCE EQUATIONS

Rather than representing $\{x\}_t$ by equation (5.1) or (5.2), often the dynamics of the components of the series are given. So far, the components are considered as quantities at certain points in time. However, it may sometimes be more convenient to represent the evolution of $\{x\}_t$ by *difference equations* of its components. The four components in difference equation form could be thought of as

$$\Delta x_t = x_t - x_{t-1} = \Delta T_t + \Delta I_t + \Delta S_t \qquad (5.3)$$

with the change in the linear trend $\Delta T_t = c$ where c is a constant, and

$$\Delta I_t = \phi\left(I_{t-1} - I_{t-2}\right) + \xi_t$$

where ξ are disturbances themselves, and

$$\Delta T_t + \Delta S_t = h(t) \qquad (5.4)$$

where $h(t)$ is some deterministic function of time. The symbol Δ indicates change in value from one period to the next.

The concept that the disturbance terms are *i.i.d.* means that the ξ behave in a manner common to all ξ (i.e., *identically distributed*) though *independently* of each other. The concept of statistical independence is explained in Appendix A while for random variables, this is done in Appendix B.

In general, difference equations are some functions of lagged values, time, and other stochastic variables. In time series analysis, one most often encounters the task of estimating difference equations such as equation (5.4). The original intent of time series analysis was to provide some reliable tools for forecasting.[4]

By forecasting, we assume that the change in value of some quantity, say x, from time t to time $t + 1$ occurs according to the difference equation (5.3). However, since we do not know the value of the disturbance in $t + 1$, ξ_{t+1}, at time t, we incorporate its expected value, that is, zero. All other quantities in equation (5.3) are deterministic and, thus, known in t. Hence, the forecast really is the expected value in $t + 1$ given the information in t.

APPLICATION: THE PRICE PROCESS

Time series analysis has grown more and more important for verifying financial models. Price processes assume a significant role among these models. In the next two subsections, we discuss two commonly encountered models for price processes given in a general setting: random walk and error

---

[4] See, for example, Walter Enders, *Applied Econometrics Time Series* (New York: John Wiley & Sons, 1995).

correction.[5] The theory behind them is not trivial. In particular, the error correction model applies expected values computed conditional on events (or information).[6]

Random Walk

Let us consider some price process given by the series $\{S\}_t$.[7] The dynamics of the process are given by

$$S_t = S_{t-1} + \varepsilon_t \tag{5.5}$$

or, equivalently, $\Delta S_t = \varepsilon_t$.

In words, tomorrow's price, S_{t+1}, is thought of as today's price plus some *random shock* that is independent of the price. As a consequence, in this model, known as the *random walk*, the increments $S_t - S_{t-1}$ from $t-1$ to t are thought of as completely undeterministic. Since the ε_t's have a mean of zero, the increments are considered fair.[8] An increase in price is as likely as a downside movement. At time t, the price is considered to contain all information available. So at any point in time, next period's price is exposed to a random shock.

Consequently, the best estimate for the following period's price is this period's price. Such price processes are called *efficient* due to their immediate information processing.

A more general model, for example, AR(p), of the form

$$S_t = \alpha_0 + \alpha_1 S_{t-1} + \ldots + \alpha_p S_{t-p} + \varepsilon_t$$

with several lagged prices could be considered as well. This price process would permit some slower incorporation of lagged prices into current prices. Now for the price to be a random walk process, the estimation would have to produce $a_0 = 0$, $a_1 = 1$, $a_2 = \ldots = a_p = 0$.

---

[5] Later in this book we will introduce an additional price process using logarithmic returns.

[6] Enders, *Applied Econometrics Time Series*.

[7] Here the price of some security at time t, S_t, ought not be confused with the seasonal component in equation (5.1).

[8] Note that since the ε assumes values on the entire real number line, the stock price could potentially become negative. To avoid this problem, logarithmic returns are modeled according to equation (5.4) rather than stock prices.

Application to S&P 500 Index Returns As an example to illustrate equation (5.4), consider the daily S&P 500 stock index prices between November 3, 2003, and December 31, 2003. The values are given in Table 5.2 along with the daily price changes. The resulting plot is given in Figure 5.4. The intuition given by the plot is roughly that, on each day, the information influencing the following day's price is unpredictable and, hence, the price change seems completely arbitrary. Hence, at first glance much in this figure seems to support the concept of a random walk. Concerning the evolution of the underlying price process, it looks reasonable to assume that the next day's price is determined by the previous day's price plus some random change. From Figure 5.4, it looks as if the changes occur independently of each other and in a manner common to all changes (i.e., with identical distribution).

Error Correction

We next present a price model that builds on the relationship between spot and forward markets. Suppose we extend the random walk model slightly by introducing some forward price for the same underlying stock S. That is, at time t, we agree by contract to purchase the stock at $t + 1$ for some price determined at t. We denote this price by $F(t)$. At time $t + 1$, we purchase the stock for $F(t)$. The stock, however, is worth S_{t+1} at that time and need not—and most likely will not—be equal to $F(t)$. It is different from the agreed forward price by some random quantity ε_{t+1}. If this disturbance has zero mean, as defined in the random walk model, then the price is fair. Based on this assumption, the reasonable forward price would equal[9]

$$F(t) = E[S_{t+1} \mid t] = E[S_t + \varepsilon_t \mid t] = S_t$$

So, on average, the difference between S and F should fulfill the following condition:

$$\Delta \equiv S_{t+1} - F(t) \approx 0$$

If, however, the price process permits some constant terms such as some upward trend, for example, the following period's price will no longer be equal to this period's price plus some random shock. The trend will spoil the fair price, and the forward price designed as the expected value of the

---

[9]Note that we employ expected values conditional on time t to express that we base our forecast on all information available at time t.

TABLE 5.2 Daily S&P 500 Stock Index Values
and Daily Changes between November 3, 2003,
and December 31, 2003

Date	P_t	Δ_t
12/31/2003	1111.92	2.28
12/30/2003	1109.64	0.16
12/29/2003	1109.48	13.59
12/26/2003	1095.89	1.85
12/24/2003	1094.04	−1.98
12/23/2003	1096.02	3.08
12/22/2003	1092.94	4.28
12/19/2003	1088.66	−0.52
12/18/2003	1089.18	12.70
12/17/2003	1076.48	1.35
12/16/2003	1075.13	7.09
12/15/2003	1068.04	−6.10
12/12/2003	1074.14	2.93
12/11/2003	1071.21	12.16
12/10/2003	1059.05	−1.13
12/09/2003	1060.18	−9.12
12/08/2003	1069.30	7.80
12/05/2003	1061.50	−8.22
12/04/2003	1069.72	4.99
12/03/2003	1064.73	−1.89
12/02/2003	1066.62	−3.50
12/01/2003	1070.12	11.92
11/28/2003	1058.20	−0.25
11/26/2003	1058.45	4.56
11/25/2003	1053.89	1.81
11/24/2003	1052.08	16.80
11/21/2003	1035.28	1.63
11/20/2003	1033.65	−8.79
11/19/2003	1042.44	8.29
11/18/2003	1034.15	−9.48
11/17/2003	1043.63	−6.72
11/14/2003	1050.35	−8.06
11/13/2003	1058.41	−0.12
11/12/2003	1058.53	11.96
11/11/2003	1046.57	−0.54
11/10/2003	1047.11	−6.10
11/07/2003	1053.21	−4.84
11/06/2003	1058.05	6.24
11/05/2003	1051.81	−1.44
11/04/2003	1053.25	−5.77
11/03/2003	1059.02	

following period's stock price conditional on this period's information will contain a systematic error. The model to be tested is, then,

$$S_{t+1} = \alpha_0 + \alpha_1 F(t) + \varepsilon_t$$

with a potential nonzero linear trend captured by α_0. A fair price would be if the estimates are $a_0 = 0$ and $a_1 = 1$. Then, the markets would be in approximate equilibrium. If not, the forward prices have to be adjusted accordingly to prohibit predictable gains from the differences in prices.

The methodology to do so is the so-called *error correction model* in the sense that today's (i.e., this period's) deviations from the equilibrium price have to be incorporated into tomorrow's (i.e., the following period's) price to return to some long-term equilibrium. The model is given by the equations system

$$S_{t+2} = S_{t+1} - \alpha\left(S_{t+1} - F(t)\right) + \varepsilon_{t+2}, \quad \alpha > 0$$
$$F(t+1) = F(t) + \beta\left(S_{t+1} - F(t)\right) + \xi_{t+1}, \quad \beta > 0$$

with

$$E[\varepsilon_{t+2} \mid t+1] = 0$$
$$E[\xi_{t+1} \mid t] = 0$$

At time $t + 2$, the term $\alpha\left(S_{t+1} - F(t)\right)$ in the price of S_{t+2} corrects for deviations from the equilibrium $\left(S_{t+1} - F(t)\right)$ stemming from time $t + 1$. Also, we adjust our forward price $F(t + 1)$ by the same deviation scaled by β. Note that, now, the forward price, too, is affected by some *innovation*, ξ_{t+1}, unknown at time t. In contrast to some disturbance or error term ε, which simply represents some deviation from an exact functional relationship, the concept of innovation such as in connection with the ξ_{t+1} is that of an independent quantity with a meaning such as, for example, new information or shock.

In general, the random walk and error correction models can be estimated using least squares regression introduced in Chapter 2. However, this is only legitimate if the regressors (i.e., independent variables) and disturbances are uncorrelated.

KEY POINTS

- A sequence of observations which are ordered in time is called a time series.
- Time series are significant in modeling price, return, or interest rate processes as well as the dynamics of economic quantities.

- Each observation comprising a time series is a pair of the components, time and value.
- Time series analysis comprises methods for analyzing time series data.
- The most traditional decomposition in time series analysis is trend, cyclical, seasonal, and disturbance (error).
- An autoregressive structure assumes that the next period's value depends on the value of prior periods.
- An autoregressive of order one structure assumes that the next period's value depends on the last prior value.
- The correlation of a time series with its own past and future values is referred to as autocorrelation.
- The random walk and error correction models are candidates for modeling security price movements.

CHAPTER 6

Regression Models with Categorical Variables

After reading this chapter you will understand:

- What a categorical variable is.
- How to handle the inclusion of one or more categorical variables in a regression when they are explanatory variables.
- How to test for the statistical significance of individual dummy variables in a regression and how to employ the Chow test.
- Models that can be used when the dependent variable is a categorical variable: the linear probability model, the logit regression model, and the probit regression model.
- The advantages and disadvantages of each type of model for dealing with situations where the dependent variable is a categorical variable.

Categorical variables are variables that represent group membership. For example, given a set of bonds, the credit rating is a categorical variable that indicates to what category—AAA, AA, A, BBB, BB, and so on—each bond belongs. A categorical variable does not have a numerical value or a numerical interpretation in itself. Thus the fact that a bond is in category AAA or BBB does not, in itself, measure any quantitative characteristic of the bond; though quantitative attributes such as a bond's yield spread can be associated with each category.

Performing a regression on categorical variables does not make sense per se. For example, it does not make sense to multiply a coefficient times AAA or times BBB. However, in a number of cases the standard tools of regression analysis can be applied to categorical variables after appropriate transformations. In this chapter, we first discuss the case when categorical variables are explanatory (independent) variables and then proceed to discuss models where categorical variables are dependent variables.

INDEPENDENT CATEGORICAL VARIABLES

Categorical input variables are used to cluster input data into different groups.[1] That is, suppose we are given a set of input-output data and a partition of the data set in a number of subsets A_i so that each data point belongs to one and only one set. The A_i represent a categorical input variable. In financial econometrics, categories might represent, for example, different market regimes, economic states, credit ratings, countries, industries, or sectors.

We cannot, per se, mix quantitative input variables and categorical variables. For example, we cannot sum yield spreads and their credit ratings. However, we can perform a transformation that allows the mixing of categorical and quantitative variables. Let's see how. Suppose first that there is only one categorical input variable that we denote by D, one quantitative input variable X, and one quantitative output variable Y. Consider our set of quantitative data, that is quantitative observations. We organize data, residuals, and parameters in matrix form as usual:

$$Y = \begin{bmatrix} Y_1 \\ \vdots \\ Y_T \end{bmatrix} \quad X = \begin{bmatrix} 1 & X_{11} \\ \vdots & \vdots \\ 1 & X_{T1} \end{bmatrix} \quad E = \begin{bmatrix} \varepsilon_1 \\ \vdots \\ \varepsilon_T \end{bmatrix} \quad B = \begin{bmatrix} \beta_0 \\ \beta_1 \end{bmatrix}$$

Suppose data belong to two categories. An explanatory variable that distinguishes only two categories is called a *dichotomous variable*. The key is to represent a dichotomous categorical variable as a numerical variable D, called a *dummy variable*, that can assume the two values 0,1. We can now add the variable D to the input variables to represent membership in one or the other group:

$$X = \begin{bmatrix} D_1 & 1 & X_{11} \\ \vdots & \vdots & \vdots \\ D_T & 1 & X_{T1} \end{bmatrix}$$

---

[1] We can also say that categorical input variables represent *qualitative* inputs. This last expression, however, can be misleading, insofar as categorical variables represent only the final coding of qualitative inputs in different categories. For example, suppose we want to represent some aspect of market psychology, say confidence level. We can categorize confidence in a number of categories, for example euphoria, optimism, neutrality, fear, or panic. The crucial question is how we can operationally determine the applicable category and whether this categorization makes sense. A categorical variable entails the ability to categorize, that is, to determine membership in different categories. If and how categorization is useful is a crucial problem in many sciences, especially economics and the social sciences.

If $D_i = 0$, the data X_{i1} belong to the first category; if $D_i = 1$, the data X_{i1} belong to the second category.

Consider now the regression equation in matrix form $Y = XB$

$$Y = XB + E$$
$$Y_1 = \beta_0 + \beta_1 X_{11} + \varepsilon_1$$
$$\vdots$$
$$Y_T = \beta_0 + \beta_1 X_{T1} + \varepsilon_T$$

(6.1)

In financial econometric applications, the index i will be time or a variable that identifies a cross section of assets, such as bond issues. Consider that we can write three separate regression equations, one for those data that correspond to $D = 1$, one for those data that correspond to $D = 0$, and one for the fully pooled data. Suppose now that the three equations differ by the intercept term but have the same slope. Let's explicitly write the two equations for those data that correspond to $D = 1$ and for those data that correspond to $D = 0$:

$$y_i = \begin{cases} \beta_{00} + \beta_1 X_{i1} + \varepsilon_1, & \text{if } D_i = 0 \\ \beta_{01} + \beta_1 X_{i1} + \varepsilon_1, & \text{if } D_i = 1 \end{cases}$$

(6.2)

where β_{00} and β_{01} are the two intercepts and i defines the observations that belong to the first category when the dummy variable D assumes value 0 and also defines the observations that belong to the second category when the dummy variable D assumes value 1. If the two categories are recession and expansion, the first equation might hold in periods of expansion and the second in periods of recession. If the two categories are investment-grade bonds and noninvestment-grade bonds, the two equations apply to different cross sections of bonds, as will be illustrated in an example later in this chapter.

Observe now that, under the assumption that only the intercept term differs in the two equations, the two equations can be combined into a single equation in the following way:

$$Y_i = \beta_{00} + \gamma D(i) + \beta_1 X_i + \varepsilon_i$$

(6.3)

where $\gamma = \beta_{01} - \beta_{00}$ represents the difference of the intercept for the two categories. In this way we have defined a single regression equation with two independent quantitative variables, X, D, to which we can apply all the usual tools of regression analysis, including the ordinary least squares (OLS) estimation method and all the tests. By estimating the coefficients of this regression, we obtain the common slope and two intercepts. Observe that we would obtain the same result if the categories were inverted.

Thus far we have assumed that there is no interaction between the categorical and the quantitative variable, that is, the slope of the regression is the same for the two categories. This means that the effects of variables are additive; that is, the effect of one variable is added regardless of the value taken by the other variable. In many applications, this is an unrealistic assumption.

Using dummy variables, the treatment is the same as that applied to intercepts. Consider the regression equation (6.1) and write two regression equations for the two categories as we did above where β_{10}, β_{11} are the slopes

$$y_i = \begin{cases} \beta_0 + \beta_{10}X_{i1} + \varepsilon_1 & \text{if } D_i = 0 \\ \beta_0 + \beta_{11}X_{i1} + \varepsilon_1 & \text{if } D_i = 1 \end{cases} \tag{6.4}$$

We can couple these two equations in a single equation as follows:

$$Y_i = \beta_0 + \beta_{10}X_i + \delta(D_iX_i) + \varepsilon_i \tag{6.5}$$

where $\delta = \beta_{11} - \beta_{10}$. In fact, equation (6.5) is identical to the first of two equations in equation (6.4) for $D_i = 0$ and to the second for $D_i = 1$. This regression can be estimated with the usual OLS methods.

In practice, it is rarely appropriate to consider only interactions and not the intercept, which is the main effect. We refer to the fact that the interaction effect is marginal with respect to the main effect as *marginalization*. However, we can easily construct a model that combines both effects. In fact we can write the following regression adding two variables, the dummy D and the interaction DX:

$$Y_i = \beta_0 + \gamma D_i + \beta_1 X_i + \delta(D_iX_i) + \varepsilon_i \tag{6.6}$$

This regression equation, which now includes three regressors, combines both effects.

The above process of introducing dummy variables can be generalized to regressions with multiple variables. Consider the following regression:

$$Y_i = \beta_0 + \sum_{j=1}^{N} \beta_j X_{ij} + \varepsilon_i \quad i = 1, \ldots, T \tag{6.7}$$

where data can be partitioned in two categories with the use of a dummy variable:

$$X = \begin{bmatrix} D_1 & 1 & X_{11} & \cdots & X_{1N} \\ \vdots & \vdots & \vdots & \ddots & \vdots \\ D_T & 1 & X_{T1} & \cdots & X_{TN} \end{bmatrix}$$

We can introduce the dummy D as well as its interaction with the N quantitative variable and thus write the following equation:

$$Y_i = \beta_0 + \gamma_i D_i + \sum_{j=1}^{N} \beta_j X_{ij} + \sum_{j=1}^{N} \delta_{ij}(D_i X_{ij}) + \varepsilon_i \qquad (6.8)$$

The above discussion depends critically on the fact that there are only two categories, a fact that allows one to use the numerical variable 0,1 to identify the two categories. However, the process can be easily extended to multiple categories by adding dummy variables. Suppose there are $K > 2$ categories. An explanatory variable that distinguishes between more than two categories is called a *polytomous variable*.

Suppose there are three categories, A, B, and C. Consider a dummy variable $D1$ that assumes a value one on the elements of A and zero on all the others. Let's now add a second dummy variable $D2$ that assumes the value one on the elements of the category B and zero on all the others. The three categories are now completely identified: A is identified by the values 1,0 of the two dummy variables, B by the values 0,1, and C by the values 0,0. Note that the values 1,1 do not identify any category. This process can be extended to any number of categories. If there are K categories, we need $K - 1$ dummy variables.

Statistical Tests

How can we determine if a given categorization is useful? It is quite obvious that many categorizations will be totally useless for the purpose of any econometric regression. If we categorize bonds in function of the color of the logo of the issuer, it is quite obvious that we obtain meaningless results. In other cases, however, distinctions can be subtle and important. Consider the question of market regime shifts or structural breaks. These are delicate questions that can be addressed only with appropriate statistical tests.

A word of caution about statistical tests is in order. As observed in Chapter 2, statistical tests typically work under the assumptions of the model and might be misleading if these assumptions are violated. If we try to fit a linear model to a process that is inherently nonlinear, tests might be misleading. It is good practice to use several tests and to be particularly attentive to inconsistencies between test results. Inconsistencies signal potential problems in applying tests, typically model misspecification.

The t-statistic applied to the regression coefficients of dummy variables offer a set of important tests to judge which regressors are significant. Recall from Chapter 2 that the t-statistics are the coefficients divided by their respective squared errors. The p-values associated with each coefficient estimate is the probability of the hypothesis that the corresponding coefficient is zero, that is, that the corresponding variable is irrelevant.

We can also use the F-test to test the significance of each specific dummy variable. To do so we can run the regression with and without that variable and form the corresponding F-test. The *Chow test*[2] is the F-test to gauge if all the dummy variables are collectively irrelevant. The Chow test is an F-test of mutual exclusion, written as follows:

$$F = \frac{\left[\text{SSR} - (\text{SSR}_1 + \text{SSR}_2) \right](n - 2k)}{(\text{SSR}_1 + \text{SSR}_2)k} \tag{6.9}$$

where SSR_1 = the squared sum of residuals of the regression run with data in the first category without dummy variables

SSR_2 = the squared sum of residuals of the regression run with data in the second category without dummy variables

SSR = the squared sum of residuals of the regression run with fully pooled data without dummy variables

The test statistic F follows an F distribution with k and $n - 2k$ degrees of freedom. Observe that $\text{SSR}_1 + \text{SSR}_2$ is equal to the squared sum of residuals of the regression run on fully pooled data but with dummy variables. Thus the Chow test is the F-test of the unrestricted regressions with and without dummy variables.

Illustration: Predicting Corporate Bond Yield Spreads To illustrate the use of dummy variables, we will estimate a model to predict corporate bond spreads.[3] The regression is relative to a cross section of bonds. The regression equation is the following:

$$\text{Spread}_i = \beta_0 + \beta_1 \text{Coupon}_i + \beta_2 \text{CoverageRatio}_i + \beta_3 \text{LoggedEBIT}_i + \varepsilon_i$$

---

[2] Gregory C. Chow, "Tests of Equality between Sets of Coefficients in Two Linear Regressions," *Econometrica* 28 (1960): 591–605.
[3] The model presented in this illustration was developed by FridsonVision and is described in "Focus Issues Methodology," *Leverage World* (May 30, 2003). The data for this illustration were provided by Greg Braylovskiy of FridsonVision. The firm uses about 650 companies in its analysis. Only 100 observations were used in this illustration.

where Spread$_i$ = option-adjusted spread (in basis points) for the bond issue of company i

Coupon$_i$ = coupon rate for the bond of company i, expressed without considering percentage sign (i.e., 7.5% = 7.5)

CoverageRatio$_i$ = earnings before interest, taxes, depreciation and amortization (EBITDA) divided by interest expense for company i

LoggedEBIT$_i$ = logarithm of earnings (earnings before interest and taxes, EBIT, in millions of dollars) for company i

The dependent variable, Spread, is not measured by the typically nominal spread but by the option-adjusted spread. This spread measure adjusts for any embedded options in a bond.[4]

Theory would suggest the following properties for the estimated coefficients:

- The higher the coupon rate, the greater the issuer's default risk and hence the larger the spread. Therefore, a positive coefficient for the coupon rate is expected.
- A coverage ratio is a measure of a company's ability to satisfy fixed obligations, such as interest, principal repayment, or lease payments. There are various coverage ratios. The one used in this illustration is the ratio of the *earnings before interest, taxes, depreciation, and amortization* (EBITDA) divided by interest expense. Since the higher the coverage ratio the lower the default risk, an inverse relationship is expected between the spread and the coverage ratio; that is, the estimated coefficient for the coverage ratio is expected to be negative.
- There are various measures of earnings reported in financial statements. Earnings in this illustration is defined as the trailing 12-months *earnings before interest and taxes* (EBIT). Holding other factors constant, it is expected that the larger the EBIT, the lower the default risk and therefore an inverse relationship (negative coefficient) is expected.

We used 100 observations at two different dates, June 6, 2005, and November 28, 2005; thus there are 200 observations in total. This will allow us to test if there is a difference in the spread regression for

---

[4] See Chapter 18 in Frank J. Fabozzi, *Bond Markets, Analysis, and Strategies*, 8th ed. (Upper Saddle River, NJ: Prentice-Hall, 2013).

investment-grade and noninvestment grade bonds using all observations. We will then test to see if there is any structural break between the two dates. We organize the data in matrix form as usual. Data are shown in Table 6.1. The columns labeled "CCC+ and Below" indicate that data belong to two categories and suggests the use of one dummy variable. Another dummy variable is used later to distinguish between the two dates. Let's first estimate the regression equation for the fully pooled data, that is, all data without any distinction in categories. The estimated coefficients for the model and their corresponding t-statistics are shown as follows:

Coefficient	Estimated Coefficient	Standard Error	t-Statistic	p-Value
β_0	157.01	89.56	1.753	0.081
β_1	61.27	8.03	7.630	9.98E-13
β_2	−13.20	2.27	−5.800	2.61E-08
β_3	−90.88	16.32	−5.568	8.41E-08

TABLE 6.1 Regression Data for the Bond Spread Application, November 28, 2005, and June 6, 2005

Issue #	Spread, 11/28/05	CCC+ and Below	Coupon	Coverage Ratio	Logged EBIT	Spread, 6/6/05	CCC+ and Below	Coupon	Coverage Ratio	Logged EBIT
1	509	0	7.400	2.085	2.121	473	0	7.400	2.087	2.111
2	584	0	8.500	2.085	2.121	529	0	8.500	2.087	2.111
3	247	0	8.375	9.603	2.507	377	0	8.375	5.424	2.234
4	73	0	6.650	11.507	3.326	130	0	6.650	9.804	3.263
5	156	0	7.125	11.507	3.326	181	0	7.125	9.804	3.263
6	240	0	7.250	2.819	2.149	312	0	7.250	2.757	2.227
7	866	1	9.000	1.530	2.297	852	1	9.000	1.409	1.716
8	275	0	5.950	8.761	2.250	227	0	5.950	11.031	2.166
9	515	0	8.000	2.694	2.210	480	0	8.000	2.651	2.163
10	251	0	7.875	8.289	1.698	339	0	7.875	8.231	1.951
11	507	0	9.375	2.131	2.113	452	0	9.375	2.039	2.042
12	223	0	7.750	4.040	2.618	237	0	7.750	3.715	2.557
13	71	0	7.250	7.064	2.348	90	0	7.250	7.083	2.296
14	507	0	8.000	2.656	1.753	556	0	8.000	2.681	1.797
15	566	1	9.875	1.030	1.685	634	1	9.875	1.316	1.677
16	213	0	7.500	11.219	3.116	216	0	7.500	10.298	2.996
17	226	0	6.875	11.219	3.116	204	0	6.875	10.298	2.996
18	192	0	7.750	11.219	3.116	201	0	7.750	10.298	2.996

TABLE 6.1 (*continued*)

Issue #	Spread, 11/28/05	CCC+ and Below	Coupon	Coverage Ratio	Logged EBIT	Spread, 6/6/05	CCC+ and Below	Coupon	Coverage Ratio	Logged EBIT
19	266	0	6.250	3.276	2.744	298	0	6.250	3.107	2.653
20	308	0	9.250	3.276	2.744	299	0	9.250	3.107	2.653
21	263	0	7.750	2.096	1.756	266	0	7.750	2.006	3.038
22	215	0	7.190	7.096	3.469	259	0	7.190	6.552	3.453
23	291	0	7.690	7.096	3.469	315	0	7.690	6.552	3.453
24	324	0	8.360	7.096	3.469	331	0	8.360	6.552	3.453
25	272	0	6.875	8.612	1.865	318	0	6.875	9.093	2.074
26	189	0	8.000	4.444	2.790	209	0	8.000	5.002	2.756
27	383	0	7.375	2.366	2.733	417	0	7.375	2.375	2.727
28	207	0	7.000	2.366	2.733	200	0	7.000	2.375	2.727
29	212	0	6.900	4.751	2.847	235	0	6.900	4.528	2.822
30	246	0	7.500	19.454	2.332	307	0	7.500	16.656	2.181
31	327	0	6.625	3.266	2.475	365	0	6.625	2.595	2.510
32	160	0	7.150	3.266	2.475	237	0	7.150	2.595	2.510
33	148	0	6.300	3.266	2.475	253	0	6.300	2.595	2.510
34	231	0	6.625	3.266	2.475	281	0	6.625	2.595	2.510
35	213	0	6.690	3.266	2.475	185	0	6.690	2.595	2.510
36	350	0	7.130	3.266	2.475	379	0	7.130	2.595	2.510
37	334	0	6.875	4.310	2.203	254	0	6.875	5.036	2.155
38	817	1	8.625	1.780	1.965	635	0	8.625	1.851	1.935
39	359	0	7.550	2.951	3.078	410	0	7.550	2.035	3.008
40	189	0	6.500	8.518	2.582	213	0	6.500	13.077	2.479
41	138	0	6.950	25.313	2.520	161	0	6.950	24.388	2.488
42	351	0	9.500	3.242	1.935	424	0	9.500	2.787	1.876
43	439	0	8.250	2.502	1.670	483	0	8.250	2.494	1.697
44	347	0	7.700	4.327	3.165	214	0	7.700	4.276	3.226
45	390	0	7.750	4.327	3.165	260	0	7.750	4.276	3.226
46	149	0	8.000	4.327	3.165	189	0	8.000	4.276	3.226
47	194	0	6.625	4.430	3.077	257	0	6.625	4.285	2.972
48	244	0	8.500	4.430	3.077	263	0	8.500	4.285	2.972
49	566	1	10.375	2.036	1.081	839	1	10.375	2.032	1.014
50	185	0	6.300	7.096	3.469	236	0	6.300	6.552	3.453
51	196	0	6.375	7.096	3.469	221	0	6.375	6.552	3.453
52	317	0	6.625	3.075	2.587	389	0	6.625	2.785	2.551
53	330	0	8.250	3.075	2.587	331	0	8.250	2.785	2.551
54	159	0	6.875	8.286	3.146	216	0	6.875	7.210	3.098
55	191	0	7.125	8.286	3.146	257	0	7.125	7.210	3.098
56	148	0	7.375	8.286	3.146	117	0	7.375	7.210	3.098
57	112	0	7.600	8.286	3.146	151	0	7.600	7.210	3.098

(*continued*)

TABLE 6.1 *(continued)*

Issue #	Spread, 11/28/05	CCC+ and Below	Coupon	Coverage Ratio	Logged EBIT	Spread, 6/6/05	CCC+ and Below	Coupon	Coverage Ratio	Logged EBIT
58	171	0	7.650	8.286	3.146	221	0	7.650	7.210	3.098
59	319	0	7.375	3.847	1.869	273	0	7.375	4.299	1.860
60	250	0	7.375	12.656	2.286	289	0	7.375	8.713	2.364
61	146	0	5.500	5.365	3.175	226	0	5.500	5.147	3.190
62	332	0	6.450	5.365	3.175	345	0	6.450	5.147	3.190
63	354	0	6.500	5.365	3.175	348	0	6.500	5.147	3.190
64	206	0	6.625	7.140	2.266	261	0	6.625	5.596	2.091
65	558	0	7.875	2.050	2.290	455	0	7.875	2.120	2.333
66	190	0	6.000	2.925	3.085	204	0	6.000	3.380	2.986
67	232	0	6.750	2.925	3.085	244	0	6.750	3.380	2.986
68	913	1	11.250	2.174	1.256	733	0	11.250	2.262	1.313
69	380	0	9.750	4.216	1.465	340	0	9.750	4.388	1.554
70	174	0	6.500	4.281	2.566	208	0	6.500	4.122	2.563
71	190	0	7.450	10.547	2.725	173	0	7.450	8.607	2.775
72	208	0	7.125	2.835	3.109	259	0	7.125	2.813	3.122
73	272	0	6.500	5.885	2.695	282	0	6.500	5.927	2.644
74	249	0	6.125	5.133	2.682	235	0	6.125	6.619	2.645
75	278	0	8.750	6.562	2.802	274	0	8.750	7.433	2.785
76	252	0	7.750	2.822	2.905	197	0	7.750	2.691	2.908
77	321	0	7.500	2.822	2.905	226	0	7.500	2.691	2.908
78	379	0	7.750	4.093	2.068	362	0	7.750	4.296	2.030
79	185	0	6.875	6.074	2.657	181	0	6.875	5.294	2.469
80	307	0	7.250	5.996	2.247	272	0	7.250	3.610	2.119
81	533	0	10.625	1.487	1.950	419	0	10.625	1.717	2.081
82	627	0	8.875	1.487	1.950	446	0	8.875	1.717	2.081
83	239	0	8.875	2.994	2.186	241	0	8.875	3.858	2.161
84	240	0	7.375	8.160	2.225	274	0	7.375	8.187	2.075
85	634	0	8.500	2.663	2.337	371	0	8.500	2.674	2.253
86	631	1	7.700	2.389	2.577	654	1	7.700	2.364	2.632
87	679	1	9.250	2.389	2.577	630	1	9.250	2.364	2.632
88	556	1	9.750	1.339	1.850	883	1	9.750	1.422	1.945
89	564	1	9.750	1.861	2.176	775	1	9.750	1.630	1.979
90	209	0	6.750	8.048	2.220	223	0	6.750	7.505	2.092
91	190	0	6.500	4.932	2.524	232	0	6.500	4.626	2.468
92	390	0	6.875	6.366	1.413	403	0	6.875	5.033	1.790
93	377	0	10.250	2.157	2.292	386	0	10.250	2.057	2.262
94	143	0	5.750	11.306	2.580	110	0	5.750	9.777	2.473
95	207	0	7.250	2.835	3.109	250	0	7.250	2.813	3.122
96	253	0	6.500	4.918	2.142	317	0	6.500	2.884	1.733
97	530	1	8.500	0.527	2.807	654	1	8.500	1.327	2.904

TABLE 6.1 (*continued*)

Issue #	Spread, 11/28/05	CCC+ and Below	Coupon	Coverage Ratio	Logged EBIT	Spread, 6/6/05	CCC+ and Below	Coupon	Coverage Ratio	Logged EBIT
98	481	0	6.750	2.677	1.858	439	0	6.750	3.106	1.991
99	270	0	7.625	2.835	3.109	242	0	7.625	2.813	3.122
100	190	0	7.125	9.244	3.021	178	0	7.125	7.583	3.138

Notes:
Spread = option-adjusted spread (in basis points).
Coupon = coupon rate, expressed without considering percentage sign (i.e., 7.5% = 7.5).
Coverage Ratio = EBITDA divided by interest expense for company.
Logged EBIT = logarithm of earnings (EBIT in millions of dollars).

Other regression results are:

SSR: 2.3666e+006
F-statistic: 89.38
p-value: 0
R^2: 0.57

Given the high value of the F-statistic and the p-value close to zero, the regression is significant. The coefficient for the three regressors is statistically significant and has the expected sign. However, the intercept term is not statistically significant. The residuals are given in the second column of Table 6.2.

TABLE 6.2 Illustration of Residuals and Leverage for Corporate Bond Spread

Issue #	Residuals	Residuals Dummy 1	Residuals Dummy 2
1	118.79930	148.931400	162.198700
2	126.39350	183.097400	200.622000
3	−68.57770	−39.278100	−26.716500
4	−37.26080	−60.947500	−71.034400
5	16.63214	4.419645	−3.828890
6	−128.76600	−104.569000	−92.122000
7	386.42330	191.377200	217.840000
8	73.53972	48.516800	56.58778
9	104.15990	146.400600	160.438900
10	−124.78700	−98.020100	−71.374300
11	−4.28874	73.473220	94.555400
12	−117.58200	−88.168700	−82.883100
13	−223.61800	−213.055000	−202.748000

(*continued*)

TABLE 6.2 (*continued*)

Issue #	Residuals	Residuals Dummy 1	Residuals Dummy 2
14	54.13075	99.735710	123.153000
15	−29.42160	−132.755000	−179.955000
16	27.74192	26.913670	24.308960
17	79.04072	63.114850	58.091160
18	−8.57759	−3.366800	−5.003930
19	18.62462	13.109110	9.664499
20	−123.21000	−56.256500	−48.090100
21	−181.64800	−140.494000	−118.369000
22	26.43157	27.457990	14.487850
23	71.79254	84.897050	73.862080
24	63.73623	93.025400	84.583560
25	−23.09740	−22.603200	−3.106990
26	−146.00700	−112.938000	−110.018000
27	53.72288	78.075810	78.781050
28	−99.29780	−84.003500	−84.749600
29	−46.31030	−41.105600	−43.489200
30	98.22006	79.285040	96.588250
31	32.05062	37.541930	41.075430
32	−167.12000	−148.947000	−143.382000
33	−127.03400	−129.393000	−127.118000
34	−63.94940	−58.458100	−54.924600
35	−85.93250	−78.871000	−75.085900
36	24.10520	41.795380	47.283410
37	12.86740	23.326060	33.884440
38	333.53890	101.376800	173.584400
39	58.02881	82.472150	77.040360
40	−19.14100	−32.550700	−29.298900
41	118.41190	67.990200	81.986050
42	−169.48100	−90.625700	−64.883800
43	−38.74030	13.936980	39.950520
44	62.91014	86.397490	80.392250
45	102.84620	127.541400	121.729700
46	−153.47300	−122.739000	−127.583000
47	−30.81510	−32.968700	−41.285200
48	−95.711400	−52.572300	−53.631800
49	−101.678000	−219.347000	−237.977000
50	50.969050	30.496460	14.081700
51	57.373200	38.712320	22.587840
52	29.717770	34.958870	36.101100
53	−56.859100	−12.364200	−4.932630
54	−23.959100	−31.659900	−38.650000
55	−7.278620	−8.940330	−14.962800
56	−65.598100	−61.220800	−66.275700
57	−115.386000	−105.573000	−109.757000
58	−59.449600	−48.429300	−52.419900
59	−69.299000	−43.044000	−23.885700
60	15.946800	13.880220	28.513500

TABLE 6.2 *(continued)*

Issue #	Residuals	Residuals Dummy 1	Residuals Dummy 2
61	11.362190	–21.353800	–35.607900
62	139.148000	129.380400	118.803100
63	158.084100	149.524300	139.140600
64	–56.785300	–60.952000	–51.339900
65	153.651800	194.149900	205.750200
66	–15.653600	–28.630900	–40.227500
67	–19.612200	–14.472300	–23.166100
68	209.488200	144.261600	67.891100
69	–185.659000	–100.217000	–63.396000
70	–91.541800	–92.646100	–91.015000
71	–36.623800	–33.937000	–29.003400
72	–65.586300	–51.301800	–59.080100
73	39.294110	32.661770	32.391920
74	28.197460	14.759650	12.952710
75	–73.910000	–28.902200	–22.353300
76	–78.608000	–47.733800	–48.902600
77	5.711553	30.546620	28.410290
78	–10.926100	22.258560	38.888810
79	–71.611400	–69.462200	–67.416900
80	–10.848000	3.505179	15.383910
81	–78.195700	32.775440	61.748590
82	123.041000	191.738700	213.938800
83	–223.662000	–160.978000	–142.925000
84	–58.977600	–47.671100	–33.850800
85	203.727300	257.223800	270.556600
86	267.904600	–65.208100	89.636310
87	220.923600	–4.162260	42.473790
88	–12.621600	–142.213000	–168.474000
89	31.862060	–127.616000	–134.267000
90	–53.593800	–57.028600	–45.579800
91	–70.794900	–73.470000	–70.669700
92	24.164780	34.342730	62.098550
93	–171.291000	–73.744300	–52.943000
94	17.439710	–22.092800	–20.420000
95	–74.246100	–56.942100	–64.236600
96	–42.690600	–42.602900	–31.958300
97	114.168900	–66.109500	–66.049500
98	114.578500	129.177300	145.600600
99	–34.225400	–7.862790	–13.705900
100	–6.958960	–10.488100	–13.508000
101	81.920940	112.117900	101.420600
102	70.515070	127.283800	120.844000
103	–18.587600	24.683610	20.132390
104	–8.443100	–26.784100	–28.884400
105	13.449820	6.582981	6.321103

(continued)

TABLE 6.2 *(continued)*

Issue #	Residuals	Residuals Dummy 1	Residuals Dummy 2
106	−50.430600	−26.617000	−36.781100
107	318.056000	133.403000	130.828300
108	47.876010	16.919350	5.068270
109	64.341610	107.038200	99.281600
110	−14.573200	10.557760	3.393970
111	−66.995600	11.539420	7.987728
112	−113.425000	−82.640800	−88.147800
113	−209.054000	−198.177000	−205.892000
114	107.522000	152.737700	142.464600
115	41.638860	−76.825800	−145.458000
116	7.647833	10.327540	9.887700
117	33.946630	21.528710	18.669900
118	−22.671700	−13.952900	−13.425200
119	40.107630	35.729610	24.798540
120	−142.727000	−74.636000	−73.956000
121	−63.286100	−31.013100	−33.970100
122	61.774140	64.481450	64.302480
123	87.135110	101.920500	103.676700
124	62.078800	93.048860	97.398200
125	48.320900	45.935300	36.150130
126	−121.736000	−90.029000	−92.609500
127	87.253680	111.626800	105.229900
128	−106.767000	−91.452500	−99.300700
129	−28.566900	−22.540100	−29.135400
130	108.560100	98.752280	95.570570
131	64.418690	71.586810	60.886980
132	−95.752300	−75.902200	−84.570100
133	−27.665900	−28.348600	−40.306300
134	−19.581300	−12.413200	−23.113000
135	−119.564000	−110.826000	−121.274000
136	47.473260	66.840260	58.094960
137	−61.953700	−53.237800	−64.316600
138	149.786400	211.505100	204.226300
139	90.609530	118.184700	114.258300
140	55.650810	29.860840	23.239180
141	126.240500	78.712630	79.050720
142	−107.826000	−27.243600	−31.116800
143	7.614932	60.121850	50.036220
144	−65.174500	−41.979400	−42.794500
145	−22.238400	2.164489	1.542950
146	−108.558000	−78.116000	−77.769900
147	20.679750	19.696850	12.963030
148	−88.216600	−43.906700	−43.383600
149	165.253100	48.262590	−23.500200
150	93.311620	74.519920	70.896340
151	73.715770	56.735780	53.402470
152	94.629570	100.961000	90.629950

TABLE 6.2 (*continued*)

Issue #	Residuals	Residuals Dummy 1	Residuals Dummy 2
153	−62.947300	−17.362000	−21.403800
154	14.480140	10.216950	6.659433
155	40.160620	41.936480	39.346550
156	−115.159000	−107.344000	−108.966000
157	−94.946500	−81.696400	−82.447900
158	−28.010400	−13.552500	−14.110500
159	−110.127000	−85.111400	−96.632900
160	9.959282	18.682370	12.662020
161	89.889700	57.689740	48.509480
162	150.675500	141.424000	135.920500
163	150.611600	142.567900	137.258000
164	−38.040900	−36.521000	−48.754100
165	55.443990	95.437610	88.132530
166	−4.652580	−18.233400	−27.698600
167	−10.611100	−6.074840	−12.637200
168	35.778970	164.163000	162.921500
169	−215.328000	−131.013000	−135.422000
170	−59.986400	−60.605400	−70.729300
171	−74.693600	−66.782400	−69.716200
172	−13.734800	0.523639	−3.905600
173	45.295840	38.898770	30.164940
174	30.476800	13.024800	3.159872
175	−67.888500	−25.271900	−23.635500
176	−135.061000	−103.830000	−107.375000
177	−90.741200	−65.550000	−70.062300
178	−28.683300	4.187387	−4.706060
179	−103.027000	−97.290000	−106.078000
180	−88.975000	−66.845700	−77.367900
181	−177.281000	−67.904100	−66.493200
182	−43.044700	24.059160	18.696920
183	−212.505000	−152.131000	−155.963000
184	−38.210800	−25.916400	−34.173800
185	−66.764700	−12.702000	−17.886300
186	295.611300	−36.578800	106.036400
187	176.630300	−47.533000	−13.126100
188	324.060100	189.413000	136.666400
189	221.951100	76.029960	34.046210
190	−58.422000	−59.380500	−70.254000
191	−37.907200	−39.303500	−49.850800
192	53.841660	65.166450	51.559780
193	−166.323000	−68.275700	−66.904900
194	−45.521100	−79.888400	−90.959200
195	−30.394500	−13.116600	−17.062000

(*continued*)

TABLE 6.2 (*continued*)

Issue #	Residuals	Residuals Dummy 1	Residuals Dummy 2
196	–42.709500	–33.855500	–50.285700
197	257.550200	34.224540	70.337910
198	90.307160	102.727000	89.148700
199	–61.373800	–35.037300	–37.531400
200	–30.310400	–29.889500	–32.034600

Notes:
Residuals: residuals from the pooled regression without dummy variables for investment grade.
Residuals Dummy 1: inclusion of dummy variable for investment grade.
Residuals Dummy 2: inclusion of dummy variable to test for regime shift.

Let's now analyze whether we obtain a better fit if we consider the two categories of investment-grade and below-investment-grade bonds. It should be emphasized that this is only an exercise to show the application of regression analysis. The conclusions we reach are not meaningful from an econometric point of view given the small size of the database. The new equation is written as follows:

$$\text{Spread}_i = \beta_0 + \beta_1 D1_i + \beta_2 \text{Coupon}_i + \beta_3 D1_i \text{Coupon}_i + \beta_4 \text{CoverageRatio}_i$$
$$+ \beta_5 D1_i \text{CoverageRatio}_i + \beta_6 \text{LoggedEBIT}_i$$
$$+ \beta_7 D1_i \text{LoggedEBIT}_i + \varepsilon_i$$

There are now seven variables and eight parameters to estimate. The estimated model coefficients and the *t*-statistics are shown as follows:

Coefficient	Estimated Coefficient	Standard Error	*t*-Statistic	*p*-Value
β_0	284.52	73.63	3.86	0.00
β_1	597.88	478.74	1.25	0.21
β_2	37.12	7.07	5.25	3.96E-07
β_3	–45.54	38.77	–1.17	0.24
β_4	–10.33	1.84	–5.60	7.24E-08
β_5	50.13	40.42	1.24	0.22
β_6	–83.76	13.63	–6.15	4.52E-09
β_7	–0.24	62.50	–0.00	1.00

Other regression results are:

SSR: 1.4744e + 006
F-statistic: 76.83
p-value: 0
$R^2 = 0.73$

The Chow test has the value 16.60. The *F*-statistic and the Chow test suggest that the use of dummy variables has greatly improved the goodness-of-fit of the regression, even after compensating for the increase in the number of parameters. The residuals of the model without and with dummy variable $D1$ are shown, respectively, in the second and third columns of Table 6.2.

Now let's use dummy variables to test if there is a regime shift between the two dates. This is a common use for dummy variables in practice. To this end, we create a new dummy variable that has the value 0 for the first date November 28, 2005, and 1 for the second date June 6, 2005. The new equation is written as in the previous case but with a different dummy variable:

$$\text{Spread}_i = \beta_0 + \beta_1 D2_i + \beta_2 \text{Coupon}_i + \beta_3 D2_i \text{Coupon}_i + \beta_4 \text{CoverageRatio}_i$$
$$+ \beta_5 D2_i \text{CoverageRatio}_i + \beta_6 \text{LoggedEBIT}_i$$
$$+ \beta_7 D2_i \text{LoggedEBIT}_i + \varepsilon_i$$

There are seven explanatory variables and eight parameters to estimate. The estimated model coefficients and *t*-statistics are shown as follows:

Coefficient	Estimated Coefficient	Standard Error	*t*-Statistic	*p*-Value
β_0	257.26	79.71	3.28	0.00
β_1	82.17	61.63	1.33	0.18
β_2	33.25	7.11	4.67	5.53E-06
β_3	28.14	2.78	10.12	1.45E-19
β_4	−10.79	2.50	−4.32	2.49E-05
β_5	0.00	3.58	0.00	1.00
β_6	−63.20	18.04	−3.50	0.00
β_7	−27.48	24.34	−1.13	0.26

Other regression statistics are:

SSR: 1.5399e + 006
F-statistic: 72.39
p-value: 0
R^2: 0.71

The Chow test has the value 14.73. The F-statistics and the Chow test suggest that there is indeed a regime shift and that the spread regressions at the two different dates are different. Again, the use of dummy variables has greatly improved the goodness-of-fit of the regression, even after compensating for the increase in the number of parameters. The residuals of the model with dummy variable $D2$ are shown in the last column of Table 6.2.

Illustration: Testing the Mutual Fund Characteristic Lines in Different Market Environments   In the previous chapter, we calculated the characteristic line of two large-cap mutual funds. Let's now perform a simple application of the use of dummy variables by determining if the slope (beta) of the two mutual funds is different in a rising stock market ("up market") and a declining stock market ("down market"). To test this, we can write the following multiple regression model:

$$y_{it} = \alpha_i + \beta_{1i}x_t + \beta_{2i}(D_tx_t) + e_{it}$$

where D_t is the dummy variable that can take on a value of 1 or 0. We will let

$D_t = 1$ if period t is classified as an up market
$D_t = 0$ if period t is classified as a down market

The coefficient for the dummy variable is β_{2i}. If that coefficient is statistically significant, then for the mutual fund:

In an up market: $\beta_i = \beta_{1i} + \beta_{2i}$
In a down market: $\beta_i = \beta_{1i}$

If β_{2i} is not statistically significant, then there is no difference in β_i for up and down markets.

In our illustration, we have to define what we mean by an up and a down market. We will define an up market precisely as one where the average excess return (market return over the risk-free rate or $(r_M - r_{ft})$) for the prior three months is greater than zero. Then

$D_t = 1$ if the average $(r_{Mt} - r_{ft})$ for the prior three months > 0
$D_t = 0$ otherwise

The regressor will then be

$D_tx_t = x_t$ if $(r_M - r_{ft})$ for the prior three months > 0
$D_tx_t = 0$ otherwise

We use the S&P 500 as a proxy for the market returns and the 90-day Treasury rate as a proxy for the risk-free rate. The data are presented in Table 6.3, which shows each observation for the variable $D_t x_t$. The regression results for the two mutual funds are as follows:

Coefficient	Coefficient Estimate	Standard Error	t-Statistic	p-Value
Fund A				
α	−0.23	0.10	−2.36	0.0198
β_1	0.75	0.03	25.83	4E-50
β_2	0.18	0.04	4.29	4E-05
Fund B				
α	0.00	0.14	−0.03	0.9762
β_1	0.75	0.04	18.02	2E-35
β_2	0.13	0.06	2.14	0.0344

The adjusted R^2 is 0.93 and 0.83 for mutual funds A and B, respectively.

TABLE 6.3 Data for Estimating Mutual Fund Characteristic Line with a Dummy Variable

Month Ended	r_M	r_{ft}	Dummy D_t	$r_M - r_{ft} = x_t$	$D_t x_t$	Mutual Fund A r_t	B r_t	A y_t	B y_t
01/31/1995	2.60	0.42	0	2.18	0	0.65	1.28	0.23	0.86
02/28/1995	3.88	0.40	0	3.48	0	3.44	3.16	3.04	2.76
03/31/1995	2.96	0.46	1	2.50	2.5	2.89	2.58	2.43	2.12
04/30/1995	2.91	0.44	1	2.47	2.47	1.65	1.81	1.21	1.37
05/31/1995	3.95	0.54	1	3.41	3.41	2.66	2.96	2.12	2.42
06/30/1995	2.35	0.47	1	1.88	1.88	2.12	2.18	1.65	1.71
07/31/1995	3.33	0.45	1	2.88	2.88	3.64	3.28	3.19	2.83
08/31/1995	0.27	0.47	1	−0.20	−0.2	−0.40	0.98	−0.87	0.51
09/30/1995	4.19	0.43	1	3.76	3.76	3.06	3.47	2.63	3.04
10/31/1995	−0.35	0.47	1	−0.82	−0.82	−1.77	−0.63	−2.24	−1.10
11/30/1995	4.40	0.42	1	3.98	3.98	4.01	3.92	3.59	3.50
12/31/1995	1.85	0.49	1	1.36	1.36	1.29	1.73	0.80	1.24
01/31/1996	3.44	0.43	1	3.01	3.01	3.36	2.14	2.93	1.71
02/29/1996	0.96	0.39	1	0.57	0.57	1.53	1.88	1.14	1.49
03/31/1996	0.96	0.39	1	0.57	0.57	0.59	1.65	0.20	1.26
04/30/1996	1.47	0.46	1	1.01	1.01	1.46	1.83	1.00	1.37
05/31/1996	2.58	0.42	1	2.16	2.16	2.17	2.20	1.75	1.78
06/30/1996	0.41	0.40	1	0.01	0.01	−0.63	0.00	−1.03	−0.40

(*continued*)

TABLE 6.3 (*continued*)

Month Ended	r_M	r_{ft}	Dummy D_t	$r_M - r_{ft} = x_t$	$D_t x_t$	Mutual Fund A r_t	B r_t	A y_t	B y_t
07/31/1996	-4.45	0.45	1	-4.90	-4.9	-4.30	-3.73	-4.75	-4.18
08/31/1996	2.12	0.41	0	1.71	0	2.73	2.24	2.32	1.83
09/30/1996	5.62	0.44	0	5.18	0	5.31	4.49	4.87	4.05
10/31/1996	2.74	0.42	1	2.32	2.32	1.42	1.34	1.00	0.92
11/30/1996	7.59	0.41	1	7.18	7.18	6.09	5.30	5.68	4.89
12/31/1996	-1.96	0.46	1	-2.42	-2.42	-1.38	-0.90	-1.84	-1.36
01/31/1997	6.21	0.45	1	5.76	5.76	4.15	5.73	3.70	5.28
02/28/1997	0.81	0.39	1	0.42	0.42	1.65	-1.36	1.26	-1.75
03/31/1997	-4.16	0.43	1	-4.59	-4.59	-4.56	-3.75	-4.99	-4.18
04/30/1997	5.97	0.43	1	5.54	5.54	4.63	3.38	4.20	2.95
05/31/1997	6.14	0.49	1	5.65	5.65	5.25	6.05	4.76	5.56
06/30/1997	4.46	0.37	1	4.09	4.09	2.98	2.90	2.61	2.53
07/31/1997	7.94	0.43	1	7.51	7.51	6.00	7.92	5.57	7.49
08/31/1997	-5.56	0.41	1	-5.97	-5.97	-4.40	-3.29	-4.81	-3.70
09/30/1997	5.48	0.44	1	5.04	5.04	5.70	4.97	5.26	4.53
10/31/1997	-3.34	0.42	1	-3.76	-3.76	-2.76	-2.58	-3.18	-3.00
11/30/1997	4.63	0.39	0	4.24	0	3.20	2.91	2.81	2.52
12/31/1997	1.72	0.48	1	1.24	1.24	1.71	2.41	1.23	1.93
01/31/1998	1.11	0.43	1	0.68	0.68	-0.01	-0.27	-0.44	-0.70
02/28/1998	7.21	0.39	1	6.82	6.82	5.50	6.84	5.11	6.45
03/31/1998	5.12	0.39	1	4.73	4.73	5.45	3.84	5.06	3.45
04/30/1998	1.01	0.43	1	0.58	0.58	-0.52	1.07	-0.95	0.64
05/31/1998	-1.72	0.40	1	-2.12	-2.12	-1.25	-1.30	-1.65	-1.70
06/30/1998	4.06	0.41	1	3.65	3.65	3.37	4.06	2.96	3.65
07/31/1998	-1.06	0.40	1	-1.46	-1.46	0.10	-1.75	-0.30	-2.15
08/31/1998	-14.46	0.43	1	-14.89	-14.89	-15.79	-13.44	-16.22	-13.87
09/30/1998	6.41	0.46	0	5.95	0	5.00	4.86	4.54	4.40
10/31/1998	8.13	0.32	0	7.81	0	5.41	4.56	5.09	4.24
11/30/1998	6.06	0.31	0	5.75	0	5.19	5.56	4.88	5.25
12/31/1998	5.76	0.38	1	5.38	5.38	7.59	7.18	7.21	6.80
01/31/1999	4.18	0.35	1	3.83	3.83	2.60	3.11	2.25	2.76
02/28/1999	-3.11	0.35	1	-3.46	-3.46	-4.13	-3.01	-4.48	-3.36
03/31/1999	4.00	0.43	1	3.57	3.57	3.09	3.27	2.66	2.84
04/30/1999	3.87	0.37	1	3.50	3.5	2.26	2.22	1.89	1.85
05/31/1999	-2.36	0.34	1	-2.70	-2.7	-2.12	-1.32	-2.46	-1.66
06/30/1999	5.55	0.40	1	5.15	5.15	4.43	5.36	4.03	4.96
07/31/1999	-3.12	0.38	1	-3.50	-3.5	-3.15	-1.72	-3.53	-2.10
08/31/1999	-0.50	0.39	0	-0.89	0	-1.05	-2.06	-1.44	-2.45
09/30/1999	-2.74	0.39	1	-3.13	-3.13	-2.86	-1.33	-3.25	-1.72
10/31/1999	6.33	0.39	0	5.94	0	5.55	2.29	5.16	1.90
11/30/1999	2.03	0.36	1	1.67	1.67	3.23	3.63	2.87	3.27
12/31/1999	5.89	0.44	1	5.45	5.45	8.48	7.09	8.04	6.65
01/31/2000	-5.02	0.41	1	-5.43	-5.43	-4.09	-0.83	-4.50	-1.24
02/29/2000	-1.89	0.43	1	-2.32	-2.32	1.43	2.97	1.00	2.54
03/31/2000	9.78	0.47	0	9.31	0	6.84	5.86	6.37	5.39
04/30/2000	-3.01	0.46	1	-3.47	-3.47	-4.04	-4.55	-4.50	-5.01

TABLE 6.3 (*continued*)

Month Ended	r_M	r_{ft}	Dummy D_t	$r_M - r_{ft} =$ x_t	$D_t x_t$	Mutual Fund A r_t	B r_t	A y_t	B y_t
05/31/2000	−2.05	0.50	1	−2.55	−2.55	−2.87	−4.47	−3.37	−4.97
06/30/2000	2.46	0.40	1	2.06	2.06	0.54	6.06	0.14	5.66
07/31/2000	−1.56	0.48	0	−2.04	0	−0.93	1.89	−1.41	1.41
08/31/2000	6.21	0.50	0	5.71	0	7.30	6.01	6.80	5.51
09/30/2000	−5.28	0.51	1	−5.79	−5.79	−4.73	−4.81	−5.24	−5.32
10/31/2000	−0.42	0.56	0	−0.98	0	−1.92	−4.84	−2.48	−5.40
11/30/2000	−7.88	0.51	0	−8.39	0	−6.73	−11.00	−7.24	−11.51
12/31/2000	0.49	0.50	0	−0.01	0	2.61	3.69	2.11	3.19
01/31/2001	3.55	0.54	0	3.01	0	0.36	5.01	−0.18	4.47
02/28/2001	−9.12	0.38	0	−9.50	0	−5.41	−8.16	−5.79	−8.54
03/31/2001	−6.33	0.42	0	−6.75	0	−5.14	−5.81	−5.56	−6.23
04/30/2001	7.77	0.39	0	7.38	0	5.25	4.67	4.86	4.28
05/31/2001	0.67	0.32	0	0.35	0	0.47	0.45	0.15	0.13
06/30/2001	−2.43	0.28	1	−2.71	−2.71	−3.48	−1.33	−3.76	−1.61
07/31/2001	−0.98	0.30	1	−1.28	−1.28	−2.24	−1.80	−2.54	−2.10
08/31/2001	−6.26	0.31	0	−6.57	0	−4.78	−5.41	−5.09	−5.72
09/30/2001	−8.08	0.28	0	−8.36	0	−6.46	−7.27	−6.74	−7.55
10/31/2001	1.91	0.22	0	1.69	0	1.01	2.30	0.79	2.08
11/30/2001	7.67	0.17	0	7.50	0	4.49	5.62	4.32	5.45
12/31/2001	0.88	0.15	1	0.73	0.73	1.93	2.14	1.78	1.99
01/31/2002	−1.46	0.14	1	−1.60	−1.6	−0.99	−3.27	−1.13	−3.41
02/28/2002	−1.93	0.13	1	−2.06	−2.06	−0.84	−2.68	−0.97	−2.81
03/31/2002	3.76	0.13	0	3.63	0	3.38	4.70	3.25	4.57
04/30/2002	−6.06	0.15	0	−6.21	0	−4.38	−3.32	−4.53	−3.47
05/31/2002	−0.74	0.14	0	−0.88	0	−1.78	−0.81	−1.92	−0.95
06/30/2002	−7.12	0.13	0	−7.25	0	−5.92	−5.29	−6.05	−5.42
07/31/2002	−7.80	0.15	0	−7.95	0	−6.37	−7.52	−6.52	−7.67
08/31/2002	0.66	0.14	0	0.52	0	−0.06	1.86	−0.20	1.72
09/30/2002	−10.87	0.14	0	−11.01	0	−9.38	−6.04	−9.52	−6.18
10/31/2002	8.80	0.14	0	8.66	0	3.46	5.10	3.32	4.96
11/30/2002	5.89	0.12	0	5.77	0	3.81	1.73	3.69	1.61
12/31/2002	−5.88	0.11	1	−5.99	−5.99	−4.77	−2.96	−4.88	−3.07
01/31/2003	−2.62	0.10	1	−2.72	−2.72	−1.63	−2.34	−1.73	−2.44
02/28/2003	−1.50	0.09	0	−1.59	0	−0.48	−2.28	−0.57	−2.37
03/31/2003	0.97	0.10	0	0.87	0	1.11	1.60	1.01	1.50
04/30/2003	8.24	0.10	0	8.14	0	6.67	5.44	6.57	5.34
05/31/2003	5.27	0.09	1	5.18	5.18	4.96	6.65	4.87	6.56
06/30/2003	1.28	0.10	1	1.18	1.18	0.69	1.18	0.59	1.08
07/31/2003	1.76	0.07	1	1.69	1.69	1.71	3.61	1.64	3.54
08/31/2003	1.95	0.07	1	1.88	1.88	1.32	1.13	1.25	1.06
09/30/2003	−1.06	0.08	1	−1.14	−1.14	−1.34	−1.12	−1.42	−1.20
10/31/2003	5.66	0.07	1	5.59	5.59	5.30	4.21	5.23	4.14
11/30/2003	0.88	0.07	1	0.81	0.81	0.74	1.18	0.67	1.11

(*continued*)

TABLE 6.3 (*continued*)

Month Ended	r_M	r_{ft}	Dummy D_t	$r_M - r_{ft} =$ x_t	$D_t x_t$	Mutual Fund A r_t	B r_t	A y_t	B y_t
12/31/2003	5.24	0.08	1	5.16	5.16	4.87	4.77	4.79	4.69
01/31/2004	1.84	0.07	1	1.77	1.77	0.87	2.51	0.80	2.44
02/29/2004	1.39	0.06	1	1.33	1.33	0.97	1.18	0.91	1.12
03/31/2004	−1.51	0.09	1	−1.60	−1.6	−0.89	−1.79	−0.98	−1.88
04/30/2004	−1.57	0.08	1	−1.65	−1.65	−2.59	−1.73	−2.67	−1.81
05/31/2004	1.37	0.06	0	1.31	0	0.66	0.83	0.60	0.77
06/30/2004	1.94	0.08	0	1.86	0	1.66	1.56	1.58	1.48
07/31/2004	−3.31	0.10	1	−3.41	−3.41	−2.82	−4.26	−2.92	−4.36
08/31/2004	0.40	0.11	0	0.29	0	−0.33	0.00	−0.44	−0.11
09/30/2004	1.08	0.11	0	0.97	0	1.20	1.99	1.09	1.88
10/31/2004	1.53	0.11	0	1.42	0	0.33	1.21	0.22	1.10
11/30/2004	4.05	0.15	1	3.90	3.9	4.87	5.68	4.72	5.53
12/31/2004	3.40	0.16	1	3.24	3.24	2.62	3.43	2.46	3.27

Notes:
1. The following information is used for determining the value of the dummy variable for the first three months:

	r_m	r_f	$r_m - r_f$
Sep–1994	−2.41	0.37	−2.78
Oct-1994	2.29	0.38	1.91
Nov-1994	−3.67	0.37	−4.04
Dec-1994	1.46	0.44	1.02

2. The dummy variable is defined as follows:
$D_t x_t = x_t$ if $(r_M - r_{ft})$ for the prior three months > 0
$D_t x_t = 0$ otherwise

For both funds, β_{2i} is statistically significantly different from zero. Hence, for these two mutual funds, there is a difference in the β_i for up and down markets.[5] From the results reported above, we would find that:

	Mutual Fund A	Mutual Fund B
Down market β_i (= β_{1i})	0.75	0.75
Up market β_i (= $\beta_{1i} + \beta_{2i}$)	0.93 (= 0.75 + 0.18)	0.88 (= 0.75 + 0.13)

---

[5] We specifically selected funds that had this characteristic so one should not infer that all mutual funds exhibit this characteristic.

DEPENDENT CATEGORICAL VARIABLES

Thus far we have discussed models where the explanatory variables can be either quantitative or categorical while the dependent variable is quantitative. Let's now discuss models where the dependent variable is categorical.

Recall that a regression model can be interpreted as a conditional probability distribution. Suppose that the dependent variable is a categorical variable Y that can assume two values, which we represent conventionally as 0 and 1. The probability distribution of the dependent variable is then a discrete function:

$$\begin{cases} P(Y = 1) = p \\ P(Y = 0) = q = 1 - p \end{cases}$$

A regression model where the dependent variable is a categorical variable is therefore a probability model; that is, it is a model of the probability p given the values of the explanatory variables $\mathbf{X}$:

$$P(Y = 1|\mathbf{X}) = f(\mathbf{X})$$

In the following sections we will discuss three probability models: the linear probability model, the probit regression model, and the logit regression model.

Linear Probability Model

The *linear probability model* assumes that the function $f(\mathbf{X})$ is linear. For example, a linear probability model of default assumes that there is a linear relationship between the probability of default and the factors that determine default:

$$P(Y = 1|\mathbf{X}) = f(\mathbf{X})$$

The parameters of the model can be obtained by using ordinary least squares applying the estimation methods of multiple regression models discussed in the previous chapter. Once the parameters of the model are estimated, the predicted value for $P(Y)$ can be interpreted as the event probability such as the probability of default in our previous example. Note, however, that when using a linear probability model, the R^2 is used as described in the previous chapter only if all the explanatory variables are also binary variables.

A major drawback of the linear probability model is that the predicted value may be negative. In the probit regression and logit regression models described below, the predicted probability is forced to be between 0 and 1.

Probit Regression Model

The *probit regression model* is a nonlinear regression model where the dependent variable is a binary variable. Due to its nonlinearity, one cannot estimate this model with least squares methods. Instead, it is necessary to use the maximum likelihood (ML) method described in Chapter 13. Because what is being predicted is the standard normal cumulative probability distribution, the predicted values are between 0 and 1.

The general form for the probit regression model is

$$P(Y = 1 \mid X_1, X_2, \ldots, X_K) = N(a + b_1X_1 + b_2X_2 + \ldots + b_KX_K)$$

where N is the cumulative standard normal distribution function.

Suppose that the following parameters are estimated as follows:

$$\beta = -2.1 \quad \beta_1 = 1.9 \quad \beta_2 = 0.3 \quad \beta_3 = 0.8$$

Then

$$N(a + b_1X_1 + b_2X_2 + b_3X_3) = N(-2.1 + 1.9X_1 + 0.3X_2 + 0.8X_3)$$

Now suppose that the probability of default of a company with the following values for the explanatory variables is sought:

$$X_1 = 0.2 \quad X_2 = 0.9 \quad X_3 = 1.0$$

Substituting these values, we get

$$N(-2.1 + 1.9(0.2) + 0.3(0.9) + 0.8(1.0)) = N(-0.65)$$

The standard normal cumulative probability for $N(-0.65)$ is 25.8%. Therefore, the probability of default for a company with this characteristic is 25.8%.

Illustration: Hedge Fund Survival   An illustration of probit regression is provided by Malkiel and Saha who use it to calculate the probability of the demise of a hedge fund.[6] The dependent variable in the regression is 1 if a

---

[6] Burton G. Malkiel and Atanu Saha, "Hedge Funds: Risk and Return," *Financial Analysts Journal* 22 (November–December 2005): 80–88.

fund is defunct (did not survive) and 0 if it survived. The explanatory variables, their estimated coefficient, and the standard error of the coefficient using hedge fund data from 1994 to 2003 are given as follows:

Explanatory Variable	Coefficient	Standard Deviation
1. Return for the first quarter before the end of fund performance.	–1.47	0.36
2. Return for the second quarter before the end of fund performance.	–4.93	0.32
3. Return for the third quarter before the end of fund performance.	–2.74	0.33
4. Return for the fourth quarter before the end of fund performance.	–3.71	0.35
5. Standard deviation for the year prior to the end of fund performance.	17.76	0.92
6. Number of times in the final three months the fund's monthly return fell below the monthly median of all funds in the same primary category.	0.00	0.33
7. Assets of the fund (in billions of dollars) estimated at the end of performance.	–1.30	–7.76
Constant term	–0.37	0.07

For only one explanatory variable, the sixth one, the coefficient is not statistically significant from zero. That explanatory variable is a proxy for peer comparison of the hedge fund versus similar hedge funds. The results suggest that there is a lower probability of the demise of a hedge fund if there is good recent performance (the negative coefficient of the first four variables above) and the more assets under management (the negative coefficient for the last variable above). The greater the hedge fund performance return variability, the higher the probability of demise (the positive coefficient for the fifth variable above).

Logit Regression Model

As with the probit regression model, the *logit regression model* is a nonlinear regression model where the dependent variable is a binary variable and the predicted values are between 0 and 1. The predicted value is also a cumulative probability distribution. However, rather than being a standard normal cumulative probability distribution, it is standard cumulative probability distribution of a distribution called the *logistic distribution*.

The general formula for the logit regression model is

$$P(Y = 1 | X_1, X_2, \ldots, X_N) = F(a + b_1 X_1 + b_2 X_2 + \ldots + b_N X_N)$$
$$= 1 / [1 + e^{-W}]$$

where $W = a + b_1 X_1 + b_2 X_2 + \ldots + b_N X_N$.

As with the probit regression model, the logit regression model is estimated with ML methods.

Using our previous illustration, $W = -0.65$. Therefore

$$1/[1 + e^{-W}] = 1/[1 + e^{-(-0.65)}] = 34.3\%$$

The probability of default for the company with these characteristics is 34.3%.

KEY POINTS

- Categorical variables are variables that represent group membership and are used to cluster input data into groups.
- An explanatory variable that distinguishes only two categories is called a dichotomous variable. The key is to represent a dichotomous categorical variable as a numerical variable called a dummy variable that can assume the value of either 0 or 1.
- An explanatory variable that distinguishes between more than two categories is called a polytomous variable.
- In a regression where there are dummy variables, the t-statistic applied to the regression coefficients of dummy variables offer a set of important tests to judge which explanatory variables are significant. The p-value associated with each coefficient estimate is the probability of the hypothesis that the corresponding coefficient is zero, that is, that the corresponding dummy variable is irrelevant.
- The Chow test is an F-test that is used to gauge if all the dummy variables are collectively irrelevant. The Chow test is the F-test of the unrestricted regressions with and without dummy variables.
- A regression model can be interpreted as a conditional probability distribution. A regression model where the dependent variable is a categorical variable is therefore a probability model.
- Three probability models most commonly used are the linear probability model, the probit regression model, and the logit regression model.

- A linear probability model assumes that the function to be estimated is linear and, as a result, it is possible to obtain negative probabilities.
- Unlike the linear probability model, the predicted probability of the probit regression and logit regression models is forced to be between 0 and 1.
- The probit regression model and logit regression model are nonlinear regression models where the dependent variable is a binary variable and the predicted value is a cumulative probability distribution.
- The logit regression model differs from the probit model because rather than the predicted value being a standard normal cumulative probability distribution, it is a standard cumulative probability distribution of a distribution called the logistic distribution.

CHAPTER 7

Quantile Regressions

A fter reading this chapter you will understand:

- How simple and multiple regressions show that the mean of the dependent variable changes with independent variables.
- How conclusions drawn at the mean may not completely describe the data if the data contain outliers or exhibit a skewed distribution.
- The concept of a quantile regression.
- How to model time series data using quantile regressions.
- How to model cross-sectional data using quantile regressions.
- How to statistically verify if the coefficients across the quantiles in a quantile regression are different.

Many empirical studies have identified that financial time series data exhibit asymmetry (skewness) and fat-tail phenomena (presence of outliers). These observed statistical properties may result in an incomplete picture of the relationship between the dependent and independent variable(s) when classical regression analysis is employed. In addition, events such as global financial crises make understanding, modeling, and managing left-tail return distributions (i.e., unfavorable returns) all the more important. A tool that would allow researchers to explore the entire distribution of the data is the *quantile regression*. Introduced by Koenker and Bassett,[1] a quantile regression involves estimating the functional relations between variables for all portions of the probability distribution. For example, if we want to examine the relationship between the dependent and independent variable at the 5th, the median, or at the 95th percentile, we will be able to test this relationship with quantile regressions. Thus, one can establish the relationship between the dependent and independent variables for a particular quantile or for each quantile using the quantile regression, and thereby allow risk managers to manage the tail risk better.

---

[1] Roger Koenker and Gilbert Bassett, "Regression Quantiles," *Econometrica* 46 (1978): 33–50.

LIMITATIONS OF CLASSICAL REGRESSION ANALYSIS

Before discussing quantile regressions, let's first illustrate the limitations of regression analysis introduced in Chapters 2 and 3, which we will refer to as classical regression analysis.

Classical regression analysis is concerned with predicting the mean value of the dependent variables on the basis of given values of the independent variable. For example, a simple regression between the moving monthly S&P 500 stock index returns over the prior 12 months and its dividend yield from January of 1926 through December of 2012 (1,030 observations) would show that the regression slope coefficient for the dividend yield is 16.03 with a t-statistic of 5.31. This slope coefficient, which is statistically and economically significant, implies that a percentage point increase in expected dividend yield on average leads to a 16.03% increase in the index returns over the next 12 months. As long as the regression errors are normally distributed, the inferences made about the regression coefficients are all valid. However, when outliers are present in the data, the assumption of normal distribution is violated, leading to a fat-tailed residual error distribution.[2] In the presence of outliers and fat tails, the inferences made at the average may not apply to the entire distribution of returns. In these instances quantile regression is a robust estimation to study the entire distribution of returns.

PARAMETER ESTIMATION

The aim of simple classical regression analysis is to minimize the sum of squared errors, given by

$$\min_{\alpha, \beta} = \sum_{i=1}^{t} (y_i - \alpha - X_i \beta)^2 \tag{7.1}$$

where y_i is the dependent variable, X_i is the independent variable, and α and β are the estimated intercept and slope parameters, respectively.

---

[2]When the observed returns are five standard deviations away from the mean, the distribution will have fat tails. For example, the monthly mean and standard deviation of the S&P 500 returns are 0.31% and 4.58%, respectively. In the data set there is a month in which the S&P index had a return of 51.4% (the maximum return) and a month with a return of −26.47% (the minimum return). These two observed returns are more than five standard deviations away from the mean, causing the return distribution to have fat tails.

The objective is to find values of β that would minimize the error. While the idea of quantile regression is similar, it aims at minimizing absolute deviations from τ th conditional quantile and it is given as:

$$\min_{\beta \in R_p} = \sum_{i=1}^{T} \rho_\tau (y_i - \xi(X_i, \beta)) \tag{7.2}$$

where ξ is the conditional quantile and ρ_τ is the so-called *check function*, which weights positive and negative values asymmetrically (giving varying weights to positive and negative residuals).

For example, to obtain conditional median parameter estimates, τ should be set at 0.5 (since τ ranges between 0 and 1, 0.5 represents the median quantile) and an optimization model is employed to find values of β that minimize the weighted sum of absolute deviations between the dependent variable and the independent variables. However, unlike in a simple regression where calculus can be used to obtain the formula for β, the constraints imposed requires that linear programming, a type of mathematical programming optimization model, must be used.

In a regression format, the relationship between the dependent and independent variable can be summarized as follows:

$$\min_{\alpha^\tau \beta^\tau} \sum_{i=1}^{T'} \left| y_i - \alpha^\tau - X_i \beta^\tau \right| \tag{7.3}$$

where α^τ is the intercept for a specified quantile and β^τ is the corresponding slope coefficient.

β^τ shows the relationship between X_i and y_i for a specified quantile. A linear program is used where different values of α and β are plugged into the above equation until the weighted sum of the absolute deviations are minimized.

For illustrative purposes, a median regression (τ = 0.5) between the S&P 500 returns over the prior 12 months and the dividend yield would result in estimated values for α and β of −0.64 and 12.24, respectively, and with corresponding *t* values of −0.64 and 4.05. The slope coefficient of 12.24 implies that the median return will go up by 12.24% for a percentage point increase in the expected dividend yield. Comparing the results provided in a simple regression described earlier in the chapter, the median response of index returns to changes in the dividend yield is about 4 percentage points below that of the mean response presented in a simple regression. The reason for this difference is that the simple regression, in an attempt to accommodate outliers, fits a line that overestimates the regression coefficients. This finding clearly demonstrates that inferences made at the mean may not describe the entire distribution of the data. Hence, it might be useful to estimate the relationship over the entire return distribution.

QUANTILE REGRESSION PROCESS

The advantage of a quantile regression is that we can see how the returns respond to the expected dividend yield over different return quantiles. The process of estimating more than a quantile at a time is defined as a *quantile process*. The results of the quantile process between the S&P 500 index returns over the prior 12 months and the expected dividend yield are presented in Table 7.1.

TABLE 7.1   Quantile Regressions, Sample from January 1926 through December 2012

	Quantile	Coefficient	Std. Error	*t*-Statistic
Constant	0.100	−23.04	2.26	−10.1
	0.200	−19.84	2.81	−7.05
	0.300	−12.20	3.34	−3.65
	0.400	−5.22	2.35	−2.21
	0.500	−0.93	1.74	−0.53
	0.600	1.28	1.61	0.79
	0.700	4.31	1.99	2.15
	0.800	6.19	1.84	3.35
	0.900	10.62	2.19	4.84
Dividend Yield	0.100	3.94	4.83	0.81
	0.200	17.35	6.12	2.83
	0.300	14.47	6.53	2.21
	0.400	12.69	4.73	2.68
	0.500	14.38	3.60	3.99
	0.600	16.98	3.49	4.85
	0.700	22.64	4.80	4.71
	0.800	32.02	4.19	7.63
	0.900	37.14	4.91	7.55

Note: α is the constant for each quantile, β is the slope coefficient of the dividend yield for each quantile, y_i is the S&P 500 stock index returns over the prior 12 months, and X_i is the expected dividend yield.

The results for nine quantiles are presented in Table 7.1. The intercept term reflects returns received on the S&P 500 index if there are no dividends. Not surprisingly, it is monotone upwards and it is positive and statistically significant at and above the 70th return percentile. But our main interest is in how expected dividend yield influences returns. For example, the effect of expected dividend yield at the 10th return percentile is statistically not different from zero. The effect of the dividend yield sharply increases at the 20th return percentile. A 1% increase in expected dividend yield will cause a 17.35% increase in the annualized S&P 500 returns. However, in spite of its statistical significance, the effect of dividend yield drops off at the 30th and 40th return quantiles. The coefficient of dividend yield grows monotonically from 14.38 at the 50th return percentile to 37.14 at the 90th return percentile.

Table 7.1 shows that coefficients of the dividend yield change across different quantiles. Now the question is are they statistically different. Koenker and Bassett proposed a Wald test to verify this across the quantiles.[3] The null hypothesis that the slope coefficients are all the same is given by

$$H_0: \beta_1 \tau_1 = \beta_1 \tau_2 = \ldots = \beta_1 \tau_k$$

where β are slope coefficients and τ are quantiles. The null hypothesis imposes k restrictions on the coefficients and a Wald statistic[4] is calculated which is distributed as χ^2 with degrees of freedom equal to number of restrictions.

In our example, we have a total of eight restrictions ($\beta_1 \tau_1 = \beta_1 \tau_2$, $\beta_1 \tau_2 = \beta_1 \tau_3, \ldots, \beta_1 \tau_9 = \beta_1 \tau_{10}$). The calculated Wald test statistic is 42.40 and the critical χ^2 with eight degrees of freedom is 15.51. Since the test statistic is greater than the critical value, we reject the null hypothesis that the slope coefficients are the same across the quantiles.

Therefore, it is important to understand that to use quantile regressions, we have to first empirically verify that the data are skewed with fat tails. Second, using the quantile process, we have to examine the relationship between the dependent and independent variables at each quantile. Finally, it is important to statistically verify if the coefficients across the quantiles are different.

---

[3] Roger Koenker and Gilbert Bassett, "Tests of Linear Hypotheses and L_1 Estimation," *Econometrica* 50 (1982): 1577–1584.

[4] This statistic is provided by software packages such as SAS, R, and Eviews. To calculate the Wald statistic, a restricted regression model with same βs across the quantiles is estimated to obtain sum of squared errors. This sum of squared errors statistic would then be compared to the statistic of sum of squared errors of regressions where the βs are allowed to vary across the quantiles. If the difference in the two sum of squared statistics is not different from zero then we will be unable to reject the null hypothesis.

APPLICATIONS OF QUANTILE REGRESSIONS IN FINANCE

One of the first applications of quantile regressions was in the area of risk management, especially in the context of the popular risk measure *value at risk* (VaR). VaR is a statistical measure that indicates under a certain set of assumptions the most that a portfolio manager can lose within a reasonable bound. For example, if the one-month VaR (0.05) of a portfolio is $55 million, one can infer with 95% confidence that there is only a 5% chance that the portfolio's value will decrease more than $55 million in one month. Several approaches have been proposed for measuring VaR. A quantile regression is a natural tool to handle VaR problems because this type of regression can be used to examine the relationship between portfolio returns and its determinants over the entire return distribution. Engle and Manganelli were among the first to consider the quantile regression for the VaR model.[5] Using daily stock return data for General Motors, IBM, and the S&P 500, they show that the tails follow a different behavior than the middle of the distribution. They conclude that VaR calculations using a quantile regression outperform the alternate approaches that have been proposed.

There are studies that suggest how quantile regressions can be used to create portfolios that outperform traditional portfolio construction methodologies. For instance, Ma and Pohlman employ a quantile regression to forecast returns and construct portfolios.[6] Using time series data on 1,100 individual stock returns, they showed that portfolios constructed based on return forecasts generated by a quantile regression outperformed the portfolios created based on traditional approaches. Quantile regressions can also be used to test the performance of a portfolio between higher and lower return quantiles. For example, Gowland, Xiao, and Zeng, using a sample of small cap stocks, showed that the performance of a 90th return quantile differs from that of a 10th return quantile of a portfolio created on the basis of book-to-market.[7]

Below we provide two illustrations of applications to finance in more detail. In the first, we look at how a quantile regression can be used to

---

[5] Robert Engle and Simone Manganelli, "CAViaR: Conditional Autoregressive Value at Risk by Regression Quantiles," *Journal of Business and Economic Statistics* 22 (2004): 367–387.

[6] Lingjie Ma and Larry Pohlman, "Return Forecasts and Optimal Portfolio Construction: A Quantile Regression Approach," *European Journal of Finance* 14 (2008): 409–425.

[7] Chris Gowland, Zhijie Xiao, and Qi Zeng, "Beyond the Central Tendency: Quantile Regression as a Tool in Quantitative Investing," *Journal of Portfolio Management* 35, no. 3 (2009): 106–119.

determine a portfolio manager's style. The data used in this application are times series data. In our second illustration, we look at how a quantile regression can be used to empirically investigate the determinants of a corporation's capital structure. In this application, cross-sectional data are used.

Determining a Portfolio Manager's Style

A quantile regression can be applied to identify a portfolio manager's investment style. The manager's performance is compared to a benchmark. The benchmark selected should be consistent with a portfolio manager's investment style. For example, a portfolio of stocks categorized as value stocks may appear to have an unsatisfactory performance relative to a broad stock index, but its performance could be outstanding relative to a value stock benchmark. Such performance is attributed to the portfolio manager's stock selection skill.

To classify the investment style of a manager, a regression-based approach has been proposed by Sharpe and is discussed in Chapter 3.[8] This approach regresses a fund's time series return on the returns to a variety of equity indexes. The statistical significance and the magnitude of the estimated coefficients represent the fund's style. However, as noted earlier, in the presence of outliers, the inferences made about the style of the manager at the average may not apply to the entire distribution of returns.

As an illustration, quantile regressions are applied to Fidelity Mid Cap Value mutual fund returns to identify the investment style of the manager across the distribution of returns. As the name suggests, the proclaimed investment style of the fund is to invest in a portfolio of mid cap stocks. The monthly returns of the fund from December 2001 through March 2013 (136 observations) are regressed against the equity index returns of large cap value, large cap growth, small cap value, small cap growth, and the Russell's Mid Cap Value Index. The data for all these variables are obtained from Morningstar EnCorr database.

The results are presented in Table 7.2. The slope coefficients of the regression show, other things being equal, the impact of a change in the index returns on the fund's return. If a mutual fund manager sticks to the fund's stated style, the index that represents the stated style should be the only factor that would influence the fund's return. The regression results show that only the mid cap value index has a statistical and positive effect on the returns of Fidelity Mid Cap Value Fund. A 1% increase in the index will

---

[8]William F. Sharpe, "Asset Allocation: Management Style and Performance Measurement," *Journal of Portfolio Management* 16, no. 2 (1992): 7–19.

TABLE 7.2 Multivariate and Quantile Regressions, Sample from December 2001 through March 2013

	Multivariate Regression	Q(0.1)	Q(0.3)	Q(0.5)	Q(0.7)	Q(0.9)
Constant	−0.077	−1.022	−0.393	−0.092	0.261	0.986
	−0.987	−7.094	−4.338	−1.014	2.505	5.501
Large Value	−0.053	0.058	0.016	−0.039	−0.086	−0.100
	−1.026	2.122	0.369	−0.829	−2.447	−4.128
Large Growth	−0.014	−0.054	−0.055	0.002	−0.042	−0.035
	−0.386	−1.580	−1.074	0.028	−0.847	−1.068
Small Value	0.037	−0.154	−0.125	−0.091	−0.024	−0.028
	0.974	−4.770	−2.573	−1.696	−0.356	−0.634
Small Growth	−0.084	0.051	0.013	0.017	0.069	0.056
	−2.384	1.758	0.324	0.405	1.456	1.799
Mid Cap	1.040	0.928	1.009	1.028	1.078	1.114
	18.395	19.112	15.624	14.925	14.497	22.085

Fidelity Mid Cap Value return = Large value index returns
+ Large growth index returns
+ Small value index returns
+ Small growth index returns
+ Mid cap value index returns

These data are obtained from Morningstar EnCorr.

cause an average increase of 1.04% in the fund's return. Since the classical multivariate regression only captures the mean change in returns, the above results may not capture the investment style of the manager across the distribution of returns. Furthermore, the Jarque-Bera (JB) normality test[9] shows that regression errors are not normally distributed.

Quantile regressions provide a complete view of investment style of the fund. The following quantile regression model is estimated:

Q_τ(Fidelity Mid Cap Value Fund return) = Large value index returns
+ Large growth index returns
+ Small value index returns
+ Small growth index returns
+ Mid cap value index returns

where Q is the quantile and τ represents the quantile levels. For the purpose of this illustration, the selected quantile levels are 0.10, 0.30, 0.50, 0.70, and 0.90.

---

[9]The Jarque-Bera normality test is explained in Chapter 4.

The results of this quantile process are shown in Table 7.2. The results show that the mid cap value index is statistically significant across the quantiles reported in the table. Other indexes are small in magnitude and statistically insignificant. If the intercept is a measure of manager's talent, it is large in magnitude and statistically significant only in higher return quantiles. Since Russell's Mid Cap Value Index influences the entire return distribution, it is safe to assume that the Fidelity Mid Cap Value Fund did not deviate from its stated style.

To ensure that inferences made across quantiles are meaningful, a Wald test is implemented. There are four restrictions[10] for each coefficient and five estimated coefficients for a total of 20 restrictions. The estimated test statistic is 23.93 and the critical χ^2 value with 20 degrees of freedom at the 5% significance level is 31.41. Thus, the null hypothesis that the coefficients are the same cannot be rejected. This is an additional evidence that the Fidelity Mid Cap Value Fund did not deviate from its stated style across the distribution of returns.

Determining the Factors That Impact Capital Structure

A key issue in corporate finance theory is how management determines the firm's capital structure (i.e., the mixture of debt and equity). Empirical evidence suggests that a firm's size, profitability, asset utilization, liquidity, and growth prospects have a significant effect on the capital structure decision. Furthermore, it has been found that leverage or debt structure (debt to assets) varies across industries, indicating that specific industry factors are at work.

To see how quantile regressions can be used to assess the factors that impact a firm's capital structure, we use company-specific fundamental data as reported each year by Bloomberg Financial.[11] We will focus on the petroleum industry for the year 2010. Our sample in this illustration is 189 firms in the petroleum industry. Since we are looking at information about firms in a given year, this is an illustration of an application using cross-sectional data.

We need firm-level data on debt and total assets. For the purpose of this illustration, we used the book value of total debt (short- and long-term debt) and divided it by the total assets. This is defined as the leverage ratio. The mean leverage ratio for the petroleum industry in 2010 was 31.1% with a standard deviation of 31% and the median was 22%. The range for the

---

[10]The restrictions are $(\beta_1 Q_{0.1} - \beta_1 Q_{0.3}, \beta_1 Q_{0.3} - \beta_1 Q_{0.5}, \beta_1 Q_{0.5} - \beta_1 Q_{0.7}, \beta_1 Q_{0.7} - \beta_1 \beta Q_{0.9})$.

[11]www.bloomberg.com/markets.

leverage ratio for the 189 firms was zero (i.e., no leverage) to 99%. The data also reveal that the leverage ratio is positively skewed (skewness of 83%) and with a kurtosis of 252%. These statistical features of the data reveal that the leverage ratio data are not normally distributed. As explained in Chapter 4, a formal way of testing normality of data is proposed by Jarque and Bera,[12] appropriately referred to as the *Jarque-Bera* (JB) *test*. In simple terms, this test verifies whether the sample data have values of skewness and kurtosis matching a normal distribution. If the distribution is normal, the skewness and the excess kurtosis (or kurtosis of 3) should jointly be zero. The calculated JB statistic[13] has a χ^2 distribution with 2 degrees of freedom (skewness being zero and excess kurtosis being zero). The calculated JB statistic is 23.50 and the critical χ^2 with 2 degrees of freedom at a 5% significance level is 5.99. Thus, the null hypothesis that the leverage ratio data came from a normal distribution is resoundingly rejected.

Since the leverage data did not come from a normal distribution, the use of classical regression analysis to explain the leverage ratio may not fully describe important determinants of capital structure. In other words, classical regression analysis may determine the leverage ratio at the mean, but the analysis may not be useful in explaining the debt structure at the top or the bottom quantiles of the leverage ratio. If an investment analyst or chief financial officer is interested in understanding the determinants of leverage across the entire distribution, then a quantile regression might be an appropriate tool.

Capital structure studies show that companies with higher free cash flow[14] tend to have higher debt in their capital structure. The explanation offered for such a relationship is that the owners by using debt are effectively reducing the availability of cash for discretionary spending by the firm's managers. It is also argued that firms with a higher percentage of fixed assets tend to have higher debt in their capital structure. The presence of fixed assets makes it easier for the firms to borrow at a lower interest cost because these fixed assets can be used as collateral. Thus, a priori one might expect a positive relationship between a firm's fixed asset ratio[15] and its leverage ratio. Finally, it is also argued that capital structure depends on the size of the firm. Since

---

[12] Carlos Jarque and Anil Bera, "Efficient Tests of Normality, Homoscedasticity and Serial Independence of Regression Residuals," *Economics Letters* 3 (1980): 255–259.
[13] Standard statistical packages routinely provide the Jarque-Bera test statistic.
[14] Free cash flow is the money available to shareholders after expenses are taken out to maintain or expand the firm's asset base. The formula is Free cash flow = Earnings before interest and taxes – Change in networking capital – Change in capital expenditure + Depreciation and amortization.
[15] Fixed asset ratio is defined as fixed assets divided by total assets.

larger firms tend to have diversified investments and easier access to capital, it would be easier for these firms to borrow at a favorable interest rate. Hence one expects a positive relationship between large capitalized firms and debt. Here we define the size of the firm by its market cap and since market cap is given in millions of dollars, it is normalized by taking its logged values. The source of firm-specific data on free cash flows, fixed asset ratio, and market capitalization for 2010 was obtained from Bloomberg Financial.[16]

The first task is to run a multivariate regression to determine the factors that influence the debt ratio. The result of this classical regression analysis was

Leverage Ratio = 0.23 + 0.00006 Free cash flow
+ 0.57 (Fixed Assets/Total Assets) − 0.05 log(Market Cap)

The free cash flow term is not statistically significant. The t-value for the market cap factor is −8.7. The relationship between between the firm's size and leverage ratio, instead of being positive, is negative and different from what is hypothesized. It shows that large cap firms in the petroleum industry have lower debt ratio than small cap firms. This finding could be unique to this industry. Finally, the results show that the fixed asset ratio is statistically significant with a t-value of 6.92. This shows that the firms with a higher ratio of fixed assets tend to have a higher leverage ratio.

Since a classical multivariate regression only captures the mean change, the above results may not be informative and may not provide a complete view of how capital structure is determined. Quantile regressions provide a complete view of the factors that determine the capital structure. The following quantile regression model is estimated:

$$Q_\tau(\text{Leverage Ratio}) = \text{Free cash flow} + \text{Fixed Assets/Total Assets} + \log(\text{Market Cap})$$

where Q is the quantile and τ represents the quantile levels. The selected quantile levels are 0.10, 0.20, 0.30, 0.40, 0.50, 0.60, 0.70, 0.80, and 0.90.

The results of this quantile process, presented in Table 7.3, show the leverage ratio for different quantiles. The results indicate that free cash flow has very little effect on the leverage ratio across all quantiles. The results also show that the fixed asset ratio is statistically significant across all quantiles and the coefficient is monotonically increasing. This finding indicates that firms with a higher ratio of fixed assets tend to have a higher leverage ratio. Instead of a positive relationship between the market cap and the leverage ratio, the relationship is negative across all quantiles implying that as

---

[16] www.bloomberg.com/markets.

TABLE 7.3 Estimated Parameters by Quantiles to Determine the Capital Structure of Petroleum

	Q(0.10)	Q(0.20)	Q(0.30)	Q(0.40)	Q(0.50)	Q(0.60)	Q(0.70)	Q(0.80)	Q(0.90)
Constant	0.00	0.01	0.03	0.06	0.22	0.32	0.45	0.49	0.50
	0.01	0.22	0.35	0.67	2.21	3.34	4.96	5.39	6.77
Free Cash Flow	0.00	0.00	0.00	0.00	0.00	0.00	0.00	0.00	0.00
	1.82	1.60	1.40	1.18	1.60	1.08	0.69	-0.13	-0.59
Fixed Assets/Total Assets	0.14	0.32	0.49	0.58	0.72	0.67	0.59	0.59	0.62
	1.55	3.37	4.24	4.01	6.06	6.16	5.51	5.50	7.06
log(Market Cap)	-0.01	-0.03	-0.04	-0.05	-0.08	-0.07	-0.07	-0.07	-0.07
	-1.02	-2.06	-2.71	-2.44	-8.93	-9.73	-10.89	-10.38	-11.66

Q_τ(Leverage Ratio) = Free cash flow + (Fixed Assets/Total Assets) + log(Market Cap).

market cap increases the debt in the capital structure declines. This finding may be unique to the petroleum industry. These findings across the distribution could not have been observed with a classical multivariate regression analysis.

As explained earlier, in order to make meaningful inferences across quantiles, it is important to verify that coefficients estimated at each quantile are statistically different. The null hypothesis that the slope coefficients are all the same is given by

$$H_o: \begin{matrix} \beta_1\tau_1 = \beta_1\tau_2 = \beta_1\tau_{10} \\ \beta_2\tau_1 = \beta_2\tau_2 = \beta_2\tau_{10} \\ \beta_3\tau_1 = \beta_3\tau_2 = \beta_3\tau_{10} \end{matrix}$$

where β_1, β_2, and β_3 are coefficients associated with free cash flow, fixed asset ratio, and the market cap. There are eight restrictions for each coefficient and with three coefficients there are a total of 24 (3 × 8) restrictions. The calculated Wald test statistic is 60.49. The critical χ^2 value with 24 degrees of freedom at a 5% significance level is 36.41. Since the test statistic is greater than the critical value, we reject the null hypothesis that the slope coefficients are the same across the quantiles. Thus, conclusions drawn for each quantile are statistically valid.

KEY POINTS

- In the presence of outliers and a skewed distribution, inferences made with classical regression analysis may not fully describe the data.
- The regression tool applied in the presence of non-normal distributions is the quantile regression.
- Quantile regressions find parameters that would minimize the weighted sum of absolute deviations between the dependent and the independent variables at each quantile.
- Quantile regressions describe relationships between dependent and independent variables within the context of time series and cross-sectional data.
- In order to make meaningful inferences across quantiles, it is important to verify that coefficients are different across the quantiles.
- Quantile regressions are useful tools for risk managers to manage the tail risk.
- Applications of quantile regressions to asset management include generating forecasted returns that can be used in constructing portfolios and determining the investment style of a portfolio manager.

CHAPTER 8

Robust Regressions

A fter reading this chapter you will understand:

- Under what conditions standard regression parameter estimates are sensitive to small changes in the data.
- The concept of robust estimates of regression parameters.
- How to construct robust regression estimators.
- How to apply robust regressions to problems in finance.

Broadly speaking, statistics is the science of describing and analyzing data and making inferences on a population based on a sample extracted from the same population. An important aspect of statistics is the compression of the data into numbers that are descriptive of some feature of the distribution. Classical statistics identifies several single-number descriptors such as mean, variance, skewness, kurtosis, and higher moments. These numbers give a quantitative description of different properties of the population.

Classical statistics chooses single-number descriptors that have nice mathematical properties. For example, if we know all the moments of a probability distribution, we can reconstruct the same distribution. In a number of cases (but not always), the parameters that identify a closed-form representation of a distribution correspond to these descriptive concepts. For example, the parameters that identify a normal distribution correspond to the mean and to the variance. However, in classical statistics, most of these descriptive parameters are not "robust." Intuitively, robustness means that small changes in the sample or small mistakes in identifying the distribution do not affect the descriptive parameters.

Robust statistics entails a rethinking of statistical descriptive concepts; the objective is to find descriptive concepts that are little affected by the choice of the sample or by mistakes in distributional assumptions. Robust statistics is not a technical adjustment of classical concepts but a profound rethinking of how to describe data. For example, robust statistics identifies parameters that represent the center or the spread of a distribution and that are robust with respect to outliers and to small changes in the distributions. Robust statistics seeks descriptive concepts that are optimal from the point of view of being insensitive to small errors in the data or assumptions.

The notion of robust statistics carries over to statistical modeling. Statistical models such as regression models are theoretically elegant but not robust. That is, small errors in distributional assumptions or small data contamination might have unbounded effects on the overall model. Robust statistics is a technique to find models that are robust (i.e., to find models that yield approximately the same results even if samples change or the assumptions are not correct). For example, robust regressions are not very sensitive to outliers.

In Appendix F we provide a more detailed explanation of robust statistics, providing the basic concepts used in this chapter. In this chapter, we cover robust regression estimators and robust regression diagnostics.

ROBUST ESTIMATORS OF REGRESSIONS

Let's begin by applying the concept of robust statistics described in Appendix F to the estimation of regression coefficients that are insensitive to outliers.

Identifying robust estimators of regressions is a rather difficult problem. In fact, different choices of estimators, robust or not, might lead to radically different estimates of slopes and intercepts. Consider the following linear regression model:

$$y = \beta_0 + \sum_{i=1}^{N} \beta_i x_i + \varepsilon$$

If data are organized in matrix form as usual,

$$Y = \begin{pmatrix} Y_1 \\ \vdots \\ Y_T \end{pmatrix} \quad X = \begin{pmatrix} 1 & X_{11} & \cdots & X_{1N} \\ \vdots & \vdots & \ddots & \vdots \\ 1 & X_{T1} & \cdots & X_{TN} \end{pmatrix} \quad \beta = \begin{pmatrix} \beta_0 \\ \vdots \\ \beta_N \end{pmatrix} \quad \varepsilon = \begin{pmatrix} \varepsilon_1 \\ \vdots \\ \varepsilon_T \end{pmatrix}$$

then the regression equation takes the form,

$$Y = X\beta + \varepsilon \qquad (8.1)$$

The standard nonrobust least squares (LS) estimation of regression parameters minimizes the sum of squared residuals,

$$\vartheta\left(\beta_0,\ldots,\beta_N\right) = \sum_{t=1}^{T}\varepsilon_t^2 = \sum_{t=1}^{T}\left(Y_t - \sum_{j=1}^{N}\beta_j X_{tj}\right)^2 \qquad (8.2)$$

or, equivalently, equating to zero their derivatives which imply solving the system of $N+1$ equations,

$$\frac{\partial\vartheta}{\partial\beta_k} = \sum_{t=1}^{T}\left(Y_t - \sum_{j=1}^{N}\beta_j X_{tj}\right)X_{tk} = 0 \quad k = 0,1,\ldots,N \qquad (8.3)$$

or, in matrix notation, $\mathbf{X'X\beta} = \mathbf{X'Y}$. The solution of this system is

$$\hat{\beta} = (\mathbf{X'X})^{-1}\mathbf{X'Y} \qquad (8.4)$$

From equation (8.1), the fitted values (i.e., the LS estimates of the expectations) of the $\mathbf{Y}$ are

$$\hat{\mathbf{Y}} = \mathbf{X(X'X)}^{-1}\mathbf{X'Y} = \mathbf{HY} \qquad (8.5)$$

The $\mathbf{H}$ matrix is called the *hat matrix* because it puts a hat on; that is, it computes the expectation $\hat{\mathbf{Y}}$ of the $\mathbf{Y}$. The hat matrix $\mathbf{H}$ is a symmetric $T \times T$ projection matrix; that is, the following relationship holds: $\mathbf{HH} = \mathbf{H}$. The matrix $\mathbf{H}$ has N eigenvalues equal to 1 and $T - N$ eigenvalues equal to 0. Its diagonal elements, $h_i \equiv h_{ii}$ satisfy:

$$0 \le h_i \le 1$$

and its trace (i.e., the sum of its diagonal elements)[1] is equal to N:

$$\text{tr}(\mathbf{H}) = N$$

Under the assumption that the errors are independent and identically distributed with mean zero and variance σ^2, it can be demonstrated that the $\hat{\mathbf{Y}}$ are consistent, that is, $\hat{\mathbf{Y}} \rightarrow E(\mathbf{Y})$ in probability when the sample becomes infinite if and only if $h = \max(h_i) \rightarrow 0$. Points where the h_i have large values are called *leverage points*. It can be demonstrated that the presence of leverage points signals that there are observations that might have a decisive influence on the estimation of the regression parameters. A rule of thumb, reported in Huber,[2] suggests that values $h_i \le 0.2$ are safe, values $0.2 \le h_i \le 0.5$ require careful attention, and higher values are to be avoided.

---

[1] See Appendix D.
[2] Peter J. Huber, *Robust Statistics* (New York: John Wiley & Sons, 1981).

Thus far we have discussed methods to ascertain regression robustness. Let's now discuss methods to "robustify" the regression estimates, namely, methods based on M-estimators and W-estimators.

Robust Regressions Based on M-Estimators

Let's first discuss how to make *robust regressions* with Huber M-estimators. The LS estimators are M-estimators because they are obtained by minimizing the sum of the squared residuals. However they are not robust. We can generalize equation (8.3) by introducing the weighting function:

$$\rho = \rho\left(Y_t - \sum_{j=1}^{N} \beta_j X_{tj} \right) \tag{8.6}$$

We rewrite the M-estimator as follows:

$$M(\beta_0, \ldots, \beta_N) = \sum_{t=1}^{T} \rho(\varepsilon_t) = \sum_{t=1}^{T} \rho\left(Y_t - \sum_{j=1}^{N} \beta_j X_{tj} \right)$$

And we generalize the LS by minimizing the M-estimator with respect to the coefficients β. To determine the minimum, we equate to zero the partial derivatives of the M-estimator. If we define the functions:

$$\psi(x) = \frac{d\rho(x)}{dx}, \quad w(x) = \frac{\psi(x)}{x}$$

We can write the following conditions:

$$\frac{\partial \vartheta}{\partial \beta_k} = \sum_{t=1}^{T} \frac{\partial \rho\left(Y_t - \sum_{j=1}^{N} \beta_j X_{tj} \right)}{\partial \beta_k} = \sum_{t=1}^{T} \psi\left(Y_t - \sum_{j=1}^{N} \beta_j X_{tj} \right) X_{tk} = 0 \quad k = 0, 1, \ldots, N$$

$$\sum_{t=1}^{T} \psi\left(Y_t - \sum_{j=1}^{N} \beta_j X_{tj} \right) X_{tk} = \sum_{t=1}^{T} w\left(Y_t - \sum_{j=1}^{N} \beta_j X_{tj} \right)\left(Y_t - \sum_{j=1}^{N} \beta_j X_{tj} \right) X_{tk} = 0$$

or, in matrix form

$$\mathbf{X}'\mathbf{W}\mathbf{X}\beta = \mathbf{X}'\mathbf{W}\mathbf{Y}$$

where $\mathbf{W}$ is a diagonal matrix.

The above is not a linear system because the weighting function is in general a nonlinear function of the data. A typical approach is to determine iteratively the weights through an iterative *reweighted least squares* (RLS) procedure. Clearly the iterative procedure depends numerically on the choice of the weighting functions. Two commonly used choices are the *Huber weighting function, $w_H(e)$*, defined as

$$w_H(e) = \begin{cases} 1 & \text{for } |e| \le k \\ k \,/\, |e| & \text{for } |e| > k \end{cases}$$

and the *Tukey bisquare weighting function, $w_T(e)$*, also referred to as biweight function, defined as

$$w_T(e) = \begin{cases} (1 - (e \,/\, k)^2)^2 & \text{for } |e| \le k \\ 0 & \text{for } |e| > k \end{cases}$$

where k is a tuning constant often set at $1.345 \times$ (standard deviation of errors) for the Huber function, and at $4.685 \times$ (standard deviation of errors) for the Tukey function. (Note that $w = 1$ [constant function] recovers the case of ordinary least squares.)

ILLUSTRATION: ROBUSTNESS OF THE CORPORATE BOND YIELD SPREAD MODEL

To illustrate robust regressions, let's continue with our illustration of the spread regression used in Chapter 6 to show how to incorporate dummy variables into a regression model. Recall that there are 200 issues in the sample studied. Table 8.1 shows the diagonal elements of the hat matrix called leverage points. These elements are all very small, much smaller than the safety threshold 0.2. We therefore expect that the robust regression does not differ much from the standard regression.

We ran two robust regressions with the Huber and Tukey weighting functions. The tuning parameter k is set as suggested earlier. The estimated coefficients of both robust regressions were identical to the coefficients of the standard regression. In fact, with the Huber weighting function, we obtained the parameters estimates shown in the second column of Table 8.2. The tuning parameter was set at 160, that is, 1.345 the standard deviation of errors. The algorithm converged at the first iteration.

With the Tukey weighting function, we obtained the beta parameters shown in the third column of Table 8.2, with the tuning parameter set at 550, that is, 4.685 the standard deviation of errors. The algorithm converged at the second iteration.

TABLE 8.1 Leverage for Corporate Bond Spread Illustration

Issue #	Leverage Point	Issue #	Leverage Point	Issue #	Leverage Point	Issue #	Leverage Point
1	0.013702	31	0.013795	61	0.025113	91	0.011934
2	0.010794	32	0.008615	62	0.014047	92	0.044409
3	0.019632	33	0.018478	63	0.013732	93	0.034539
4	0.025846	34	0.013795	64	0.014753	94	0.029392
5	0.028057	35	0.012994	65	0.009094	95	0.014565
6	0.012836	36	0.008759	66	0.023258	96	0.019263
7	0.014437	37	0.013293	67	0.015577	97	0.019100
8	0.027183	38	0.013522	68	0.063569	98	0.027901
9	0.008394	39	0.013767	69	0.033131	99	0.015033
10	0.026077	40	0.012888	70	0.012423	100	0.013543
11	0.017687	41	0.171633	71	0.016903	101	0.013887
12	0.005725	42	0.020050	72	0.014743	102	0.010884
13	0.008469	43	0.019344	73	0.010000	103	0.008541
14	0.017604	44	0.014446	74	0.015290	104	0.018612
15	0.028824	45	0.014750	75	0.018074	105	0.019873
16	0.024891	46	0.016669	76	0.010866	106	0.011579
17	0.021291	47	0.012692	77	0.010507	107	0.020055
18	0.027499	48	0.019541	78	0.009622	108	0.036536
19	0.017078	49	0.051719	79	0.007122	109	0.008974
20	0.022274	50	0.020500	80	0.008845	110	0.017905
21	0.020021	51	0.020222	81	0.040731	111	0.017995
22	0.021077	52	0.013348	82	0.015223	112	0.005809
23	0.025114	53	0.008207	83	0.011651	113	0.009238
24	0.034711	54	0.013002	84	0.012244	114	0.016268
25	0.027129	55	0.013384	85	0.009014	115	0.028688
26	0.008034	56	0.014434	86	0.008117	116	0.018651
27	0.009757	57	0.015949	87	0.019357	117	0.016205
28	0.011686	58	0.016360	88	0.024764	118	0.020799
29	0.008090	59	0.017263	89	0.023501	119	0.017949
30	0.095189	60	0.031493	90	0.015906	120	0.020301

TABLE 8.1 *(Continued)*

Issue #	Leverage Point	Issue #	Leverage Point	Issue #	Leverage Point	Issue #	Leverage Point
121	0.015754	141	0.157105	161	0.025706	181	0.041400
122	0.020207	142	0.020563	162	0.014594	182	0.013532
123	0.023941	143	0.018518	163	0.014276	183	0.011638
124	0.033133	144	0.016334	164	0.018527	184	0.015537
125	0.021344	145	0.016663	165	0.008675	185	0.009148
126	0.007491	146	0.018707	166	0.020882	186	0.008451
127	0.009683	147	0.011602	167	0.012834	187	0.020417
128	0.011631	148	0.016474	168	0.062460	188	0.023978
129	0.008184	149	0.054354	169	0.031092	189	0.023629
130	0.067155	150	0.020168	170	0.012731	190	0.018335
131	0.015243	151	0.019845	171	0.010213	191	0.012962
132	0.009928	152	0.014368	172	0.015083	192	0.025442
133	0.020009	153	0.008312	173	0.010233	193	0.034161
134	0.015243	154	0.010802	174	0.014593	194	0.026897
135	0.014425	155	0.010850	175	0.019872	195	0.014917
136	0.010076	156	0.011566	176	0.011204	196	0.037224
137	0.013824	157	0.012781	177	0.010866	197	0.019013
138	0.013863	158	0.013124	178	0.010313	198	0.022461
139	0.014560	159	0.017243	179	0.008397	199	0.015419
140	0.032351	160	0.011670	180	0.012101	200	0.012067

Leverage Point: In robust regressions, signals that the corresponding observations might have a decisive influence on the estimation of the regression parameters.

TABLE 8.2 Robust Estimates of Parameters Using Huber and Tukey Weighting Functions

Coefficient	Huber	Tukey
β_0	157.0116	157.0138
β_1	61.2781	61.2776
β_2	−13.2054	−13.2052
β_3	−90.8871	−90.8871

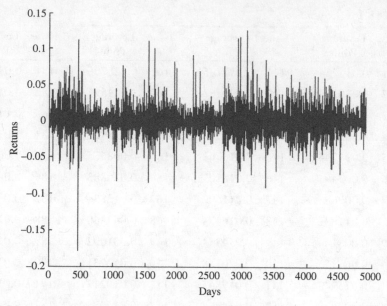

FIGURE 8.1 Daily Returns of the Japan Index: 1986–2005

Let's illustrate the robustness of regression through another example. Let's create an equally weighted index with the daily returns of 234 Japanese firms. Note that this index is created only for the sake of this illustration; no econometric meaning is attached to this index. The daily returns for the index for period 1986 to 2005 are shown in Figure 8.1.

Now suppose that we want to estimate the regression of Nippon Oil on this index; that is, we want to estimate the following regression:

$$R_{NO} = \beta_0 + \beta_1 R_{Index} + \text{Errors}$$

Estimation with the standard least squares method yields the following regression parameters:

R^2: 0.1349
Adjusted R^2: 0.1346
Standard deviation of errors: 0.0213

	Beta	t-Statistic	p-Value
β_0	0.0000	0.1252	0.9003
β_1	0.4533	27.6487	0.0000

When we examined the diagonal of the hat matrix, we found the following results:

Maximum leverage = 0.0189
Mean leverage   = 4.0783e–004

suggesting that there is no dangerous point. Robust regression can be applied; that is, there is no need to change the regression design. We applied robust regression using the Huber and Tukey weighting functions with the following parameters:

$$\text{Huber } (k = 1.345 \times \text{standard deviation})$$

and

$$\text{Tukey } (k = 4.685 \times \text{standard deviation})$$

The robust regression estimate with Huber weighting functions yields the following results:

R^2 = 0.1324
Adjusted R^2 = 0.1322
Weight parameter   = 0.0287
Number of iterations = 39

	Beta	t-Statistic	Change in p-Value
β_0	–0.000706	–0.767860	0.442607
β_1	0.405633	7.128768	0.000000

The robust regression estimate with Tukey weighting functions yields the following results:

R^2 = 0.1315
Adjusted R^2 = 0.1313
Weight parameter   = 0.0998
Number of iterations = 88

	Beta	t-Statistic	Change in p-Value
β_0	–0.000879	–0.632619	0.527012
β_1	0.400825	4.852742	0.000001

We can conclude that all regression slope estimates are highly significant; the intercept estimates are insignificant in all cases. There is a considerable difference between the robust (0.40) and the nonrobust (0.45) regression coefficient.

ROBUST ESTIMATION OF COVARIANCE AND CORRELATION MATRICES

Variance-covariance matrices are central to financial modeling. In fact, the estimation of the variance-covariance matrices is critical for portfolio management and asset allocation. Suppose the logarithm of returns is a multivariate random vector written as

$$\mathbf{r}_t = \mathbf{\mu} + \mathbf{\varepsilon}_t$$

The random disturbances ε_t is characterized by a covariance matrix Ω.

The correlation coefficient between two variables X and Y is defined as:

$$\rho_{X,Y} = \mathrm{corr}(X, Y)$$

$$= \frac{\mathrm{cov}(X, Y)}{\sqrt{\mathrm{var}(X)\mathrm{var}(Y)}} = \frac{\sigma_{X,Y}}{\sigma_X \sigma_Y}$$

The correlation coefficient fully represents the dependence structure of multivariate normal distribution. More in general, the correlation coefficient is a valid measure of dependence for elliptical distributions (i.e., distributions that are constants on ellipsoids). In other cases, different measures of dependence are needed (e.g., copula functions).[3]

The empirical covariance between two variables, X and Y, is defined as

$$\hat{\sigma}_{X,Y} = \frac{1}{N-1} \sum_{i=1}^{N} (X_i - \bar{X})(Y_i - \bar{Y})$$

where X_i and Y_i are N samples of the variables X and Y and:

$$\bar{X} = \frac{1}{N} \sum_{i=1}^{N} X_i \quad \bar{Y} = \frac{1}{N} \sum_{i=1}^{N} Y_i$$

are the empirical means of the variables.

---

[3] Paul Embrechts, Filip Lindskog, and Alexander McNeil, "Modelling Dependence with Copulas and Applications to Risk Management," in *Handbook of Heavy Tailed Distributions in Finance*, ed. S. T. Rachev (Amsterdam: Elsevier/North-Holland, 2003).

The empirical correlation coefficient is the empirical covariance normalized with the product of the respective empirical standard deviations:

$$\hat{\rho}_{X,Y} = \frac{\hat{\sigma}_{X,Y}}{\hat{\sigma}_X \hat{\sigma}_Y}$$

The empirical standard deviations are defined as

$$\hat{\sigma}_X = \sqrt{\frac{1}{N-1}\sum_{i=1}^{N}(X_i - \bar{X})^2} \quad \hat{\sigma}_Y = \sqrt{\frac{1}{N-1}\sum_{i=1}^{N}(Y_i - Y)^2}$$

Empirical covariances and correlations are not robust as they are highly sensitive to tails or outliers. Robust estimators of covariances and/or correlations are insensitive to the tails. However, it does not make sense to robustify correlations if dependence is not linear.

Different strategies for robust estimation of covariances exist; among them are:

- Robust estimation of pairwise covariances
- Robust estimation of elliptic distributions

Here we discuss only the robust estimation of pairwise covariances. As detailed in Huber,[4] the following identity holds:

$$\mathrm{cov}(X,Y) = \frac{1}{4ab}[\mathrm{var}(aX+bY) - \mathrm{var}(aX-bY)]$$

Assume S is a robust scale functional:

$$S(aX+b) = |a|S(X)$$

A robust covariance is defined as

$$C(X,Y) = \frac{1}{4ab}[S(aX+bY)^2 - S(aX-bY)^2]$$

Choose

$$a = \frac{1}{S(X)} \quad b = \frac{1}{S(Y)}$$

---

[4] Huber, *Robust Statistics*.

A robust correlation coefficient is defined as

$$c = \frac{1}{4}[S(aX + bY)^2 - S(aX - bY)^2]$$

The robust correlation coefficient thus defined is not confined to stay in the interval $[-1, +1]$. For this reason, the following alternative definition is often used:

$$r = \frac{S(aX + bY)^2 - S(aX - bY)^2}{S(aX + bY)^2 + S(aX - bY)^2}$$

APPLICATIONS

As explained in Chapter 3, regression analysis has been used to estimate the market risk of a stock (beta) and to estimate the factor loadings in a factor model. Robust regressions have been used to improve estimates in these two areas.

Martin and Simin provide the first comprehensive analysis of the impact of outliers on the estimation of beta.[5] Moreover, they propose a weighted least squares estimator with data-dependent weights for estimating beta, referring to this estimate as "resistant beta," and report that this beta is a superior predictor of future risk and return characteristics than the beta calculated using the method of least squares described in Chapter 13. To demonstrate the potential dramatic difference between the ordinary least squares (OLS) beta and the resistant beta, the estimates of beta and the standard error of the estimate for four companies reported by Martin and Simin are shown as follows:[6]

	OLS Estimate		Resistant Estimate	
	Beta	Standard Error	Beta	Standard Error
AW Computer Systems	2.33	1.13	1.10	0.33
Chief Consolidated Mining Co.	1.12	0.80	0.50	0.26
Oil City Petroleum	3.27	0.90	0.86	0.47
Metallurgical Industries Co.	2.05	1.62	1.14	0.22

---

[5] R. Douglas Martin and Timothy T. Simin, "Outlier Resistant Estimates of Beta," *Financial Analysts Journal* 59 (September–October 2003): 56–69.
[6] Reported in Table 1 of the Martin-Simin study. Various time periods were used from January 1962 to December 1996.

Martin and Simin provide a feeling for the magnitude of the *absolute* difference between the OLS beta and the resistant beta using weekly returns for 8,314 companies over the period January 1992 to December 1996. A summary of the distribution follows:

Absolute Difference in Beta	No. of Companies	Percent
0.0 + to 0.3	5,043	60.7
0.3 + to 0.5	2,206	26.5
0.5 + to 1.0	800	9.6
Greater than 1.0+	265	3.2

Studies by Fama and French find that market capitalization (size) and book-to-market are important factors in explaining cross-sectional returns.[7] These results are purely empirically based since there is no equilibrium asset pricing model that would suggest either factor as being related to expected return. The empirical evidence that size may be a factor that earns a risk premia (popularly referred to as the "small-firm effect" or "size effect") was first reported by Banz.[8] Knez and Ready reexamined the empirical evidence using robust regressions, more specifically the least-trimmed squares regression discussed earlier.[9] Their results are twofold. First, they find that when 1% of the most extreme observations are trimmed each month, the risk premia found by Fama and French for the size factor disappears. Second, the inverse relation between size and the risk premia reported by Banz and Fama and French (i.e., the larger the capitalization, the smaller the risk premia) no longer holds when the sample is trimmed. For example, the average monthly risk premia estimated using OLS is –12 basis points. However, when 5% of the sample is trimmed, the average monthly risk premia is estimated to be +33 basis points; when 1% of the sample is trimmed, the estimated average risk premia is +14 basis points.

[7] Eugene F. Fama and Kenneth R. French, "The Cross-Section of Expected Stock Returns," *Journal of Finance* 47 (1992): 427–466, and Eugene F. Fama and Kenneth R. French, "Common Risk Factors in the Returns on Stocks and Bonds," *Journal of Financial Economics* 33 (1993): 3–56.
[8] Rolf W. Banz, "The Relationship between Return and Market Value of Common Stocks," *Journal of Financial Economics* 9 (1981): 3–18.
[9] Peter J. Knez and Mark J. Ready, "On the Robustness of Size and Book-to-Market in Cross-Sectional Regressions," *Journal of Finance* 52 (1997): 1355–1382.

KEY POINTS

- Robust statistics addresses the problem of obtaining estimates that are less sensitive to small changes in the basic assumptions of the statistical models used. It is also useful for separating the contribution of the tails from the contribution of the body of the data.
- Identifying robust estimators of regressions is a rather difficult problem. Different choices of estimators, robust or not, might lead to radically different estimates of a model's parameters.
- The expected values of the regression's dependent variables are obtained by multiplying the data and the hat matrix.
- Leverage points are large values of the hat matrix such that small changes in the data lead to large changes in expectations.
- To make a regression robust, the least squares method can be generalized by using weighting functions that trim residuals.

CHAPTER 9

Autoregressive Moving Average Models

After reading this chapter you will understand:

- The concept of autoregression and autoregressive models.
- How to identify autoregressive models.
- The concept of moving average process and moving average models.
- How to identify moving average models.
- How to model autoregressive moving average (ARMA) models.
- How to use information criteria for ARMA model selection.
- How to apply ARMA in modeling stock returns.
- How to use autoregressive models, moving average models, and ARMA models to forecast stock returns and how to evaluate the forecasting performance of these models.
- The concept of vector autoregression.

In Chapter 5 we introduced time series analysis where variables change over time. As discussed in that chapter, the foundation of time series models is based on the assumption that the disturbance term is a *white noise process*. The implication of this assumption is that the last period's disturbance term cannot be used to predict the current disturbance term and that the disturbance term has constant variance. In other words, the implication of this assumption is the absence of serial correlation (or predictability) and homoscedasticity (or conditional constant variance).

However, in empirical applications the white noise assumption is often violated. That is, successive observations show *serial dependence*. Under these circumstances, forecasting tools such as *exponential smoothing*[1] may

---

[1] See, for example, Svetlozar T. Rachev, Stefan Mittnik, Frank J. Fabozzi, Sergio M. Focardi, and Teo Jasic, *Financial Econometrics* (Hoboken, NJ: John Wiley & Sons, 2007).

be inefficient and sometimes inappropriate because they may not take advantage of the serial dependence in the most effective way. In this chapter, we will introduce *autoregressive moving average* (ARMA) models that allow for serial dependence in the observations.

AUTOREGRESSIVE MODELS

In finance, some asset returns show serial dependence. Such dependence can be modeled as an autoregressive process. For example, a first-order autoregressive model can be represented as

$$y_t = c + \rho y_{t-1} + \varepsilon_t \qquad (9.1)$$

where y_t is the asset return c and ρ are parameters ε_t is assumed to be independent and identically distributed (i.i.d). The i.i.d process is a white noise process with mean zero and variance σ_ε^2.
In words, equation (9.1) says that this period's return depends on the prior period's return scaled by the value of ρ.

For example, an estimation of equation (9.1) using CRSP value-weighted weekly index returns[2] for the period from January 1998 through October 2012 (774 observations) yields

$$y_t \qquad = 0.15 - 0.07 y_{t-1}$$
$$t\text{-statistic} \quad (1.65)\,(1.97)$$

The fact that last week's return has a statistically significant coefficient shows that lagged weekly returns might be useful in predicting weekly returns. In other words, next period's forecast is a weighted average of the mean of the weekly return series and the current value of the return.

The first-order autoregressive model can be generalized to an nth order autoregressive model and can be written as

$$y_t = c + \rho_1 y_{t-1} + \rho_2 y_{t-2} + \ldots + \rho_n y_{t-n} + \varepsilon_t \qquad (9.2)$$

---

[2]The CRSP value-weighted index, created by the Center for Research in Security Prices, is a value-weighted index composed of all New York Stock Exchange (NYSE), American Stock Exchange (AMEX), and NASDAQ stocks. By "value-weighted" it is meant each stock in the index is weighted by its market capitalization (i.e., number of common stock shares outstanding multiplied by the stock price).

The order n for an autoregressive model is unknown and must be determined. Two approaches are available for determining the value of n:

1. Partial autocorrelation function
2. The use of some information criterion

Partial Autocorrelation

The *partial autocorrelation* (PAC) measures the correlation between y_t and y_{t-n} after controlling for correlations at intermediate lags. In other words, the PAC at lag n is the regression coefficient on y_{t-n} when y_t is regressed on a constant and $y_{t-1}, \ldots, y_{t-n}$.

How does one test for the statistical significance of the PAC for each lag? This is done by using the *Ljung-Box Q-statistic*, or simply *Q-statistic*. The Q-statistic tests whether the joint statistical significance of accumulated sample autocorrelations up to any specified lags are all zero. For example, the Q-statistic for lag 3 is measured as:

$$\text{Q-statistics}(3) = T(T+2)\left(\frac{y_1^2}{(T-1)} + \frac{y_2^2}{(T-2)} + \frac{y_3^2}{(T-3)} \right)$$

where T is the sample size. The statistic is asymptotically distributed as a chi-square (χ^2) with degrees of freedom equal to the number of lags.

If the computed Q-statistic exceeds the critical value from the χ^2 distribution, the null hypothesis of no autocorrelation at the specified lag length is rejected. Thus, the Q-statistic at lag n is a test statistic for the null hypothesis that there is no autocorrelation up to order n.

The PAC for 24 lags for our earlier illustration using the CRSP value-weighted weekly index returns are presented in Table 9.1 along with the results of the Q-statistic. The computed Q-statistic for lags 1 and 2 are 3.67 and 5.85, respectively. The critical values from the χ^2 distribution with 1 and 2 degrees of freedom at the 5% level of significance is 3.84 and 5.99, respectively. The null hypothesis of no autocorrelation at lags 1 and 2 is therefore rejected. While the null hypothesis is not rejected at lag 3, it is again rejected at lags 4 and 5. Given that the results are yielding mixed lag lengths for an autoregressive model, more formal approaches may provide us with a better model.

Information Criterion

Another approach of selecting an autoregressive model is the use of some information criterion such as the *Akaike information criterion* (AIC) or

TABLE 9.1 Partial Autocorrelations (PAC) for the Weekly Sample Returns of CRSP Value-Weighted Index from January 1998 through October 2012

Lags	PAC	Q-Statistic	ρ-Value
1	−0.069	3.667	0.055
2	0.048	5.851	0.054
3	−0.046	7.971	0.047
4	−0.051	9.324	0.053
5	0.046	11.033	0.051
6	0.076	14.520	0.024
7	−0.086	20.094	0.005
8	0.009	20.566	0.008
9	−0.034	23.042	0.006
10	0.010	23.399	0.009
11	0.022	23.997	0.013
12	−0.046	25.739	0.012
13	−0.002	25.739	0.018
14	0.015	25.818	0.027
15	0.095	31.608	0.007
16	0.008	31.810	0.011
17	0.010	31.931	0.015
18	−0.004	32.319	0.020
19	0.005	32.341	0.029
20	0.018	32.647	0.037
21	0.012	33.218	0.044
22	0.019	33.259	0.058
23	0.003	33.260	0.077
24	−0.033	34.742	0.072

Bayesian (or Schwarz) information criterion (BIC). By selecting an autoregressive model, we mean determining number of lags. The AIC and BIC are described in Appendix E, where we discuss model selection. Both information criteria involve finding the minimum value of a measure.

Table 9.2 shows the results when the calculations for the AIC and BIC are applied to the CRSP value-weighted weekly index returns. The second and third columns show the AIC and BIC, respectively, at different lags. The AIC shows that the model is optimal (i.e., the n that provides the minimum

TABLE 9.2 Autoregressive Model: Akaike Information Criterion (AIC) and Bayesian Information Criterion (BIC) for the Weekly Sample Returns of CRSP Value-Weighted Index (y_t) from January 1998 through October 2012

Lags	AIC	BIC
1	2.032	2.044*
2	2.030	2.048
3	2.030	2.054
4	2.031	2.061
5	2.033	2.069
6	2.029	2.071
7	2.025*	2.074
8	2.029	2.083
9	2.031	2.092
10	2.035	2.102
11	2.038	2.111
12	2.039	2.118
13	2.043	2.128
14	2.046	2.137
15	2.041	2.138
16	2.045	2.148
17	2.048	2.158
18	2.052	2.169
19	2.056	2.179
20	2.060	2.189
21	2.064	2.199
22	2.066	2.208
23	2.070	2.218
24	2.073	2.227

A model is selected based on the calculated minimum of either AIC or BIC.
* Denotes minimum values.

AIC) when there are seven lags—denoted by AR(7). For the BIC, however, the model is optimal is when n is one (i.e., AR(1)).

In practice it is important to check for the adequacy of the selected model. If the model is adequate, the residual series of the model should behave as white noise or should have no autocorrelation. For this purpose, the Q-statistic can be employed. The Q-statistic tests whether the joint statistical significance of accumulated sample autocorrelations up to any specified lags are all zero.

We can test the residual series from the AR(1) and AR(7) models to see if there is serial correlation in the residuals using the Q-statistic. For illustrative purposes, the test statistic for 12 lags is presented. The computed Q-statistic of the residuals for the AR(1) and AR(7) models are Q-statistic(12) = 19.83 and Q-statistic(12) = 3.29, respectively. The critical value at the 5% significance level from the χ^2 distribution is 18.54. Based on these values, the null hypothesis of no autocorrelation at the 5% significance level is rejected for the AR(1) model but not for the AR(7) model. Although the autoregressive model AR(7) is adequate in explaining the behavior of the weekly index returns series, we do not know if this model does a good job of explaining the dynamic structure of the data.

MOVING AVERAGE MODELS

The autoregressive models just described for modeling the weekly CRSP value-weighted index return series may not be the only process that generates the return series. Suppose we model weekly returns, y, as:

$$y_t = \mu + \varepsilon_t + \delta_1 \varepsilon_{t-1} \qquad (9.3)$$

where μ = the mean of the series
           δ_1 = the parameter of the model
     $\varepsilon_t, \varepsilon_{t-1}$ = the white noise error terms

In the model given by equation (9.3), y at time t is equal to a constant plus a moving average of the current and past error terms. In this case, y_t follows a first-order *moving average* (denoted by MA(1)) process. The moving average (MA) models are treated as simple extensions of a white noise series. In other words, an MA model is a linear regression model of the current value of the series against the unobserved white noise error terms or shocks. A qth order moving average model is represented as

$$y_t = \mu + \varepsilon_t + \delta_1 \varepsilon_{t-1} + \ldots + \delta_q \varepsilon_{t-q} \qquad (9.4)$$

Since the error terms in equation (9.4) are not observable, MA models are usually estimated using the maximum likelihood estimation method described in Chapter 13. The initial values needed for the shocks in the likelihood function are obtained recursively from the model, starting with $\varepsilon_1 = y_1 - \mu$ and $\varepsilon_2 = y_2 - \mu - \delta_1\varepsilon_1$ and so on.

For example, an estimation of a MA(1) model for CRSP value-weighted weekly index returns for the period from January 1998 through October 2012 yields

$$y_t = 0.14 + \varepsilon_t - 0.063\,\varepsilon_{t-1}$$
$$t\text{-statistics} \quad (1.48) \qquad (-1.76)$$

The results show that the first-order moving average term is not statistically significant. Thus, the MA(1) model in this case is not adequate. Consequently, different lag lengths for the moving average term must be tried.

As with autoregressive models, either the AIC or BIC can be employed to select the optimal lag length. For the CRSP value-weighted weekly index returns, Table 9.3 shows that the AIC identifies MA(7) as the optimal model while the BIC identifies MA(1) as optimal. Since the MA(1) model is not adequate for the return series that we are studying, we tested the residuals of the MA(7) model for serial correlation. With a computed Q-statistic(12) of 5.97 and with a critical value of 18.54 from the χ^2 distribution, we are unable to reject the null hypothesis of no autocorrelation. Hence, the MA(7) model appears to be adequate in modeling the weekly stock index return series.

TABLE 9.3 Moving Average Model: Akaike Information Criterion (AIC) and Bayesian Information Criterion (BIC) for the Weekly Sample Returns of CRSP Value-Weighted Index (y_t) from January 1998 through October 2012

Lags	AIC	BIC
1	2.033	2.045*
2	2.033	2.051
3	2.034	2.058
4	2.034	2.064
5	2.034	2.070
6	2.031	2.073
7	2.026*	2.074
8	2.029	2.083
9	2.030	2.090
10	2.033	2.099

(continued)

TABLE 9.3   (*continued*)

Lags	AIC	BIC
11	2.035	2.107
12	2.035	2.113
13	2.038	2.122
14	2.041	2.130
15	2.034	2.131
16	2.036	2.138
17	2.039	2.147
18	2.041	2.155
19	2.044	2.164
20	2.046	2.172
21	2.049	2.181
22	2.051	2.189
23	2.053	2.198
24	2.055	2.205

A model is selected based on the calculated
minimum of either AIC or BIC.
*Denotes minimum values.

AUTOREGRESSIVE MOVING AVERAGE MODELS

Because in practical applications higher-order models may be required
to describe the dynamic structure of the data, AR and MA models may
require estimation of a large number of parameters. In 1938, Herman Wold
showed that a combined AR and MA process, referred to as an *autoregressive moving average* (ARMA) process, can effectively describe the time
series structure of the data as long as the appropriate number of AR and
MA terms are specified.[3] This means that any time series y_t can be modeled
as a combination of past y_t values and/or past ε_t errors. More formally, an
ARMA model can be expressed as

$$y_t = c + \rho_1 y_{t-1} + \rho_2 y_{t-2} + \ldots + \rho_n y_{t-n} + \varepsilon_t + \delta_1 \varepsilon_{t-1} + \ldots + \delta_q \varepsilon_{t-q} \quad (9.5)$$

where n and q are the number of AR and MA terms, respectively.

---

[3]Herman Wold, *A Study in the Analysis of Stationary Time Series* (Stockholm,
Sweden: Almgrist & Wiksell, 1938).

The benefit of ARMA models is a higher-order AR or MA model may have a parsimonious ARMA representation that is much easier to identify and estimate. In other words, ARMA models represent observed data with fewer parameters than suggested by AR or MA models. In the 1970s, George Box and Gwilym Jenkins popularized the estimation of the ARMA process given by equation (9.5).[4] Their methodology for estimating ARMA models, referred to as the *Box-Jenkins estimation model*, requires the following three steps:

Step 1. Test the series for stationarity.

Step 2. Identify the appropriate order of AR and MA terms.

Step 3. Once an appropriate lag order is identified, determine whether the model is adequate or not. If the model is adequate, the residuals (ε_t) of the model are expected to be white noise.

Let's look at these three steps and use our return time series that we have studied earlier in this chapter to illustrate them.

The first step is to check for stationarity. There are several methodologies for doing so and these are discussed in Chapter 10 where we describe the econometric tool of cointegration. For our discussion here, if fluctuations in the variable exhibit no pattern over time, then we temporarily consider the variable to be stationary. As an example, Figure 9.1 shows the plot of the weekly CRSP value-weighted index returns. Although the return series shown in the figure indicate considerable fluctuations over time, the returns meander around a constant level close to zero. Thus, the returns exhibit no pattern over time, and for the purpose of this chapter, we regard this as stationary and proceed to Step 2 in the methodology for estimating an ARMA process.

The second step involves identifying the order of AR and MA terms. For illustrative purposes, we start out with AR(1) and MA(1) model which is referred to as a first-order ARMA(1, 1) model and expressed as

$$y_t = c + \rho_1 y_{t-1} + \varepsilon_t + \delta_1 \varepsilon_{t-1} \tag{9.6}$$

Our estimated results of the above model using the weekly index returns for the period from January 1998 through October 2012 are:

$$y_t = 0.13 - 0.79\, y_{t-1} + \varepsilon_t + 0.65\, \varepsilon_{t-1}$$
$$t\text{-statistics} \quad (1.40) \quad (-4.17) \qquad (3.54)$$

These results clearly show that the first-order autoregressive term for the index weekly returns is statistically significant and inversely related to the

---

[4] George Box and Gwilym Jenkins, *Time Series Analysis: Forecasting and Control* (San Francisco: Holden-Day, 1970).

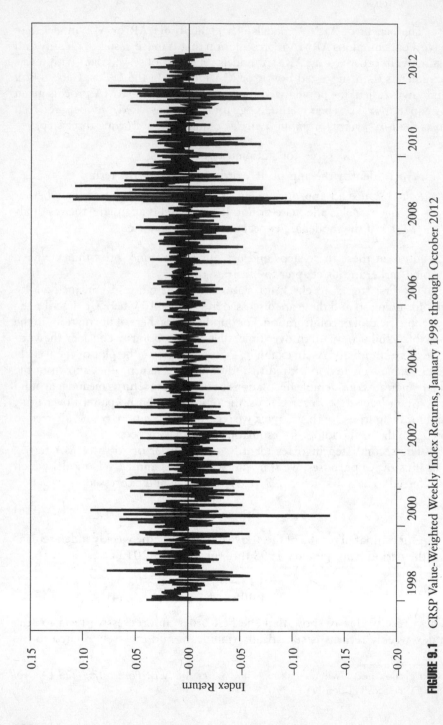

FIGURE 9.1 CRSP Value-Weighted Weekly Index Returns, January 1998 through October 2012

current weekly return. The moving average is positively related to this week's returns and the coefficient is statistically significant. Hence, both AR(1) and MA(1) are statistically significant.

Now the issue is the identification of optimal lags. To identify the optimal lag, a combination of ARMA models up to a specified number of lags is calculated and then one of the information criteria is calculated for each of these models. For our weekly return series, we tried up to 12 lags and then used the AIC. The results are presented in Table 9.4. For the weekly return series, the AIC is at its minimum when the model has five autoregressive terms and four moving average terms.

The third and final step in ARMA modeling involves using the AR and MA terms found in Step 2 and then testing the residuals. If the model is adequate, the residuals should not exhibit serial correlation. This is done by testing whether the residuals can be characterized as being white noise. In our illustration, in Step 2 we have identified five AR terms and four MA terms as optimal lags. Table 9.5 shows the results when we fit an ARMA(5,4) to the time series of weekly returns. As can be seen, the first and the second AR terms are statistically significant and the first three MA terms are statistical significant.

To ensure that the model is describing the data adequately, we checked to see if the residuals of the model are white noise. With a Q-statistic(12) of 8.93, we are unable to reject the null hypothesis of no autocorrelation. Hence, the ARMA(5,4) model appears to be adequate in modeling the weekly stock index return series.

ARMA MODELING TO FORECAST
S&P 500 WEEKLY INDEX RETURNS

As long as asset returns exhibit trends,[5] ARMA modeling can be employed to predict these trends. There are investors who believe that stock returns, commodity returns, and currency returns exhibit trends and these trends can be forecasted and then used to design highly profitable trading strategies. Those investors who seek to capitalize on trends are said to be technical traders and follow an investment approach known as technical analysis. For illustrative purposes, we will use an ARMA[6] model to forecast weekly S&P 500 stock index returns. The weekly S&P 500 returns from January

---

[5] See Chapter 5 for the definition of trends.
[6] ARMA modeling is only one of the ways trends can be predicted and technical traders may or may not use ARMA to extract trends.

TABLE 9.4 Autoregressive Moving Average Models, Akaike Information Criterion (AIC) for the Weekly Sample Returns of CRSP Value-Weighted Index from January 1998 through October 2012

AR(n)	MA(q)												
	0	1	2	3	4	5	6	7	8	9	10	11	12
0	3772	3771	3771	3770	3770	3769	3769	3768	3769	3767	3769	3770	3771
1	3770	3770	3772	3771	3775	3773	3766	3768	3770	3769	3769	3771	3773
2	3770	3772	3768	3770	3775	3771	3767	3770	3767	3770	3771	3773	3770
3	3771	3772	3769	3771	3770	3774	3768	3771	3769	3771	3777	3774	3771
4	3771	3774	3776	3780	3774	3773	3765	3771	3769	3781	3770	3771	3775
5	3771	3772	3768	3771	3763*	3768	3769	3775	3770	3775	3777	3779	3774
6	3768	3766	3767	3769	3767	3769	3766	3768	3773	3771	3786	3774	3775
7	3765	3767	3768	3770	3767	3773	3768	3767	3783	3773	3772	3778	3776
8	3767	3769	3767	3770	3767	3768	3769	3791	3770	3778	3775	3776	3786
9	3768	3770	3770	3771	3771	3782	3776	3786	3773	3778	3774	3776	3796
10	3770	3772	3769	3773	3771	3771	3770	3775	3770	3769	3774	3780	3772
11	3771	3772	3773	3775	3778	3773	3779	3778	3779	3779	3776	3781	3778
12	3772	3774	3771	3772	3777	3779	3778	3778	3780	3798	3788	3784	3776

A model is selected based on the calculated minimum AIC.
*Denotes minimum values.

TABLE 9.5 Autoregressive Moving Average Model, Weekly Sample Returns of CRSP Value-Weighted Index from January 1998 through October 2012

Variable	Coefficient	t-Statistic	p-Value
c	0.12	1.23	0.22
ρ_1	0.94	3.60	0.00
ρ_2	−0.72	−2.30	0.02
ρ_3	0.34	1.51	0.13
ρ_4	0.19	1.03	0.30
ρ_5	0.02	0.34	0.73
δ_1	−1.00	−3.81	0.00
δ_2	0.84	2.52	0.01
δ_3	−0.51	−1.97	0.05
δ_4	−0.10	−0.48	0.63

of 1998 through December 2012 (783 observations) used in our illustration are obtained from DataStream.[7]

The first step is to check for stationarity in the S&P 500 index returns. The plotted weekly S&P 500 index returns are presented in Figure 9.2. The returns fluctuate considerably but always around a constant level close to zero and exhibit no pattern over time. As stated earlier, for the purpose of this chapter, we regard this as stationary and proceed to Step 2 in the methodology of estimating an ARMA process.

The next step is to identify a possible model that best fits the data. We tried a combination of 12 AR and MA models and used the AIC to select the model that describes the data optimally. The results are presented in Table 9.6. For the weekly S&P 500 return series, the AIC is at its minimum when the model has three autoregressive terms and two moving average terms.

The final step involves estimating the model identified in Step 2 and testing the residuals for the presence of autocorrelation. Table 9.7 shows the results when we fit an ARMA(3,2) to the weekly S&P 500 index return series. As can be seen, the first and second AR terms and both MA terms are statistically significant. To ensure that the model is describing the data adequately, we checked to see if the residuals of the model are white noise. With a computed Q-statistic(12) of 3.75 and with a critical value of 18.54

---

[7]DataStream is a comprehensive time series database available from Thomson Reuters.

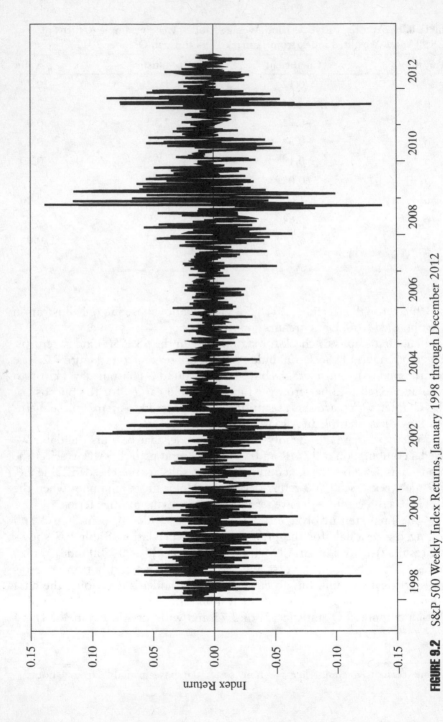

FIGURE 9.2 S&P 500 Weekly Index Returns, January 1998 through December 2012

TABLE 9.6 Autoregressive Moving Average Models, Akaike Information Criterion (AIC) for the Weekly Sample Returns of S&P 500 Index from January 1998 through December 2012

AR(n)	MA(q)												
	0	1	2	3	4	5	6	7	8	9	10	11	12
0	−3378	−3391	−3389	−3387	−3387	−3386	−3384	−3384	−3383	−3382	−3381	−3383	−3381
1	−3391	−3389	−3387	−3386	−3385	−3383	−3382	−3383	−3381	−3379	−3382	−3382	−3381
2	−3389	−3387	−3394	−3383	−3383	−3392	−3390	−3385	−3387	−3386	−3384	−3381	−3251
3	−3388	−3387	−3394*	−3394	−3391	−3386	−3383	−3383	−3385	−3385	−3382	−3380	−3370
4	−3388	−3386	−3394	−3390	−3394	−3388	−3382	−3391	−3387	−3381	−3381	−3375	−3383
5	−3386	−3384	−3392	−3390	−3394	−3392	−3385	−3147	−3381	−3376	−3384	−3374	−3369
6	−3384	−3384	−3390	−3389	−3392	−3387	−3386	−3386	−3385	−3376	−3373	−3379	−3371
7	−3386	−3384	−3389	−3383	−3373	−3383	−3383	−3373	−3371	−3127	−3384	−3307	−3376
8	−3384	−3382	−3387	−3385	−3374	−3390	−3386	−3383	−3377	−3374	−3378	−3377	−3374
9	−3382	−3381	−3378	−3380	−3382	−3375	−3373	−3370	−3379	−3369	−3373	−3350	−3333
10	−3383	−3379	−3377	−3380	−3377	−3371	−3378	−3377	−3382	−3367	−3376	−3354	−3377
11	−3383	−3383	−3381	−3382	−3376	−3383	−3377	−3380	−3379	−3373	−3309	−3356	−3354
12	−3381	−3379	−3381	−3379	−3384	−3369	−3377	−3368	−3367	−3373	−3369	−3363	−3358

A model is selected based on the calculated minimum AIC.
*Denotes minimum values.

TABLE 9.7 Autoregressive Moving Average Model, Weekly Sample Returns of S&P 500 Index from January 1998 through December 2012

Variable	Coefficient	t-Statistic	p-Value
c	0.00	1.25	0.21
ρ_1	−1.10	−7.44	0.00
ρ_2	−0.83	−5.44	0.00
ρ_3	−0.03	−0.68	0.50
δ_1	0.97	6.79	0.00
δ_2	0.72	5.72	0.00

from the χ^2 distribution, we are unable to reject the null hypothesis that there is no autocorrelation. Hence, the ARMA(3,2) model appears to be adequate in modeling the weekly S&P 500 index return series.

While the model seems adequate, we don't yet know if it does a good job of forecasting the data. In order to judge the forecasting performance of the ARMA(3,2) model, we need a set of competing models. For the purpose of illustration, we used an AR(1) and an MA(1) model and compared the forecasting performance of ARMA(3,2) against these two models. A good approach of model evaluation is to divide the sample into an *in-sample* estimation period and a *holdout* sample. The in-sample period is used to estimate the model parameters and the holdout sample will be used to construct out-of-sample forecasts. For our illustration, we use an estimation period for the three models from January 1998 through December 2011 (730 observations), holding back the last 52 observations to construct out-of-sample forecasts.

It is possible to forecast 52 weeks forward, but long-term time series forecasts tend to be less reliable than short-term forecasts. One way to get around this problem is to compute long-term forecasts by iterating forward by one-step forecasts. This involves estimating the models from January 1998 through December 2011 and forecasting the S&P 500 returns for the first week of January 2012. Then we add the first week's realized return to the estimation period and then forecast the second week's return. This iterative process continues until we use up the entire holdout sample. This exercise will yield 52 forecasts with 52 realizations (i.e., observed values). The results of these forecasts and the S&P weekly returns are presented in Figure 9.3. The FORECAST_AR1 shown in the figure denotes the forecasts generated by the AR(1) model. The FORECAST_MA1 indicates the forecasts generated by the MA(1) model, while the FORECAST_AR3MA2 denotes the forecasts generated by the ARMA(3,2) model. In 2012, the S&P

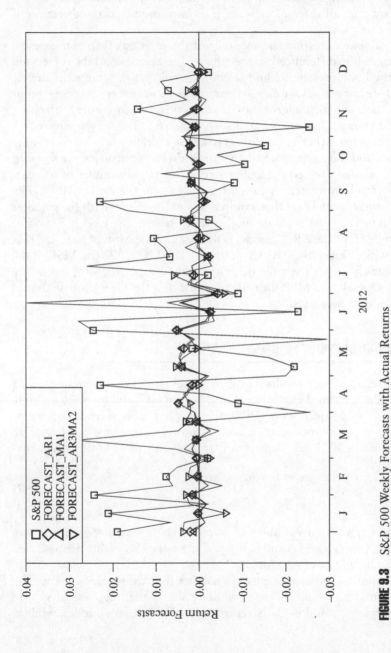

FIGURE 9.3 S&P 500 Weekly Forecasts with Actual Returns

S&P 500 is the realized weekly returns. The FORECAST_AR1 reported in the figure denotes the forecasts generated by the AR(1) model. The FORECAST_MA1 denotes the forecasts generated by the MA(1) model, while the FORECAST_AR3MA2 denotes the forecasts generated by the ARMA(3,2) model.

500 returns fluctuated considerably more than the prediction made by the models. However, all three models seem to have predicted the direction of the change fairly well.

A formal way of testing the accuracy of the forecasts is to compare the forecast errors (the difference between the realized values and the forecasted values of the holdout sample) and select a model that generates the lowest aggregate forecast error. One cannot just add the forecast errors of the holdout sample because such aggregation leads to positive differences offsetting negative differences, leaving a small forecast error. One way to overcome this problem is to either square the errors or to take the absolute value of the errors and then aggregate them. For illustrative purposes, we squared the errors and then divided the aggregated value by the number of forecast errors. The resulting metric is called the *mean squared error* (MSE). The MSE of the three models are then compared and the model with the smallest MSE would be the most accurate model. In the case of the weekly S&P 500 returns, the MSE of the AR(1) model is 0.000231. The MSE of the MA(1) is 0.000237 while that of the ARMA(3,2) model is 0.000247. The MSE of the AR(1) is slightly better than the other two models, but the differences are very small. Overall, the MSE measures suggest that the three models should provide adequate forecasts.

VECTOR AUTOREGRESSIVE MODELS

So far in the chapter we examined how to model and forecast one single time series variable. A natural extension would be to model and forecast multiple time series variables jointly. In 1980, Christopher Sims introduced *vector autoregression* (VAR) modeling or *vector autoregressive models* to analyze multiple time series.[8] A first-order two-variable VAR model takes the form

$$
\begin{aligned}
y_t &= b_1 + b_2 y_{t-1} + b_3 z_{t-1} + \varepsilon_{yt} \\
z_t &= c_1 + c_2 y_{t-1} + c_3 z_{t-1} + \varepsilon_{zt}
\end{aligned}
\tag{9.7}
$$

where y_t and z_t are two variables of interest. The parameter estimates are shown by the letters b and c, and ε shows white noise errors that are assumed to be uncorrelated with each other.

Notice that y_t and z_t influence each other. For example, b_3 shows the effect of a unit change in z_{t-1} on y_t while c_2 shows the influence of y_{t-1} on z_t. For example, y_t could be daily returns on some U.S. stock index while z_t

---

[8] Christopher Sims, "Macroeconomics and Reality," *Econometrica* 48 (1980): 1–48.

could be some Japanese daily stock index returns. These returns are not only affected by their own past values but will also influence each other. Thus, the advantage of VAR modeling is not only that one can estimate multiple time series variables simultaneously but one can also study interrelationships among variables.

The main drawback of VAR is that as the number of variables/lags increases, the number of parameters to be estimated will increase significantly. For example, to estimate a system of three variables with three lags, we need to estimate a total of 30 parameters.[9] This may lead to having many lags with statistically insignificant coefficients. In addition, the signs of the coefficients may change across the lags making it difficult to interpret the coefficient.

Thus, to study the interrelationship among variables, the estimated VAR could be used to check for block significance tests, impulse responses, and variance decompositions.[10] However, one significant benefit of VAR was discovered by Granger and Engle when they introduced the concept of cointegration, which is the subject of the next chapter.

KEY POINTS

- Often financial time series exhibit trends where the current values are related to the past or lagged values.
- The models that use past observations to predict the current value are the autoregressive (AR) and moving average (MA) models.
- An AR model is appropriate when the current value is determined by the values of variables in the recent past.
- An MA model is appropriate when the current value is influenced by a recent shock and shocks in the recent past.
- Sometimes AR and MA models may require estimation of a large number of parameters to describe the data. In such circumstances, an autoregressive moving average (a mixture of AR and MA terms, or ARMA) model is recommended.
- The ARMA model has the advantage of requiring fewer estimated parameters.
- Regardless if it is an AR, MA, or ARMA model, it is important to select the correct number of lags to describe the data.

---

[9] The number of parameters to be estimated is determined by $k + nk^2$ where k is number of variables and n is number of lags.

[10] For a further discussion of these topics, see Rachev et al., *Financial Econometrics*.

- The appropriate number of lags can be selected either by using a partial autocorrelation function or by using some information criterion. This often requires considerable experimentation.
- A model is selected if the residuals of the model are white noise.
- It is important to evaluate models based on the accuracy of forecasts.
- A model's forecast performance is judged adequate when its mean squared error is small relative to competing models.
- Using vector autoregressions it is possible to model multiple time series variables.

CHAPTER 10

Cointegration

After reading this chapter you will understand:

- The concept of cointegration.
- The concept of spurious regressions.
- How to test for stationarity.
- How to test for cointegration using the Engle-Granger cointegration test.
- How to test for cointegration using the Johansen-Juselius cointegration test.
- How to identify multiple cointegration relations.

Financial time series data tend to exhibit trends. Trends can be deterministic or stochastic. In Chapter 5 we introduced the concept of a deterministic trend. To uncover a relationship among financial variables it is important to model changes in stochastic trends over time. Cointegration can be used to identify common stochastic trends among different financial variables. If financial variables are cointegrated, it can also be shown that the variables exhibit a long-run relationship. If this long-run relationship is severed, this may indicate the presence of a financial bubble.[1]

The long-term relationships among financial variables, such as short-term versus long-term interest rates and stock prices versus dividends, have long interested finance practitioners. For certain types of trends, multiple regression analysis needs modification to uncover these relationships. A trend represents a long-term movement in the variable. One type of trend, a *deterministic trend*, has a straightforward solution. Since a deterministic trend is a function of time, we need merely include this time function in the regression. For example, if the variables are increasing or decreasing as a linear function of time, we may simply include time as a variable in the

---

[1] A financial bubble is defined as a situation where asset price increases are sharper than justified by the fundamental investment attributes of the asset.

regression equation. The issue becomes more complex when the trend is stochastic. As defined in Chapter 5, a *stochastic trend* is a persistent but random long-term movement. Thus a variable with a stochastic trend may exhibit prolonged long-run increases followed by prolonged long-run declines and perhaps another period of long-term increases.

Most financial theorists believe stochastic trends better describe the behavior of financial variables than deterministic trends. For example, if stock prices are rising, there is no reason to believe they will continue to do so in the future. Or, even if they continue to increase in the future, that they may not do so at the same growth rate as in the past. This is because stock prices are driven by a variety of economic factors and the impact of these factors may change over time. One way of capturing these common stochastic trends is by using an econometric technique usually referred to as *cointegration*.

In this chapter, we explain the concept of cointegration. There are two major ways of testing for cointegration. We outline both econometric methods and the underlying theory for each method. We illustrate the first technique with an example of the first type of cointegration problem, testing market price efficiency. Specifically, we examine the present value model of stock prices. We illustrate the second technique with an example of the second type of cointegration problem, examining market linkages. In particular, we test the linkage and the dynamic interactions among stock market indices of three European countries.

STATIONARY AND NONSTATIONARY VARIABLES AND COINTEGRATION

The presence of stochastic trends may lead a researcher to conclude that two economic variables are related over time when in fact they are not. This problem is referred to as *spurious regression*. For example, during the 1980s the U.S. stock market and the Japanese stock market were both rising. An ordinary least squares (OLS) regression of the U.S. Morgan Stanley Stock Index on the Japanese Morgan Stanley Stock Index (measured in U.S. dollars) for the time period 1980–1990 using monthly data yields

Japanese Stock index = 76.74 + 19 U.S. Stock Index
  t-statistic   (–13.95)   (26.51) $R^2 = 0.86$

The t-statistic on the slope coefficient (26.51) is quite large, indicating a strong positive relationship between the two stock markets. This strong relationship is reinforced with a very high R^2 value. However estimating the same regression over a different time period, 1990–2007, reveals

Japanese Stock index = 2905.67 − 0.29 U.S. Stock Index
t-statistic   (30.54)   (2.80) $R^2 = 0.04$

This regression equation suggests there is a strong negative relationship between the two stock market indices. Although the t-statistic on the slope coefficient (2.80) is large, the low R^2 value suggests that the relationship is very weak.

The reason behind these contradictory results is the presence of stochastic trends in both series. During the first time span, these stochastic trends were aligned, but not during the second time period. Since different economic forces influence the stochastic trends and these forces change over time, during some periods they will line up and in some periods they will not. In summary, when the variables have stochastic trends, the OLS technique may provide misleading results. This is the *spurious regression problem*.

Recall that the OLS method requires that the observations are independent and identically distributed, and because the monthly values of the Japanese stock index (as well as those of the U.S. stock index) are not independent and identically distributed, the use of OLS regression for such monthly series is meaningless.

Another problem is that when the variables contain a stochastic trend, the t-values of the regressors no longer follow a normal distribution, even for large samples. Standard hypothesis tests are no longer valid for these nonnormal distributions.

At first, researchers attempted to deal with these problems by removing the trend through differencing these variables. That is, they focused on the change in these variables, $X_t - X_{t-1}$, rather than the level of these variables, X_t. Although this technique was successful for univariate Box-Jenkins analysis, there are two problems with this approach in a multivariate scenario. First, we can only make statements about the changes in the variables rather than the level of the variables. This will be particularly troubling if our major interest is the level of the variable. Second, if the variables are subject to a stochastic trend, then focusing on the changes in the variables will lead to a specification error in our regressions.

The cointegration technique allows researchers to investigate variables that share the same stochastic trend and at the same time avoid the spurious regression problem. Cointegration analysis uses regression analysis to study the long-run linkages among economic variables and allows us to consider the short-run adjustments to deviations from the long-run equilibrium.

The use of cointegration in finance has grown significantly. Surveying this vast literature would take us beyond the scope of this chapter. To narrow our focus, we note that cointegration analysis has been used for mainly two types of problems in finance. First, it has been used to evaluate the price efficiency of financial markets in a wide variety of contexts. For example, Enders used cointegration to evaluate the validity of Purchasing Power Parity Theory.[2] As another example, Campbell and Shiller used cointegration to test both the rational expectations theory of the term structure of interest rates and the present value model of stock prices.[3] The second type of cointegration study investigates market linkages. For example, there have been a good number of studies that have looked at the linkage between equity markets of different countries and regions.[4]

Before explaining cointegration it is first necessary to distinguish between stationary and nonstationary variables. A variable X is said to be *stationary* (more formally, *weakly stationary*) if its mean and variance are constant and its autocorrelation depends on the lag length, that is,

Constant mean: $E(X_t) = \mu$

Constant variance: $var(X_t) = \sigma^2$

Autocorrelation depends on the lag length: $cov(X_t, X_{t-l}) = \gamma(l)$

Stationary means that the variable X fluctuates about its mean with constant variation. Another way to put this is that the variable exhibits mean reversion and so displays no stochastic trend. In contrast, *nonstationary variables* may wander arbitrarily far from the mean. Thus, only nonstationary variables exhibit a stochastic trend.

---

[2] Walter Enders, "ARIMA and Cointegration Tests of Purchasing Power Parity," *Review of Economics and Statistics* 70 (1988): 504–508.

[3] John Campbell and Robert Shiller, "Stock Prices, Earnings and Expected Dividends," *Journal of Finance* 43 (1988): 661–676.

[4] See, for example, Theodore Syriopoulos, "International Portfolio Diversification to Central European Stock Markets," *Applied Financial Economics* 14 (2004): 1253–1268; Paresh K. Narayan and Russell Smyth, "Modeling the Linkages between the Australian and G7 Stock Markets: Common Stochastic Trends and Regime Shifts," *Applied Financial Economics* 14 (2004): 991–1004; Eduardo D. Roca, "Short-Term and Long-Term Price Linkages between the Equity Markets of Australia and Its Major Trading Partners," *Applied Financial Economics* 9 (1999): 501–511; Angelos Kanas, "Linkages between the US and European Equity Markets: Further Evidence From Cointegration Tests," *Applied Financial Economics* 8 (1999): 607–614; Kenneth Kasa, "Common Stochastic Trends in International Stock Markets," *Journal of Monetary Economics* 29 (1992): 95–124; and, Mark P. Taylor and Ian Tonks, "The Internationalization of Stock Markets and Abolition of UK Exchange Control," *Review of Economics and Statistics* 71 (1989): 332–336.

The simplest example of a nonstationary variable is a *random walk*. A variable is a random walk if

$$X_t = LX_t + e_t$$

where e_t is a random error term with mean 0 and standard deviation σ. L is defined as a lag operator, so that LX_t is X_{t-1}.[5]

It can be shown that the standard deviation $\sigma(X_t) = t\sigma$, where t is time. Since the standard deviation depends on time, a random walk is nonstationary.

Nonstationary time series often contain a *unit root*. The unit root reflects the coefficient of the X_{t-1} term in an autoregressive relationship of order one. In higher-order autoregressive models, the condition of nonstationarity is more complex. Consider the p-order autoregressive model

$$(1 - a_1L^1 - \ldots - a_pL^p)X_t = e_t + a_0 \tag{10.1}$$

where a_i terms are coefficients
       L^i is the lag operator

If the sum of polynomial coefficients equals 1, then the X_t series are nonstationary.

If all the variables under consideration are stationary, then there is no spurious regression problem and the standard OLS estimation method can be used. If some of the variables are stationary, and some are nonstationary, then no economically significant relationships exist. Since nonstationary variables contain a stochastic trend, they will not exhibit any relationship with the stationary variables that lack this trend. The spurious regression problem occurs only when all the variables in the system are nonstationary.

If the variables share a common stochastic trend, we may overcome the spurious regression problem. In this case, cointegration analysis may be used to uncover the long-term relationship and the short-term dynamics. Two or more nonstationary variables are cointegrated if there exists a linear combination of the variables that is stationary. This suggests cointegrated variables share long-run links. They may deviate in the short run but are likely to get back to some sort of equilibrium in the long run. It is important to note that, here, the term "equilibrium" is not the same as used in economics. To economists, equilibrium means the desired amount equals the actual amount and there is no inherent tendency to change. In contrast,

---

[5] Similarly $L^2X_t = L(LX_t) = X_{t-2}$ and more generally, $L^pX_t = X_{t-p}$, for $p = 0,1,2,\ldots$

equilibrium in cointegration analysis means that if variables are apart, they show a greater likelihood to move closer together than further apart.

More formally, consider two time series x_t and y_t. Assume that both series are nonstationary and integrated order one. (*Integrated order one* means that if we difference the variable one time, the resultant series is stationary.) These series are cointegrated if

$$z_t = x_t - ay_t$$

z_t is stationary for some value of a.

In the multivariate case, the definition is similar but vector notation must be used. Let A and Y be vectors $(a_1, a_2, \ldots, a_n)$ and $(y_{1t}, y_{2t}, \ldots, y_{nt})'$. Then the variables in Y are cointegrated if each of the $y_{1t}, \ldots, y_{nt}$ are nonstationary and, $Z = AY$, Z is stationary. A represents a cointegrating vector.

Finding cointegration between two variables represents a special case. We should not expect most nonstationary variables to be cointegrated. If two variables lack cointegration, then they do not share a long-run relationship or a common stochastic trend because they can move arbitrarily far away from each other. In terms of the present value model of stock prices, suppose stock prices and dividends lack cointegration, then stock prices could rise arbitrarily far above the level of their dividends. Using a U.S. stock index and dividend data from 1887 through 2003, Gurkaynak illustrated that whenever stock prices are not cointegrated with dividends, stock prices rose far above the level justified by the level of dividends.[6] This would be consistent with a stock market bubble. Even if it is not a bubble, it is still inconsistent with the efficient market theory.

In terms of stock market linkages, if the stock price indices of different countries lack cointegration, then stock prices can wander arbitrarily far apart from each other. This possibility lends support to proponents who argue that investors would benefit from international portfolio diversification.

TESTING FOR COINTEGRATION

There are two popular methods of testing for cointegration: the Engle-Granger tests and the Johansen-Juselius tests. We illustrate both in the remainder of this chapter.

---

[6] Refet Gurkaynak, "Econometric Tests of Asset Price Bubbles: Taking Stock," *Journal of Economic Surveys* 22 (2008): 166–186.

Engle-Granger Cointegration Tests

The *Engle-Granger conintegration test*, developed by Engle and Granger,[7] involves the following four-step process:

Step 1. Determine whether the time series variables under investigation are stationary. We may consider both informal and formal methods for investigating stationarity of a time series variable. Informal methods entail an examination of a graph of the variable over time and an examination of the autocorrelation function. The *autocorrelation function* describes the autocorrelation of the series for various lags. The correlation coefficient between x_t and x_{t-i} is called the *lag i autocorrelation*. For nonstationary variables, the lag 1 autocorrelation coefficient should be very close to one and decay slowly as the lag length increases. Thus, examining the autocorrelation function allows us to determine a variable's stationarity.

Unfortunately, the informal method has its limitations. For stationary series that are very close to unit root processes, the autocorrelation function may exhibit the slow-fading behavior as lag length increases. If more formal methods are desired, the *Dickey-Fuller statistic*, the *Augmented Dickey-Fuller statistic*,[8] or the *Phillips-Perron statistic*[9] can be employed. These statistics test the hypothesis that the variables have a unit root, against the alternative that they do not. The Phillips-Perron test makes weaker assumptions than the Dickey-Fuller and augmented Dickey-Fuller statistics and is generally considered more reliable. If it is determined that the variable is nonstationary and the differenced variable is stationary, proceed to Step 2.

Step 2. Estimate the following regression:

$$y_t = c + dx_t + z_t \tag{10.2}$$

To make this concrete, let y_t represent some U.S. stock market index, x_t represents stock dividends on that stock market index, and z_t the error term. Let c and d represent regression parameters. For

[7] Robert Engle and Clive Granger, "Cointegration and Error-Correction: Representation, Estimation, and Testing," *Econometrica* 55 (1987): 251–276.

[8] David Dickey and Wayne Fuller, "Distribution of the Estimates for Autoregressive Time Series with a Unit Root," *Journal of the American Statistical Association* 74 (1979): 427–431.

[9] Peter Phillips and Pierre Perron, "Testing for a Unit Root in Time Series Regression," *Biometrica* 75 (1988): 335–346.

cointegration tests, the null hypothesis states that the variables lack cointegration and the alternative claims that they are cointegrated.

Step 3. To test for cointegration, test for the stationarity in z_t. The most often used stationarity test is the Dickey-Fuller test. That is, the following autoregression of the error term should be considered:

$$\Delta z_t = p\ z_{t-1} + u_t \tag{10.3}$$

where z_t is the estimated residual from equation (10.2). The Dickey-Fuller test focuses on the significance of the estimated p. If the estimate of p is statistically negative, we conclude that the residuals, z_t, are stationary and reject the hypothesis of no cointegration.

The residuals of equation (10.3) should be checked to ensure the residuals are not autocorrelated. If they are, the augmented Dickey-Fuller test should be employed. The augmented Dickey-Fuller test is analogous to the Dickey-Fuller test but includes additional lags of Δz_t as shown in the following equation:

$$\Delta z_t = p\ z_{t-1} + a_1 \Delta z_{t-1} + \ldots + a_n \Delta z_{t-n} + u_t \tag{10.4}$$

The augmented Dickey-Fuller test for stationarity, like the Dickey-Fuller test, tests the hypothesis of $p = 0$ against the alternative hypothesis of $p < 0$ for equation (10.4).

Generally, the OLS-produced residuals tend to have as small a sample variance as possible, thereby making residuals look as stationary as possible. Thus, the standard t-statistic or augmented Dickey-Fuller test may reject the null hypothesis of nonstationarity too often. Hence, it is important to have correct statistics. Fortunately, Engle and Yoo provide the correct statistics.[10] Furthermore, if it is believed that the variable under investigation has a long-run growth component, it is appropriate to test the series for stationarity around a deterministic time trend for both the Dickey-Fuller and augmented Dickey-Fuller tests. This is accomplished by adding a time trend to equations (10.3) or (10.4).

Step 4. The final step for the Engle-Granger conintegration test involves estimating the *error-correction model*. Engle and Granger showed that if two variables are cointegrated, then these variables can be

---

[10] Robert Engle and Byung Yoo, "Forecasting and Testing in Co-integrated Systems," *Journal of Econometrics* 35 (1987): 143–159.

described in an error-correction format described in the following two equations:

$$\Delta y_t = b_{10} + \sum_{i=1}^{n} b_{1i} \Delta y_{t-i} + \sum_{j=1}^{n} c_{1j} \Delta x_{t-j} + d_1(y_{t-1} - ax_{t-1}) + e_{1t} \qquad (10.5)$$

$$\Delta y_t = b_{20} + \sum_{i=1}^{n} b_{2i} \Delta y_{t-i} + \sum_{j=1}^{n} c_{2j} \Delta x_{t-j} + d_2(y_{t-1} - ax_{t-1}) + e_{2t} \qquad (10.6)$$

Equation (10.5) tells us that the changes in y_t depend on

- Its own past changes.
- The past changes in x_t.
- The disequilibrium between x_{t-1} and y_{t-1}, $(y_{t-1} - ax_{t-1})$.

The size of the error-correction term, d_1 in equation (10.5), captures the speed of adjustment of x_t and y_t to the previous period's disequilibrium. Equation (10.6) has a corresponding interpretation for the error-correction term d_2.

The appropriate lag length is found by experimenting with different lag lengths. For each lag the Akaike information criterion (AIC) or the Bayesian (or Schwarz) information criterion (BIC) is calculated and the lag with the lowest value of the criteria is employed.[11]

The value of $(y_{t-1} - ax_{t-1})$ is estimated using the residuals from the cointegrating equation (10.3), z_{t-1}. This procedure is only legitimate if the variables are cointegrated. The error-correction term, z_{t-1}, will be stationary by definition if and only if the variables are cointegrated. The remaining terms in the equation (i.e., the lag difference of each variable) are also stationary because the levels were assumed nonstationary. This guarantees the stationarity of all the variables in equations (10.5) and (10.6) and justifies the use of the OLS estimation method.

Empirical Illustration of the Engle-Granger Procedure The dividend growth model of stock price valuation asserts that the fundamental value of a stock

---

[11] For a summary of these criteria, see Appendix E.

is determined by the present value (discounted value) of its expected future dividend stream. This model may be represented as:

$$P_0 = \Sigma D_i/(1+r) \tag{10.7}$$

where P_0 = the current stock price
D_i = a dividend in period i
r = the discount rate

If the discount rate exceeds the growth rate of dividends and the discount rate remains constant over time, then one can test for cointegration between stock prices and dividends. In brief, if the present value relationship as given by equation (10.7) holds, one does not expect stock prices and dividends to meander arbitrarily far from each other.

Before starting any analysis, it is useful to examine the plot of the underlying time series variables. Figure 10.1 presents a plot of stock prices and dividends for the years 1962 through 2006. Stock prices are represented by the S&P 500 index and the dividends represent the dividend received by the owner of $1,000 worth of the S&P 500 index. The plot shows that the variables move together until the early 1980s. As a result of this visual analysis, we will entertain the possibility that the variables were cointegrated until the 1980s. After that, the common stochastic trend may have dissipated. We will first test for cointegration in the 1962–1982 period and then for the whole 1962–2006 period.

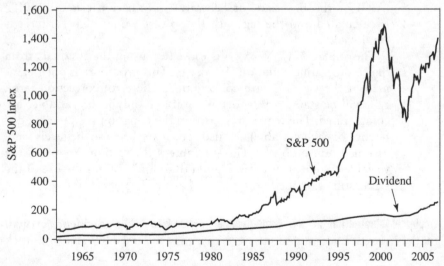

FIGURE 10.1   S&P 500 Index and Dividends 1962–2006
Note: Dividends are multiplied by 10 for a scale effect.

In accordance with Step 1 of the four-step Engle-Granger conintegration test, it is necessary to establish the nonstationarity of the two variables—stock prices as proxied by the S&P 500 and dividends. To identify nonstationarity, we will use both formal and informal methods. The first informal test consists of analyzing the plot of the series shown in Figure 10.1. Neither series appears to exhibit mean reversion. The dividend series wanders less from its mean than the stock price series. Nevertheless, neither series appears stationary.

The second informal method involves examining the autocorrelation function. Table 10.1 shows the autocorrelation function for 36 lags of the S&P 500 index and the dividends for the 1962–2006 period using monthly data. The autocorrelations for the early lags are quite close to 1. Furthermore, the autocorrelation function exhibits a slow decay at higher lags. This provides sufficient evidence to conclude that stock prices and dividends are nonstationary. When we inspect the autocorrelation function of their first differences (not shown in Table 10.1), the autocorrelation of the first lag is not close to one. A fair conclusion is that the series are stationary in the first differences.

TABLE 10.1   Autocorrelation Functions of the S&P 500 Index and Dividends

Lag Autocorrelation	1	2	3	4	5	6	7	8
S&P 500 Index	0.993	0.986	0.979	0.973	0.967	0.961	0.954	0.948
Dividends	0.991	0.983	0.974	0.966	0.958	0.979	0.941	0.933

Lag Autocorrelation	9	10	11	12	13	14	15	16
S&P 500 Index	0.940	0.933	0.926	0.918	0.911	0.903	0.896	0.889
Dividends	0.925	0.916	0.908	0.900	0.891	0.883	0.876	0.868

Lag Autocorrelation	17	18	19	20	21	22	23	24
S&P 500 Index	0.881	0.874	0.866	0.858	0.851	0.843	0.835	0.827
Dividends	0.860	0.852	0.845	0.837	0.830	0.822	0.815	0.808

Lag Autocorrelation	25	26	27	28	29	30	31	32
S&P 500 Index	0.819	0.811	0.804	0.796	0.789	0.782	0.775	0.768
Dividends	0.801	0.794	0.788	0.781	0.775	0.769	0.763	0.758

Lag Autocorrelation	33	34	35	36				
S&P 500 Index	0.761	0.754	0.748	0.741				
Dividends	0.753	0.747	0.743	0.738				

TABLE 10.2 Stationarity Test for the S&P 500 Index and Dividends, 1962–2006

Variable	Augmented Dickey-Fuller	Phillips-Perron	Critical Value of Test Statistics at 1%, 5%, 10% Significance
S&P 500	1.22	1.12	–3.44 (1%)
Δ S&P 500	–19.07	–19.35	–2.87 (5%)
Dividends	1.52	4.64	–2.56 (10%)
Δ Dividends	–2.13	–31.68	

Notes
- Null hypothesis: Variable is nonstationary.
- The lag length for the ADF test was determined by the Bayesian criterion. For the S&P 500 index and its first difference, the lag length was 1. For the dividends and its first difference, the lag lengths were 12 and 11, respectively.

In Table 10.2, we present the results of formal tests of nonstationarity. The lag length for the augmented Dickey-Fuller test was determined by the Bayesian criterion. The null hypothesis is that the S&P 500 stock index (dividends) contains a unit root; the alternative is that it does not. For both the augmented Dickey-Fuller and the Phillips-Perron tests, the results indicate that the S&P 500 index is nonstationary and the changes in that index are stationary. The results for the dividends are mixed. The augmented Dickey-Fuller statistic supports the presence of a unit root in dividends, while the Phillips-Perron statistic does not. Since both the autocorrelation function and the augmented Dickey-Fuller statistic conclude there is a unit root process, we shall presume that the dividend series is nonstationary. In sum, our analysis suggests that the S&P 500 index and dividend series each contain a stochastic trend in the levels, but not in their first differences.

In Step 2 of the Engle-Granger conintegration test, whether the S&P 500 index and dividends are cointegrated is tested. This is accomplished by estimating the long-run equilibrium relation by regressing the logarithm (log) of the S&P 500 index on the log of the dividends. We use the logarithms of both variables to help smooth the series. The results using monthly data are reported in Table 10.3 for both the 1962–1982 and 1962–2006 periods. We pay little attention to the high t-statistic on the

TABLE 10.3 Cointegration Regression: S&P 500 and Dividends Log S&P $500 = a + b \log \text{dividends} + z_t$

Period	Constant	Coefficient of Dividends	t-Stat Dividends
1962–1982	4.035	0.404	17.85
1962–2006	2.871	1.336	68.54

dividends variable because the *t*-test is not appropriate unless the variables are cointegrated. This is, of course, the issue that we are investigating.

Once we estimate the regression in Step 2, the next step involves testing the residuals of the regression, z_t, for stationarity from equation (10.3). By definition, the residuals have a zero mean and lack a time trend. This simplifies the test for stationarity. This is accomplished by estimating equation (10.4). The null hypothesis is that the variables lack cointegration. If we conclude that p in equation (10.4) is negative and statistically significant, then we reject the null hypothesis and conclude that the evidence is consistent with the presence of cointegration between the stock index and dividends. The appropriate lag lengths may be determined by the Akaike information criterion or theoretical and practical considerations. We decided to use a lag length of three periods representing one quarter. The results are presented in Table 10.4. For the 1962–1982 period, the null hypothesis of no

TABLE 10.4   Augmented Dickey-Fuller Tests of Residuals for Cointegration
Panel A. 1962–1982 $n = 248$

Variable	Coefficient	*t*-Stat	*p*-Value
z_t	−0.063	−3.23	0.001
Δz_{t-1}	0.272	4.32	0.000
Δz_{t-2}	−0.030	−0.46	0.642
Δz_{t-3}	0.090	1.40	0.162

t-statistic of $p = -3.23$; critical values at 5% and 10% are −3.36 and −3.06 respectively.

Panel B. 1962–2006 $n = 536$

Variable	Coefficient	*t*-Stat	*p*-Value
z_t	−0.008	−1.81	0.070
Δz_{t-1}	0.265	6.13	0.000
Δz_{t-2}	−0.048	−1.08	0.280
Δz_{t-3}	0.031	0.71	0.477

t-statistic of $p = -1.81$; critical values at 5% and 10% are 3.35 and 3.05, respectively.

The critical values of the augmented Dickey-Fuller (ADF) statistic are from Engle and Yoo (1987). The cointegration equation errors used to perform the ADF test are based on the following regression:

$$\Delta z_t = -p z_{t-1} + a \Delta z_{t-1} + b \Delta z_{t-2} + c \Delta z_{t-3} + e_t$$

where Δz_t is the change in the error term from the cointegration regression and e_t is a random error. If p is positive and significantly different from zero, the z residuals from the equilibrium equation are stationary so we may accept the null hypothesis of cointegration. In both equations the error terms are white noise, so no further stationarity tests were performed.

cointegration is rejected at the 10% level of statistical significance. For the entire period (1962–2006), the null hypothesis ($p = 0$) of no cointegration cannot be rejected. Apparently, the relationship between stock prices and dividends unraveled in the 1980s and the 1990s. This evidence is consistent with the existence of an Internet stock bubble in the 1990s.

Having established that the S&P 500 index and dividends are cointegrated from 1962–1982, the interaction between stock prices and dividends in the final step (Step 4) of the Engle-Granger cointegration test is examined by estimating the error-correction model given by equations (10.5) and (10.6). It is useful at this point to review our interpretation of equations (10.5) and (10.6). Equation (10.5) claims that changes in the S&P 500 index depend upon past changes in the S&P 500 index and past changes in dividends and the extent of disequilibrium between the S&P 500 index and dividends. Equation (10.6) has a similar statistical interpretation. However, from a theoretical point of view, equation (10.6) is meaningless. Financial theory does not claim that changes in dividends are impacted either by past changes in stock prices or the extent of the disequilibrium between stock prices and dividends. As such, equation (10.6) degenerates into an autoregressive model of dividends.

We estimated the error-correction equations using three lags. The error term, z_{t-1}, used in these error-correction regressions was obtained from OLS estimation of the cointegration equation reported in Table 10.3. Estimates of the error-correction equations are reported in Table 10.5. By construction, the error-correction term represents the degree to which the stock prices

TABLE 10.5 Error Correction Model: S&P 500 Index and Dividends, 1962–1982

	Equation (10.5)			Equation (10.6)	
	Coefficient	t-Stat		Coefficient	t-Stat
b_{01}	−0.009	−2.42	b_{20}	0.001	2.91
b_{11}	0.251	4.00	b_{21}	0.002	0.63
b_{12}	−0.043	−0.66	b_{22}	−0.003	−0.88
b_{13}	0.081	1.27	b_{23}	0.004	1.07
c_{11}	0.130	0.11	c_{21}	0.939	14.60
c_{12}	−0.737	−0.46	c_{22}	−0.005	−0.06
c_{13}	−0.78	−0.65	c_{23}	−0.006	0.87
d_1	−0.07	−3.64	d_2	0.000	0.30

The change in the S&P 500 index is denoted as ΔY_t and the change in dividends is denoted as ΔX_t.

and dividends deviate from long-run equilibrium. The error-correction term is included in both equations to guarantee that the variables do not drift too far apart. Engle and Granger showed that, if the variables are cointegrated, the coefficient on the error-correction term, $(y_{t-1} - ax_{t-1})$, in at least one of the equations must be nonzero.[12] The t-value of the error-correction term in equation (10.5) is statistically different from zero. The coefficient of -0.07 is referred to as the *speed of adjustment coefficient*. The estimated value for the coefficient suggests that 7% of the previous month's disequilibrium between the stock index and dividends is eliminated in the current month. In general, the higher the speed of adjustment coefficient, the faster the long-run equilibrium is restored. Since the speed of adjustment coefficient for the dividend equation is statistically indistinguishable from zero, all of the adjustment falls on the stock price.

An interesting observation from Table 10.5 relates to the lag structure of equation (10.5). The first lag on past stock price changes is statistically significant. This means that the change in the stock index this month depends upon the change during the last month. This is inconsistent with the efficient market hypothesis. On the other hand, the change in dividend lags is not statistically different from zero. The efficient market theory suggests, and the estimated equation confirms, that past changes in dividends do not affect the current changes in stock prices.

Johansen-Juselius Cointegration Test

The Engle-Granger cointegration test has some problems. These problems are magnified in a multivariate (three or more variables) context. In principle, when the cointegrating equation is estimated (even in a two-variable problem), any variable may be utilized as the dependent variable. In illustration of the application of the Engle-Granger cointegration test, this would entail placing dividends on the left-hand side of equation (10.2) and the S&P 500 index on the right-hand side. As the sample size approaches infinity, Engle and Granger showed that the cointegration tests produce the same results irrespective of what variable is used as the dependent variable. The question is then: How large a sample is large enough?

A second problem is that the errors we use to test for cointegration are only estimates and the not the true errors. Thus any mistakes made in estimating the error term, z_t, in equation (10.2) are carried forward into the regression given by equation (10.3). Finally, the Engle-Granger cointegration test is unable to detect multiple cointegrating relationships.

---

[12] Engle and Granger, "Cointegration and Error-Correction."

The Johansen-Juselius cointegration test[13] avoids these problems. Consider the following multivariate model:

$$y_t = Ay_{t-1} + u_t \tag{10.8}$$

where y_t = an $n \times 1$ vector $(y_{1t}, y_{2t}, \ldots, y_{nt})$ of variables
  u_t = an n-dimensional error term at t
  A = an $n \times n$ matrix of coefficients

If the variables display a time trend, we may wish to add the matrix A_0 to equation (10.8). This matrix would reflect a deterministic time trend. (The same applies to equation (10.9) presented below.) It does not change the nature of our analysis.

The model (without the deterministic time trend) can then be represented as:

$$\Delta y_t = B\, y_{t-1} + u_t \tag{10.9}$$

where $B = I - A$, and I is the identity matrix of dimension n variables

The cointegration of the system is determined by the rank of B matrix. The highest rank of B that can be obtained is n, the number of variables under consideration. If B is zero, that means that there are no linear combinations of y_t that are stationary and so there are no cointegrating vectors.

If the rank of B is n, then each y_{it} is an autoregressive process. This means each y_{it} is stationary and the relationship can be tested using a vector autoregression model, which we cover in Chapter 9. For any rank between 1 and $n - 1$, the system is cointegrated and the rank of the matrix is the number of cointegrating vectors.

The Johansen-Juselius cointegration test employs two statistics to test for cointegration:

1. λ trace test statistic
2. maximum eigenvalue test

The λ *trace test statistic* verifies the null hypothesis that there are no cointegration relations. The alternative hypothesis is that there is at least one

---

[13] Soren Johansen and Katarina Juselius, "Maximum Likelihood Estimation and Inference on Cointegration with Application to the Demand for Money," *Oxford Bulletin of Economics and Statistics* 52 (1990): 169–209.

cointegration vector. The *maximum eigenvalue test*, so-named because it is based on the largest eigenvalue, tests the null hypothesis that there are i cointegrating vectors against the alternative hypothesis of $i + 1$ cointegrating vectors.

Johansen and Juselius derive critical values for both test statistics. The critical values are different if there is a deterministic time trend A_0 included. Enders provides tables for both critical statistics with and without the trend terms.[14] Software programs often provide critical values and the relevant *p*-values.

Empirical Illustration of Johansen-Juselius Procedure Many financial advisors and portfolio managers argue that investors would be able to improve their risk/return profile by investing internationally rather than restricting their holding to domestic stocks (i.e., following a policy of international diversification). If stock market returns in different countries are not highly correlated, then investors could obtain risk reduction without significant loss of return by investing in different countries. But with the advent of globalization and the simultaneous integration of capital markets throughout the world, the risk-diversifying benefits of international investing have been challenged. Here, we illustrate how cointegration can shed light on this issue and apply the Johansen-Juselius cointegration test.

The idea of a common currency for the European countries is to reduce transactions costs and more closely link the economies. We shall use cointegration to examine whether the stock markets of France, Germany, and the Netherlands are linked following the introduction of the euro in 1999. We use monthly data for the period 1999–2006.

Although testing for cointegration requires that the researcher test for stationarity in the series, Johansen states that testing for stationarity is redundant since stationarity is revealed through a cointegration vector.[15] However, it is important to establish the appropriate lag length for equation (10.9). This is typically done by estimating a traditional vector autoregressive (VAR) model (see Chapter 9) and applying a multivariate version of the Akaike information criterion or Bayesian information criterion. For our model, we use one lag, and thus the model takes the form:

$$y_t = A_0 + A_1 y_{t-1} + u_t \tag{10.10}$$

where y_t is the $n \times 3$ vector $(y_{1t}, y_{2t}, \ldots, y_{3t})'$ of the logs of the stock market index for France, Germany, and the Netherlands (i.e., element y_{1t} is the log

---

[14] Enders, "ARIMA and Cointegration Tests of Purchasing Power Parity."
[15] Soren Johansen, *Likelihood-Based Inference in Cointegrated Vector Autoregressive Models* (New York: Oxford University Press, 1995).

TABLE 10.6   Cointegration Test

Hypothesized No. of Cointegrating Vectors	Characteristic Roots	Trace Statistics λ_{trace}	5% Critical Value	p-Value	Max-Statistic λ_{max}	5% Critical Value	p-Value
None	0.227	33.05	29.80	0.02	24.72	21.13	0.01
At most 1	0.057	8.32	15.49	0.43	5.61	14.26	0.66
At most 2	0.028	2.72	3.84	0.10	2.72	3.84	0.10

of the French stock index at time t; y_{2t} is the log of the German stock index at time t; and y_{3t} is the log of the Netherlands stock index at time t). We use logs of the stock market indices to smooth the series. A_0 and A_1 are $n \times n$ matrices of parameters and u_t is the $n \times n$ error matrix.

The next step is to estimate the model. This means fitting equation (10.9). We incorporated a linear time trend, hence the inclusion of the matrix A_0. Since there are restrictions across the equations, the procedure uses a maximum likelihood estimation procedure and not OLS. (We explain the maximum likelihood estimation method in Chapter 13.) The focus of this estimation is not on the parameters of the A matrices. Few software programs present these estimates, rather the emphasis is on the matrix B which is estimated to determine the number of cointegrating vectors.

The estimates are presented in Table 10.6. We want to establish whether i indices are cointegrated. Thus, we test the null hypothesis that the stock indices lack cointegration. To accomplish this, the λ trace test statistic, denoted by $\lambda_{\text{trace}}(0)$, is calculated (0 is included to indicate that there are zero cointegrating vectors). Table 10.6. also provides this statistic. To insure comprehension of this important statistic, we detail its calculation.

We have 96 usable observations.

$$\lambda_{\text{trace}}(0) = -T[\ln(1 - \lambda_i^*) + \ln(1 - \lambda_2^*) + \ln(1 - \lambda_3^*)]$$
$$= -96[\ln(1 - 0.227) + \ln(1 - 0.057) + \ln(1 - 0.028)] = 33.05$$

As reported in Table 10.6, this exceeds the critical value for 5% significance of 29.80[16] and has a p-value of 0.02. Thus, the null hypothesis at a 5% level of significance is rejected with the evidence consistent with at least one cointegrating vector. Next we can examine $\lambda_{\text{trace}}(1)$ to test the null hypothesis of at most one cointegrating vector against the alternative of two cointegrating vectors. Table 10.6 shows that λ_1 at 8.33 is less than the critical value of

---

[16]The critical values for this cointegration method are obtained from Johansen, *Likelihood-Based Inference in Cointegrated Vector Autoregressive Models*.

15.49 necessary to establish statistical significance at the 5% level. We do not reject the null hypothesis. We therefore conclude that there is at least one cointegrating vector. There is no need to evaluate λ_{trace} (2).

The maximum eigenvalue statistic, denoted λ_{max}, reinforces the conclusion from the λ trace test statistic. We can use $\lambda_{max}(0, 1)$ to test the null hypothesis that the variables lack (0) cointegration against the alternative that they are cointegrated with one (1) cointegrating vector. Table 10.6 presents the value of $\lambda_{max}(0, 1)$. Again, for pedagogic reasons, we outline the calculation of $\lambda_{max}(0, 1)$:

$$\lambda_{max}(0,1) = (-T \ln(1 - \lambda_i^*))$$
$$= -96 \ln(1 - 0.227) = 24.72$$

The computed value of 24.72 exceeds the critical value of 21.13 at the 5% significance level and has a p-value of 0.01. Once again, this leads to rejection of the null hypothesis that the stock indices lack cointegration. The conclusion is that there exists at least one cointegrating vector.

The next step requires a presentation of the cointegrating equation and an analysis of the error-correction model. Table 10.7 presents both. The cointegrating equation is a multivariate representation of z_{t-1} in the Engle-Granger cointegration test. This is presented in Panel A of Table 10.7. The error-correction model takes the following representation:

$$\Delta y_t = b_{10} + \sum_{i=1}^{n} b_{1i} \Delta y_{t-i} + \sum_{j=1}^{n} c_{1j} \Delta x_{t-j} + d_1 (y_{t-1} - a x_{t-1}) + e_{1t} \qquad (10.11)$$

The notation of equation (10.11) differs somewhat from the notation of equations (10.5) and (10.6). The notation used in equation (10.11) reflects the matrix notation adopted for the Johansen-Juselius cointegration test in equation (10.9). Nevertheless, for expositional convenience, we did not use the matrix notation for the error-correction term. The notation Δ means the first difference of the variable; thus Δy_{1t-1} means the change in the log of the French stock index in period $t - 1$, $(y_{1t-1} - y_{1t-2})$. Equation (10.11) claims that changes in the log of the French stock index are due to changes in the French stock index during the last two periods; changes in the German stock index during the last two periods; changes in the Netherlands stock index during the last two periods; and finally deviations of the French stock index from its stochastic trend with Germany and the Netherlands.[17] An analogous equation could be written for both Germany and the Netherlands.

---

[17] Lag length of two periods is determined on the basis of information criteria such as the Bayesian information criterion and it is provided in statistical software programs.

TABLE 10.7 Cointegration Equation and Error Correction Equations, 1999–2007

Panel A. Cointegrating Equation

France = 4.82 + 2.13 Germany − 1.71 Netherlands
[8.41]   [5.25]

Panel B. Error-Correction Equations

Country	A(France)	A(Germany)	A(Netherlands)
Z_{t-1}	−0.151477	−0.057454	−0.179129
	[−2.21]	[−0.66]	[−2.52]
Δ(France(−1))	0.087360	0.245750	0.225357
	[0.27]	[0.60]	[0.67]
Δ(France(−2))	−0.200773	−0.218331	−0.324250
	[−0.68]	[−0.58]	[−1.06]
Δ(Germany(−1))	−0.189419	−0.024306	−0.094891
	[−0.82]	[−0.08]	[−0.39]
Δ(Germany(−2))	−0.155386	−0.109070	−0.127301
	[−0.67]	[−0.37]	[−0.53]
Δ(Netherlands(−1))	0.079881	−0.189775	−0.188295
	[0.34]	[−0.64]	[−0.77]
Δ(Netherlands(−2))	0.439569	0.446368	0.483929
	[1.89]	[1.52]	[2.00]
C	0.005967	0.002575	0.002688
	[1.02]	[0.35]	[0.44]

France(−1) represents the log return of the French stock index from the previous month. Germany(−1) and Netherlands(−1) have a similar interpretation. Numbers in brackets represent the t-statistic.

Panel B of Table 10.7 presents the error-correction model estimates for each of the three countries. The error-correction term in each equation reflects the deviation from the long-run stochastic trend of that stock index in the last period. It should be noted that in contrast to the Engle-Granger cointegration test, the Johansen-Juselius cointegration test estimates the long-run and short-run dynamics in one step. The speed of adjustment coefficient provides insight into the short-run dynamics. This coefficient is insignificant (at the 5% level) for Germany. This means that stock prices in Germany do not change in response to deviations from their stochastic trend with France and the Netherlands. Because the variables are cointegrated, we are guaranteed that at least one speed of adjustment coefficient will be significant. In fact, the speed of adjustment coefficients of both France and the Netherlands attain statistical significance (at the 5% level) and are about the same size. This shows that when the economies of France and the Netherlands deviate from the common stochastic trend, they adjust. In France about 15% and in Netherlands about 17% of the last period deviation is corrected during this period.

KEY POINTS

- Many of the variables of interest to finance professionals are nonstationary.
- The relationships among nonstationary variables can be analyzed if they share a common stochastic trend. A way of capturing this common stochastic trend is the application of cointegration.
- Cointegration analysis can reveal interesting long-run relationships between variables.
- When the variables have stochastic trends, there is a spurious regression problem and, as a result, the ordinary least squares estimation method may provide misleading results.
- Cointegration analysis has been used in testing market price efficiency and international stock market linkages.
- It is possible that cointegrating variables may deviate in the short run from their relationship, but the error-correction model shows how these variables adjust to the long-run equilibrium.
- There are two important methods of testing for cointegration: the Engle-Granger cointegration test and the Johansen-Juselius test.
- The most often used method to test cointegration between two variables is the Engle-Granger cointegration test.
- The Johansen-Juselius test is employed to test cointegration among multiple variables.

CHAPTER 11

Autoregressive Heteroscedasticity Model and Its Variants

After reading this chapter you will understand:

- The concepts of homoscedasticity and heteroscedasticity.
- The concept of conditional heteroscedasticity.
- The empirical basis for conditional heteroscedasticity.
- Autoregressive modeling of conditional heteroscedasticity.
- Autoregressive conditional heteroscedasticity (ARCH) models.
- Extensions of ARCH models: generalized autoregressive conditional heteroscedasticity (GARCH) models and multivariate ARCH models.
- How to apply estimation software for ARCH models.

In Chapter 9, we described a time series tool, the autoregressive moving average (ARMA) model, that focuses on estimating and forecasting the mean. Now we turn to financial econometric tools that are used to estimate and forecast an important measure in finance: the variance of a financial time series. The variance is an important measure used in the quantification of risk for a portfolio or a trading position, strategies for controlling the risk of a portfolio or a trading position (i.e., determination of the hedge ratio), and as an input in an option pricing model.

Among the financial econometric tools used for forecasting the conditional variance, the most widely used are the autoregressive conditional heteroscedasticity (ARCH) model and the generalized autoregressive conditional heteroscedasticity (GARCH) model.[1] These tools are described in this chapter along with a brief description of variants of these models. Estimation of the forecasted correlation between major asset classes or any two financial assets in the same asset class is calculated based on the forecasted

---

[1] Other tools include stochastic volatility models and Markov switching models.

variance of each one and their covariances. Thus a time series tool for estimating conditional covariances is needed in portfolio construction. Forecasts of conditional covariances can be done using multivariate ARCH and multivariate GARCH models which we very briefly describe at the end of this chapter.

ESTIMATING AND FORECASTING VOLATILITY

The simplest approach for measuring historical volatility involves using a sample of prices or returns observed over a recent, short time period to calculate the variance and standard deviation. Variants of historical volatility depend on how much weight is given to each observation. Assigning each sample observation equal weight means that the most recent observations are given the same influence as the observations at the beginning of the time period. This approach is referred to as the *equally weighted average approach*. The drawback of this approach is that more recent observations may contain more information regarding future volatility than more distant observations. To overcome this drawback, the *exponentially weighted moving average* (EWMA) approach can be used. This approach assigns more weight to more recent observations. By assigning more weight to recent observations, extreme observations that occurred in the past are given less importance in the calculation of the variance. This approach involves the selection of a process for weighting observations so as to give more weight to recent observations and less weight to the more distant observations. An exponentially weighted scheme is used for this purpose and hence the use of the term in describing this approach. The user must specify the weighting scheme (i.e., how much weight should be assigned to recent and distant observations).[2]

The drawbacks of the two approaches just described are that they are historical volatility or realized volatility measures and therefore not necessarily a measure of expected future volatility. The use of a "realized" volatility measure for forecasting future volatility is based on the assumption that volatility will remain constant (unchanged) in the future from what it was during the sample time period. In addition, because it is a sample estimate, it is subject to sampling error. This means that historical volatility depends on the sample time period used.

---

[2]For a detailed explanation of how to apply estimate and forecast volatility using the equally weighted average and EWMA approaches, see Carol Alexander, "Moving Average Models for Volatility and Correlation, and Covariance Matrices," in *Handbook of Finance*, ed. Frank J. Fabozzi, vol. 3 (Hoboken, NJ: John Wiley & Sons, 2008): 711–724.

Although the EMWA approach for forecasting future volatility is superior to the equally weighted average, there is no model that provides a structure for the expected behavior of volatility. In looking for this type of structure for the variance in the case of the returns on financial assets, practitioners can be guided by two stylized facts: (1) volatility tends to be time varying and (2) volatility exhibits clustering. By time varying volatility, it is meant that there are turbulent periods (i.e., periods of high volatility) and tranquil periods (i.e., periods of low volatility). By volatility clustering it is meant that when volatility is low it tends to remain low and when volatility is high it tends to remain high.

The two statistical models described in this chapter, ARCH and GARCH models (and its variants), are derived by imposing a structure on volatility that is consistent with observations about the volatility observed in a market. For example, a GARCH model asserts that the best predictor for future volatility for the next period is made up of three components: (1) a long-run variance which is constant, (2) a forecast of volatility in the prior period, and (3) new information not available when the prior forecast of volatility was made. (The last component is obtained in the square of the prior forecasts residual.) The many extensions of the GARCH model involve adapting models to the structure of the behavior of the variance that has been observed. For example, in the stock market it is observed that bad news tends to be more important than good news in terms of its influence on price. This is referred to as the *leverage effect*. An extension of the GARCH model to incorporate this is the threshold GARCH model.

With this understanding of the objective of forecasting future volatility by providing a structure for the variance, we now move on to describing ARCH and GARCH models.

ARCH BEHAVIOR

Autoregressive conditional heteroscedasticity models, referred to as ARCH models, are used in financial econometrics to represent time-varying conditional volatility. Considered a major achievement of modern econometrics, ARCH models were first described by Robert Engle, who was awarded the 2003 Nobel Memorial Prize in Economic Sciences for his work in time series econometrics.[3]

---

[3] Robert F. Engle, "Autoregressive Conditional Heteroscedasticity with Estimates of the Variance of United Kingdom Inflation," *Econometrica* 50, no. 4 (1982): 987–1007. Engle's development of the ARCH model was only one of his major contributions to time series econometrics. The corecipient of the award that year was Clive Granger who jointly with Robert Engle formulated the cointegration technique that we describe in Chapter 10.

The key idea behind ARCH models is the following:

Unpredictable fluctuations of asset prices as well as of economic time series do not have a constant average magnitude. Periods when unpredictable fluctuations are large alternate with periods when they are small.

This type of behavior of unpredictable fluctuations is almost universal in financial and economic time series data.

ARCH modeling can be applied to a large class of financial and economic variables. In order to gain an understanding of ARCH modeling, we will consider asset returns. Let's first assume that returns behave as a sequence of independent and identically distributed random variables, commonly referred to as an i.i.d. sequence. As explained in Chapter 2, an i.i.d. sequence is the simplest model of returns. It implies that returns are unpredictable: the returns at any given time are random values independent from previous returns; they are extracted from the same distribution.

Figure 11.1 represents the plot of simulated returns of a hypothetical asset. Returns are assumed to be an i.i.d. sequence formed with 1,000 independent

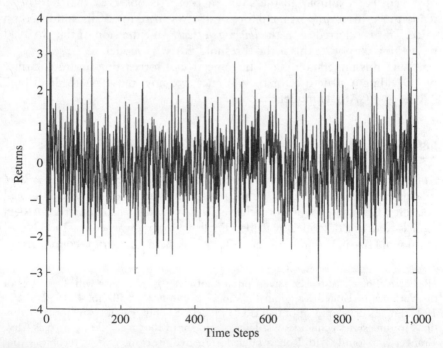

FIGURE 11.1   Plot of Simulated Returns as a Sequence of 1,000 i.i.d. Variables

random draws from a standard normal distribution. Recall that a standard normal distribution has a mean equal to zero and a variance equal to one. The assumption of normal distribution of returns is an approximation which simplifies simulations. (We will examine this assumption later in this book.) The main points are (1) the magnitude of returns in the plot varies randomly and (2) the plot does not seem to follow any regular pattern. In particular, the magnitude of simulated returns oscillates from a minimum of approximately –0.3 (–30%) to a maximum of +0.3 (+30%) but we cannot recognize any extended periods when the absolute value of returns is larger or smaller.

The simulated plot in Figure 11.1 is only an approximation of what is observed in real-world financial markets. In fact, stock returns are only approximately i.i.d. variables. Empirically, researchers have found that although the direction of the fluctuations (i.e., the sign of the returns) is almost unpredictable, it is possible to predict the absolute value of returns. In other words, given past returns up to a given time t, we cannot predict the sign of the next return at time $t + 1$ but we can predict if the next return will be large or small in absolute value. This is due to the fact that the average magnitude of returns, that is, their average absolute value, alternates between periods of large and small average magnitude.

Consider, for example, Figure 11.2, which represents the returns of the stock of Oracle Corporation in the period from January 12, 2008, to December 30, 2011. That period includes 1,000 trading days. The plot in Figure 11.2 has more structure than the plot in Figure 11.1. By looking at the plot in Figure 11.2, we can recognize that extended periods where fluctuations are small alternate with extended periods where fluctuations are large. The average magnitude of unpredictable fluctuations is called *volatility*. Volatility is a measure of risk. Therefore we can say that periods of high risk alternate with periods of lower risk.

Let's review a few terms that we introduced in our discussion of regression analysis in Chapter 4 regarding the assumptions of the general linear model. A sequence of random variables is said to be *homoscedastic* if all variables have the same measure of dispersion, in particular the same variance. An i.i.d. sequence is homoscedastic because it is formed with random variables that are identical and therefore have the same variance or any other measure of dispersion. A sequence of random variables is said to be *heteroscedastic* if different variables have different variance or other measures of dispersion.

Recall that a time series, that is a sequence of random variables, is called covariance-stationary or weakly stationary[4] if (1) all first- and second-order

---

[4] A covariance stationary series is often called simply "stationary." A time series is called "strictly stationary" if all finite distributions are time independent. A strictly stationary series is not necessarily weakly stationary because the finite distributions might fail to have first and second moments.

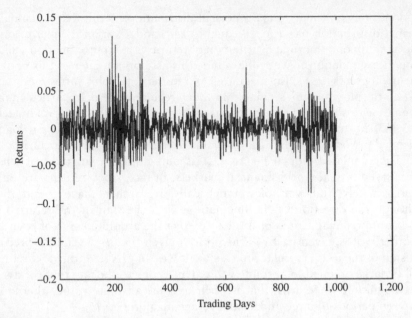

FIGURE 11.2 Plot of 1,000 Returns of the Oracle Corporation Stock in the Period from January 12, 2008, to December 30, 2011

moments exist and (2) they are constant and not time-dependent. That is, a covariance-stationary series has a constant mean, a constant variance, and constant autocovariances.

A time series is said to be *homoscedastic* if it has a constant variance. A homoscedastic time series is not necessarily stationary because its mean can be time dependent. A heteroscedastic sequence of random variables is not a stationary series because the variance of the sequence is not constant in time (i.e., the variance depends on time).

Now, consider a sequence such as that represented in Figure 11.2. The sequence exhibits periods in which returns are large in absolute value and periods in which returns are small. Given that the magnitude of returns in absolute value is persistent, we can predict, albeit in a probabilistic sense, when returns will be large in absolute value and when they will be small. That is, we can predict if returns will be large or small in absolute value *conditionally on previous returns.* We say that the sequence is *conditionally heteroscedastic,* because the variance of returns at any moment depends on previous returns. A sequence is conditionally heteroscedastic if we can predict the value of future variance of returns in function of past returns (i.e., conditional on previous returns).

However, it has been demonstrated that—and this is a key point— *a sequence can be conditionally heteroscedastic though it is stationary.* Though it might seem counterintuitive, a sequence might be stationary, with constant unconditional variance, and still its observed values (referred to as *realizations*) might exhibit periods when fluctuations are larger and periods when fluctuations are smaller. That is, the variance changes in time *conditionally to previous values of the series.*

Modeling ARCH Behavior

Robert Engle first introduced a model of conditional heteroscedasticity in 1982. Engle's choice was to model conditional heteroscedasticity as an autoregressive process, hence the model is called autoregressive conditional heteroscedasticity.

To explain how to model ARCH behavior, we will use asset returns (although the modeling can be applied to any financial variable), denoting the return at time t by R_t. Assume that the behavior of asset returns R_t is described by the following process:

$$R_t = \sigma_t \varepsilon_t \tag{11.1}$$

where σ_t is the standard deviation of the return at time t and ε_t is a sequence of independent normal variables with mean zero and variance one. In equation (11.1) we assume that returns have mean zero or, realistically, that a constant mean has been subtracted from returns.

The simplest ARCH model requires that the following relationship holds:

$$\sigma_t^2 = c + a_1 R_{t-1}^2 \tag{11.2}$$

where σ_t^2 is the variance of the return at time t and c and a_1 are constants to be determined via estimation. In plain English, this model states that the variance of an asset's return at any time t depends on a constant term plus the product of a constant term and the square of the previous time period's return. Because this model involves the return for one prior time period (i.e., one-period lag), it is referred to as an *ARCH(1) model* where (1) denotes a one-period lag.

We need to impose conditions on the parameters c and a_1 to ensure that the variance σ_t^2 is greater than 0 and that the returns R_t are stationary. A process that assumes only values greater than 0 is called a *positive process*.

If we require that $c > 0$ and that $0 < a_1 < 1$, then the return process R_t is stationary with variance equal to $\sigma^2 = c/(1-a_1)$ and the variance process is positive.

To illustrate the above, Figure 11.3 provides a plot of simulated returns that follow an ARCH(1) process assuming that $c = 0.1$ and $a_1 = 0.1$. Figure 11.4 shows that the volatility of the series changes in time and oscillates between low and high values.

To improve the ability of ARCH models to fit realistic time series, we can use a larger number of lags. We use the notation ARCH(m) model to denote a model with m lags and describe this form of the model as follows:

$$R_t = \sigma_t \varepsilon_t \tag{11.3}$$

$$\sigma_t^2 = c + a_1 R_{t-1}^2 + \cdots + a_m R_{t-m}^2 \tag{11.4}$$

In equation (11.3) a random error, ε_t, is multipled by the time-varying volatility σ_t; equation (11.4) prescribes that current volatility is a weighted average of past squared returns plus a constant. In order to ensure that σ_t^2 is nonnegative and the model stationary, we require that

1. The parameters $a_1, \ldots, a_m$ be nonnegative
2. $a_1 + \ldots + a_m < 1$

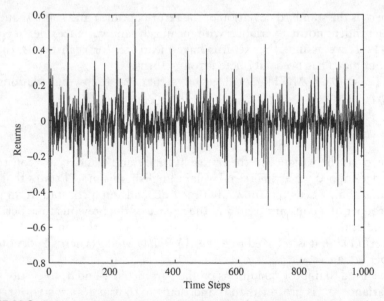

FIGURE 11.3 Simulated ARCH(1) Return Process with Parameters $c = 0.1$ and $a_1 = 0.1$

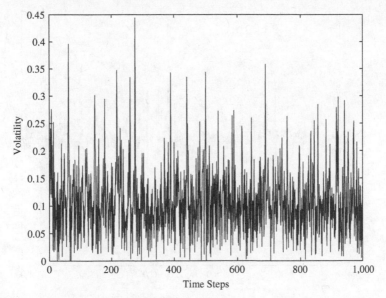

FIGURE 11.4 Plot of Volatility Relative to Figure 11.3
Note: Periods of high and low volatility alternate but the frequency of changes is high.

Figures 11.5 and 11.6 provide the plot of a simulated series of returns that follow an ARCH(3) process; that is, a process that follows an ARCH model with three lags. The model's coefficients assumed in the plots are $c = 0.1$, $a_1 = 0.6$, $a_2 = 0.2$, and $a_3 = 0.1$. Notice that the assumed values for the parameters satisfy the two conditions for the model to be positive stationary: (1) the assumed value for the three parameters for three lags are all positive and (2) their sum is 0.9 which is less than one. It can be shown that R_t^2 is an autoregressive process.[5] By establishing that R_t^2 is an autoregressive process, if returns follow an ARCH process, we prove that squared returns

---

[5] Let's substitute $\sigma_t^2 = c + a_1 R_{t-1}^2 + \cdots + a_m R_{t-m}^2$ into $R_t = \sigma_t \varepsilon_t$ and take conditional expectations. As lagged values of R_t are known and ε_t has zero mean and unit variance, we obtain:

$$E\left(R_t^2 \mid R_{t-1}^2 \cdots R_{t-m}^2\right) = \left(c + a_1 R_{t-1}^2 + \cdots + a_m R_{t-m}^2\right) E\left(\varepsilon_t^2\right) = c + a_1 R_{t-1}^2 + \cdots + a_m R_{t-m}^2$$

This relationship shows that R_t^2 is an autoregressive process. The process R_t^2 represents squared returns and therefore must be positive. To ensure that R_t^2 be positive, we require that $c > 0$, $a_i \geq 0$, $i = 1,\ldots,m$. It can be demonstrated that this condition guarantees stationarity. Taking expectations, we see that the unconditional variance is:

$$c / \left(1 - \sum a_i\right)$$

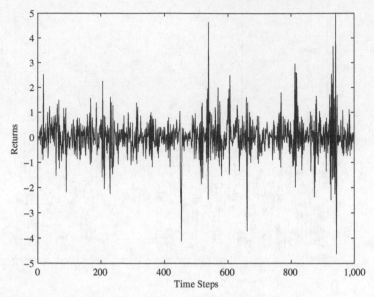

FIGURE 11.5 Simulated ARCH(3) Return Process with Parameters $c = 0.1$, $a_1 = 0.6$, $a_2 = 0.2$, and $a_3 = 0.1$

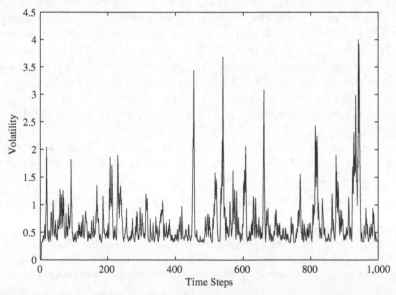

FIGURE 11.6 Plot of Volatility Relative to Figure 11.5

are predictable and we can determine explicit formulas to make predictions. In particular, we can make predictions of volatility, which is a key measure of risk.

ARCH in the Mean Model

The *ARCH in the mean model*, denoted ARCH-M model, is a variant of the ARCH model suggested by the consideration that investors require higher returns to bear higher risk and, therefore, periods when the conditional variance is higher should be associated with higher returns.[6] The ARCH-M model is written as follows:

$$R_t = d\sigma_t + u_t \tag{11.5}$$

$$u_t = \sigma_t \varepsilon_t \tag{11.6}$$

$$\sigma_t^2 = c + a_1 u_{t-1}^2 + \cdots + a_m u_{t-m}^2 \tag{11.7}$$

Equation (11.5) states that returns at time t are the sum of two components: $d\sigma_t$, and u_t. The first component $d\sigma_t$ is proportional to volatility at time t while the second component u_t has the same form of the ARCH(m) model. If we set $d = 0$ the ARCH in the mean model becomes the standard ARCH(m) model given by equations (11.3) and (11.4).

Recall that standard ARCH models represent zero-mean returns; we assume that if returns have a constant mean, the mean has been subtracted. Because of the addition of the (always positive) term $d\sigma_t$ in equation (11.5) in the ARCH-in-the-mean model the conditional mean of returns is not zero but is time varying. The conditional mean is bigger when volatility is high, smaller when volatility is low.

GARCH MODEL

Figures 11.5 and 11.6 show how adding lags allows one to reduce the frequency of switching between low and high volatility. Of course, in a practical application, all constants need to be estimated. The need to estimate constants is the key weakness of models with many parameters: estimation

---

[6] Robert F. Engle, David V. Lilien, and Russell P. Robins, "Estimating Time Varying Risk Premia in the Term Structure: The ARCH-M Model," *Econometrica* 55 (1987): 391–407.

is noisy and unreliable. To avoid too many lags, Tim Bollerslev introduced a variant of ARCH models called the *generalized autoregressive conditional heteroscedasticity* model or GARCH model.[7]

In a GARCH model, volatility depends not only on the past values of the process as in ARCH models but also on the past values of volatility. The GARCH(p, q) model, where p is the number of lags or the past value of R_t^2 and q the number of lags for the variance in the model, is described by the following pair of equations:

$$R_t = \sigma_t \varepsilon_t + d \tag{11.8}$$

$$\sigma_t^2 = c + a_1 R_{t-1}^2 + \cdots + a_p R_{t-p}^2 + b_1 \sigma_{t-1}^2 + \cdots + b_q \sigma_{t-q}^2 \tag{11.9}$$

Conditions to ensure that σ is positive and that the process is stationary are the same as for ARCH models; that is

1. $c > 0$
2. All parameters $a_1, \ldots, a_p, b_1, \ldots, b_q$ must be nonnegative
3. The sum of all parameters must be less than 1:

$$a_1 + \cdots + a_p + b_1 + \cdots + b_q < 1$$

If these conditions are met, then the squared returns can be represented as an autoregressive process as follows:

$$R_t^2 = c + (a_1 + b_1) R_{t-1}^2 + \cdots + (a_m + b_m) R_{t-m}^2 + w_t \tag{11.10}$$

To illustrate, let's simulate a GARCH(1,1) process assuming that $c = 0.1$, $a_1 = 0.4$, and $b_1 = 0.4$. Figure 11.7 shows 1,000 simulated returns obtained for this GARCH(1,1) process. Figure 11.8 represents the corresponding volatility. As can be seen, the conditional heteroscedasticity effect is quite strong. In fact, we can see from this figure that volatility periodically goes to a minimum of about 0.4 and then rises again to higher values. This periodic oscillation of the value of volatility is the essence of ARCH/GARCH models.

---

[7]Tim Bollerslev, "Generalized Autoregressive Conditional Heteroscedasticity," *Journal of Econometrics* 31 (1986): 307–327.

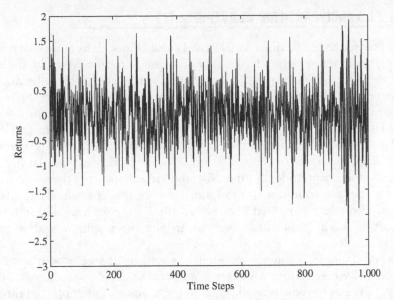

FIGURE 11.7 Simulated Returns Obtained with a GARCH(1,1) Process Assuming $c = 0.1$, $a_1 = 0.4$, and $b_1 = 0.4$

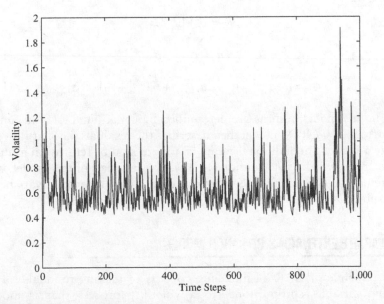

FIGURE 11.8 Plot of Volatility Relative to Figure 11.7

WHAT DO ARCH/GARCH MODELS REPRESENT?

Thus far we have described ARCH and GARCH models as models of returns or of financial time series. In these models, volatility coincides with the magnitude of returns or of some other financial time series. This is because we assume that the series to be modeled is proportional to a zero-mean i.i.d. sequence as given by equation (11.5).

However, in many applications this is not the case. In fact, ARCH/GARCH models might describe the behavior of the errors of some more fundamental model of the conditional mean. In this case, volatility represents the magnitude of unpredictable residuals. In other words, we first model the conditional mean and then we model residuals as ARCH/GARCH models. Note that because we are dealing with weakly stationary processes, both the unconditional mean and the unconditional volatility are constants.

For example, we might represent the returns of stocks with some factor model where returns are regressed over a number of predictors. In this case, forecasts of returns conditional to the predictors are obtained through the primary regressions over the factors; volatility is the magnitude of fluctuations of the residuals of the factor model. The ARCH/GARCH model applies to the residuals from previous modeling of the conditional mean. The model would be written as follows:

$$R_t = \alpha + \beta f_t + u_t \tag{11.11}$$

$$u_t = \sigma_t \varepsilon_t + d \tag{11.12}$$

$$\sigma_t^2 = c + a_1 u_{t-1}^2 + \cdots + a_p u_{t-p}^2 + b_1 \sigma_{t-1}^2 + \cdots + b_q \sigma_{t-q}^2 \tag{11.13}$$

In this model, returns are determined by equation (11.11) in function of factors. A GARCH model then describes the residuals u_t. That is, we first write a model of conditional mean as a regression of returns on a number of factors, given by the equation (11.11). The residuals of this model, which represent the unpredictable component, do not have a constant variance but are subject to GARCH modeling.

UNIVARIATE EXTENSIONS OF GARCH MODELING

The principle of GARCH modeling consists of making residuals (or economic variables) proportional to a volatility process that is modeled separately. Subsequent to the initial introduction of GARCH models, many

TABLE 11.1 Univariate Extensions of GARCH Models

Model	About the Model
Normal GARCH (NGARCH) Also called nonlinear GARCH	Introduced by Engle and Ng,[a] is a non linear asymmetric GARCH specification where negative and positive returns have different effects on future volatility.
Exponential GARCH (EGARCH)	Introduced by Nelson,[b] models the logarithm of the conditional variance. It addresses the same leverage effect as the NGARCH; that is, a negative return affects volatility more than a positive return.
GJR-GARCH/ Threshold GARCH (TGARCH)	The GARCH model by Glosten, Jagannathan, and Runkle (and bearing their initials)[c] and by Zakoian,[d] models the asymmetries in the effects of positive and negative returns.
Integrated GARCH (IGARCH)	A specification of GARCH models in which conditional variance behaves like a random walk and in which shocks to the variance are therefore permanent.[e]

[a] Robert Engle and Victor K. Ng, "Measuring and Testing the Impact of News on Volatility," *Journal of Finance* 48 (1993): 1749–78.
[b] Daniel B. Nelson, "Conditional Heteroscedasticity in Asset Returns: A New Approach," *Econometrica* 59 (1991): 347–70.
[c] Lawrence R. Glosten, Ravi Jagannathan, and David E. Runkle, "On the Relation between the Expected Value and the Volatility of the Nominal Excess Return on Stocks," *Journal of Finance* 48 (1993): 1779–1801.
[d] Jean-Michele Zakoian, "Threshold Heteroscedastic Models," *Journal of Economic Dynamics and Control* 18 (1994): 931–55.
[e] Robert F. Engle and Tim Bollerslev, "Modeling the Persistence of Conditional Variances," *Econometric Reviews* 5 (1986): 1–50.

similar models have been proposed. Table 11.1 lists some of the most common variants of GARCH models and their general properties.

The first three models shown in Table 11.1 address the *leverage effect*—initially identified by Fischer Black—by which negative returns have a larger impact on volatility than positive returns.[8] This asymmetric impact of returns on volatility has been subsequently confirmed in many studies.

These variants use various nonlinear specifications of the GARCH model. In the classical GARCH model, equation (11.9) shows that the squared

---

[8] Fischer Black,"Studies of Stock Price Volatility Changes," in *Proceedings of the 1976 American Statistical Association*, Business and Economical Statistics Section (1976), 177–181.

TABLE 11.2 Prediction of Monthly Volatility Using GARCH, EGARCH, and GJR-GARCH Models for Oracle Corporation, Coca Cola Corporations, and Caterpillar, Monday, December 17, 2012

	Model GARCH	Model EGARCH	Model GJR-GARCH
ORACLE Corp			
Average volatility (1 Month)	19.56%	18.49%	20.60%
1-day forecast	19.18%	18.80%	20.42%
Coca Cola Corp			
Average volatility (1 Month)	13.66%	15.03%	15.16%
1-day forecast	14.87%	14.04%	14.05%
Caterpillar			
Average volatility (1 Month)	25.33%	26.60%	26.23%
1-day forecast	23.89%	24.23%	24.62%

Predictions are from the site of V-Lab at Stern University The V-Lab site can be accessed at: http://vlab.stern.nyu.edu/analysis/VOL.KO:US-R.EGARCH

volatility at time t is a weighted average of past squared volatilities and past squared returns. Note that the square is a symmetric function while we have just remarked on asymmetric impact of returns on volatility. Therefore, the first three models in Table 11.1 replace the square with nonlinear asymmetric functions that give more weight to negative returns than to positive returns. Thus, returns at time $t - 1$ produce larger volatility at time t if they are negative than if they are positive even if their absolute value is the same.

In all models described thus far, volatility is mean reverting to a long-term value. However, for some financial time series this property might not be applicable. In these cases, one might use the IGARCH model, which makes volatility shocks persistent.

How different are volatility predictions in different GARCH models? To gain an understanding of the differences, let's look at the predictions on Monday, December 17, 2012, for one-month average volatility and one-day return volatility for the return on the stock of Oracle Corporation, Coca Cola Corporations, and Caterpillar using the standard GARCH model, EGARCH model, and GJR-GARCH model. The estimated volatilities are shown in Table 11.2. The predictions for the three models reported in the table were obtained from the Web site of V-Lab at Stern School of Business of New York University.[9]

---

[9] We thank V-Lab for letting us show their predictions. The V-Lab site can be accessed at http://vlab.stern.nyu.edu/analysis/VOL.KO:US-R.EGARCH.

ESTIMATES OF ARCH/GARCH MODELS

ARCH/GARCH models can be estimated with the maximum likelihood estimation (MLE) method described in Chapter 13. To illustrate, consider the MLE method applied to the simplest ARCH(1) model described in equations (11.1) and (11.2). The MLE method seeks the values of the model's parameters that maximize the probability computed on the data (likelihood).

It is convenient to condition on the first observation and compute the conditional likelihood given the first observation. The assumptions of the ARCH(1) model imply that each return has the following normal conditional distribution:

$$f(R_t|R_{t-1},\ldots,R_0) = \frac{1}{\sqrt{2\pi}\sigma_t}\exp\left(-\frac{R_t^2}{2\sigma_t^2}\right)$$

If the ARCH model is correctly specified, all these conditional probabilities are mutually independent and therefore the likelihood is simply the product of the likelihoods:

$$L = \prod_{t=1}^{T}\frac{1}{\sqrt{2\pi}\sigma_t}\exp\left(-\frac{R_t^2}{2\sigma_t^2}\right)$$

And the log-likelihood is

$$\log L = -\frac{T}{2}\log(2\pi) - \sum_{t=1}^{T}\log(\sigma_t) - \sum_{t=1}^{T}\frac{1}{2}\frac{R_t^2}{\sigma_t^2} \tag{11.14}$$

This expression contains the variable σ_t, which can be recovered for every t from equation (11.2):

$$\sigma_t = \sqrt{c + a_1 R_{t-1}^2}$$

We have therefore the expression of the log-likelihood in function of the parameters c, a_1. These parameters can be determined as those values that maximize the log-likelihood. Maximization is performed with numerical methods.

In practice, estimation is performed by most standard econometric packages such as E-Views and by software such as MATLAB. The user needs only to input the time series of residuals, the specification of the model (i.e., ARCH, GARCH, E-GARCH, or the other models described in this chapter), and the number of lags and the software performs the estimation and the volatility forecasts.

APPLICATION OF GARCH MODELS TO OPTION PRICING

An option is a derivative instrument that grants the buyer of the option the right to buy (call) or sell (put) the underlying at the strike price at or before the option expiration date. Options are called European options if they can be exercised only at the expiration date, American options if they can be exercised at any time. The most well-known model for pricing European options is the Black-Scholes model.[10] In this model, the return distribution is assumed to be a normal distribution and the price of a European call and put option is given by a closed form that depends on only one unknown parameter: the variance of the return. The assumption of the Black-Scholes model is that the volatility is constant.

Instead of assuming a constant volatility (as in the case of the Black-Scholes model) what has been proposed in the literature is the use of either a stochastic volatility model or a GARCH model. Stochastic volatility models were first proposed by Hull and White.[11] The approach using a GARCH model has been proposed in a number of studies.[12]

As we have seen, standard GARCH models assume residuals are normally distributed. When fitting GARCH models to a return series, it is often found that the residuals tend to be heavy tailed. One reason is that the normal distribution is insufficient to describe the residual of return distributions. In general, the skewness and leptokurtosis observed for financial data cannot be captured by a GARCH model assuming residuals are normally distributed. To allow for particularly heavy-tailed conditional (and unconditional) return distributions, GARCH processes with non normal distribution have been considered.[13] Although asset

---

[10] Fischer Black and Myron Scholes, "The Pricing of Options and Corporate Liabilities," *Journal of Political Economy* 81 (1973): 637–659.
[11] John Hull and Alan White, "The Pricing of Options on Assets with Stochastic Volatilities," *Journal of Finance* 42 (1987): 281–300.
[12] See, for example, Jaesun Noh, Robert F. Engle, and Alex Kane, "Forecasting Volatility and Option Prices of the S&P 500 Index," *Journal of Derivatives* 2, no. 1 (1994): 17–30; Jan Kallsen and Murad S. Taqqu, "Option Pricing in ARCH-Type Models," *Mathematical Finance* 8 (1998): 13–26; Christian M. Hafner and Helmut Herwartz, "Option Pricing under Linear Autoregressive Dynamics Heteroscedasticity and Conditional Leptokurtosis," *Journal of Empirical Finance* 8 (2001): 1–34; Christian M. Hafner and Arle Preminger, "Deciding between GARCH and Stochastic Volatility Using Strong Decision Rules," *Journal of Statistical Planning and Inference* 140 (2010): 791–805; and Jeroen Rombouts and Lars Stentoft, "Multivariate Option Pricing with Time Varying Volatility and Correlations," *Journal of Banking and Finance* 35 (2011): 2267–2281.
[13] Stefan Mittnik, Marc S. Paolella, and Svetlozar T. Rachev, "Unconditional and Conditional Distributional Models for the Nikkei Index," *Asia-Pacific Financial Markets* 5, no. 2 (1998): 99–128.

return distributions are known to be conditionally leptokurtotic, only a few studies have investigated the option pricing problem with GARCH dynamics and non-Gaussian innovations using alternative assumptions about the residuals.[14]

MULTIVARIATE EXTENSIONS OF ARCH/GARCH MODELING

Thus far we have applied ARCH and GARCH models to univariate time series. Let's now consider multivariate time series, for example the returns of an ensemble of stocks or of stock indexes.

Let's assume that returns are normally distributed. Although a univariate normal distribution is completely characterized by two parameters—a mean and a variance—a multivariate normal is characterized by a vector of means and by a matrix of covariances.

Empirical studies of time series of stock returns find that the conditional covariance matrix is time-varying. Not only is the variance of each individual return time-varying, the strength of correlations between stock returns also time-varying. For example, Figure 11.9 illustrates the time-varying nature of correlations of the S&P 500 universe. We computed correlations between daily returns of stocks that belong to the S&P 500 universe over a 100-day moving window from May 25, 1989, to December 30, 2011. Between these dates there are 5,699 trading days. As correlations are symmetrical in the sense that correlation between returns of stocks A and B is the same as correlations between returns of stocks B and A, for each trading day there are $500 \times 499/2 = 12,4750$ correlations. We average all these correlations to obtain an average daily correlation C.

Figure 11.9 illustrates that correlations are not time constant. Average correlation ranges from a minimum of 0.1 to a maximum of 0.7 and exhibits an upward trend. In addition there are periodic fluctuations around the trend. These facts suggest modeling the covariance matrix with ARCH/GARCH-like models.

---

[14] See Christian Menn and Svetlozar T. Rachev, "Smoothly Truncated Stable Distributions, GARCH-Models, and Option Pricing," *Mathematical Methods of Operations Research* 63, no. 3 (2009): 411–438; Peter Christoffersen, Redouane Elkamhi, Bruno Feunou, and Kris Jacobs, "Option Valuation with Conditional Heteroscedasticity and Nonnormality," *Review of Financial Studies* 23 (2010): 2139–2183; and Young-Shin Kim, Svetlozar T. Rachev, Michele Bianchi, and Frank J. Fabozzi, "Tempered Stable and Tempered Infinitely Divisible GARCH Models," *Journal of Banking and Finance* 34, no. 9 (2010): 2096–2109.

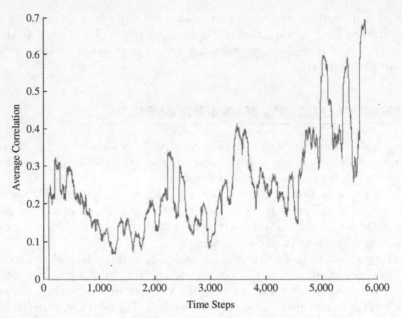

FIGURE 11.9   Plot of Average Correlations between Stocks in the S&P 500 Universe in the Period from May 25, 1989, to December 30, 2011

It is possible to define theoretically a multivariate ARCH/GARCH model called the *VEC-GARCH model*.[15] The model replaces the volatility parameter with the covariance matrix and models the covariance matrix. The problem is that in a multivariate GARCH model each individual element of the covariance matrix is regressed over every other element and every other product between past returns. To see this, consider a simple bivariate return process:

$$R_{1,t} = \varepsilon_{1t}$$
$$R_{2,t} = \varepsilon_{2t}$$

---

[15] The VEC model in the ARCH framework was proposed in Robert F. Engle, Clive Granger, and Dennis Kraft, "Combining Competing Forecasts of Inflation Using a Bivariate ARCH Model," *Journal of Economic Dynamics and Control* 8 (1984): 151–165; and Dennis Kraft and Robert F. Engle, "Autoregressive Conditional Heteroscedasticity in Multiple Times Series," (Unpublished manuscript, Department of Economics, University of California, San Diego, 1983). The first GARCH version was proposed in Tim Bollerslev, Robert F. Engle, and Jeffrey M. Wooldridge, "A Capital Asset Pricing Model with Time-Varying Covariances," *Journal of Political Economy* 96 (1998): 116–131.

The form of the process is similar to the univariate ARCH in equation (11.1) but the two residuals $\varepsilon_{1t}, \varepsilon_{2t}$ are now characterized by different variances $\sigma_{1t}^2, \sigma_{2t}^2$ plus a covariance term σ_{12t}. Analogous to the univariate ARCH, we assume that variances and covariances are time-dependent autoregressive processes. But in this case every term depends on all lagged squared returns and all products of lagged returns. For example, for one lag we can write:

$$\sigma_{1t}^2 = c_1 + a_{11}R_{1,t-1}^2 + a_{12}R_{1,t-1}R_{2,t-1} + a_{13}R_{2,t-1}^2$$

$$\sigma_{12t} = c_2 + a_{21}R_{1,t-1}^2 + a_{22}R_{1,t-1}R_{2,t-1} + a_{23}R_{2,t-1}^2 \qquad (11.15)$$

$$\sigma_{2t}^2 = c_3 + a_{31}R_{1,t-1}^2 + a_{32}R_{1,t-1}R_{2,t-1} + a_{33}R_{2,t-1}^2$$

Hence, the simplest bivariate ARCH model with one lag implies estimating 12 parameters. For three time series and one lag it is necessary to estimate 42 parameters. Clearly the number of parameters to estimate becomes prohibitive for any except bivariate processes.

In practice, the number of parameters to estimate is too large to allow models to be estimated with samples of the size available in financial time series, implying that the VEC model can be used only in the case of two series. Therefore simplifications are needed. Several simplifying approaches have been proposed.[16] A popular approach proposed by Bollerslev assumes that conditional correlations are constant and models the variance of each series with a GARCH model.[17] With this approach, we need to estimate a constant correlation matrix plus the GARCH parameters for each series.

KEY POINTS

- Variance is a measure of volatility. Because in many financial applications variance is commonly used as a proxy measure for risk, an important application of financial econometrics is the forecasting of the variance.

---

[16] Other approaches are described in Luc Bauwens, Sébastien Laurent, and Jeroen V. K. Rombouts, "Multivariate GARCH Models: A Survey," *Journal of Applied Econometrics* 21 (2006): 79–109; and Robert F. Engle, Sergio M. Focardi, and Frank J. Fabozzi, "ARCH/GARCH Models in Applied Financial Econometrics," in *Handbook of Finance,* ed. Frank J. Fabozzi, vol. 3 (Hoboken, NJ: John Wiley & Sons, 2008): 689–700.

[17] Tim Bollerslev, "Modeling the Coherence in Short-Run Nominal Exchange Rates: A Multivariate Generalized ARCH Approach," *Review of Economics and Statistics* 72 (1990): 498–505.

- The simplest approach for measuring historical volatility involves calculating the variance from a sample of prices or returns observed over a recent short-time period.
- Historical volatility can be computed by assigning an equal weight to each observation or assigning different weights such that more recent observations are given a greater weight than more distant observations.
- The drawback of using historical volatility as a forecast of future volatility is that it is based on the assumption that volatility will remain unchanged in the future from what it was during the sample time period used to calculate the variance.
- The approach commonly used in financial econometrics for predicting future volatility is to impose a structure on the conditional variance based on stylized facts observed about the variance in the market: (1) volatility tends to be time varying and (2) volatility exhibits clustering.
- A time series is called conditionally heteroscedastic if its variance can be predicted based on past values of the series.
- The autoregressive conditional heteroscedasticity (ARCH) model predicts the conditional variance as a linear combination of past squared returns.
- The generalized autoregressive conditional heteroscedasticity (GARCH) model extends ARCH to include past squared returns and past variances.
- Several extensions of ARCH/GARCH models have been proposed, in particular to account for asymmetries in the effect of positive and negative returns on future variance.
- Multivariate extensions of ARCH/GARCH models have been proposed but drastic simplifications are needed to reduce the number of parameters of the model that must be estimated.

CHAPTER 12

Factor Analysis and Principal Components Analysis

After reading this chapter you will understand:

- What factor analysis is.
- What a factor model is.
- How a factor model might or might not be the result of factor analysis.
- The difference between a factor model and a multiple regression.
- How to estimate the parameters of a factor model.
- How to estimate factor scores.
- What principal components analysis is.
- How to construct principal components.
- The difference between a factor model and principal components analysis.

In this chapter we describe factor models and principal components analysis (PCA). Both techniques are used to "simplify" complex data sets composed of multiple time series as a function of a smaller number of time series. Factor models and PCA find many applications in portfolio management, risk management, performance measurement, corporate finance, and many other areas of financial analytics.

In Chapter 3 we described multiple regression analysis, a statistical model that assumes a simple linear relationship between an observed dependent variable and one or more explanatory variables. Although factor models and PCA share many similarities with linear regression analysis, there are also significant differences. In this chapter, we will distinguish between linear regressions, factor models, factor analysis, and PCA. We begin with a review of the fundamental properties and assumptions about linear regressions.

ASSUMPTIONS OF LINEAR REGRESSION

First recall from Chapter 3 that all variables in a linear regression are observable. In general, the explanatory variables, denoted by x_i, are assumed to be either deterministic or random variables while the dependent variable, denoted by y, is assumed to be a random variable. This implies that the observed values of the explanatory variables x_i are assumed to be the true values of the variables while the dependent variable y is only known with some error.

Note that assuming that regressors are random variables is not the same as assuming that there are errors in the regressors. Assuming random regressors simply means assuming that the sample regressors data are not fixed but can change with a given distribution. This fact leaves estimation techniques unchanged but impacts the accuracy of estimates. Regression models with errors in the regressors cannot be handled with the same estimation techniques as models without errors.

A fundamental assumption of linear regression analysis is that the residuals, denoted by ε, carry no information: residuals are assumed to be independent draws from the same distribution. A critical assumption is that residuals and regressors are uncorrelated. Under this assumption, the same methods can be used to estimate deterministic or random regressors.

The estimation framework for linear regression assumes that we have a sample formed by S observations y_s, $s = 1, \ldots, S$ of the scalar dependent variable y and by S observations $[x_{1i}, \ldots, x_{pi}]'$, $i = 1, \ldots, S$ of the p-vector of explanatory variables $[x_1, \ldots, x_p]'$. The regression equation is:

$$y = a + b_1 x_1 + \cdots b_p x_p + \varepsilon$$

Linear regression does not place constraints on the number of observations that are required. Estimation follows the usual rules of statistics according to which we make better estimates if we have larger samples. As we will see later in this chapter, some factor models can be defined only in the limit of infinite samples.

We can look at a regression equation as a static relationship between variables without any temporal ordering involved. For example, suppose we want to investigate whether there is a relationship between the earnings of a firm as the dependent variable, and its level of capitalization and debt as independent variables. We collect observations of earnings, capitalization, and debt of N firms and estimate a regression. There is no temporal order involved in our observations.

However, in many financial applications there is a temporal ordering of observations. Suppose we have a sample formed by T observations

y_t, $t = 1, \ldots$, T of the scalar dependent variable and by T observations $[x_{1t}, \ldots, x_{pt}]'$, $t = 1, \ldots, T$ of the p-vector of independent variables indexed by time. As explained in Chapter 5, variables indexed by time are called *time series*. In this setting, a linear regression is a relationship between time series. For example, if we want to investigate whether there is a linear relationship between the returns RI_t of a stock index I, the rate of inflation IN_t, and the economic growth rate GR_t, we might write a linear regression equation as follows:

$$RI_t = \alpha_0 + \alpha_1 IN_t + \alpha_2 GR_t + \varepsilon_t$$

The theory of regression can be generalized to multiple regressions formed by N regression equations with the same regressors and with error terms that are serially uncorrelated but can be cross correlated

$$y_i = a + b_{i1}x_1 + \cdots b_{ip}x_p + \varepsilon_i, \quad i = 1, \ldots, N \qquad (12.1)$$

Assuming that all the error terms are uncorrelated with the regressors and that no equation is a linear combination of the others, it can be demonstrated that the usual ordinary least squares (OLS) estimators are efficient estimators of the equations given by (12.1).

BASIC CONCEPTS OF FACTOR MODELS

Suppose now that instead of the full set of dependent and independent variables y_t, $x_{1t}, \ldots$, x_{qt} we are given only a multivariate time series $y_t = (y_{1t}, \ldots, y_{Nt})'$. For example, suppose we are given a set of stock returns. The question that leads to *factor analysis* (the process of estimating factor models) and to factor models is whether the structure of the data, in particular the correlation structure of the data, can be simplified. With factor analysis we try to understand if and how we can explain our variables as a multiple linear regression on a reduced number of independent variables. We will start by defining factor models and factor analysis and then look at some other ways of creating factor models.

Linear factor models assume that the observed variables y_t can be represented as a multiple linear regression on a number q of *unobserved*, or *hidden variables* f_{it}, $i = 1, \ldots, q$ called *factors*.

We can write a factor model in various forms. Here are three common forms for representing a factor model.

Explicit form. We can write a factor model explicitly as a set of N equations:

$$y_{1t} = a_1 + b_{11}f_{1t} + \cdots + b_{1q}f_{qt} + \varepsilon_{1t}$$
$$\vdots$$
$$y_{it} = a_i + b_{i1}f_{1t} + \cdots + b_{iq}f_{qt} + \varepsilon_{it} \quad i = 1,\ldots,N, t = 1,\ldots,T \qquad (12.2)$$
$$\vdots$$
$$y_{Nt} = a_N + b_{N1}f_{1t} + \cdots + b_{Nq}f_{qt} + \varepsilon_{Nt}$$

The a_i are the constant terms, the coefficients b_{jt} are called *factor loadings*, the f_{jt} are the hidden factors, and the ε_{it} are the error terms or the residuals.

Vector form. We can write a factor model more compactly in vector form as follows:

$$y_t = a + Bf_t + \varepsilon_t, \quad t = 1,\ldots,T \qquad (12.3)$$

where $y_t = \begin{bmatrix} y_{1t} \cdots y_{Nt} \end{bmatrix}'$ is the $N \times 1$ vector of observed variables at time t

         $a = \begin{bmatrix} a_1 \cdots a_N \end{bmatrix}'$ is the $N \times 1$ vector of constant terms

         $f_t = \begin{bmatrix} f_{1t} \cdots f_{qt} \end{bmatrix}'$ is the $q \times 1$ vector of factors at time t

$$B = \begin{bmatrix} b_{11} & \cdots & b_{1q} \\ \vdots & \ddots & \vdots \\ b_{N1} & \cdots & b_{Nq} \end{bmatrix} \text{ is the } N \times q \text{ matrix of factor loadings}$$

and $\varepsilon_t = \begin{bmatrix} \varepsilon_{1t} \cdots \varepsilon_{Nt} \end{bmatrix}'$ is the $N \times 1$ vector of residuals

Matrix form. Equations (12.2) and (12.3) represent a factor model in terms of variables. However, we can also represent a factor model in terms of realizations of sample data in the following matrix form which is analogous to the matrix form of regression, equation (12.2):

$$Y = FC + E \qquad (12.4)$$

where

$$
Y = \begin{bmatrix} y_{11} & \cdots & y_{N1} \\ \vdots & \cdots & \vdots \\ y_{1t} & \ddots & y_{Nt} \\ \vdots & \cdots & \vdots \\ y_{1T} & \cdots & y_{NT} \end{bmatrix}
$$

is the matrix of the data, in which every row corresponds to an observation of all N variables, and each column corresponds to all T observations of each variable; and where

$$
F = \begin{bmatrix} 1 & f_{11} & \cdots & f_{q1} \\ \vdots & \vdots & \cdots & \vdots \\ 1 & f_{1t} & \ddots & f_{qt} \\ \vdots & \vdots & \cdots & \vdots \\ 1 & f_{1T} & \cdots & f_{qT} \end{bmatrix}
$$

is the matrix of factors where we add a column of ones to include the constant terms a (note that the terms of this matrix are not observable)

$$
C = \begin{bmatrix} a_1 & \cdots & a_N \\ b_{11} & \cdots & b_{N1} \\ \vdots & \ddots & \vdots \\ b_{1q} & \cdots & b_{Nq} \end{bmatrix}
$$

is the matrix of factor loadings plus the terms a in the first row.

$$
E = \begin{bmatrix} \varepsilon_{11} & \cdots & \varepsilon_{N1} \\ \vdots & \cdots & \vdots \\ \varepsilon_{1t} & \ddots & \varepsilon_{Nt} \\ \vdots & \cdots & \vdots \\ \varepsilon_{1T} & \cdots & \varepsilon_{NT} \end{bmatrix}
$$

is the matrix of error terms, which are not observable.

Alternatively, we could subtract the mean from the data and write factor models in terms of *de-meaned data* $x_t = y_t - \mu$ where μ is the mean of y. In this case, the constant terms a_i are all equal to zero.

In terms of de-meaned data x_t, the factor model in vector form, equation (12.3), becomes

$$x_t = Bf_t + \varepsilon_t, \ t = 1, \ldots, T \tag{12.5}$$

The vector model written in matrix form, equation (12.4), $Y = FB + E$ becomes:

$$X = FB' + E \tag{12.6}$$

where

$$X = \begin{bmatrix} x_{11} & \cdots & x_{N1} \\ \vdots & \cdots & \vdots \\ x_{t1} & \ddots & x_{Nt} \\ \vdots & \cdots & \vdots \\ x_{T1} & \cdots & x_{NT} \end{bmatrix}$$

is the matrix of demeaned data;

$$F = \begin{bmatrix} f_{11} & \cdots & f_{q1} \\ \vdots & \cdots & \vdots \\ f_{1t} & \ddots & f_{qt} \\ \vdots & \cdots & \vdots \\ f_{1T} & \cdots & f_{qT} \end{bmatrix}$$

is the matrix of factors without a column of ones.

ASSUMPTIONS AND CATEGORIZATION OF FACTOR MODELS

As is the case with a linear regression, specific assumptions about factors and error terms need to be made, otherwise factor models are void of empirical content. We will define different categories of factor models, but common to all factor models are the following two assumptions:

1. Both factors and residuals are zero-mean variables
2. Residuals are uncorrelated with factors, that is:

$$E(f_t) = 0, \ E(\varepsilon_{t'}) = 0, \ E(f_t{}'\varepsilon_{t'}) = 0 \text{ for any } t \tag{12.7}$$

A factor model is called a *strict factor model* if the residuals are uncorrelated; that is, if the covariance matrix of the residuals is a diagonal matrix.[1] A factor model is called a *scalar factor model* if, in addition, all variances of residuals are identical.

Strict and scalar factor models with a finite number of samples and time series are called *classical factor models*. Later in this chapter we will define a different type of factor models called *approximate factor models*.

SIMILARITIES AND DIFFERENCES BETWEEN FACTOR MODELS AND LINEAR REGRESSION

Factor models have the same form as a multiple linear regression. However, there are two major differences between factor models and multiple regressions:

Difference 1. Factors are *unobserved* variables, determined by the data, while in multiple regressions regressors are given *observed* variables.

Difference 2. Although in both multiple regressions and factor models the error terms are assumed to be serially uncorrelated, residuals of multiple regressions can be mutually correlated while residuals of strict factor models are assumed to be uncorrelated.

To understand the difference between the two models, consider the monthly returns of the 500 stocks comprising the S&P 500 index over the past 30 years. A factor model would try to reveal if the monthly returns of these 500 stocks can be explained in terms of a smaller number of hidden factors, say two. In this case, both the model parameters and the factors have to be estimated from the monthly return series for the 500 stocks. Now suppose that the objective is to try to see if there is a linear relationship

---

[1] For an explanation of the different types of matrices, see Appendix D.

between the monthly returns series for the 500 stocks and some macroeconomic variables such as the change in gross domestic product, the rate of inflation, and the yield spread between high-grade and low-grade corporate bonds. This is a multiple regression.

PROPERTIES OF FACTOR MODELS

Let's now discuss some properties of factor models. Consider a factor model as defined in equation (12.3) with the assumptions given by equation (12.7). We will adopt the following notation:

1. Ω denotes the covariance matrix of factors, $\Omega = \text{cov}(f_t) = E(f_t f_t')$.
2. $\Sigma = E((y_t - a)(y_t - a)')$ denotes the covariance matrix of the observed variables.
3. $\Psi = E(\varepsilon_t \varepsilon_t')$ denotes the covariance matrix of the residuals.

The three covariance matrices of factors, observed variables, and residuals are supposed to be constant matrices, independent of t. From the definition of covariance we can write:

$$\Sigma = E((y_t - a)(y_t - a)') = E((Bf_t)(Bf_t)') + 2E(f_t'\varepsilon_t) + E(\varepsilon_t'\varepsilon_t)$$

Because we assume that factors and residuals are uncorrelated (i.e., $E(f_t'\varepsilon_t) = 0$), we can write:

$$\Sigma = B\Omega B' + \Psi \qquad (12.8)$$

Equation (12.8) is the fundamental relationship that links the covariance matrix of the observed variables to the covariance matrices of factors and residuals. It is sometimes referred to as the *fundamental theorem of factor models*.

From equation (12.3) we can see that a factor model is not identified. This means that observed variables do not univocally determine factors and model parameters. To see this, consider any nonsingular $q \times q$ matrix T. From matrix algebra we know that a nonsingular matrix T is a matrix that admits an inverse matrix T^{-1} such that $T^{-1}T = I$. Given that multiplication by the identity matrix leaves any matrix unchanged and given that matrix multiplication is associative, we can write

$$y_t = a + Bf_t + \varepsilon_t = a + BIf_t + \varepsilon_t = a + BT^{-1}Tf_t + \varepsilon_t = a + (BT^{-1})(Tf_t) + \varepsilon_t$$

Hence, given any set of factors f_t, if we multiply them by any nonsingular $q \times q$ matrix T, we obtain a new set of factors $g_t = Tf_t$. If we multiply the

$N \times q$ matrix of factor loadings B by the matrix inverse of T, we obtain a new $N \times q$ loading matrix $L = BT^{-1}$, such that the new factor model

$$y_t = a + Lg_t + \varepsilon_t$$

is observationally equivalent to the original model.

Given any set of factors f_t, we can always find a nonsingular matrix T such that the new factors $g_t = Tf_t$ are uncorrelated and have unit variance; that is, $E(g_t g_t{}') = I$. Uncorrelated factors are often called *orthogonal factors*. Therefore, we can always choose factors such that their covariance matrix is the identity matrix $\Omega = I$ so that equation (12.8) becomes

$$\mathrm{cov}(\Omega) = I, \quad \Sigma = BB' + \Psi \tag{12.9}$$

This is a counterintuitive conclusion. Given a set of observable variables, if they admit a factor representation, we can always choose factors that are mutually uncorrelated variables with unit variance.

In a strict factor model, the correlation structure of observed variables is due uniquely to factors; there is no residual correlation. For a large covariance matrix, this is a significant simplification. For example, in order to estimate the covariance matrix of 500 stock return processes as in the S&P 500 universe, we have to estimate $(500 \times 501)/2 = 125{,}250$ different entries (covariances). However, if we can represent the same return processes with 10 factors, from equation (12.9) we see that we would need to estimate only the $500 \times 10 = 5{,}000$ factor loadings plus 500 diagonal terms of the matrix Ψ.

This is a significant advantage for estimation. For example, if our sample includes four years of daily return data (250 trading days per year or 1,000 observations for four years), we would have approximately $500 \times 1{,}000 = 500{,}000$ individual return data. If we have to estimate the entire covariance matrix we have only $500{,}000/125{,}250 \approx 4$ data per estimated parameter, while in the case of a 10-factor model we have $500{,}000/5{,}500 \approx 90$ data per parameter.

We can now compare the application of regression models and factor models. If we want to apply a multiple regression model we have to make sure that (1) regressors are not collinear and (2) that residuals are serially uncorrelated and uncorrelated with all the observed variables. If we want to apply a multiple regression model, we assume that residuals are serially uncorrelated but we accept that residuals are cross correlated.

However, if we want to investigate the strict factor structure of a set of observed variables, we have to make sure that residuals are not only serially uncorrelated but also mutually uncorrelated. In fact, a strict factor model explains the correlation between variables in terms of regression on a set of common factors. We will see later in this chapter how this requirement can be relaxed.

ESTIMATION OF FACTOR MODELS

After defining the two fundamental classical factor models—that is, strict and scalar factor models—we can now ask three important questions:

1. Given the data, how do we determine the number of factors?
2. Given the data, how do we estimate parameters and factors?
3. Are parameters and factors uniquely determined by our data?

Problem of Factor Indeterminacy

Suppose for a moment we know the number of factors. Can we estimate parameters and factors? The somewhat surprising conclusion is that we can determine the model's parameters but we cannot uniquely determine factors. This is the well-known problem of *factor indeterminacy*.

Historically, factor indeterminacy provoked much debate in the literature on statistics. The reason is that factor models were initially proposed in the area of psychometrics, with factors being the determinant of personality. Based on factor analysis, psychologists claimed that personality can be explained almost deterministically in terms of a number of basic factors. The discovery of factor indeterminacy weakened this proposition.

Finite and Infinite Factor Models   In practice, every quantity we deal with in our personal and professional lives is finite, that is, it can be measured with an ordinary number. For example, the universe of potential stocks from which a portfolio can be constructed consists of a finite number of stocks. The number of candidate stocks can be very large, say in the range of thousands, but still it is finite. The number of dates, or even instants of trading, is finite.

However, many mathematical properties can be better stated in the limit of an infinite number of time series or an infinite number of dates and time points. Mathematicians distinguish many different types of infinity, and many different types of infinite processes. We cannot go into the details of the mathematics of infinite quantities. However, the intuition behind infinite numbers can be stated as follows. To be concrete, let's define what is meant by an infinite market formed by infinitely many stock return processes.

Essentially an *infinite market* means that whatever large number we choose, as large as we want, the market will have more stocks. A market is infinite if no ordinary number, regardless of how big we choose it, will be able to count the market. The same concept can be applied to the concept of an infinitely long time series: whatever number we choose, the series will have more points.

Obviously this is a mathematical abstraction because no real market is infinite. However, it is a useful abstraction because it simplifies the statement of many properties. In practice, we use the concept of both infinite markets and infinite factor models to approximate the behavior of very large markets. If a market is very large, say, thousands of stocks, we assume that its properties can be well approximated by the properties of the abstract infinite market. We will see in the following sections a number of properties that apply to infinite markets.

Estimating the Number of Factors

There are several criteria for determining the number of factors but there is no rigorous method that allows one to identify the number of factors of classical factor models. Rigorous criteria exist in the limit of an infinite number of series formed by an infinite number of time points.

For finite models, a widely used criterion is the Cattell scree plot, which can be described as follows. In general, there are as many eigenvalues as stocks. Therefore, we can make a plot of these eigenvalues in descending order. An example is in Table 12.1. In general, we empirically observe that the plot of eigenvalues exhibits an elbow, that is, it goes down rapidly, but it slows down at a certain point. Heuristically, we can assume there are as many factors as eigenvalues to the right of the elbow, assuming eigenvalues grow from left to right. However, the scree plot is a heuristic criterion, not a formal criterion. The Akaike information criterion and the Bayesian information criterion are also used, especially to determine the number of factors for large models. We describe these two information criteria in Appendix E.

Estimating the Model's Parameters

Let's start by estimating the model's parameters. The usual estimation method for factor models is *maximum likelihood estimation* (MLE) which we explain in Chapter 13. However, MLE requires that we know, or that we make an assumption on the probability distribution of the observed variables. We will therefore make the additional assumption that variables are normally distributed. Other distributional assumptions can be used but the assumption of normal distribution simplifies calculations.

As explained in Chapter 13, the *likelihood* is defined as the probability distribution computed on the data. MLE seeks those values of the parameters that maximize the likelihood. As we assume that data are normally distributed, the likelihood depends on the covariance matrix. From equation (12.9) we know that $\Sigma = BB' + \Psi$ and we can therefore determine the parameters B, Ψ maximizing the likelihood with respect to these parameters.

TABLE 12.1 A Sample of Stock Daily Returns for the Period December 2, 2011, to December 30, 2011

Dates	ORCL	MSFT	TROW	HON	EMC	FO	LLTC	ADM
02-Dec-2011	−0.01	0.00	0.02	0.00	0.00	0.00	0.00	−0.01
05-Dec-2011	0.02	0.02	0.01	0.01	0.01	0.01	0.02	0.00
06-Dec-2011	−0.01	0.00	0.00	0.00	0.00	0.00	0.00	−0.01
07-Dec-2011	−0.01	0.00	0.03	−0.01	0.00	0.00	0.00	0.00
08-Dec-2011	−0.03	−0.01	−0.04	−0.02	−0.02	−0.01	−0.03	−0.03
09-Dec-2011	0.03	0.01	0.02	0.02	0.01	0.02	0.00	0.01
12-Dec-2011	−0.01	−0.01	−0.02	−0.02	−0.02	−0.02	−0.02	−0.03
13-Dec-2011	−0.02	0.01	−0.02	−0.01	−0.02	−0.02	−0.02	−0.02
14-Dec-2011	−0.03	−0.01	−0.02	−0.01	−0.02	−0.01	−0.02	−0.01
15-Dec-2011	−0.03	0.00	0.00	0.02	0.00	0.00	0.00	0.02
16-Dec-2011	0.01	0.02	0.01	0.01	0.00	−0.01	0.01	−0.01
19-Dec-2011	−0.02	−0.02	−0.01	−0.02	−0.02	−0.01	−0.02	−0.02
20-Dec-2011	0.02	0.02	0.05	0.04	0.02	0.02	0.05	0.04
21-Dec-2011	−0.12	−0.01	0.00	0.00	−0.04	0.01	−0.01	0.01
22-Dec-2011	0.00	0.00	0.00	0.01	0.01	0.00	0.02	0.00
23-Dec-2011	0.01	0.01	0.01	0.01	0.01	0.01	0.01	0.01
27-Dec-2011	−0.02	0.00	0.00	0.00	−0.01	0.01	0.00	0.00
28-Dec-2011	0.00	−0.01	−0.02	−0.02	−0.01	0.00	−0.01	−0.02
29-Dec-2011	0.01	0.01	0.02	0.01	0.01	0.01	0.00	0.01
30-Dec-2011	−0.01	0.00	−0.01	−0.01	0.00	0.00	0.00	0.00

Ticker	Company
ORCL	Oracle Corp.
MSFT	Microsoft Corp
TROW	T. Rowe Price Group
HON	Honeywell International
EMC	EMC/MA
FO	Fortune Brands Inc.
LLTC	Linear Technology Corp
ADM	Archer-Daniels Midland Co.

We can thus estimate the factor loadings and the residual variances under the assumptions that factors are uncorrelated with unitary variances.

While we can estimate the factor loadings and the residuals' variances with MLE methods, we cannot estimate factors with maximum likelihood. There is a fundamental factor indeterminacy so that, in finite models, factors cannot be uniquely determined. The usual solution consists in estimating a set of factor scores. This is done by interpreting equation (12.2) as a regression equation, which allows one to determine factor scores f.

Before proceeding to illustrate other factor models it is useful to illustrate the above with an example. Table 12.1 lists eight series of 20 daily stock returns $R_{ti}, t = 1, \ldots, 20$, $i = 1, \ldots, 8$. The first row reports the stock symbols, the rows that follow give stock daily returns from December 2, 2011, to December 30, 2011.

Let's begin by standardizing the data. The matrix X of *standardized data* is obtained by subtracting the means and dividing by the standard deviations as follows:

$$
\begin{aligned}
\mu_i &= E(R_{ti}) \\
\sigma_i &= \sqrt{E(R_{ti} - \mu)^2} \\
X_{ti} &= \frac{R_{ti} - \mu_i}{\sigma_i} \\
X_i &= [X_{1i} \cdots X_{ti} \cdots X_{Ti}]' \\
X &= [\ X_1 \ \cdots \ X_N \ ] = \{X_{ti}\}
\end{aligned}
\tag{12.10}
$$

The empirical covariance matrix Σ_X of the standardized data, which is the same as the correlation matrix of the original data, is the following 8×8 matrix:

$$
\Sigma_X =
\begin{bmatrix}
1.0000 & 0.6162 & 0.3418 & 0.3991 & 0.8284 & 0.2040 & 0.4461 & 0.1273 \\
0.6162 & 1.0000 & 0.5800 & 0.7651 & 0.6932 & 0.4072 & 0.7145 & 0.5209 \\
0.3418 & 0.5800 & 1.0000 & 0.7925 & 0.6807 & 0.7864 & 0.8715 & 0.8312 \\
0.3991 & 0.7651 & 0.7925 & 1.0000 & 0.7410 & 0.7449 & 0.8656 & 0.8771 \\
0.8284 & 0.6932 & 0.6807 & 0.7410 & 1.0000 & 0.5630 & 0.7577 & 0.5496 \\
0.2040 & 0.4072 & 0.7864 & 0.7449 & 0.5630 & 1.0000 & 0.7480 & 0.8420 \\
0.4461 & 0.7145 & 0.8715 & 0.8656 & 0.7577 & 0.7480 & 1.0000 & 0.7952 \\
0.1273 & 0.5209 & 0.8312 & 0.8771 & 0.5496 & 0.8420 & 0.7952 & 1.0000
\end{bmatrix}
$$

Assume that the standardized data X can be represented with four factors. Hence, we can use equation (12.9) to represent the above covariance matrix as $\Sigma_X = B'B + \Psi$ where B is a 4×8 matrix of factor loadings and Ψ is an 8×8 diagonal matrix of variances. Using the function factoran of MATLAB, we estimate B and Ψ:

$$
B = \begin{bmatrix}
0.7411 & -0.5245 & 0.1871 & -0.1707 \\
0.9035 & -0.0440 & -0.4202 & -0.0107 \\
0.7614 & 0.5634 & 0.2033 & -0.2069 \\
0.8630 & 0.3504 & -0.0092 & 0.2900 \\
0.9215 & -0.1575 & 0.3477 & 0.0137 \\
0.6028 & 0.5476 & 0.2658 & 0.1600 \\
0.8503 & 0.3637 & 0.0898 & -0.0025 \\
0.6616 & 0.6449 & 0.1086 & 0.2814
\end{bmatrix}
$$

$$
\Psi = \begin{bmatrix}
0.1115 & 0 & 0 & 0 & 0 & 0 & 0 & 0 \\
0 & 0.0050 & 0 & 0 & 0 & 0 & 0 & 0 \\
0 & 0 & 0.0188 & 0 & 0 & 0 & 0 & 0 \\
0 & 0 & 0 & 0.0482 & 0 & 0 & 0 & 0 \\
0 & 0 & 0 & 0 & 0.0050 & 0 & 0 & 0 \\
0 & 0 & 0 & 0 & 0 & 0.2405 & 0 & 0 \\
0 & 0 & 0 & 0 & 0 & 0 & 0.1367 & 0 \\
0 & 0 & 0 & 0 & 0 & 0 & 0 & 0.0553
\end{bmatrix}
$$

We can see that

$$
BB' + \Psi = \begin{bmatrix}
1.0000 & 0.6159 & 0.3421 & 0.4046 & 0.8283 & 0.1819 & 0.4566 & 0.1244 \\
0.6159 & 1.0000 & 0.5800 & 0.7651 & 0.6932 & 0.4072 & 0.7145 & 0.5208 \\
0.3421 & 0.5800 & 1.0000 & 0.7926 & 0.6806 & 0.7884 & 0.8710 & 0.8309 \\
0.4046 & 0.7651 & 0.7926 & 1.0000 & 0.7408 & 0.7561 & 0.8597 & 0.8776 \\
0.8283 & 0.6932 & 0.6806 & 0.7408 & 1.0000 & 0.5638 & 0.7574 & 0.5497 \\
0.1819 & 0.4072 & 0.7884 & 0.7561 & 0.5638 & 1.0000 & 0.7352 & 0.8259 \\
0.4566 & 0.7145 & 0.8710 & 0.8597 & 0.7574 & 0.7352 & 1.0000 & 0.8061 \\
0.1244 & 0.5208 & 0.8309 & 0.8776 & 0.5497 & 0.8259 & 0.8061 & 1.0000
\end{bmatrix}
$$

is a good estimate of the covariance matrix of the standardized data. To see this point, in order to make a quantitative evaluation of how well the matrix $B'B + \Psi$ approximates the covariance matrix of the standardized data, we introduce the concept of the *Frobenius norm of a matrix*. Given any matrix $A = \{a_{ij}\}$, the Frobenius norm of A, written as $\|A\|_F$, is the square root of the sum of the squares of the absolute value of its terms:

$$\|A\|_F = \sqrt{\sum_{i,j} |a_{ij}|^2}$$

The Frobenius norm is a measure of the average magnitude of the terms of a matrix.

We can now compute the ratio between the Frobenius norm of the difference $\Sigma_X - (BB' + \Psi)$ and that of Σ_X. We obtain the value

$$\frac{\|\Sigma_X - (BB' + \Psi)\|_F}{\|\Sigma_X\|_F} = 0.0089$$

which shows that the magnitude of the difference $\Sigma_X - (BB' + \Psi)$ is less than 1% of the magnitude of Σ_X itself; hence, it is a good approximation.

Estimation of Factors

Having determined the factor loadings with MLE, we can now estimate the factors. As observed above, factors are not unique and cannot be estimated with MLE methods. The estimated factors are called *factor scores* or simply *scores*. In the literature and in statistical software, estimates of factor scores might be referred to as *predictions* so that estimated factors are called *predicted scores*. There are several methods to estimate factor scores.

The most commonly used method is to look at equation (12.5) as a multiple regression equation with x as regressors. After estimating the matrix B in equation (12.5), we can look at the variables x_t, f_t as variables with a joint normal distribution. Recall that from equation (12.7),

$$E(x_t) = 0$$
$$E(f_t) = 0$$
$$\text{cov}(f_t, \varepsilon_{t'}) = E(f_t' \varepsilon_{t'}) = 0$$

while from equation (12.9),

$$\text{cov}(x_t) = B'B + \Psi$$
$$\text{cov}(f_t) = I$$

and therefore $\text{cov}(x_t, f_t) = \text{cov}(Bf_t + \varepsilon_t, f_t) = B$.

Because $x_t = Bf_t + \varepsilon_t$, the vector $[x_t \ f_t]$ has a normal distribution with mean zero and the following covariance matrix:

$$\text{cov}\left(\begin{bmatrix} x_t \\ f_t \end{bmatrix}\right) = \begin{bmatrix} B'B + \Psi & B' \\ B & I \end{bmatrix}$$

From this it can be demonstrated that an estimate of factor scores is given by

$$\hat{f}_t = B(B'B + \Psi)x_t \tag{12.11}$$

Scores are only an estimate of factors and, in general, do not have the properties of factors; that is, scores do not have unit variance and are not orthogonal. For example, using the MATLAB function factoran, in our illustration, we obtain the following 20×4 matrix estimate of the matrix of scores F:

$$F = \begin{bmatrix}
0.1307 & 0.1885 & 1.1355 & -1.1246 \\
1.3760 & -0.8360 & -0.9245 & -0.2546 \\
-0.0302 & -0.5621 & 0.6448 & -0.0978 \\
0.0744 & 0.6716 & 1.0122 & -2.4148 \\
-1.1057 & -1.5757 & -0.1156 & 0.9868 \\
1.1724 & -0.0423 & 0.1176 & 0.5556 \\
-1.1110 & -0.7784 & -0.3086 & -0.5283 \\
-0.2808 & -0.8173 & -2.3988 & -0.3218 \\
-1.0935 & 0.1184 & -0.5359 & -0.1613 \\
0.2160 & 0.1450 & 0.9409 & 2.5238 \\
0.8722 & -0.4340 & -1.6825 & -0.5003 \\
-1.3746 & 0.1600 & 1.4673 & -0.2178 \\
2.0655 & 1.5356 & 0.1549 & 0.1682 \\
-1.6935 & 3.0525 & -1.3063 & 0.5341 \\
0.4430 & -0.2481 & 0.7989 & 0.5219 \\
0.7366 & 0.0515 & -0.0451 & 0.0660 \\
-0.2023 & 0.3304 & -0.2513 & 0.2079 \\
-0.8073 & -0.8878 & 0.6037 & -0.1950 \\
0.7959 & 0.3830 & 0.1956 & 0.0616 \\
-0.1836 & -0.4548 & 0.4972 & 0.1904
\end{bmatrix}$$

If we compute the covariance matrix of F, we obtain:

$$\Sigma_F = \begin{bmatrix} 0.9975 & 0.0000 & 0.0000 & -0.0000 \\ 0.0000 & 0.9737 & 0.0000 & -0.0000 \\ 0.0000 & 0.0000 & 0.9843 & 0.0000 \\ -0.0000 & -0.0000 & 0.0000 & 0.8548 \end{bmatrix}$$

To summarize, our illustration demonstrates what is done in practice. We started with a matrix of eight series of 20 standardized daily return data series and tried to find a smaller set of four series of factors that explain the data as a multiple regression. To do so, we first determine with MLE, B, and Ψ, and then estimate factors.

Factors are not observed; they are reconstructed from data and are abstract. For example, in the factor model that we have estimated, it would be difficult to interpret factors. We can say that the original returns are exposed to four risk factors but we cannot easily interpret these factors. As we have remarked, we cannot say that our risk factors are unique. We will see later how we can partially modify this proposition.

Other Types of Factor Models

In financial modeling, there are factor models that are not obtained through factor analysis. These models are multiple regressions on specific families of regressors. Widely used regressors include macroeconomic variables, fundamental information on companies such as market capitalization and book-to-value ratio, as well as countries and sectors. In factor models based on countries and sectors, stock return time series are partitioned into countries and/or industrial sectors. The factor loadings are equal to unity if a stock belongs to a country or a sector, zero in all other cases (just as when using categorical variables in regression analysis as explained in Chapter 6) and factor scores are obtained through regressions.

PRINCIPAL COMPONENTS ANALYSIS

Let's now look at *principal components analysis* (PCA). PCA is used to parsimoniously represent data. There are similarities and differences between PCA and factor analysis. The main difference is that PCA is a data-reduction technique: PCA can be applied to any set of data without assuming any statistical model while factor analysis assumes a statistical model for the data. In addition, principal components are linear combinations of the data and therefore are observable while factors are generally non observable variables. There are other differences that will be made clear after describing PCA.

Step-by-Step PCA

The key idea of PCA is to find linear combinations of the data, called *principal components*, that are mutually orthogonal and have maximum variance. The use of the term "orthogonal" requires explanation. Earlier in this chapter we defined orthogonal factors as uncorrelated factors. But in defining PCA we do not, as mentioned, assume a statistical model for the data; principal components are vectors of data without any associated probability distribution. We say that two different principal components are orthogonal if their scalar product as vectors is equal to zero.

Given two vectors $x = [x_1, \ldots, x_N]'$ and $y = [y_1, \ldots, y_N]'$, of the same length N and such that the average of their components is zero, their *scalar product* is defined as:

$$(x', y) = [x_1, \ldots, x_N] \begin{bmatrix} y_1 \\ \vdots \\ y_N \end{bmatrix} = \sum_{i=1}^{N} x_i y_i \qquad (12.12)$$

The reason we want to find principal components that are orthogonal and have maximum variance is that, as will become clearer later in this section, we want to represent data as linear combinations of a small number of principal components. This objective is better reached if principal components are orthogonal and have maximum variance.

Perhaps the simplest way to describe this process is to illustrate it through a step-by-step example using the same data that were used to illustrate factor analysis. Let's therefore consider the standardized data X and its covariance matrix Σ_X in equation (12.9).

Step 1: Compute Eigenvalues and Eigenvectors of the Covariance Matrix of Data In Appendix D we review the basics of matrix algebra. There we explain that the *eigenvalues* and *eigenvectors* of the matrix Σ_X are those vectors V and those numbers λ_i that satisfy the condition $\Sigma_X V_i = \lambda V_i$. In general, an $N \times N$ covariance matrix has N distinct, real-valued eigenvalues and eigenvectors. We can therefore form a matrix V whose columns are the eigenvectors and a diagonal matrix D with the eigenvalues on the main diagonal.

Eigenvalues and eigenvectors are computed using a statistical or mathematical package. Let's compute the eigenvalues and eigenvectors of the matrix Σ_X using the eig function of MATLAB. We obtain the following matrices:

$$V = \begin{bmatrix}
-0.3563 & 0.4623 & -0.1593 & 0.0885 & -0.0951 & -0.3155 & -0.6800 & 0.2347 \\
0.2721 & -0.0733 & -0.1822 & 0.4334 & -0.0359 & 0.7056 & -0.3014 & 0.3311 \\
-0.1703 & -0.2009 & -0.5150 & 0.0241 & 0.6772 & -0.1653 & 0.1890 & 0.3784 \\
-0.6236 & -0.3148 & 0.0961 & -0.3693 & -0.3385 & 0.2945 & 0.0895 & 0.3963 \\
0.5319 & -0.4428 & 0.0909 & -0.3693 & -0.0972 & -0.3284 & -0.3586 & 0.3611 \\
-0.0088 & -0.1331 & 0.0672 & 0.6355 & -0.4031 & -0.4157 & 0.3484 & 0.3422 \\
0.0075 & 0.2697 & 0.7580 & 0.0421 & 0.4326 & 0.0557 & 0.0579 & 0.3966 \\
0.3131 & 0.5957 & -0.2823 & -0.3540 & -0.2395 & 0.0693 & 0.3869 & 0.3610
\end{bmatrix}$$

and

$$D = \begin{bmatrix}
0.0381 & 0 & 0 & 0 & 0 & 0 & 0 & 0 \\
0 & 0.0541 & 0 & 0 & 0 & 0 & 0 & 0 \\
0 & 0 & 0.1131 & 0 & 0 & 0 & 0 & 0 \\
0 & 0 & 0 & 0.1563 & 0 & 0 & 0 & 0 \\
0 & 0 & 0 & 0 & 0.2221 & 0 & 0 & 0 \\
0 & 0 & 0 & 0 & 0 & 0.4529 & 0 & 0 \\
0 & 0 & 0 & 0 & 0 & 0 & 1.3474 & 0 \\
0 & 0 & 0 & 0 & 0 & 0 & 0 & 5.6160
\end{bmatrix}$$

Note that the product VV' is a diagonal matrix with ones on the main diagonal. This means that the eigenvectors are mutually orthogonal vectors; that is, their scalar product is 0 if the vectors are different, with length equal to 1.

Step 2: Construct Principal Components by Multiplying Data by the Eigenvectors   If we multiply the data X by any of the eigenvectors (i.e., any of the columns of the matrix V), we obtain a new time series formed by a linear combination of the data. For example, suppose we multiply the data X by the first eigenvector; we obtain our first principal component (denoted by PC_1):

$$PC_1 = XV_1$$
$$= -X_1 \times 0.3563 + X_2 \times 0.2721 - X_3 \times 0.1703 - X_4 \times 0.6236$$
$$+ X_5 \times 0.5319 - X_6 \times 0.0088 + X_7 \times 0.0075 + X_8 \times 0.3131$$

We can therefore construct a new 20×8 matrix

$$PC = XV \tag{12.13}$$

where each column is the product of the data X and the corresponding eigenvector. The columns of the matrix PC are what we referred to earlier as the principal components. Table 12.2 shows the eight principal components.

Principal components are linear combinations of the original data. Because the original data are a series of stock returns, we can think of principal components as portfolios formed with those same stocks. The values of principal components are therefore the returns of these portfolios.

Step 3: Getting the Data Back Exactly from Principal Components Thus far we have transformed the original time series into a new set of mutually uncorrelated time series are called principal components. We can now ask if and how we can reconstruct data from principal components. Since $VV' = I$, we can write the following:

$$X = XVV' = (XV)V' = PCV' \qquad (12.14)$$

TABLE 12.2 The Set of All Principal Components of the Sample Standardized Data

PC_1	PC_2	PC_3	PC_4	PC_5	PC_6	PC_7	PC_8
0.03	−0.61	−0.25	−0.13	0.48	−0.60	0.09	0.19
0.23	−0.19	0.24	0.67	−0.11	0.39	−1.11	2.28
−0.04	−0.30	0.13	−0.18	0.07	−0.28	−0.51	−0.43
0.31	0.06	−0.49	0.00	1.18	−0.78	0.08	0.27
0.19	−0.20	0.07	−0.05	−0.71	0.04	−0.72	−3.60
−0.27	−0.11	−0.50	0.28	−0.86	−0.33	−0.42	2.82
−0.17	0.32	0.23	−0.17	0.42	0.15	−0.91	−3.10
0.12	0.17	−0.44	−0.04	0.11	1.60	−1.14	−2.23
−0.13	0.14	−0.14	0.21	−0.07	0.08	0.34	−2.41
0.22	0.00	0.10	−1.14	−0.73	0.20	0.86	0.90
−0.28	−0.23	0.17	−0.07	0.46	1.38	−1.21	0.96
−0.36	0.12	−0.10	−0.38	0.11	−1.01	0.30	−2.50
−0.12	0.24	0.28	−0.04	0.30	0.12	0.76	6.03
0.00	−0.11	0.04	0.34	0.11	0.83	4.19	−1.77
0.05	−0.01	0.76	−0.36	0.25	−0.14	−0.16	1.20
0.21	0.40	−0.20	0.11	−0.15	−0.12	−0.24	1.77
−0.06	0.06	0.07	0.54	−0.34	−0.21	0.59	0.06
−0.04	0.06	0.48	0.50	−0.12	−0.83	−0.52	−1.90
−0.13	0.04	−0.50	−0.24	−0.16	−0.03	−0.11	1.98
0.24	0.14	0.07	0.14	−0.22	−0.50	−0.15	−0.48

That is, we can exactly obtain the data multiplying principal components by the transpose of the matrix of eigenvectors. Let's write it down explicitly:

$$X_1 = PC(V')_1 = PC_1V_{11} + PC_2V_{12} + \cdots + PC_8V_{18}$$
$$\vdots$$
$$X_i = PC(V')_i = PC_1V_{i1} + PC_2V_{i2} + \cdots + PC_8V_{i8} \qquad (12.15)$$
$$\vdots$$
$$X_8 = PC(V')_8 = PC_1V_{81} + PC_2V_{82} + \cdots + PC_8V_{88}$$

That is, the ith data time series is a weighted sum of principal components, with the jth weight equal to the ith component of the jth eigenvector. Contrast these weights with those of the representation of PCs in terms of data:

$$PC_1 = X(V)_1 = X_1V_{11} + X_2V_{21} + \cdots + X_8V_{81}$$
$$\vdots$$
$$PC_i = X(V)_i = X_1V_{1i} + X_2V_{2i} + \cdots + X_8V_{8i}$$
$$\vdots$$
$$PC_8 = X(V)_8 = X_1V_{18} + X_2V_{28} + \cdots + X_8V_{88}$$

where the ith principal component is a weighted sum of data, with the jth weight equal to the jth component of the ith eigenvector.

If we compute the variance of each principal component, we obtain the following vector:

$$\text{var} = [0.0381\ 0.0541\ 0.1131\ 0.1563\ 0.2221\ 0.4529\ 1.3474\ 5.6160]' \quad (12.16)$$

We can immediately see that the variance of each principal component is equal to the corresponding eigenvalue: $\text{var}(PC_i) = D_{ii} = \lambda_i$. This is a general property: *variance of a principal component is equal to the corresponding eigenvalue of the covariance matrix of data.*

Step 4: Look at the Decay of the Variances of Principal Components The magnitude of the variances of principal components differs greatly across different principal components. The smallest variance, corresponding to $PC1$, is 0.0381 while the largest, corresponding to $PC8$, is 5.6. Panels A and B of Figure 12.1 show the plots of the first and last principal components and a plot of the eigenvalues.

We now understand why it is important that principal components be orthogonal vectors. Because principal components are orthogonal vectors,

A. Value of First and Last Principal Components

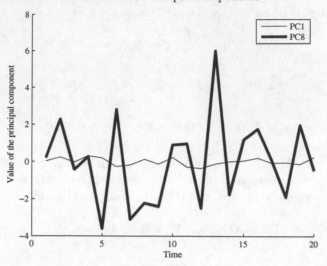

B. Eigenvalues of the Covariance Matrix of Data

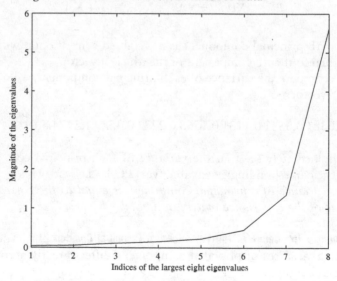

FIGURE 12.1 Plot of Principal Components and Eigenvalues

we can represent the variance of the ith data time series X_i as a weighted sum of the eigenvalues (each eigenvalue is equal to the variance of the relative principal component) as follows:

$$\text{var}(X_1) = \lambda_1 V_{11} + \lambda_2 V_{12} + \cdots + \lambda_8 V_{18}$$
$$\vdots$$
$$\text{var}(X_i) = \lambda_1 V_{i1} + \lambda_2 V_{i2} + \cdots + \lambda_8 V_{i8} \qquad (12.17)$$
$$\vdots$$
$$\text{var}(X_8) = \lambda_1 V_{81} + \lambda_2 V_{82} + \cdots + \lambda_8 V_{88}$$

Step 5: Using Only Principal Components with Largest Variances   From equation (12.16), we see that in our illustration there are more than two orders of magnitude (>100) between the smallest and the largest eigenvalues, and that there is a rapid decay of the magnitude of eigenvalues after the first three eigenvalues. Therefore, we can represent data approximately using only a reduced number of principal components that have the largest variance. Equivalently, this means using only those principal components that correspond to the largest eigenvalues.

Suppose we use only four principal components. We can write the following approximate representation:

$$X_1 \approx PC_5 V_{15} + \cdots + PC_8 V_{18}$$
$$\vdots$$
$$X_i \approx PC_5 V_{i5} + \cdots + PC_8 V_{i8} \qquad (12.18)$$
$$\vdots$$
$$X_8 \approx PC_5 V_{85} + \cdots + PC_8 V_{88}$$

or

$$X_1 = PC_5 V_{15} + \cdots + PC_8 V_{18} + e_1$$
$$\vdots$$
$$X_i = PC_5 V_{i5} + \cdots + PC_8 V_{i8} + e_i \qquad (12.19)$$
$$\vdots$$
$$X_8 = PC_5 V_{85} + \cdots + PC_8 V_{88} + e_8$$

where e represents the approximation error. The error terms are linear combinations of the first four principal components. Therefore, they are orthogonal to the last four principal components but, in general, they will be mutually correlated. To see this point, consider, for example,

$$X_1 = PC_5 V_{15} + \cdots + PC_8 V_{18} + e_1 \text{ and } X_8 = PC_5 V_{85} + \cdots + PC_8 V_{88} + e_8$$

From equation (12.12):

$$X_1 = PC_1 V_{11} + PC_2 V_{12} + \cdots + PC_8 V_{18} \text{ and } X_8 = PC_1 V_{81} + PC_2 V_{82} + \cdots + PC_8 V_{88}$$

Therefore,

$$e_1 = PC_1 V_{11} + PC_2 V_{12} + \cdots + PC_4 V_{14} \text{ and } e_8 = PC_1 V_{81} + PC_2 V_{82} + \cdots + PC_4 V_{84}$$

Consider, for example, the scalar product

$$\left(e_1 ' V_{15} \right) = PC_1 V'_{11} V_{15} + \cdots + PC_4 V'_{14} V_{15}$$

Each of the products $V'_{11} V_{15}, \ldots, V'_{14} V_{15}$ is equal to zero because the eigenvectors are orthogonal. The same reasoning can be repeated for any product $\left(e_i ' V_{1j} \right)$, $i = 1,2,3,4, j = 5,6,7,8$, which shows that the error terms are orthogonal to the last four principal components.

Consider now the scalar product $\left(e_1 ' e_8 \right)$. This scalar product is a weighted sum of products $V'_{1i} V_{1j}$, $i = 1,2,3,4, j = 1,2,3,4$. These products are zero if $i \neq j$ but they are different from zero when $i = j$. Hence the covariance and the correlations between residuals are not zero. For example, in our illustration, the covariance of the residuals is:

$$\Sigma_e = \begin{bmatrix}
0.0205 & 0.0038 & 0.0069 & -0.0062 & -0.0250 & 0.0044 & -0.0064 & 0.0108 \\
0.0038 & 0.0362 & 0.0113 & -0.0322 & -0.0196 & 0.0421 & -0.0138 & -0.0173 \\
0.0069 & 0.0113 & 0.0334 & 0.0005 & -0.0053 & -0.0000 & -0.0470 & 0.0066 \\
-0.0062 & -0.0322 & 0.0005 & 0.0425 & 0.0172 & -0.0335 & 0.0010 & -0.0002 \\
-0.0250 & -0.0196 & -0.0053 & 0.0172 & 0.0436 & -0.0330 & -0.0009 & 0.0096 \\
0.0044 & 0.0421 & -0.0000 & -0.0335 & -0.0330 & 0.0646 & 0.0080 & -0.0417 \\
-0.0064 & -0.0138 & -0.0470 & 0.0010 & -0.0009 & 0.0080 & 0.0692 & -0.0178 \\
0.0108 & -0.0173 & 0.0066 & -0.0002 & 0.0096 & -0.0417 & -0.0178 & 0.0515
\end{bmatrix}$$

which is not a diagonal matrix. Hence the fundamental equation of factor models $\Sigma = B'B + \Psi$ (equation (12.7)) does not, in general, hold for principal components.

It can be demonstrated that the weights of the last four principal components in equation (12.14) minimize the sum of squared residuals. Therefore, the weights in equation (12.14) are the same as those one would obtain estimating a linear regression of the data on the last four principal components.

For example, if we estimate a linear regression using MATLAB's regress function

$$X_1 = \alpha_1 PC_5 + \alpha_2 PC_5 + \alpha_3 PC_5 + \alpha_4 PC_8 + \varepsilon$$

we obtain the following estimate for the regression coefficients:

$$\begin{bmatrix} \alpha_1 \\ \alpha_2 \\ \alpha_3 \\ \alpha_4 \end{bmatrix} = \begin{bmatrix} -0.0951 \\ -0.3155 \\ -0.6800 \\ 0.2347 \end{bmatrix}$$

If we look at the matrix V, we see that the estimated regression coefficients are equal to $V_{15}, V_{16}, V_{17}, V_{18}$ as in equation (12.15).

The eight panels in Figure 12.2 illustrate the approximation obtained with four principal components.

The Process of PCA

The example we have provided in this section can be generalized to any set of data. We can therefore establish the following general process for PCA. Given a set of data formed by time series of the same length, with nonsingular covariance matrix, PCA involves the following steps:

1. Compute the covariance matrix Σ_X of the data.
2. Compute the eigenvalues D and eigenvectors V of the covariance matrix Σ_X.
3. Compute the principal components PC multiplying data by the eigenvectors: $PC = XV$.
4. Look at how eigenvalues decay (i.e., look at the plot of their magnitude).
5. Choose a (small) number of PCs corresponding to the largest eigenvalues.
6. Represent data approximately as weighted sums of these PCs.

DIFFERENCES BETWEEN FACTOR ANALYSIS AND PCA

There are clearly similarities between factor analysis and PCA. In both cases, data are parsimoniously represented as a weighted sum of a (generally small) number of factors or principal components. But there are also three important differences that we can summarize as follows:

1. PCA is a data-reduction technique; that is, it is a parsimonious representation that can be applied to any data set with a nonsingular covariance

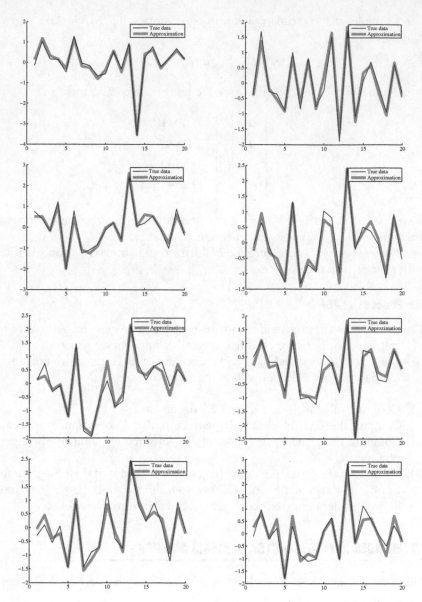

FIGURE 12.2 Approximation to the True Data Obtained with Four Principal Components

Note: Data go from X1 top left to X8 bottom right.

matrix. PCA per se does not assume any probabilistic model for the data. Factor models, in contrast, assume a statistical model for the data. To appreciate the difference, suppose we split our data into two parts, one to estimate data and one to test the model. If data follow a factor model, then the same model applies to both estimation and sample data. There is, however, no reason to assume that PCA works with similar parameters for both sets of data.

2. Principal components are observable time series. In our example, they are portfolios, while factors might be nonobservable.

3. Residuals of PCA will not, in general, be uncorrelated and therefore equation (12.7) does not hold for PCA.

We might ask if principal components are an estimate of the factors of factor models. Recall that thus far we have considered data sets that are finite in both the time dimension (i.e., time series are formed by a finite number of time points) and the number of time series. Under these assumptions, it has been demonstrated that principal components are a consistent estimate of factors only in the case of scalar models (i.e., only if the variance of residuals is the same for all residuals).[2] If the variances of residuals are not all equal, then principal components are not a consistent estimate of factors.

Scalar models are the only case where finite factor models and PCA coincide; in this case, we can estimate factors with principal components. In all other cases (1) principal components analysis gives results similar to but not identical with factor analysis and (2) principal components are not consistent estimates of factors, though they might approximate factors quite well. In the next section, we will see that principal components do approximate factors well in large factor models.

APPROXIMATE (LARGE) FACTOR MODELS

Thus far we have considered factor models where residuals are uncorrelated, and therefore the covariance between the data is due only to factors. In this case, equation (12.7) $\Sigma = B'B + \Psi$ (where Ψ is a diagonal matrix) holds. We can now ask if we can relax this assumption and accept that Ψ is a nondiagonal matrix. This question is suggested by the fact that, in practice, large factor models, for example factor models of returns of realistic data sets, do not yield a diagonal matrix of residuals. After estimating any reasonable number of factors, residuals still exhibit cross correlations.

---

[2] See Hans Schneeweiss and Hans Mathes, "Factor Analysis and Principal Components," *Journal of Multivariate Analysis* 55 (1995): 105–124.

If we look at the fundamental relationship $\Sigma = B'B + \Psi$, it is easy to see that there is no simple solution to this question. In fact, if Ψ is not a diagonal matrix, we could nest another factor structure that might yield $\Psi = HH' + \Omega$. But nesting another factor structure would increase the number of factors. That is, if we accept that residuals be correlated, then the original factors cannot be the only factors given that residuals will also exhibit a factor structure.

Intuitively, we could split the eigenvalues into two groups, "large" and "small" eigenvalues so that $\Sigma = B'B + \Psi$ is the sum of two parts, one $B'B$ due to large eigenvalues and the other Ψ due to small eigenvalues. However, this is not a theoretically satisfactory solution because the splitting into large and small eigenvalues is ultimately arbitrary.

In order to find a theoretically rigorous solution, the setting of factor models was modified by assuming that both the number of time points T and the number of time series are *infinite*. This solution was developed by Stephen Ross, whose arbitrage pricing theory (APT) published in the mid 1970s makes use of infinite factor models.[3] Factor models with correlated residuals are called *approximate factor models*. The theory of approximate factor models was developed in the early 1980s, again in the setting of an infinite number of both time points and time series.[4] Approximate factor models allow residuals to be correlated but they are defined for infinite markets.

The assumption of infinite markets is essential for defining approximate factor models. This is because the assumption of infinite markets allows for the distinction between those eigenvalues that grow without bounds from those eigenvalues that remain bounded. Roughly speaking, in an infinite market, *true global factors* are those that correspond to infinite eigenvalues while *local factors* are those that correspond to bounded eigenvalues.

Of course this distinction requires a carefully defined limit structure. In order to define approximate factor models, Chamberlain and Rothschild first defined an infinite sequence of factor models with an increasing number of series and data points.[5] It is assumed that as the size of the model increases, only a finite and fixed number of eigenvalues grow without limits while the others remain bounded. This assumption allows one to define an approximate factor model as a sequence of factor models such that a

[3] Stephen Ross, "The Arbitrage Theory of Capital Asset Pricing," *Journal of Economic Theory* 13 (1976): 341–360.
[4] Gary Chamberlain and Michael Rothschild, "Arbitrage, Factor Structure, and Mean-Variance Analysis in Large Asset Markets," *Econometrica* 51 (1983): 1305–1324.
[5] See Chamberlain and Rothschild, "Arbitrage, Factor Structure, and Mean-Variance Analysis."

finite number of eigenvalues grows without bounds, all other eigenvalues are bounded and residuals are correlated.

Note that APT can be rigorously defined only for an infinite market. The theory of approximate factor models has been extended to allow a more general setting where residuals and factors can be autocorrelated.[6]

APPROXIMATE FACTOR MODELS AND PCA

A key finding of the theory of approximate factor models is that factors of approximate factor models are unique and can be estimated and identified with principal components. Of course, a limit structure has to be defined. In fact, per se, it does not make sense to define principal components of an infinite market. However, one can define a limit process so that the limit of principal components of growing markets coincides, in some sense, with the limit of factors. Hence we can say that, in infinite approximate factor models, factors are unique and can be estimated with principal components.

How can we realistically apply the theory of approximate factor models? For example, how can we apply the theory of approximate factor models to stock returns given that any market is finite? The answer is that the theory of approximate factor models is a good approximation for large factor models with a large number of long time series. For example, it is not unusual at major investment management firms to work with a universe of stocks that might include more than 1,000 return processes, each with more than 1,000 daily returns.

When working with large models, global factors are associated with large eigenvalues and local factors with small eigenvalues. The separation between large and small eigenvalues is not as clear cut as the theoretical separation between infinite and bounded eigenvalues. However, criteria have been proposed to make the distinction highly reasonable. Some criteria are essentially model selection criteria. Model selection criteria choose the optimal number of factors as the optimal compromise between reducing the magnitude of the residuals and the complexity of the model, that is, the number of parameters to estimate. This is the strategy adopted in Bai and Ng.[7] Other criteria are based on the distribution of the eigenvalues of large matrices, as in Onatsky.[8]

---

[6] Jushan Bai, "Inferential Theory for Factor Models of Large Dimensions," *Econometrica* 71 (2003): 135–171.

[7] Jushan Bai and Serena Ng, "Determining the Number of Factors in Approximate Factor Models," *Econometrica* 70 (2002): 191–221.

[8] Alexei Onatski, "Determining the Number of Factors from Empirical Distribution of Eigenvalues," *Review of Economics and Statistics* 92 (2010): 1004–1016.

To summarize, both factor models and principal components analysis try to find a parsimonious representation of data. Factor models assume a statistical model for data while PCA is a pure data-reduction technique. The two techniques are essentially equivalent in large models but there might be significant differences in small models.

KEY POINTS

- The statistical techniques of factor analysis and principal component analysis are used to reduce a large number of observed variables to a smaller number of factors or principal components.
- Principal component analysis involves creating a linear combination of a set of explanatory variables to form a set of principal components.
- Classical factor models assume that there are a finite number of series and a finite number of observations.
- Classical factor models assume that residuals are uncorrelated. In this case, the variance of the data is due only to factors.
- Factor analysis is the process of estimating factor models.
- Although maximum likelihood estimation methods can be employed to estimate the parameters of a model, factors are not uniquely determined and cannot be estimated with these methods.
- Factor scores can be used to approximate factors.
- Factor models are similar to multiple regressions but factors are generally nonobservable and residuals are uncorrelated.
- In addition to factor analysis, the parsimonious representation of data can be done using principal components analysis.
- PCA is a data-reduction technique, not a statistical model.
- To perform PCA, (1) the eigenvectors and eigenvalues of the covariance matrix are computed, (2) principal components are then computed by multiplying data and eigenvectors, and (3) a small number of principal components corresponding to the largest eigenvectors are chosen and data as regressions on the chosen principal components are represented.
- Principal components estimate factors only in the limit of very large models.
- The main differences between factor analysis and PCA are (1) residuals of PCA are correlated and (2) PCA is not a statistical model.
- In large factor models, factors can be estimated with good approximation with principal components.

CHAPTER 13

Model Estimation

After reading this chapter you will understand:

- The concept of estimation and estimators.
- The properties of estimators.
- The least-squares estimation method.
- How to apply the least-squares method.
- The use of ordinary least squares, weighted least squares, and generalized least squares.
- The maximum likelihood estimation method.
- How to apply the maximum likelihood method.
- The instrumental variables approach to estimation.
- The method of moments and its generalizations.
- How to apply the method of moments.

In the previous chapters of this book, we have described the most commonly used financial econometric techniques. However, with the exception of our discussion of the simple linear regression in Chapter 2, we purposely did not focus on methods for estimating parameters of the model. As we mentioned in the preface, we did not do so because most users of financial econometric techniques utilize commercial software where the vendor utilizes the latest estimation techniques. Nevertheless, it is still important to understand the various estimation methods that can be applied to specific models. In this chapter, we discuss these methods. We begin by discussing the concept of estimation and the concept of sampling distributions.

STATISTICAL ESTIMATION AND TESTING

All of the financial econometric models that we have described in this book have parameters that must be estimated. *Statistical estimation* is a set of criteria and methodologies for determining the best estimates of parameters.

Testing is complementary to estimation. Critical parameters are often tested before the estimation process starts in earnest, although some tests of the adequacy of models can be performed after estimation.

In general terms, statistics is a way to make inferences from a sample to the entire population from which the sample is taken. This area within the field of statistics is called *inferential statistics* (or *inductive statistics*) and is explained in more detail in Appendix C. In financial econometrics, the sample is typically an empirical time series. Data may be returns, prices, interest rates, credit spreads, default rates, company-specific financial data, or macroeconomic data. The objective of estimation techniques is to estimate the parameters of models that describe the empirical data.

The key concept in estimation is that of estimators. An *estimator* is a function of sample data whose value is close to the true value of a parameter in a distribution. For example, the empirical average (i.e., the sum of the sample's values for a variable divided by the number of samples) is an estimator of the mean; that is, it is a function of the empirical data that approximates the true mean. Estimators can be simple algebraic expressions; they can also be the result of complex calculations.

Estimators must satisfy a number of properties. In particular, estimators

- Should get progressively closer to the true value of the parameter to be estimated as the sample size becomes larger.
- Should not carry any systematic error.
- Should approach the true values of the parameter to be estimated as rapidly as possible.

The question related to each estimation problem should be what estimator would be best suited for the problem at hand. Estimators suitable for the very same parameters can vary quite remarkably when it comes to quality of their estimation. In Appendix C we explain some of the most commonly employed quality criteria for evaluating estimators.

Being a function of sample data, an estimator is a random (i.e., stochastic) variable. Therefore, the estimator has a probability distribution referred to as the *sampling distribution*. In general, the probability distribution of an estimator is difficult to compute accurately from small samples but is simpler for large samples.[1]

The sampling distribution is important. Decisions such as determining whether a process is integrated must often be made on the basis of estimators. Because estimators are random variables, decisions are based on

---

[1] See Appendix C for a discussion of how the behavior of estimators changes as the size of the sample varies.

comparing empirical estimators with *test statistics* or *critical values* computed from the sampling distribution.[2] A test statistic is used in hypothesis testing to decide whether to accept or reject a hypothesis.[3]

ESTIMATION METHODS

Because estimation methods involve criteria that cannot be justified by themselves, they are subject to some arbitrariness. The crucial point is that, whereas an estimation process must "fit" a distribution to empirical data, any distribution can, with a few restrictions, be fitted to any empirical data. The choice of distributions thus includes an element of arbitrariness. Suppose we want to determine the probability distribution of the faces of a tossed coin, and in 1,000 experiments, heads comes out 950 times. We probably would conclude that the coin is highly biased and that heads has a 95% probability of coming up. We have no objective way, however, to rule out the possibility that the coin is fair and that we are experiencing an unlikely event. Ultimately, whatever conclusion we draw is arbitrary.

Four estimation methods are commonly used in financial econometrics:

- Least squares method
- Maximum likelihood method
- Method of moments method
- Bayesian method

The four methods listed above are the fundamental estimation methods. These methods have been generalized in broad estimation frameworks that, however, overlap, making it difficult to create a simple taxonomy of estimation methods. In fact, the least squares method and the maximum likelihood method are instances of a more general approach called the M-estimator method. The method of moments has been generalized into the generalized method of moments. The least squares method and the maximum likelihood method are also instances of the generalized method of moments. The Bayesian estimation method is based on a different interpretation of statistics and will not be discussed in this chapter.[4] The instrumental variables

---

[2] Hypothesis testing is explained in Appendix C.

[3] Test statistics or critical values of the autoregressive parameters are tabulated and are available in all major time-series software packages.

[4] For readers interested in learning more about Bayesian estimation, see Svetlozar T. Rachev, John S. J. Hsu, Biliana Bagasheva, and Frank J. Fabozzi, *Bayesian Methods in Finance* (Hoboken, NJ: John Wiley & Sons, 2008).

method is an approach to estimation that is essentially based on changing the observed variables when the original ones cannot be estimated with any of the above methods. The instrumental variables method is also an instance of the generalized method of moments.

As will be explained in this chapter, there are variants of the methods that are used when assumptions of a model fail. The choice between different estimation methods depends on the data and the modeling assumptions we make. More specifically, when the assumptions of the general linear regression model that were described in Chapter 4 hold, the ordinary least squares method—a type of least squareds method—and the maximum likelihood method are appropriate. An additional consideration in selecting an estimation method is the computational cost that might favor one or another method.

LEAST-SQUARES ESTIMATION METHOD

The *least-squares* (LS) *estimation method* is a best-fit technique adapted to a statistical environment. As a data-fitting technique, LS methods can always be used. When LS methods are applied to linear regressions they are called *ordinary least squares* (OLS). OLS methods require that the standard assumptions of regressions are satisfied. As we will see, when some assumptions of standard regression are violated, two alternative methods described in this chapter—weighted least squares or generalized least squares—are applicable.

Let's begin with the basic task of fitting data. Suppose we observe a set of data and we want to find the straight line that best approximates these points. A sensible criterion in this case is to compute the distance of each point from a generic straight line, compute the sum of the squares of these distances, and choose the line that minimizes this sum—in short, the LS method.

To illustrate, suppose that we are given the set of 10 data points listed in Table 13.1. We can think of these data as 10 simultaneous observations of two variables. Figure 13.1 represents the scatterplot of the data, which is a figure with a point corresponding to each coordinate.

Suppose we want to draw the optimal straight line that minimizes the sum of squared distances. A straight line is represented by all points that satisfy a linear relationship

$$y = a + bx$$

After choosing a and b, a straight line will take the values $y_i = a + b_i$, $i = 1, \ldots, 10$ in correspondence with our sample data. For example, Figure 13.2

TABLE 13.1   Sample Data for Illustration

Observation	Y	X
1	0.8	0.7
2	1.8	1.3
3	1.1	2.9
4	1.7	4.2
5	1.6	5.5
6	1.4	6.7
7	1.6	7.4
8	1.7	8.1
9	2.1	9.2
10	2.4	10.6

represents the sample data in Table 13.1 and a straight line corresponding to $a = 0.05$, $b = 0.1$.

It is evident that this straight line is not the closest possible to the sample points because it remains entirely on one side of the points. To find the optimal line we have to find a and b that minimize the sum of the squared distances between the sample points and the corresponding

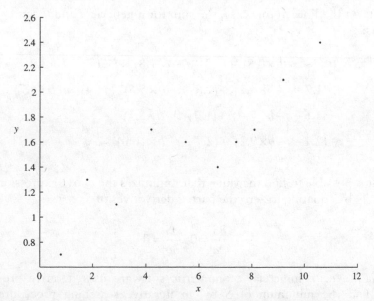

FIGURE 13.1   Scatterplot of the 10 Sample Data in Table 13.1

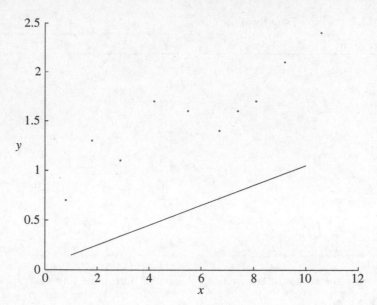

FIGURE 13.2 Scatterplot of Sample Data and the Plot of the Straight Line $y = 0.05 + 0.1x$

points on the line. In this case, the sum for a generic a and b can be written as:

$$
\begin{aligned}
S =&\ (0.7 - a - b \times 0.8)^2 + (1.3 - a - b \times 1.8)^2 + (1.1 - a - b \times 2.9)^2 \\
&+ (1.7 - a - b \times 4.2)^2 + (1.6 - a - b \times 5.5)^2 + (1.4 - a - b \times 6.7)^2 \\
&+ (1.6 - a - b \times 7.4)^2 + (1.7 - a - b \times 8.1)^2 \\
&+ (2.1 - a - b \times 9.2)^2 + (2.4 - a - b \times 10.6)^2
\end{aligned}
$$

It is possible to find the value that minimizes the above expression analytically by equating to zero the partial derivatives of S:

$$
\frac{\partial S}{\partial a} = 0 \quad \frac{\partial S}{\partial b} = 0
$$

However, commercial econometric software uses iterative programs that find the minimum of S by an iterative searching procedure. For example, we can perform the above operation in MATLAB using the polyfit function. With the function polyfit (X,Y,1) we obtain the following solution: $a = 0.1317$, $b = 0.8065$. Figure 13.3 represents the scatterplot of data and the best fitting straight line

$$y = 0.1317 + 0.8065x$$

We can measure how accurately the straight line represents the sample data with the square root of sum of squared residuals, which is the sum S evaluated for $a = 0.1317$, $b = 0.8065$. For our sample data, we obtain $\sqrt{S} = 0.6566$.

Looking at the scatterplot of sample data shown in Figure 13.3, we might ask if a polynomial of second degree could better approximate the data. We can repeat the above process but using

$$y = a + bx + cx^2$$

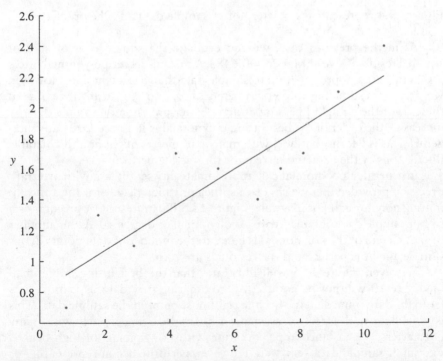

FIGURE 13.3   Scatterplot of Sample Data and Plot of the Best Fitting Straight Line

instead of $y = a + bx$. We therefore compute the sum S as follows:

$$S = \left(0.7 - a - b \times 0.8 - c \times 0.8^2\right)^2 + \left(1.3 - a - b \times 1.8 - c \times 1.8^2\right)^2$$
$$+ \left(1.1 - a - b \times 2.9 - c \times 2.9^2\right)^2 + \left(1.7 - a - b \times 4.2 - c \times 4.2^2\right)^2$$
$$+ \left(1.6 - a - b \times 5.5 - c \times 5.5^2\right)^2 + \left(1.4 - a - b \times 6.7 - c \times 6.7^2\right)^2$$
$$+ \left(1.6 - a - b \times 7.4 - c \times 7.4^2\right)^2 + \left(1.7 - a - b \times 8.1 - b \times 8.1^2\right)^2$$
$$+ \left(2.1 - a - b \times 9.2 - c \times 9.2^2\right)^2 + \left(2.4 - a - b \times 10.6 - c \times 10.6^2\right)^2$$

As in the previous case, we can find the minimum of the sum S by equating to zero the partial derivatives of the above equation. However, commercial software generally uses iterative optimizers. For example, if we again use the function polyfit of MATLAB, specifying a polynomial of second degree, we obtain the polynomial

$$y = 0.0038 + 0.0889x + 0.8893x^2$$

Figure 13.4 represents the scatterplot of sample data and the optimal polynomial.

As in the previous case, we can evaluate the square root of sum of squared residuals. We obtain $\sqrt{S} = 0.6483$. A second-degree polynomial offers a slightly better approximation to sample data than a straight line. However, we are now estimating three parameters, a, b, and c, instead of two as in the case of the straight line. Obtaining a better precision on sample data by increasing the order of the best fitting polynomial is not necessarily advantageous. This is because a model with many parameters might fit unpredictable fluctuations of the data and have poor forecasting performance.

In general, a polynomial can approximate any set of data with arbitrary precision provided that we choose a sufficiently high degree for the approximating polynomial. For example, Figure 13.5 illustrates the approximation to our sample data obtained with a polynomial of degree 10. As the number of parameters of the polynomial is equal to the number of data points in our sample, the fit is perfect and the residuals are zero.

However, Figure 13.5 well illustrates that the best fitting polynomial of degree 10 will not be good at approximating new data as it moves far from the data immediately after the rightmost point in the sample data. This is a fundamental aspect of estimation methods. Using models with many parameters, for instance approximating with polynomials of high degree, we can fit sample data very well. However, performance in representing or forecasting out-of-sample data will be poor. Model estimation is always a compromise between accuracy of estimates in-sample and model parsimony.

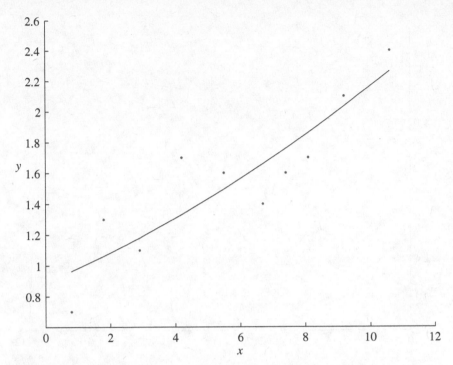

FIGURE 13.4 Scatterplot of Sample Data and Plot of the Best Fitting Polynomial of Second Degree

In order to decide what approximation is the best, we could use AIC or BIC criteria as discussed in Appendix E.

In the preceding illustration we used two different functional forms, a straight line, which is a polynomial of degree one, and a polynomial of degree two. The LS method can be adapted to any set of data points and to different functional forms (straight lines, polynomial functions, and so on). The choice of the functional form depends on both theoretical and statistical considerations. Theoretical considerations might suggest a specific functional form to approximate the data. For example, suppose our objective is to model a series of market capitalization data of some firm. Theoretical considerations on firm growth will probably suggest that we try an exponential function.

Ordinary Least Squares Method

Thus far we have illustrated LS methods as a technique to find an optimal approximation to data and we have not made any statistical assumptions. However, the LS method also applies to statistical models, in particular to regressions, as we have seen in Chapter 3. As explained above, the LS

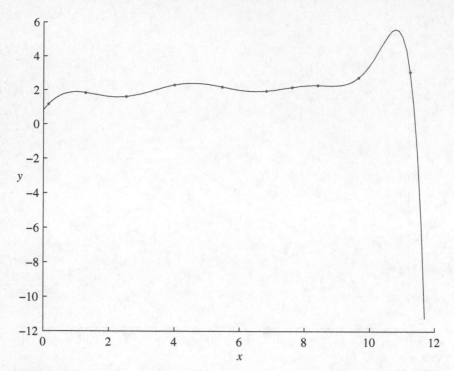

FIGURE 13.5 Scatterplot of Sample Data and Plot of the Best Fitting Polynomial of Degree 10

method applied to simple or multiple regressions under standard assumptions is the OLS method to distinguish it from weighted and generalized least squares that we will describe shortly.

Standard assumptions of simple and multiple regression require that residuals have the same variances and that they are mutually uncorrelated and uncorrelated with the regressors. Under these assumptions, the OLS method estimates the regression parameters by minimizing the sum of squared residuals. We have seen in Chapter 3 that the regression equation (3.8), which is reproduced as equation (13.1):

$$y = X\beta + e \qquad (13.1)$$

This can be estimated by finding the value of b that minimizes the sum of squared residuals:

$$S = \sum_{i=1}^{n} e_i^2 \qquad (13.2)$$

We have also seen that the estimated regression parameters can be represented in terms of the sample data by expression (3.10) in Chapter 3, which is reproduced here as equation (13.3):

$$b = (X'X)^{-1} X'y \qquad (13.3)$$

where $\quad y = \begin{bmatrix} y_1 \\ \vdots \\ y_n \end{bmatrix} \quad X = \begin{bmatrix} 1 & x_{11} & \cdots & x_{1k} \\ \vdots & \vdots & \ddots & \vdots \\ 1 & x_{n1} & \cdots & x_{nk} \end{bmatrix}$

n = the number of samples
k = the number of regressors

The column of 1s in matrix X corresponds to the constant intercept term.

To illustrate, let's use the data in Table 13.1. In this case, the matrix X has two columns, one column of 1s and the data in Table 13.1 The estimated regression coefficients can be computed from equation (13.3). If we compute this expression (or if we perform the regression estimation with commercial software, for example using the MATLAB regress function) we obtain the following estimate for the regression coefficients:

$$b = \begin{bmatrix} 0.8065 \\ 0.1317 \end{bmatrix}$$

which are the same coefficients we obtained above as the best fitting straight line.

Recall from Chapter 3 that the regressors X are assumed to be deterministic while the dependent variable y is a random variable. This means that in different samples, only the y change while the X remain fixed. Note that, if there are k regressors plus a constant term, then $(X'X)^{-1} X'$ is a $k \times n$ matrix and y is an $n \times 1$ vector in equation (13.3). Hence the vector b is the product of a $k \times n$ matrix and an $n \times 1$ vector. Each component of b is therefore a linear combination of sample data y given that the X are fixed. Hence equation (13.3) shows that the OLS estimator of b is a linear estimator.

The estimator b is a function of sample data y given that the X remain fixed. The sample data y are random data and therefore b is a random variable. Recall from Chapter 3 that we assume that the regression variables are normally distributed and therefore b is a linear combination of normal variables and is therefore a normal variable. Suppose that the true regression model is the expression shown in equation (3.1) in Chapter 3 reproduced here as equation (13.4):

$$y = \beta_0 + \beta_1 x_1 + \ldots + \beta_k x_k + \varepsilon \tag{13.4}$$

Then the difference $b - \beta$, where $\beta = (\beta_0, \beta_1, \ldots, \beta_k)'$ is the vector of true parameters, is a normally distributed random variable.

It can be demonstrated that $E(b - \beta) = 0$; that is, the expectation of the estimated regression coefficients is equal to the true parameters and the variance-covariance of the difference $b - \beta$ is $\text{cov}(b - \beta) = (X'X)^{-1} \sigma^2$ where σ^2 is the variance of the data. If the regression variables are normally distributed, the above can be concisely stated by saying that the estimator b is distributed as a normal multivariate variable with mean β and covariance matrix $(X'X)^{-1} \sigma^2$.

The variance of an estimator is a measure of its accuracy. The *Gauss-Markov theorem* states that the OLS regression estimator is the *best linear unbiased estimator* (generally referred to by the acronym BLUE) in the sense that it has the lowest possible variance among all linear unbiased estimators.

Weighted Least Squares Method

The OLS method can be generalized in different ways. The first important generalization is when all variables, X and y, are assumed to be random variables. In this case, the computation of the regression coefficients from the observed data remains unchanged. In fact, with OLS we compute the coefficients b given the data. Hence, we estimate b with the same formula as in equation (13.4):

$$b | X = (X'X)^{-1} X'y \tag{13.5}$$

This formula is numerically identical to that of equation (13.4) but the data X are now a realization of the random variables X.

Assuming that residuals and regressors are independent, the OLS estimator given by equation (13.5) is still an unbiased estimator even when regressors are stochastic. However, the covariance of the estimator is no longer $(X'X)^{-1} \sigma^2$. This expression represents the regressors' covariance matrix under the assumption that regressors X are fixed. However, if regressors are stochastic, $(X'X)^{-1} \sigma^2$ is the conditional variance given X. To obtain the final covariance we have to multiply $(X'X)^{-1} \sigma^2$ by the distribution of the regressors. In general, even if data are normally distributed, this is not a normal distribution.

Another generalization involves the case when regressors are deterministic but we relax the assumption that all errors e have the same variance. As explained in Chapter 4, this is the homoscedasticity property. In practice, many financial time series are not homoscedastic, but have different variance. Time series with different variances are said to heteroscedastic. In Chapter 11 we explained time series whose heteroscedasticity can be described through an autoregressive process. Here we consider the case where the variances of each residual are perfectly known.

Consider the regression equation given by equation (13.4) and consider the covariance matrix of residuals:

$$W = \text{cov}(\varepsilon) = E(\varepsilon\varepsilon') \tag{13.6}$$

W is an $n \times n$ matrix. Under the standard assumptions of regression given in Chapter 3, W is proportional to the identity matrix C where σ^2 is the constant variance of the residuals. Let's relax this assumption and assume that W is a diagonal matrix but with different diagonal terms:

$$W = \sigma^2 V$$

$$V = \begin{bmatrix} v_1^2 & 0 & 0 \\ 0 & \ddots & 0 \\ 0 & 0 & v_n^2 \end{bmatrix} \tag{13.7}$$

In the above case, the usual OLS formula does not work. It has been demonstrated, however, that a modified version of OLS called *weighted least squares* (WLS) works. WLS seeks the minimum of the sum of squared weighted residuals. Instead of minimizing the sum of squared residuals given by equation (13.2), it minimizes the sum of weighted squared residuals:

$$WS = \sum_{i=1}^{n} w_i e_i^2 \tag{13.8}$$

Given the regression equation $y = \beta_0 + \beta_1 x_1 + \cdots + \beta_k x_k + \varepsilon$, if the variance of each residual term is known exactly and is given by the matrix in equation (13.7), then WLS seeks to minimize

$$WS = \sum_{i=1}^{n} \frac{1}{v_i^2} e_i^2 \tag{13.9}$$

It can be demonstrated that the estimator of the regression coefficients becomes

$$b = \left(X'V^{-1}X \right)^{-1} X'V^{-1}y \tag{13.10}$$

and that this WLS estimator is unbiased and BLUE. If the residuals are homoscedastic, the matrix V becomes the identity matrix and the estimator b becomes the usual expression given by equation (13.5).

Generalized Least Squares Method

The WLS estimator can be generalized to the *generalized least squares* (GLS) *estimator*. The GLS estimator applies when residuals are both heteroscedastic and autocorrelated. In this case, equation (13.7) becomes

$$W = \sigma^2 V$$

$$V = \begin{bmatrix} v_{11}^2 & \cdots & v_{n1} \\ \vdots & \ddots & \vdots \\ v_{n1} & \cdots & v_{nn}^2 \end{bmatrix} \tag{13.11}$$

where V is now a full symmetric covariance matrix. The GLS estimator of the regression parameters, conditional on the realization X, is given by the same expression as in equation (13.10) but where now V is a full covariance matrix. The GLS estimator is linear, unbiased, and has minimum variance among the linear estimators.

The theory of WLS and that of GLS assume that the covariance matrix of residuals is perfectly known. This is the key limitation in applying WLS and GLS in practice. In practice, we have to estimate the covariance matrix of residuals. In an ad hoc iterative procedure, we first estimate a regression and residuals with OLS, then estimate the covariance matrix of residuals, and lastly estimate a new regression and relative residuals with GLS, and proceed iteratively.

THE MAXIMUM LIKELIHOOD ESTIMATION METHOD

The *maximum likelihood* (ML) *estimation method* involves maximizing the likelihood of the sample given an assumption of the underlying distribution (for example, that it is a normal distribution or a uniform distribution). *Likelihood* is the distribution computed for the sample. In order to apply ML estimation methods we must know the functional form of the distributions of the data. If we do not know the distribution, we cannot compute the likelihood function. ML methods can be difficult to apply in practice in models that include hidden variables.[5] We will first give an intuition for the method and then illustrate how MLE works for regressions.

The intuition of choosing those parameters that maximize the likelihood of the sample is simple. For example, suppose we toss a coin 1,000 times and get 950 heads and 50 tails. What can we conclude about the probability of obtaining heads or tails in tossing that coin? Although every sequence is theoretically possible, intuition tells us that the coin is biased and that it is reasonable to assume that the probability of a head is 95% and the probability of a tail is only 5%.

The MLE principle formalizes this intuition. If we let p denote the probability of heads and q the probability of tails, then any particular sequence that contains 950 heads and 50 tails has probability

$$L = p^{950} (1-p)^{50}$$

This probability L is the likelihood of the sequence. To maximize likelihood, we equate to zero the derivatives of the likelihood with respect to p:

$$\frac{dL}{dp} = 950 p^{950-1} (1-p)^{50} - 50 p^{950} (1-p)^{50-1} = p^{950} (1-p)^{50} \left(\frac{950}{p} - \frac{50}{1-p} \right) = 0$$

This equation has three solutions:

$p = 0$

$p = 1$

$\left(\dfrac{950}{p} - \dfrac{50}{1-p} \right) = 0 \Rightarrow 950(1-p) = 50p \Rightarrow 950 = 1000p \Rightarrow p = 0.95$

The first two solutions are not feasible and therefore the maximum likelihood is obtained for $p = 0.95$ as suggested by intuition.

Application of MLE to Regression Models

Let's now discuss how to apply the MLE principle to regressions, as well as factor models described in the previous chapter. Let's first see how the MLE

---

[5] A hidden variable is a variable that is not observed but can be computed in function of the data. For example, in ARCH/GARCH models described in Chapter 11, volatility is a hidden variable computed through the ARCH/GARCH model.

principle is applied to determine the parameters of a distribution. We will again use our sample in Table 13.1 and assume that sample data y are random draws from a normal distribution with mean μ and variance σ^2. Therefore, the normal distribution computed on the sample data will have the form:

$$P(y_i) = \frac{1}{\sigma\sqrt{2\pi}} \exp\left(-\frac{(y_i - \mu)^2}{2\sigma^2}\right) \quad i = 1, \ldots, 10 \qquad (13.12)$$

As the data are assumed to be independent random draws, their likelihood is the product

$$L = \prod_{i=1}^{10} P(y_i) = \prod_{i=1}^{10} \frac{1}{\sigma\sqrt{2\pi}} \exp\left(-\frac{(y_i - \mu)^2}{2\sigma^2}\right) \qquad (13.13)$$

We can simplify the expression for the likelihood by taking its logarithm. Because the logarithm is a monotonically growing function, those parameters that maximize the likelihood also maximize the logarithm of the likelihood and vice versa. The logarithm of the likelihood is called the *log-likelihood*. Given that the logarithm of a product is the sum of the logarithms, we can write

$$
\begin{aligned}
\log L &= \log \prod_{i=1}^{10} P(y_i) = \sum_{i=1}^{10} \log P(y_i) \\
&= \sum_{i=1}^{10} \log\left(\frac{1}{\sigma\sqrt{2\pi}} \exp\left(-\frac{(y_i - \mu)^2}{2\sigma^2}\right)\right) \\
&= \sum_{i=1}^{10} \log\left(\frac{1}{\sigma\sqrt{2\pi}}\right) - \sum_{i=1}^{10} \frac{(y_i - \mu)^2}{2\sigma^2} \\
&= -10\log\sqrt{2\pi} - 10\log\sigma - \frac{1}{2\sigma^2}\sum_{i=1}^{10}(y_i - \mu)^2
\end{aligned}
\qquad (13.14)
$$

We can explicitly compute the log-likelihood of the sample data:

$$
\begin{aligned}
\log L = &-10\log\sqrt{2\pi} - 10\log\sigma \\
&-\frac{1}{2\sigma^2}\left[\begin{array}{l}(0.7-\mu)^2 + (1.3-\mu)^2 + (1.1-\mu)^2 + (1.7-\mu)^2 + (1.6-\mu)^2 \\ +(1.4-\mu)^2 + (1.6-\mu)^2 + (1.7-\mu)^2 + (2.1-\mu)^2 + (2.4-\mu)^2\end{array}\right]
\end{aligned}
$$

This is the expression that needs to be maximized in order to determine the parameters of the normal distribution that fit our sample data y. Maximization can be achieved either analytically by equating to zero the derivatives of log$L$ with respect to the mean μ and variance σ^2 or using commercial software. We obtain the following estimates:

$$\mu = 1.5600$$
$$\sigma = 0.4565$$
$$\sigma^2 = 0.2084$$

Application of MLE to Regression Models

We can now discuss how to apply the MLE principle to the estimation of regression parameters. Consider first the regression equation (13.4). Assuming samples are independent, the likelihood of the regression is the product of the joint probabilities computed on each observation:

$$L = \prod_{i=1}^{n} P(y_i, x_{i1}, \ldots, x_{ik}) \tag{13.15}$$

Let's assume that the regressors are deterministic. In this case, regressors are known (probability equal to 1) and we can write

$$L = \prod_{i=1}^{n} P(y_i, x_{i1}, \ldots, x_{ik}) = \prod_{i=1}^{n} P(y_i | x_{i1}, \ldots, x_{ik}) \tag{13.16}$$

If we assume that all variables are normally distributed we can write

$$P(y_i | x_{i1}, \ldots, x_{ik}) \approx N(\beta_0 + \beta_1 x_1 + \ldots + \beta_k x_k, \sigma^2)$$

We can write this expression explicitly as

$$P(y_i | x_{i1}, \ldots, x_{ik}) = \frac{1}{\sigma\sqrt{2\pi}} \exp\left(-\frac{(y_i - \beta_0 - \beta_1 x_1 - \cdots - \beta_k x_k)^2}{2\sigma^2}\right)$$

and therefore:

$$L = \prod_{i=1}^{n} P(y_i | x_{i1}, \ldots, x_{ik})$$
$$= \prod_{i=1}^{n} \frac{1}{\sigma\sqrt{2\pi}} \exp\left(-\frac{(y_i - \beta_0 - \beta_1 x_1 - \cdots - \beta_k x_k)^2}{2\sigma^2}\right) \tag{13.17}$$

and

$$\log L = n\log\left(\frac{1}{\sqrt{2\pi}}\right) - n\log(\sigma) - \frac{1}{2\sigma^2}\sum_{i=1}^{n}(y_i - \beta_0 - \beta_1 x_1 + \cdots - \beta_k x_k)^2$$

The first term is a constant, the second and the third terms are negative; therefore, maximizing the log-likelihood is equivalent to finding the solution of the following minimization problem:

$$(\beta,\sigma) = \arg\min\left[n\log(\sigma) + \frac{1}{2\sigma^2} \sum_{i=1}^{n}(y_i - \beta_0 - \beta_1 x_1 - \cdots - \beta_k x_k)^2 \right] \quad (13.18)$$

The analytic solution to this problem requires equating to zero the partial derivatives with respect to the arguments. Computing the derivatives of equation (13.15) yields the following expressions:

$$\frac{\partial\left[\sum_{i=1}^{n}(y_i - \beta_0 - \beta_1 x_1 - \cdots - \beta_k x_k)^2 \right]}{\partial\beta_j} = 0$$

$$\sigma^2 = \frac{1}{n}\sum_{i=1}^{n}(y_i - \beta_0 - \beta_1 x_1 - \cdots - \beta_k x_k)^2$$

The first condition is exactly the same condition as that obtained with the OLS method. The second expression states that the variance σ^2 is estimated by the empirical variance of the sample residuals. We find the important result that, if variables are normally distributed, OLS and MLE estimation methods yield exactly the same estimators.

Application of MLE to Factor Models

The same reasoning applies to factor models. Consider the factor model equation (12.3) from Chapter 12:

$$y_t = a + Bf_t + \varepsilon_t, \, t = 1, \ldots, T$$

The variables y are the only observable terms. If we assume that the variables y_t are normally distributed, we can write

$$P(y_t) = N(a, \Sigma)$$

where a is the vector of averages and Σ is the covariance matrix of the y_t. Because the logarithm is a monotone function, maximizing the likelihood is equivalent to maximizing the log-likelihood

$$\log(L) = \sum_{t=1}^{T}\log\big(P(y_t)\big)$$

A normal distribution has the following multivariate probability distribution function:

$$N(a, \Sigma) = \frac{1}{(2\pi)^{\frac{N}{2}} |\Sigma|^{\frac{1}{2}}} \exp\left(-\frac{1}{2}(y-a)'\Sigma^{-1}(y-a)\right)$$

hence

$$\log(L) = \sum_{t=1}^{T} \log(P(y_t))$$

$$= -\frac{TN}{2}\log(2\pi) - \frac{T}{2}\log(|\Sigma|) - \frac{1}{2}\sum_{t=1}^{T}(y_t - a)'\Sigma^{-1}(y_t - a) \qquad (13.19)$$

From equation (13.9), we know that $\Sigma = B'B + \Psi$; we can therefore determine the parameters B, Ψ by maximizing the log-likelihood with respect to these parameters.

ML is a widely used estimation method. Note, however, that the ML method implies that one knows the form of the distribution, otherwise, one cannot compute the likelihood.

INSTRUMENTAL VARIABLES

The *instrumental variables* (IV) *estimation* approach is a strategy for changing the variables of an estimation problem that cannot be solved with any of the above methods. To understand this approach, consider that in all regression models discussed thus far, it is imperative that regressors and errors are uncorrelated. This condition ensures that the dependent variable is influenced *independently* by the regressors and the error terms. Regressors are said to be *exogenous* in the regression model. If this condition is not satisfied, the OLS estimator of regression parameters is biased.

In practice, in regressions commonly used in financial modeling the condition of independence of errors and regressors is often violated. This happens primarily because errors include all influences that are not explicitly accounted for by regressors and therefore some of these influences might still be correlated with regressors. OLS estimation is no longer suitable because the regression problem is not correctly specified.

A possible solution to this problem is given by the IV approach, which solves a different regression problem. Consider the usual regression equation (13.4) where we allow some regressors x to be correlated with the errors. Suppose there is a vector of variables z of size equal to k such that the variables z are independent from the errors ε and are correlated with x. The variables z are referred to as *instruments*.

Instruments lead to a consistent estimator of the regression parameters. In fact, it can be demonstrated that the following $(k + 1)$-vector is a consistent IV estimator of the regression parameters:

$$b = (Z'X)Z'y \quad b = (\beta_0, \ldots, \beta_k)' \tag{13.20}$$

In general, the IV estimator is not efficient. Efficiency of the IV estimators improves if the instruments are highly correlated with the regressors. In practice, it might be very difficult to find instruments for a given regression model.

METHOD OF MOMENTS

The *method of moments* (MOM) *estimation* approach is the oldest estimation method for estimating the parameters of a population. The intuition behind the MOM is simple: MOM estimates the parameters of a probability distribution by equating its moments with the empirical moments computed for the sample. The MOM assumes that (1) we know the form of the distribution of the population from which the sample has been extracted and (2) moments can be expressed in terms of the parameters of the distribution. In general, this latter condition is satisfied for all usual distributions.[6]

Given a random variable X with a given distribution $P = P(\vartheta)$, where ϑ is a k-vector of parameters, the *jth moment of P* is defined as

$$\mu_j = \mu_j(\vartheta) = E(X^j)$$

Suppose now that we have a sample of n variables independently extracted from the same distribution P. The *jth empirical moment of P*, defined as

$$m_j = \frac{\sum_{i=1}^{n} X_i^j}{n}$$

is a function of the data. It is known that empirical moments are consistent estimators of moments.

---

[6] However, theoretically it might be difficult to define a distribution in terms of parameters. For example, a distribution could be defined as the solution of a differential equation. This could make it very difficult to establish a relationship between moments and parameters.

If we have to estimate k parameters, we can compute the first k empirical moments and equate them to the corresponding first k moments. We obtain k equations the solutions for which yield the desired parameters:

$$\mu_1 = \frac{\sum_{i=1}^{n} X_i}{n}$$

$$\vdots \tag{13.21}$$

$$\mu_k = \frac{\sum_{i=1}^{n} X_i^k}{n}$$

For example, suppose we know that the Y data in our sample given by equation (13.1) are a random extraction from a normal distribution. A normal distribution is fully characterized by two parameters, the mean and the variance. The first moment is equal to the mean; the second moment is equal to the variance plus the square of the first moment. In fact:

$$\mu_1 = \mu$$

$$\sigma^2 = E\left[(X - \mu)^2\right] = E\left[X^2 - 2\mu X + \mu^2\right] = \mu_2 - \mu_1^2 \tag{13.22}$$

$$\mu_2 = \sigma^2 + \mu$$

Computing the first two empirical moments for the sample data given by equation (13.1), we obtain

$$m_1 = 1.56$$
$$m_2 = 2.642$$

and solving for σ, μ from equation (13.22) we obtain

$$\mu = 1.56$$
$$\sigma^2 = 2.642 - 1.56^2 = 0.2084$$

Therefore, the MOM estimates that our sample data are drawn from the following normal distribution: $N(1.56, 0.2084)$. This is the same result obtained above using the MLE method.

Generalized Method of Moments

MOM is a parametric method insofar as it assumes that the functional form of the distribution is known. MOM has been generalized to the *generalized method of moments* (GMM).[7] GMM does not assume complete knowledge of the distribution but seeks to optimize a number of parameters of the distribution.

To understand how the GMM works, let's first go back to the previous example and compute both the third empirical moment and the third theoretical moment in function of μ, σ. The theoretical moment is obtained by expanding the basic definition of moment as follows:

$$
\begin{aligned}
\mu_3 = E(X^3) &= E\left[\left((X-\mu)+\mu\right)^3\right] \\
&= E\left[(X-\mu)^3 + 3(X-\mu)^2\mu + 3(X-\mu)\mu^2 + \mu^3\right] \\
&= E\left[(X-\mu)^3\right] + E\left[3(X-\mu)^2\mu\right] + E\left[3(X-\mu)\mu^2\right] + E\left[\mu^3\right]
\end{aligned}
$$

Given that $E\left[(X-\mu)\right] = 0$, $E\left[(X-\mu)^2\right] = \sigma^2$, the theoretical third moment is

$$
\mu_3 = 3\sigma^2\mu + \mu^3
$$

Let's compare theoretical and empirical moments:

$$
\begin{aligned}
\mu_1 &= 1.5600 \quad m_1 = 1.5600 \\
\mu_2 &= 2.6420 \quad m_2 = 2.6420 \\
\mu_3 &= 4.7717 \quad m_3 = 4.7718
\end{aligned}
$$

The theoretical and empirical values of the first two moments are obviously identical because of equation (13.21). Note also that the theoretical and empirical values of the third moment also almost coincide. If we compute the differences,

$$
g = \begin{bmatrix} \mu_1 - m_1 \\ \mu_2 - m_2 \\ \mu_3 - m_3 \end{bmatrix} \tag{13.23}
$$

we obtain $g \approx 0$.

In order to illustrate the GMM, let's use the sample of data shown in Table 13.2. Notice that the values for X are the same as in Table 13.1 but the

---

[7]The GMM framework was proposed in 1982 by Lars Hansen, the 2013 corecipient of the Nobel Prize in Economic Sciences. See Lars P. Hansen, "Large Sample Properties of Generalized Methods of Moments Estimators," *Econometrica* 50 (1982): 1029–1054.

TABLE 13.2　Sample Data to Illustrate the GMM

Observation	Y	X
1	0.7	0.7
2	1.3	1.3
3	1.1	2.9
4	1.7	4.2
5	1.6	5.5
6	1.4	6.7
7	1.6	7.4
8	1.7	8.1
9	3.1	9.2
10	4.4	10.6

values for Y for some of the observations are different. If we repeat the same calculations as above, we find the following empirical moments:

$$m_1 = 1.8600$$
$$m_2 = 4.5220$$
$$m_3 = 13.9608$$

If we apply the MOM and equate the first two theoretical and empirical moments, using equation (13.21) we obtain

$$\mu = 1.86$$
$$\sigma^2 = 4.5220 - 1.86^2 = 1.0624$$

Using these parameters we can now compute the first three theoretical moments:

$$\mu_1 = 1.8600 \qquad m_1 = 1.8600$$
$$\mu_2 = 4.5220 \qquad m_2 = 4.5220$$
$$\mu_3 = 12.3630 \qquad m_3 = 13.9608$$

While the first two theoretical and empirical moments coincide by construction as in the previous case, there is a significant difference between the theoretical and empirical values of the third moment. The vector g in equation (13.22) assumes the following values:

$$g = \begin{bmatrix} 0 \\ 0 \\ -1.5978 \end{bmatrix}$$

Now, given that a normal distribution has only two parameters, there is no way we can fit exactly the three first moments obtaining $g = 0$. However, we can try to estimate the parameters of the normal distribution with some optimization criterion that involves the first three (or eventually more) moments. This is the essence of the GMM: optimizing using more moments than parameters. How can we define an optimization criterion? It is reasonable to base an optimization criterion on some linear combination of the products of the differences between theoretical and empirical moments. Therefore, if we write the vector of these differences as in equation (13.22), an optimization criterion could minimize the expression

$$Q(\mu, \sigma, Y) = g'Wg \qquad (13.24)$$

where W is a positive definite symmetric weighting matrix. An expression of the form in equation (13.24) is called a *quadratic form*.

The choice of the matrix W is a critical point. Each choice of W apportions the weights to each of the three moments. To illustrate, let's assume that we give the same weight to each moment and therefore we choose W equal to the identity matrix. Hence, $Q(\mu, \sigma, Y) = g'g$. If we minimize this expression, for example using the MATLAB function fminsearch, we obtain the following estimates for the model's parameters:

$$\mu = 1.7354$$
$$\sigma = 1.2930$$
$$\sigma^2 = 1.6718$$

If we compute the theoretical moments, we obtain the following comparison:

$$\mu_1 = 1.7354 \qquad m_1 = 1.8600$$
$$\mu_2 = 1.7354 \qquad m_2 = 4.5220$$
$$\mu_3 = 13.9298 \qquad m_3 = 13.9608$$

and therefore the vector g becomes:

$$g = \begin{bmatrix} -0.3411 \\ -1.9543 \\ -9.2691 \end{bmatrix}$$

and the objective function Q assumes the value $Q = 0.0425$, while its initial value was $Q = 2.5528$.

The above illustration includes the key elements of the GMM. The GMM is based on identifying a number of independent conditions that involve both the data and the parameters. These conditions typically take the form of equations where the expectation of given functions is equated to zero:

$$E\big[h_i\left(X_t,\beta\right)\big]=0$$

In our illustrations, these conditions were the conditions that defined the first three moments of a normal variable.

The GMM replaces these conditions with averages and constructs the vector:

$$g_i=\frac{1}{T}\sum_{t=1}^{T}h_i\left(X_t,\beta\right)$$

where T is the number of available samples and determines β minimizing the quadratic form: $Q\left(\mu,\sigma,Y\right)=g'Wg$.

THE M-ESTIMATION METHOD AND M-ESTIMATORS

Both LS and ML methods are based on minimizing/maximizing a function of the data. This approach has been generalized. The M-estimators are estimators obtained by maximizing given functions of the data and parameters. This generalization proved fruitful in the field of robust statistics, which is described in Appendix F and in Chapter 8 on robust regressions. In fact, by choosing appropriate functions to be minimized, estimation can give less weight to observations that fall very far from the mean, thereby making estimators robust.

KEY POINTS

- Inferential statistics infer the properties of a population from a sample.
- Estimation is a set of methods to determine population parameters from a sample. An estimator is a function of sample data.
- The estimation methods commonly used in financial econometrics are the least squares method, maximum likelihood method, method of moments, and Bayesian method.
- The least squares estimation method estimates parameters by minimizing the sum of squared residuals.
- Least squares estimators of standard regressions, called ordinary least squares (OLS) estimators, are linear functions of the sample data.
- Least squares estimators of regressions are the best linear unbiased estimators.

- The weighted least squares (WLS) estimator, used when residuals have different variance, minimizes a weighted sum of squared residuals.
- The generalized least squares (GLS) estimator, used when residuals have different variance and are correlated, minimizes a weighted sum of squared residuals.
- The maximum likelihood method estimates parameters by maximizing the probability of the distribution on the data.
- The maximum likelihood method assumes the form of the distribution is known.
- If variables are normally distributed, the maximum likelihood and least squares methods give the same results.
- When residuals are correlated with regressors, we cannot use the OLS method and instead we might use the instrumental variables (IV) approach.
- The IV approach replaces regressors correlated with the residuals with new variables that are correlated with the regressors but uncorrelated with the residuals.
- The method of moments equates empirical and theoretical moments.
- The generalized method of moments uses more conditions than parameters and replaces exact determination of parameters with optimization.

CHAPTER 14

Model Selection

A fter reading this chapter you will understand:

- The notion of machine learning.
- The difference between an approach based on theory and an approach based on learning.
- The relationship between the size of samples and the complexity of models that can be learned.
- The concept of overfitting.
- The use of penalty functions in learning.
- The concept of data snooping.
- The concept of survivorship bias.
- The concept of model risk.
- Methods for mitigating model risk.
- Model averaging.

In the previous chapters in this book, we described the most important financial econometric tools. We have not addressed how a financial modeler deals with the critical problem of selecting or perhaps building the optimal financial econometric model to represent the phenomena they seek to study. The task calls for a combination of personal creativity, theory, and machine learning. In this chapter and the one to follow we discuss methods for model selection and analyze the many pitfalls of the model selection process.

PHYSICS AND ECONOMICS: TWO WAYS OF MAKING SCIENCE

In his book, *Complexity*, Mitchell Waldrop describes the 1987 Global Economy Workshop held at The Santa Fe Institute, a research center dedicated to the study of complex phenomena and related issues.[1] Attended by

---

[1] M. Mitchell Waldrop, *Complexity* (New York: Simon & Schuster, 1992).

distinguished economists and physicists, the seminar introduced the idea that economic laws might be better understood by applying the principles of physics and, in particular, the newly developed theory of complex systems. An anecdote from the book is revealing of the issues specific to economics as a scientific endeavor. According to Waldrop, physicists attending the seminar were surprised to learn that economists used highly sophisticated mathematics. A physicist attending the seminar reportedly asked Kenneth Arrow, the corecipient of the 1972 Nobel Memorial Prize in Economics, why, given the lack of data to support theories, economists use such sophisticated mathematics. Arrow replied, "It is just because we do not have enough data that we use sophisticated mathematics. We have to ensure the logical consistency of our arguments." For physicists, in contrast, explaining empirical data is the best guarantee of the logical consistency of theories. If theories work empirically, then mathematical details are not so important and will be amended later; if theories do not work empirically, no logical subtlety will improve them.

This anecdote is revealing of one of the key problems that any modeler of economic phenomena has to confront. On the one side, as with economics, the field of financial economics is an empirical science based on empirical facts. However, as data are scarce, many theories and models fit the same data.

Given the importance of model selection, let us discuss this issue before actually discussing estimation issues. It is perhaps useful to compare again the methods of financial economics and of physics. In physics, the process of model choice is largely based on human creativity. Facts and partial theories are accumulated until scientists make a major leap forward. Physicists are not concerned with problems such as fitting the data to the same sample that one wants to predict—referred to as *data snooping* and explained later in this chapter. In general, data are overabundant and models are not determined through a process of fitting and adaptation.

Now consider financial economics, where the conceptual framework is totally different. First, though apparently many data are available, these data come in vastly different patterns. For example, the details of development of a financial system and instruments are very different from year to year and from country to country. Asset prices seem to wander about in random ways. Introducing a concept that plays a fundamental role in formulating investment strategies explained in the next chapter, we can state: From the point of view of statistical estimation, financial economic data are always scarce given the complexity of their patterns.

Attempts to discover simple deterministic laws that accurately fit empirical financial data have proved futile. Furthermore, as financial data are the product of human artifacts, it is reasonable to believe that they will not follow the same laws for very long periods of time. Simply put, the structure of any financial system and economy change too much over time to confirm that laws in financial economics are time-invariant laws of nature. One is, therefore, inclined to believe that only approximate laws can be discovered. The attention of the modeler has therefore to switch from discovering deterministic paths to determining the time evolution of probability distributions.[2]

The adoption of probability as a descriptive framework is not without a cost: discovering probabilistic laws with confidence requires working with very large populations (or samples). In physics, this is not a problem as physicists have very large populations of particles.[3] In finance, however, populations are typically too small to allow for a safe estimate of probability laws; small changes in the sample induce changes in the laws. We can, therefore, make the following general statement: Financial data are too scarce to allow one to make probability estimates with complete certainty. (The exception is the ultra high-frequency intraday data, five seconds or faster trading.)

As a result of the scarcity of financial data, many statistical models, even simple ones, can be compatible with the same data with roughly the same level of statistical confidence. For example, if we consider stock price processes, many statistical models—including the random walk—compete to describe each process with the same level of significance. Before discussing the many issues surrounding model selection and estimation, we will briefly discuss the subject of machine learning and the machine learning approach to modeling.

MODEL COMPLEXITY AND SAMPLE SIZE

Let's now discuss three basic approaches to financial modeling, namely the

1. Machine learning approach
2. Theoretical approach
3. Machine learning theoretical approach

The machine learning theoretical approach is a hybrid of the two former approaches.

---

[2] In physics, this switch was made at the end of the nineteenth century, with the introduction of statistical physics. It later became an article of scientific faith that one can arrive at no better than a probabilistic description of nature.

[3] Although this statement needs some qualification because physics has now reached the stage where it is possible to experiment with small numbers of elementary particles, it is sufficient for our discussion here.

The *machine learning approach* to financial modeling is in principle a consequence of the diffusion of low-cost high-performance computers.[4] It is based on using a family of very flexible models that can approximate sample data with unlimited precision.[5] Consider that some "machine learning" appears in most financial econometric endeavors. For example, determining the number of lags in an autoregressive model is a problem typically faced in financial econometric modeling (see Chapter 9).

However, practice has shown that if we represent sample data with very high precision, we typically obtain poor forecasting performance. Here is why. In general, the main features of the data can be described by a simple structural model plus unpredictable noise. As the noise is unpredictable, the goal of a model is to capture the structural components. A very precise model of sample data (in-sample) will also try to match the unpredictable noise. This phenomenon, called *overfitting* (discussed later in this chapter), leads to poor (out-of-sample) forecasting abilities. Obviously there is no guarantee that data are truly described by a simple structural model plus noise. Data might be entirely random or might be described by a truly complex model.

To address the problem of overfitting, the machine learning theory suggests criteria to constrain the complexity of the model so that it fits sample data only partially but, as a trade-off, retains some forecasting power. The intuitive meaning is the following: *The structure of the data and the sample size dictate the complexity of the laws that can be learned by computer algorithms.* This is typically accomplished by introducing what is called a *penalty function.* For example, determining the number of lags in an autoregressive model is typically solved with methods of machine learning theory by selecting the number of lags that minimize the sum of the loss function of the model plus a penalty function.

This is a fundamental point. If we have only a small sample data set, we can learn only simple patterns, provided that these patterns indeed exist.

---

[4] In the 1970s, a full-fledged quantitative theory of machine learning was developed in V. N. Vapnik and Y. A. Chervonenkis, *Theory of Pattern Recognition* (Moscow: Nauka, 1974). While this theory goes well beyond the scope of this chapter, the practical implication of the theory is what is important here: model complexity must be constrained in function of the sample.

[5] Neural networks are a classical example. With an unrestricted number of layers and nodes, a neural network can approximate any function with arbitrary precision. We express this fact by saying that a neural network is a *universal function approximator.* The idea of universal function approximators is well known in calculus. The Taylor series and Fourier series are universal approximators for broad classes of functions.

Learning theory constrains the dimensionality of models to make them adapt to the sample size and structure. A central idea in machine learning theory is to add a penalty term to the objective function wherein the penalty terms increases with the number of parameters but gets smaller if the number of sample points increases.[6] That is, the penalty function is a function of the size of the sample and of the complexity of the model. One compares models by adding the penalty function to the likelihood function (a definition of the likelihood function is provided in Chapter 13). In this way, one can obtain an ideal trade-off between model complexity and forecasting ability.

At the other end of the landscape, the theoretical approach is based on human creativity. In this approach, models are the result of new scientific insights that have been embodied in theories. The theoretical approach is typical of the physical sciences. Perhaps the most well-known example of a theoretical model in financial economics is the capital asset pricing model (CAPM).

The hybrid approach retains characteristics of both the theoretical and machine learning approaches. It uses a theoretical foundation to identify families of models but uses a learning approach to choose the correct model within the family. For example, the ARCH/GARCH family of models (see Chapter 11) is suggested by theoretical considerations while, in its practical application, the right model is selected through a learning approach that identifies the model parameters. Thus, ultimately, in modern computer-based financial econometrics, there is no clear-cut distinction between a learning approach versus a theory-based a priori approach.

At this point, the four key conclusions regarding model complexity and sample size are:

1. Financial data are generally scarce for statistical estimation given the complexity of their patterns.
2. Financial data are too scarce for sure statistical estimates.
3. The scarcity of financial data means that the data might be compatible with many different models.
4. There is a trade-off between model complexity and the size of the data sample.

The last two conclusions are critical.

---

[6] Several proposals have been made as regards the shape of the penalty function. Three criteria in general use are (1) the Akaike information criterion (AIC), (2) Bayesian information criterion (BIC), and (3) maximum description length principle. The first two are described in Appendix E.

DATA SNOOPING

One of the most serious mistakes that a financial econometrician seeking to formulate an investment strategy can make is to look for rare or unique patterns that look profitable in-sample but produce losses out-of-sample. This mistake is made easy by the availability of powerful computers that can explore large amounts of data: any large data set contains a huge number of patterns, many of which look very profitable. Otherwise expressed, any large set of data, even if randomly generated, can be represented by models that appear to produce large profits.

Given the scarcity of data and the basically uncertain nature of any financial econometric model, it is generally necessary to calibrate models on some data set, the so-called *training set,* and test them on another data set, the *test set*. In other words, it is necessary to perform an out-of-sample validation on a separate test set. The rationale for this procedure is that any machine learning process—or even the calibration mechanism itself—is a heuristic methodology, not a true discovery process. Models determined through a machine learning process must be checked against the reality of out-of-sample validation. Failure to do so is referred to as *data snooping*, that is, performing training and tests on the same data set.

Out-of-sample validation is typical of machine learning methods. Learning entails models with unbounded capabilities of approximation constrained by somewhat artificial mechanisms such as a penalty function. This learning mechanism is often effective but there is no guarantee that it will produce a good model. Therefore, the learning process is considered an example of *discovery heuristics*. The true validation test, say the experiments, has to be performed on the test set. Needless to say, the test set must be large and cover all possible patterns, at least in some approximate sense.

Data snooping is not always easy to understand or detect. It is a result of a defect of training processes which must be controlled but which is very difficult to avoid given the size of data samples currently available. Suppose samples in the range of 10 years are available.[7] One can partition these data and perform a single test free from data snooping biases. However, if the test fails, one has to start all over again and design a new strategy. The process of redesigning the modeling strategy might have to be repeated several times over before an acceptable solution is found. Inevitably, repeating the process on the same data includes the risk of data snooping.

---

[7]Technically much longer data sets on financial markets, up to 50 years of price data, are available. While useful for some applications, these data may be of limited use for many financial econometric applications due to problems faced by asset managers given the changes in the structure of the economy.

The real danger in data snooping is the possibility that by trial and error, one hits upon a model that casually performs well both in-sample and out-of sample but that will perform poorly in real-world forecasts. In the next chapter, we explore at length different ways in which data snooping and other biases might enter the model discovery process and we propose a methodology to minimize the risk of biases, as will be explained in the last section of this chapter.

SURVIVORSHIP BIASES AND OTHER SAMPLE DEFECTS

Let us now see how samples might be subject to biases that reduce our ability to correctly estimate model parameters. In addition to errors and missing data, a well-known type of bias in financial econometrics is *survivorship bias*, a bias exhibited by samples selected on the basis of criteria valid at the last date in the sample time series. In the presence of survivorship biases in our data, return processes relative to firms that ceased to exist prior to that date are ignored. For example, in the study of the performance of mutual funds, poorly performing mutual funds often close down (and therefore drop out of the sample) while better performing mutual funds continue to exist (and therefore remain in the sample). In this situation, estimating past returns from the full sample would result in overestimation due to survivorship bias. As another example, suppose a sample contains 10 years of price data for all stocks that are in the S&P 500 today and that existed for the last 10 years. This sample, apparently well formed, is, however, biased. The selection, in fact, is made on the stocks of companies that are in the S&P 500 today, that is, those companies that have "survived" in sufficiently good shape to still be in the S&P 500 aggregate.

Survivorship bias arises from the fact that many of the surviving entities (mutual funds or individual stocks) successfully passed through some difficult period. Surviving the difficulty is a form of reversion to the mean. An asset manager may indeed produce trading profits buying cheap when the company is facing difficulty and exploiting the subsequent recovery. At the end of the period, we know what firms recovered.

Survivorship bias is a consequence of selecting time series, asset price time series in particular, based on criteria that apply at the end of the period. Avoiding the survivorship bias seems simple in principle. It might seem sufficient to base any sample selection at the moment where the forecast begins, so that no invalid information enters the strategy prior to trading. However, the fact that companies are founded, merged, and closed plays havoc with simple models. In fact, calibrating a simple model requires data for assets that exist over the entire training period. This in itself introduces a potentially substantial training bias.

A simple model cannot handle processes that start or end in the middle of the training period. On the other hand, models that take into account the founding or closing of firms cannot be simple. Consider, for example, a simple linear autoregressive model (see Chapter 9). Any addition or deletion of companies introduces a nonlinearity effect into the model and precludes using standard tools such as the ordinary least squares method.

There is no ideal solution. Care is required in estimating possible performance biases consequent to sample biases. Suppose that we make a forecast of return processes based on models trained on the past three or four years of returns data on the same processes that we want to forecast. Clearly there is no data snooping because we use only information available prior to forecasting. However, it should be understood that we are estimating our models on data that contain biases. If the selection of companies to forecast is subject to strong criteria, for example companies that are included in a major stock index such as the S&P 500, it is likely that the model will suffer a loss of performance. This is due to the fact that models will be trained on spurious past performance. If the modeler is constrained to work on a specific stock selection, for example, in order to create an active strategy against a selected benchmark, the modeler might want to reduce the biases applying his or her own judgment.

The survivorship bias is not the only possible bias of sample data. More in general, any selection of data contains some bias. Some of these biases are intentional. For example, selecting large market capitalization companies or small market capitalization companies introduces special behavioral biases that are intentional. However, other selection biases are more difficult to appreciate. In general, any selection based on stock indexes introduces index-specific biases in addition to the survivorship bias. Consider that presently thousands of indexes are in use. Institutional investors and their consultants use these indexes to create asset allocation strategies and then give the indexes to asset managers for active management.

Anyone using financial econometrics to create active management strategies based on these stock indexes should be aware of the biases inherent in the indexes when building their strategies. Data snooping applied to carefully crafted stock selection can result in poor performance because the asset selection process inherent in the index formation process can produce very good results in sample; these results vanish out-of-sample as "snow under the sun."

Moving Training Windows

Thus far we have assumed that the data generating process (DGP) discussed in Chapter 1 exists as a time-invariant model. Can we also assume that the DGP varies and that it can be estimated on a moving window? If yes, how can it be tested? These are complex questions that do not admit an easy answer. It is often assumed that financial markets undergo "structural breaks" or "regime shifts" (i.e., that financial markets undergo discrete changes at fixed or random time points).

If financial markets are indeed subject to breaks or shifts and the time between breaks is long, models would perform well for a while and then, at the point of the break, performance would degrade until a new model is learned. If regime changes are frequent and the interval between the changes short, one could use a model that includes the changes. The result is typically a nonlinear model. Estimating models of this type is very oner-ous given the nonlinearities inherent in the model and the long training period required.

There is, however, another possibility that is common in modeling. Consider a model that has a defined structure, for example a linear vec-tor autoregressive (VAR) model (see Chapter 9), but whose coefficients are allowed to change in time with the moving of the training window. In prac-tice, most models work in this way as they are periodically recalibrated. The rationale of this strategy is that models are assumed to be approximate and sufficiently stable for only short periods of time. Clearly there is a trade-off between the advantage of using long training sets and the disadvantage that a long training set includes too much change.

Intuitively, if model coefficients change rapidly, this means that the model coefficients are noisy and do not carry genuine information. There-fore, it is not sufficient to simply reestimate the model: one must determine how to separate the noise from the information in the coefficients. For exam-ple, a large VAR model used to represent prices or returns will generally be unstable. It would not make sense to reestimate the model frequently; one should first reduce model dimensionality with, for example, factor analy-sis (see Chapter 12). Once model dimensionality has been reduced, coef-ficients should change slowly. If they continue to change rapidly, the model structure cannot be considered appropriate. One might, for example, have ignored fat tails or essential nonlinearities.

How can we quantitatively estimate an acceptable rate of change for model coefficients? Are we introducing a special form of data snooping in calibrating the training window?

Calibrating a training window is clearly an empirical question. How-ever, it is easy to see that calibration can introduce a subtle form of data snooping. Suppose a rather long set of time series is given, say six to eight years, and that one selects a family of models to capture using financial econometrics the DGP of the series and to build an investment strategy. Testing the strategy calls for calibrating a moving window. Different moving windows are tested. Even if training and test data are kept separate so that forecasts are never performed on the training data, clearly the methodology is tested on the same data on which the models are learned.

Other problems with data snooping stem from the psychology of modeling. A key precept that helps to avoid biases is the following: Modeling hunches should be based on theoretical reasoning and not on looking at the data. This statement might seem inimical to an empirical enterprise, an example of the danger of "clear reasoning" mentioned above. Still, it is true that by looking at data too long one might develop hunches that are sample-specific. There is some tension between looking at empirical data to discover how they behave and avoiding capturing the idiosyncratic behavior of the available data.

Clearly simplicity (i.e., having only a small number of parameters to calibrate) is a virtue in modeling. A simple model that works well should be favored over a complex model that might produce unpredictable results. Nonlinear models in particular are always subject to the danger of unpredictable chaotic behavior.

MODEL RISK

As we have seen, any model choice might result in biases and poor performance. In other words, any model selection process is subject to *model risk*. One might well ask if it is possible to mitigate model risk. In statistics, there is a long tradition, initiated by the eighteenth-century English mathematician Thomas Bayes, of considering uncertain not only individual outcomes but the probability distribution itself. It is therefore natural to see if ideas from Bayesian statistics and related concepts could be applied to mitigate model risk.

A simple idea that is widely used in practice is to take the average of different models. This idea can take different forms. There are two principal reasons for applying model risk mitigation. First, we might be uncertain as to which model is best, and so mitigate risk by diversification. Second, perhaps more cogent, we might believe that different models will perform differently under different circumstances. By averaging, the modeler hopes to reduce the volatility of the model's forecasts. It should be clear that averaging model results or working to produce an average model (i.e., averaging coefficients) are two different techniques. The level of difficulty involved is also different.

Averaging results is a simple matter. One estimates different models with different techniques, makes forecasts, and then averages the forecasts. This simple idea can be extended to different contexts. For example, in a financial econometric model developed for rating stocks, the modeler might want to do an exponential averaging over past ratings, so that the proposed rating today is an exponential average of the model rating today and model ratings in the past. Obviously parameters must be set correctly, which again forces a careful analysis of possible data snooping biases. Whatever the averaging process one uses, the methodology should be carefully checked for statistical consistency. The key principle is that averaging is used to eliminate noise, not genuine information.

Averaging models is more difficult than averaging results. In this case, the final result is a single model, which is, in a sense, the average of other models.[8]

MODEL SELECTION IN A NUTSHELL

It is now time to turn all the caveats into some positive approach to model selection. As explained in the next chapter, any process of model selection must start with strong economic intuition. Machine learning alone is unlikely to identify investment strategies that yield significant positive results.

Intuition applied to financial decisions clearly entails an element of human creativity. As in any other scientific and technological endeavor, it is inherently dependent on individual abilities. Is there a body of true, shared science that any modeler can use? Or do modelers have to content themselves with only partial and uncertain findings reported in the literature? At this time, the answer is probably a bit of both.

One would have a hard time identifying laws in financial economics that have the status of true scientific laws. Principles such as the absence of arbitrage are probably what comes closest to a true scientific law but are not, per se, very useful in finding, say, profitable trading strategies.[9] Most empirical findings in finance are of an uncertain nature and are conditional on the structure of the financial market and financial system. It is fair to say that intuition in finance is based on a number of broad financial principles plus a set of findings of an uncertain and local nature. Empirical findings in finance are statistically validated on a limited sample and probably hold only for a finite time span. Consider, for example, findings such as volatility clustering in asset returns. One might claim that volatility clustering is ubiquitous and that it holds for every financial market. In a broad sense this is

---

[8] Shrinkage of the covariance matrix used in computing portfolio variance is a simple example of averaging models.

[9] In finance there is arbitrage if the same financial product can be traded at different prices in different locations at the same moment. Arbitrage, if it exists, allows one to make unlimited profit, as unlimited quantity of the product can be bought where it is cheap and sold where it is expensive.

true. However, no volatility clustering model can claim the status of a law of nature as all volatility clustering models fail to explain some essential fact.

It is often argued that profitable investment strategies can be based only on secret proprietary discoveries. This is probably true but its importance should not be exaggerated. Secrecy is typically inimical to knowledge building. Secrets are also difficult to keep. Industrial projects of a non military nature are rarely based on a truly scientific breakthrough. They typically exploit existing knowledge.

Financial econometrics is probably no exception. Proprietary techniques are, in most cases, the application of more or less shared knowledge. There is no record of major breakthroughs in finance made in secrecy by investment teams of asset management firms. Some firms have advantages in terms of data. Until the recent past, availability of computing power was also a major advantage, reserved for only the biggest Wall Street firms; however, computing power is now a commodity. As a consequence, it is fair to say that intuition in finance can be based on a vast amount of shared knowledge plus some proprietary discovery or interpretation.

After using intuition to develop an ex ante hypothesis, the process of model selection and calibration begins in earnest. This implies selecting a sample free from biases and determining a quality-control methodology. In the production phase, an independent risk control mechanism will be essential. A key point is that the discovery process should be linear. If at any point the development process does not meet the quality standards, one should resist the temptation of adjusting parameters and revert to developing new intuition.

This process implies that there is plenty of intuition to work on when dealing with the various issues in finance. The modeler must have many ideas to develop. Ideas might range from the intuition that certain segments of the financial market have some specific behavior to the discovery that there are specific patterns of behavior with unexploited opportunities. In some cases it will be the application of ideas that are well known but have never been applied on a large scale.

A special feature of the model selection process is the level of uncertainty and noise. Models capture small amounts of information in a vast "sea of noise." Models are always uncertain, and so is their potential longevity. The psychology of discovery plays an important role. These considerations suggest the adoption of a rigorous objective research methodology. In the next chapter we illustrate the work flow for a sound process of discovery of profitable strategies.

A modeler working in financial econometrics is always confronted with the risk of finding an artifact that does not, in reality, exist. And, as we have seen, paradoxically one cannot look too hard at the data; this risks introducing biases formed by available but insufficient data sets. Even trying too many possible solutions, one risks falling into the trap of data snooping.

KEY POINTS

- Model selection in financial econometrics requires a blend of theory, creativity, and machine learning.
- The machine learning approach starts with a set of empirical data that we want to explain.
- There is a trade-off between model complexity and the size of the data sample. To implement this trade-off, ensuring that models have forecasting power, the fitting of sample data is constrained to avoid fitting noise.
- Financial data are generally scarce given the complexity of their patterns. This scarcity introduces uncertainty as regards statistical estimates. It means that the data might be compatible with many different models with the same level of statistical confidence.
- A serious mistake in model selection is to look for models that fit rare or unique patterns; such patterns are purely random and lack predictive power.
- Another mistake in model selection is data snooping; that is, fitting models to the same data that we want to explain. A sound model selection approach calls for a separation of sample data and test data: models are fitted to sample data and tested on test data.
- Because data are scarce, techniques have been devised to make optimal use of data; perhaps the most widely used of such techniques is bootstrapping.
- Financial data are also subject to survivorship bias; that is, data are selected using criteria known only at the end of the period. Survivorship bias induces biases in models and results in forecasting errors.
- Model risk is the risk that models are subject to forecasting errors in real data.
- A simple idea that is widely used in practice to mitigate model risk is to take the average of different models.
- A sound model selection methodology includes strong theoretical considerations, the rigorous separation of sample and testing data, and discipline to avoid data snooping.

CHAPTER 15

Formulating and Implementing Investment Strategies Using Financial Econometrics

A fter reading this chapter you will understand:

- The financial econometrics research aspect of the quantitative research process.
- The purpose of using financial econometric tools is to identify any persistent pattern in financial data and convert that information into implementable and profitable investment strategies.
- The three phases of the quantitative research process: (1) develop an ex ante justification based on financial economic theory, (2) select a survivorship-free sample, and (3) estimate a parameter-free model.
- Common fallacies in the use of financial econometrics to develop investment strategies.
- Considerations in deciding on which and how many explanatory variables should be included in a financial econometrics model.
- Why in attempting to identify profitable investment strategies there is concern with overmining of data.
- The pitfalls of using insufficient data.
- Why a safeguard against data snooping is to scrutinize the model once through time.
- Why after developing a strategy based on some financial econometric model it is always prudent to test the model against an artificial data set.

This chapter is coauthored with Christopher K. Ma of KCM Asset Management, and Professor of Finance and Director of the George Investments Institute and Roland George Investments Program at Stetson University.

In Chapters 3 and 4, we explained how to build, diagnose, and test a multiple linear regression model. In this chapter, we provide a blueprint as to how to apply financial econometrics to quantitative asset management. The objective of quantitative asset management is to identify any persistent pattern in financial data and convert that information into implementable and profitable investment strategies. We discuss the general process for converting statistical information obtained from the application of financial econometric tools into implementable investment strategies that can be employed by asset managers. Generally, this process includes developing underlying financial theories, explaining actual asset returns, and estimating expected asset returns that can be used in constructing a portfolio or a trading position. In addition, we identify some of the commonly induced biases in this process.

In Figure 15.1, we provide a flowchart that shows the process of how quantitative research is performed and converted into implementable

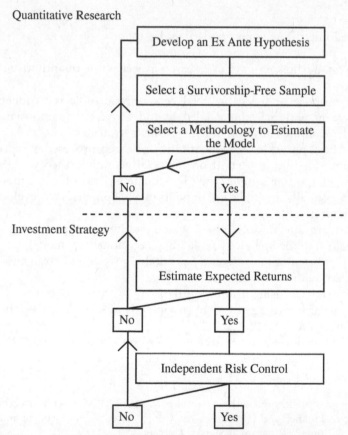

FIGURE 15.1 Process of Quantitative Research and Investment Strategy

trading strategies. The process involves two phases. The first is quantitative research utilizing financial econometrics. The second involves using the results obtained from a financial econometrics study to develop an investment strategy.

THE QUANTITATIVE RESEARCH PROCESS

As can be seen in Figure 15.1, the financial econometrics research aspect of the quantitative research process involves three phases:

1. Develop an ex ante justification based on financial economic theory.
2. Select a survivorship-free sample.
3. Select a methodology to estimate the model.

We discuss each phase in this section.

Develop an Ex Ante Justification Based on Financial Economic Theory

A sound hypothesis is a necessary condition for the successful formulation of an implementable and replicable investment strategy. Financial economics, however, can only be motivated with creative intuitions and scrutinized by strict logical reasoning, but it does not come from hindsight or prior experience. This requirement is critical since scientific conclusions can easily be contaminated by the process of data snooping, especially when a truly independent financial economic theory is not established first.

As explained in the previous chapter, data snooping is identifying seemingly significant but in fact spurious patterns in the data.[1] All empirical tests are at risk for this problem, especially if a large number of studies have been performed on the same data sets. Given enough time and trials, people who are convinced of the existence of a pattern will eventually manage to find that pattern, real or imagined. Furthermore, there is an identical life cycle of experience in data snooping. Researchers are often confronted with exactly the same issues and will have to make the same types of choices in the process.

The process of data snooping comes in several forms. At some basic but subtle level, a hypothesis based on financial economics is founded by the knowledge of past patterns in data. Researchers may establish their "prior"

---

[1] See, for example, Stephen A. Ross, "Survivorship Bias in Performance Studies," and Andrew Lo, "Data-Snooping Biases in Financial Analysis," both appearing in *Proceedings of Blending Quantitative and Traditional Equity Analysis* (Charlottesville, VA: Association for Investment Management and Research, 1994).

from their knowledge, learning, experience, or simply what others have said. A good example for a classic yet wrong way to model the excess return in equity analysis is "market capitalization should be included in the model because there is evidence of a size effect."

From then on, the problem can only get worse as long as there is more room for choices. A researcher may choose to design the same statistical tests because of what others have done using similar data. The choices in these tests include, but are not limited to, the selection of explanatory variables, how to measure them, the functional form of the model, the length of the time period, the underlying probability distribution, and test statistics. The difference in each of these artificial choices by itself may be small, but its resulting investment performance impact is often significant.

Ideally, there should be no need to make artificial selections since all of the tests should have been dictated by the underlying theories. However, even the best financial concept, being abstract and simplified, does not always fully specify its application in reality. There are many opportunities for which decision makers have to find proxies and instruments to complete the process.

A common fallacy, however, is that researchers tend to go back to the most immediate prior step in searching for solutions when the result is not what they expect to see. Of course, this attitude reflects the general human tendency to overweight the information in the most recent period in their decision making. This could easily lead to the mindless trial of numerous alternatives, which are most likely not justified.

Therefore, a direct way to control for data snooping at all levels is that the entire process will have to be reconstructed right from the beginning whenever the output at any phase of the process cannot pass the quality test. If the estimated model cannot explain the variation of excess returns to some satisfactory degree, the process needs to be stopped and abandoned. We need to go back and develop a new theory. If the predicted model does not produce acceptable excess returns, go back to the beginning. Finally, if the level of the actual risk-adjusted excess return found from following the strategy "does not cut the muster"—go back to the beginning. This "trial-and-error" process may correct for most, but not all, of the data snooping problem. As we throw away the obvious, "bad" models through testing, we learn from the experience of trial and error. This experience itself inevitably affects the seemingly independent creation of the next generation of models.

Of course, most researchers would agree that there is almost no way to completely eliminate some form of data snooping since even the most rigorous scientific process is no more than a sequence of choices, subjective or not. As suggested by Lo,[2] like someone suffering from substance addiction,

---

[2]Lo, "Data-Snooping Biases in Financial Analysis."

the first step toward recovery is the recognition of the problem. The next step is to facilitate a research environment that avoids the temptations of making choices.[3] What this conclusion also means is that researchers should be extremely disciplined at every step of the process in making choices, with the explicit understanding of the bias induced from data snooping.

Select a Sample Free from Survivorship Bias

Since all backtest research is performed on a data set that looks back in time, the entire history of an observation will not be available if it does not survive the present. The sample that researchers can work with is a set of observations that have been preselected through time by some common denominators. A sample of a sample should not pose a problem if the subset is selected randomly. But this is not the case for most samples, which suffer from survivorship bias as we described in the previous chapter. The bias becomes relevant if the common bond to survive the observation is related to the pattern for which we are looking. A finding of a statistically significant pattern merely reflects the underlying common bond that was used to construct the testing sample.

One typical point of interest, which is severely affected by the survivorship bias, is performance comparison. By only looking at the portfolios currently outstanding, it is obvious that portfolios that did not survive through time due to poor performance are excluded from the sample. By design, the sample only contains good portfolios. How can the true factors that have caused bad performance ever be identified?

Commercial data vendors are not helping on this issue. Due to cost consideration, most data sets are only provided on a live basis. That is, for a currently non existent sample observation, the common practice is to delete its entire history from the data set. To simulate the true historical situation, it is the researchers' responsibility to bring these observations back to the sample. The sample collection procedure should be reversed in time. Cases that existed at the beginning of the sample period should be included and tracked through time.

Select a Methodology to Estimate the Model

The selection of a certain methodology should pass the same quality tests as developing financial economic theories and selecting samples. Without strong intuition, researchers should choose the methodology that needs the

---

[3]This reluctance is probably the single most important reason for the recently developed machine learning techniques discussed in the previous chapter.

least amount of human inputs. A good example is the machine learning method that uses computerized algorithms to discover the knowledge (pattern or rule) inherent in data. Advances in modeling technology such as artificial intelligence, neural network, and genetic algorithms fit into this category. The beauty of this approach is its vast degree of freedom. As explained in the previous chapter, there are none of the restrictions that are often explicitly specified in traditional, linear, stationary models.

Of course, researchers should not rely excessively on the power of the method itself. Learning is impossible without knowledge. Even if a researcher wants to simply throw data into a financial econometric model and expect it to spit out the answer, he or she needs to provide some background knowledge, such as the justification and types of input variables. There are still numerous occasions that require researchers to make justifiable decisions. For example, a typical way of modeling stock returns is using the following linear form:

$$R_{it} = a + b_{1t}F1_{it} + b_{2t}F2_{it} + \ldots + b_{nt}Fn_{it} + \varepsilon_{it} \tag{15.1}$$

where R_{it} = excess return (over a benchmark return) for the ith security in period t

   Fj_{it} = jth factor return value for the ith security in period t

   b_{nt} = the market-wide payoff for factor k in period t

   ε_{it} = error (idiosyncratic) term in period t

Trade-Off between Better Estimations and Prediction Errors

Undoubtedly, in testing and estimating equation (15.1), the first task is to decide which and how many explanatory variables should be included. This decision should not be a question whether the test is justified by an ex ante hypothesis based on financial economics. Theories, in financial economics, however, are often developed with abstract concepts that need to be measured by alternative proxies. The choice of proper proxies, while getting dangerously close to data snooping, makes the determination of both the type and the number of explanatory variables an art rather than a science. The choice of a particular proxy based on the rationale "Because it works!" is not sufficient unless it is first backed up by the theory.

One rule of thumb is to be parsimonious. A big model is not necessarily better, especially in the context of predictable risk-adjusted excess return. While the total power of explanation increases with the number of variables (size) in the model, the marginal increase of explanatory power drops quickly after some threshold. Whenever a new variable is introduced, what

TABLE 15.1 Marginal Contribution of Additional Explanatory Variables

Additional Explanatory Variable	In Sample		Out of Sample		
	Explanatory Power (R^2)	Explanatory Power (Adj. R^2)	Annualized Excess Return (%)	Annualized Standard Deviation (%)	Information Ratio
1st	0.086	0.082	2.52	7.15	0.352
2nd	0.132	0.105	2.98	7.10	0.420
3rd	0.175	0.117	3.61	6.97	0.518
4th	0.188	0.165	3.82	6.82	0.560
5th	0.202	0.174	4.05	6.12	0.662
6th	0.251	0.239	3.99	6.08	0.656
7th	0.272	0.221	3.76	6.19	0.607
8th	0.282	0.217	3.71	6.22	0.596
9th	0.291	0.209	3.64	6.37	0.571
10th	0.292	0.177	3.53	6.58	0.536

comes with the benefit of the additional description is the increase of estimation error of an additional parameter.

In Table 15.1, we demonstrate the explanatory power of a typical multifactor model for stock returns by including one additional variable at a time.[4] The second and third columns clearly show that, although by design the R^2 increases with the number of variables, the adjusted R^2, which also reflects the impact of the additional estimation error, levels off and starts decreasing after some point. This illustration suggests that in the process of estimation, the cost of estimation error is even compounded when a new prediction is further extended into the forecast period.

In Table 15.2, we also perform an out-of-sample prediction based on the estimated multifactor model in each stage. The fourth and fifth columns in the table show a more striking pattern that the risk-adjusted excess return, in the form of information ratio,[5] deteriorates even more quickly when the model becomes large.

---

[4] This is based on Christopher K. Ma, "How Many Factors Do You Need?" (Research Paper #96-4, KCM Asset Management, Inc., 2005 and 2010).

[5] The information ratio is a reward-risk ratio. The reward is the average of the active return, which is the portfolio return reduced by the return on a benchmark. This is popularly referred to in finance as "alpha." The risk is the standard deviation of the active return, which is known as the tracking error. The higher the information ratio, the better the portfolio manager performed relative to the risk assumed.

TABLE 15.2 Statistical Significance and Economic Profits

Correlation Coefficient[a]	t-Value[b]	Annual Excess Return (%)	Annual Standard Deviation (%)	Information Ratio
0.10	2.10[b]	0.50	2.17	0.230
0.25	3.78[b]	1.82	4.06	0.448
0.50	7.15[b]	3.71	4.25	0.873
0.15	1.20	0.58	1.10	0.527
0.35	2.93[b]	1.98	4.55	0.435
0.60	2.75[b]	3.80	4.55	0.835

[a] Significant at the 1% level.
[b] t-value is for the significance of correlation coefficient.
Source: Christopher K. Ma, "How Many Factors Do You Need?" Research Paper #96-4, KCM Asset Management, Inc., 2010.

Influence of Emotions

It is the exact same objectivity that researchers are proud of regarding their procedures that often leads to the question, "If everyone has the financial econometric models, will they not get the same answers?" The "overmining" on the same data set using simple linear models almost eliminates the possibility of gaining excess risk-adjusted returns (or alpha in the parlance of the financial profession).

Pessimism resulting from the competition of quantitative research also justifies the need to include some form of what the economist John Maynard Keynes called "animal spirit" in the decision process—how emotions influence human behavior.[6] Being able to do so is also probably the single most important advantage that traditional security analysis can claim over quantitative approach. Casual observations provide ample examples that investor behavior determining market pricing follows neither symmetric nor linear patterns: investors tend to react to bad news much differently than to good news;[7] information in more recent periods is overweighted in the decision process;[8] investors ignore the probability of the event but emphasize the

---

[6] John Maynard Keynes, *The General Theory of Employment, Interest, and Money* (New York: Harcourt, Brace and Company, 1936).
[7] See Keith Brown, W. Van Harlow, and Seha M. Tinic, "Risk Aversion, Uncertain Information, and Market Efficiency," *Journal of Financial Economics* 22 (1988): 355–386.
[8] See Werner F. DeBondt and Richard Thaler, "Does the Stock Market Overreact?" *Journal of Finance* 40 (1985): 793–805.

magnitude of the event;[9] stocks are purchased for their glamour but not for intrinsic value;[10] and, low price-earnings stocks paying high returns do not imply that high price–earnings stocks pay low returns.[11] We are not proposing that a statistical model should include all these phenomena, but the modeling methodology should be flexible enough to entertain such possibilities if they are warranted by the theory.

Statistical Significance Does Not Guarantee Alpha

Staunch defenders of quantitative research argue that profitable investment strategies cannot be commercialized by quantitative analysis using tools such as those available to financial econometricians;[12] the production of excess returns will stay idiosyncratic and proprietary. Alpha will originate in those proprietary algorithms that outperform commercially standardized packages for data analysis. In other words, researchers will have to learn to gain confidence even if there is no statistical significance, while statistical significance does not guarantee alpha.

Since quantitative market strategists often start with the identification of a pattern that is defined by financial econometric tools, it is easy to assume alpha from conventional statistical significance. To show that there is not necessarily a link, we perform a typical momentum trading strategy that is solely based on the predictability of future returns from past returns. A simplified version of the return-generating process under this framework follows:

$$E_{t-1}(R_t) = a + b_{t-1}R_{t-1}$$

where $E_{t-1}(R_t)$ is the conditional expected return for the period t, evaluated at point $t-1$, a is time-invariant return, and b_{t-1} is the momentum coefficient observed at time $t-1$. When b_{t-1} is (statistically) significantly positive, the time-series returns are said to exhibit "persistence and positive momentum." To implement the trading strategy using the information in correlations, stocks with at least a certain level of correlation are included in portfolios at the beginning of each month, and their returns are tracked. The performance of these portfolios apparently reflects the statistical significance (or lack thereof) in correlation between successive returns. In Table 15.3, we

---

[9] See Christopher K. Ma, "Preference Reversal in Futures Markets," working paper, Stetson University, 2010.

[10] See Josef Lakonishok, Andrei Shleifer, and Robert W. Vishny, "Contrarian Investment, Extrapolation, and Risk," *Journal of Finance* 49, no. 5 (1994): 1541–1578.

[11] See Ma, "How Many Factors Do You Need?"

[12] See, for example, Russell H. Fogler, "Investment Analysis and New Quantitative Tools," *Journal of Portfolio Management* (1995): 39–47.

TABLE 15.3 Statistical Significance and Economic Profits

Correlation Coefficient[a]	t-Value[b]	Annual Excess Return (%)	Annual Standard Deviation (%)	Information Ratio
0.10	2.10[b]	0.50	2.17	0.230
0.25	3.78[b]	1.82	4.06	0.448
0.50	7.15[b]	3.71	4.25	0.873
0.15	1.20	0.58	1.10	0.527
0.35	2.93[b]	1.98	4.55	0.435
0.60	2.75[b]	3.80	4.55	0.835

[a]Significant at the 1% level.
[b]t-value is for the significance of correlation coefficient.
Source: Christopher K. Ma, "How Many Factors Do You Need?" Research Paper #96-4, KCM Asset Management, Inc., 2010.

summarize the performance of some of the representative portfolios from a study conducted and updated by Ma in 2005 and 2010.[13]

It is not surprising that higher excess returns are generally associated with higher correlation between successive returns. More importantly, higher risk seems to be also related to higher statistical significance of the relationship (correlation). The bottom line is that an acceptable level of risk-adjusted excess return, in the form of information ratio (e.g., 1), cannot always be achieved by statistical significance alone. A more striking observation, however, is that, sometime without conventional statistical significance, the portfolio was able to deliver superior risk-adjusted returns. While the driving force may yet be known, evidence is provided for the disconnection between statistical significance and abnormal risk-adjusted returns.

INVESTMENT STRATEGY PROCESS

Once the quantitative research process is completed, implementing financial econometric results involves the investment strategy process. As can be seen in Figure 15.1, this involves two phases:

1. Estimating expected returns
2. Independent risk control.

We describe each below.

---

[13] Ma, "How Many Factors Do You Need?"

A Model To Estimate Expected Returns

The estimation for the model to explain past returns from Step 3, by itself, is not enough, since the objective of the process is to predict future returns. A good model for expected return is much harder to come by since we simply don't have enough data. As pointed out by Fischer Black, people are often confused between a model to explain average returns and a model to predict expected returns.[14] While the former can be tested on a large number of historical data points, the latter requires a long time period (sometimes decades) to cover various conditions to predict the expected return. Since we do not have that time to wait, one common shortcut is to simply assume that the model to explain average returns will be the model to predict expected returns. Of course, such predictions are highly inaccurate, given the assumption of constant expected returns.

We can easily find evidence to show it is a bad assumption. For example, if one can look at the actual model that explains the cross sections of short-term stock returns, even the most naive researcher can easily conclude that there is little resemblance between the models from one period to the next. This would in turn suggest, at least in the short term, the model to explain past returns cannot be used to predict expected returns.

This calls for brand new efforts to establish an ex ante expected return model. The process has to pass the same strict tests for quality that are required for any good modeling, as discussed earlier in this chapter and in the previous chapter. These tests would include the independent formulation of the hypothesis for expected return and a methodology and sample period free from data snooping and survivorship bias. While they are not necessarily related, the process of developing hypotheses for conditional expected return models can greatly benefit from the insights from numerous models of past returns estimated over a long time period.

Largest Value Added Apparently, the final risk-adjusted returns from a strategy can be attributed to the proper execution of each step described in Figure 15.1. The entire process can be generally described in a three-step procedure consisting of economic hypothesis, model estimation, and prediction. It is only natural for researchers to ask how to allocate their efforts among the three steps to maximize the return contribution.

To answer this question, let's examine the return contribution from model estimation and prediction. For this purpose, we use a typical multifactor model to explain the return for all stocks in the Standard & Poor's 500

---

[14] Fischer Black, "Estimating Expected Return," *Financial Analysts Journal* 49 (1993): 36–38.

Index. Assume that at the beginning of each period the best model actually describing the return in the period is known to the portfolio manager. Using this information, a portfolio consisting of the predicted top quartile is formed. The excess return from this portfolio generated with perfect information would suggest the extent of return contribution from model estimation. Accordingly, based on the results of a 2010 study[15] shown in Table 15.3, the annual mean excess return of the top predicted quartile is between 12% and 26%, depending on the length of the investment horizon.

In contrast, the annual mean excess return of the actual top quartile in the S&P 500 is between 42% and 121%. The difference in excess return between the actual top quartile portfolio and the predicted top quartile portfolio, between 30% and 95%, would suggest the extent of the return contribution from model prediction. It is clear then that for all investment horizons, the return contribution from model prediction is on average two to five times the excess returns from model estimation.

Therefore, for all practical purposes, the step of identifying a predictable model is responsible for the largest potential value added in generating predictable excess returns. The implication is that resources allocated to research should be placed disproportionally toward the effort of out-of-sample prediction.

Test the Prediction Again   Another safeguard against data snooping is to scrutinize the model once more through time. That is, the conditional model to estimate expected return needs to be tested again in a "fresh" data period. As it requires multiple time periods to observe the conditional model for expected returns, the prediction model derived under a single condition has to be confirmed again. In the following figure, we specify the relationship in time periods among estimation, testing, and confirmation.

The sample period:

Estimation	Testing	Forecast	Testing	Forecast	
Period I	Period I	Period II	Period II	Period II	Now

The sequential testing of the prediction model in the forecast period would affirm that the condition that converts the model of actual returns to the model of expected returns still produces an acceptable level of performance. As the conditioning factor varies from one period to another,

---

[15]Christopher K. Ma, "Nonlinear Factor Payoffs?" (Research Paper #97-5, KCM Asset Management, Inc., 2010).

the consistent performance of the three-period process suggests that it is not driven by a constant set of artificial rules introduced by data snooping.

Test Against a Random Walk Hypothesis   After completing the modeling exercise it is always wise to test the model against an artificial data set formed from independent and identically distributed returns. Any trading strategy applied to purely random data should yield no average excess return. Of course, purely random fluctuations will produce positive and negative excess returns. However, because we can simulate very long sequences of data, we can test with high accuracy that our models do not actually introduce artifacts that will not live up to a real-life test.

Independent Risk Control

Even if the expected return is modeled properly at the individual stock level, the bottom line of implementable investment strategies is evaluated by an acceptable level of risk-adjusted portfolio excess returns. As most institutional portfolios are benchmarked, the goal is to minimize tracking error (standard deviation of active returns), given some level of portfolio excess return. Consequently, risk control becomes technically much more complex than the conventional efficient portfolio concept. As shown by Richard Roll, an optimal portfolio which minimizes tracking error subject to a level of excess return is not a mean-variance efficient portfolio.[16] It should be noted that, due to the objective and competitive nature of the quantitative approach in its strong form, most models produce similar rankings in expected returns. The variation in performance among quantitative portfolios is mainly attributed to a superior risk control technology.

One commonly used but less preferred practice in risk management is often performed right at the stage of identifying the model for expected returns. It involves revising the estimates from the model to explain the actual return. The purpose is to control the risk by attempting to reduce the estimation error for the model of expected returns. This approach has several flaws. First, in most cases, the procedure of revising the parameter estimates (from the model of actual returns) so they can be used in the model of expected returns is often performed on an ad hoc basis, and vulnerable to data snooping. Second, in revising the parameter estimates, the task of building a relevant expected model with low prediction errors is mistaken for risk control on portfolio returns. Finally, there is a lesser degree

---

[16] Richard R. Roll, "A Mean/Variance Analysis of Tracking Error," *Journal of Portfolio Management* (Summer 1992): 13–23.

of freedom in that estimates are made based on the estimates of previous steps. The "risk control" procedure becomes dependent to the process of estimating expected returns. Consequently, an independent risk control procedure, usually through an optimization process, should be performed as an overlay on the stock selections that are determined initially by the predicted expected returns.

For computing efficiency, the iterations can be significantly reduced if several other conditions are simultaneously imposed. For example, it has been shown that the largest source of tracking error is the deviation of portfolio sector weights from its benchmark sector weights.[17] Consequently, most optimal benchmarked portfolios are "sector neutral," that is, portfolios do not make sector bets against the benchmark. This consideration would indicate the need to include a constraint that sets maximum acceptable deviations of portfolio sector weights from benchmark sector weights.

Along the same line, tracking error can be further controlled when the individual stock weight is constrained to conform to its corresponding weight in the benchmark. It is also accomplished by setting a maximum allowed deviation of stock weight in the portfolio from the weight in the benchmark.

Additional realistic portfolio constraints may be considered. Examples would include specification of a (1) minimum level of market liquidity for individual stocks, (2) maximum absolute weight in which any stock is allowed to invest, (3) minimum total number of stocks held, (4) minimum number of stocks held in each sector, and (5) maximum level of portfolio turnover allowed.

KEY POINTS

- In evaluating financial econometric models for potential implementation of investment strategies, two guiding principles are model simplicity and out-of-sample validation.
- A higher level of confidence can be placed on a simple model validated on data different from those on which it has been built.
- In the quantitative process the identification of any persistent pattern in the data is sought and must then be converted into implementable and profitable investment strategies. How this is done requires the development of underlying economic theories, an explanation of actual returns, estimation of expected returns, and construction of corresponding portfolios.

---

[17] See Ma, "Nonlinear Factor Payoffs?"

- For backtesting proposed strategies, the sample used can be a set of observations that have been preselected through time by some common denominators.
- Although a sample of a sample should not pose a problem in backtesting if the subset is selected randomly, this is not the case for most samples that suffer from survivorship bias.
- A statistically significant pattern found for a strategy may merely reflect the underlying common bond that was used to construct the testing sample.
- The selection of a methodology for estimating a financial econometric model should satisfy the same quality tests as developing economic theories and selecting samples. In the absence of strong intuition, the methodology that needs the least amount of human inputs should be employed for estimating a model.
- For both testing and model estimation, the first task is to decide which and how many explanatory variables should be included.
- Economic theories underlying a model typically involve abstract concepts that need to be measured by alternative proxies.
- Selection of the appropriate proxies, while getting dangerously close to data snooping, makes the determination of both the type and the number of explanatory variables an art rather than a science. One rule of thumb is to be parsimonious.
- To safeguard against data snooping there should be a sequential testing of the prediction model in the forecast period in order to affirm that the condition that converts the model of actual returns to the model of expected returns still produces an acceptable level of performance.
- Even if the expected return is modeled properly at the individual stock level, the bottom line of implementable investment strategies is evaluated by an acceptable level of risk-adjusted portfolio excess returns.
- Because most institutional portfolios are benchmarked, the objective is to minimize tracking error given some level of portfolio excess return. For this purpose, risk control becomes technically much more complex than the conventional efficient portfolio concept.

Descriptive Statistics

In this appendix, we review descriptive statistics. In contrast to inferential statistics that we describe in Appendix C, the objective in descriptive statistics is to quantitatively describe data. In inferential statistics, the objective is to draw conclusions and make predictions based on the data.

BASIC DATA ANALYSIS

Determining the objective of the analysis is the most important task before getting started in investigating the data using financial econometric methods. Data are gathered by several methods. In the financial industry, we have market data based on regular trades recorded by the exchanges. These data are directly observable. Aside from the regular trading process, there is so-called over-the-counter (OTC) trading, for which data may be less accessible. Annual reports and quarterly reports are published by companies in print or electronically. These data are available also in the business and finance sections of most major business-oriented print media and the Internet.

If one does research on certain financial quantities of interest, one might find the data available from either free or commercial databases. Hence, one must be concerned with the quality of the data. Unfortunately, very often databases of unrestricted access such as those available on the Internet may be of limited credibility. In contrast, there are many commercial purveyors of financial data who are generally acknowledged as providing accurate data. But, as always, quality has its price.

Once the data are gathered, it is the objective of descriptive statistics to visually and computationally convert the information collected into quantities that reveal the essentials in which we are interested. Usually in this context, visual support is added since very often that allows for a much easier grasp of the information.

The field of descriptive statistics discerns different types of data. Very generally, there are two types: nonquantitative (i.e., qualitative and ordinal) and quantitative data.

If certain attributes of an item can only be assigned to categories, these data are referred to as *qualitative data*. For example, stocks listed on the New York Stock Exchange (NYSE) as items can be categorized as belonging to a specific industry sector such as "banking," "energy," "media and telecommunications," and so on. That way, we assign each item (i.e., stock) as its attribute sector one or possibly more values from the set containing "banking," "energy," "media and telecommunications," and so on.[1] Another example would be the credit ratings assigned to debt obligations by credit rating agencies such as Standard & Poor's, Moody's, and Fitch Ratings. Except for retrieving the value of an attribute, nothing more can be done with qualitative data. One may use a numerical code to indicate the different sectors, for example 1 = "banking," 2 = "energy," and so on. However, we cannot perform any computation with these figures since they are simply names of the underlying attribute sector.

On the other hand, if an item is assigned a *quantitative variable*, the value of this variable is numerical. Generally, all real numbers are eligible. Depending on the case, however, one will use discrete values only, such as integers. Stock prices or dividends, for example, are quantitative data drawing from—up to some digits—positive real numbers. Quantitative data can be used to perform transformations and computations. One can easily think of the market capitalization of all companies comprising some index on a certain day while it would make absolutely no sense to do the same with qualitative data.[2]

Cross-Sectional Data and Time Series Data

There is another way of classifying data. Imagine collecting data from one and the same quantity of interest or *variable*. A variable is some quantity that can assume values from a value set. For example, the variable "stock price" can technically assume any nonnegative real number of currency but only one value at a time. Each day, it assumes a certain value that is the day's stock price. As another example, a variable could be the dividend payments from a specific company over some period of time. In the case of dividends, the observations are made each quarter.

---

[1] Most of the time, we will use the term "variable" instead of "attribute."

[2] Market capitalization is the total market value of the common stock of a company. It is obtained by multiplying the number of shares outstanding by the market price per share.

The set of data then form what is called *time series data*. In contrast, one could pick a particular time period of interest such as the first quarter of the current year and observe the dividend payments of all companies comprising the Standard & Poor's 500 index. By doing so, one would obtain *cross-sectional data* of the universe of stocks in the S&P 500 index at that particular time.

Frequency Distributions

One of the most important aspects of dealing with data is that they are effectively organized and transformed in order to convey the essential information contained in them. This processing of the original data helps to display the inherent meaning in a way that is more accessible to intuition.

Relative Frequency Suppose that we are interested in a particular variable that can assume a set of either finite or infinitely many values. These values may be qualitative or quantitative in nature. In either case, the initial step when obtaining a data sample for some variable is to sort the values of each observation and then to determine the frequency distribution of the data set. This is done simply by counting the number of observations for each possible value of the variable. This is referred to as the *absolute frequency*. Alternatively, if the variable can assume values on all or part of the real line, the frequency can be determined by counting the number of observations that fall into nonoverlapping intervals partitioning the real line.

In our illustration, we begin with qualitative data first and then move on to the quantitative aspects. For example, suppose we want to compare the industry composition of the component stocks in the Dow Jones Industrial Average (DJIA), an index comprised of 30 U.S. stocks, the Dow Jones Global total 50 Index (DJGTI), and the S&P 500. A problem arises because the number of stocks contained in the three indices is not the same. Hence, we cannot compare the respective absolute frequencies. Instead, we have to resort to something that creates comparability of the two data sets. This is done by expressing the number of observations of a particular value as the proportion of the total number of observations in a specific data set. That means we have to compute the *relative frequency*.

Let's denote the (absolute) frequency by a and, in particular, by a_i for the ith value of the variable. Formally, the relative frequency f_i of the ith value is then defined by

$$f_i = \frac{a_i}{n}$$

where n is the total number of observations. With k being the number of the different values, the following holds:

$$n = \sum_{i=1}^{k} f_i$$

Empirical Cumulative Frequency Distribution

In addition to the frequency distribution, there is another quantity of interest for comparing data that are closely related to the absolute or relative frequency distribution.

Suppose that one is interested in the percentage of stocks in the DJIA with closing prices of less than US$50 on a specific day. One can sort the observed closing prices by their numerical values in ascending order to obtain something like the array shown in Table A.1 for market prices as of December 15, 2006. Note that since each value occurs only once, we have to assign each value an absolute frequency of 1 or a relative frequency of 1/30, respectively, since there are 30 component stocks in the DJIA.

We start with the lowest entry ($20.77) and advance up to the largest price still less than $50, which is $49 (Coca-Cola). Each time we observe less than $50, we added 1/30, accounting for the frequency of each company, to obtain an accumulated frequency of 18/30 representing the total share of closing prices below $50. This accumulated frequency is called the *empirical cumulative frequency* at the value $50. If one computes this for all values, one obtains the *empirical cumulative frequency distribution*. The word "empirical" is used because we only consider values that are actually observed. The theoretical equivalent of the cumulative distribution function where all theoretically possible values are considered will be introduced in the context of probability theory in Appendix B.

Formally, the empirical cumulative frequency distribution F_{emp} is defined as

$$F_{emp}(x) = \sum_{i=1}^{k} a_i$$

where k is the index of the largest value observed that is still less than x. In our example, k is 18.

When we use relative frequencies, we obtain the empirical relative cumulative frequency distribution defined analogously to the empirical

TABLE A.1 DJIA Stocks by Share Price in Ascending Order as of December 15, 2006

Company	Share Price
Intel Corp.	$20.77
Pfizer Inc.	25.56
General Motors Corp.	29.77
Microsoft Corp.	30.07
Alcoa Inc.	30.76
Walt Disney Co.	34.72
AT&T Inc.	35.66
Verizon Communications Inc.	36.09
General Electric Co.	36.21
Hewlett-Packard Co.	39.91
Home Depot Inc.	39.97
Honeywell International Inc.	42.69
Merck & Co. Inc.	43.60
McDonald's Corp.	43.69
Wal-Mart Stores Inc.	46.52
JPMorgan Chase & Co.	47.95
E.I. DuPont de Nemours & Co.	48.40
Coca-Cola Co.	49.00
Citigroup Inc.	53.11
American Express Co.	61.90
United Technologies Corp.	62.06
Caterpillar Inc.	62.12
Procter & Gamble Co.	63.35
Johnson & Johnson	66.25
American International Group Inc.	72.03
Exxon Mobil Corp.	78.73
3M Co.	78.77
Altria Group Inc.	84.97
Boeing Co.	89.93
International Business Machines Corp.	95.36

Source: www.dj.com/TheCompany/FactSheets.htm, December 15, 2006.

cumulative frequency distribution, this time using relative frequencies. Hence, we have

$$F_{emp}^f(x) = \sum_{i=1}^{k} f_i$$

In our example, $F_{emp}^f(\$50) = 18/30 = 0.6 = 60\%$.

Note that the empirical cumulative frequency distribution can be evaluated at any real x even though x need not be an observation. For any value x between two successive observations $x_{(i)}$ and $x_{(i+1)}$, the empirical cumulative frequency distribution as well as the empirical cumulative relative frequency distribution remain at their respective levels at $x_{(i)}$; that is, they are of constant level $F_{emp}(x_{(i)})$ and $F_{emp}^f(x_{(i)})$, respectively. For example, consider the empirical relative cumulative frequency distribution for the data shown in Table A.1.

The computation of either form of empirical cumulative distribution function is obviously not intuitive for categorical data unless we assign some meaningless numerical proxy to each value such as "Sector A" = 1, "Sector B" = 2, and so on.

Continuous versus Discrete Variables

When quantitative variables are such that the set of values—whether observed or theoretically possible—includes intervals or the entire real numbers, then the variable is said to be a *continuous variable*. This is in contrast to *discrete variables*, which assume values only from a finite or countable set. Variables on a nominal scale cannot be considered in this context. And because of the difficulties with interpreting the results, we will not attempt to explain the issue of classes for rank data either.

When one counts the frequency of observed values of a continuous variable, one notices that hardly any value occurs more than once.[3] Theoretically, with 100% chance, all observations will yield different values. Thus, the method of counting the frequency of each value is not feasible. Instead, the continuous set of values is divided into mutually exclusive intervals. Then for each such interval, the number of values falling within that interval can be counted again. In other words, one groups the data into classes for which the frequencies can be computed. Classes should be such that their respective lower and upper bounds are real numbers.

---

[3] Naturally, the precision given by the number of digits rounded may result in higher occurrences of certain values.

Moreover, whether the class bounds are elements of the classes or not must be specified. The class bounds of a class have to be bounds of the respective adjacent classes as well, such that the classes seamlessly cover the entire data. The width should be the same for all classes. However, if there are areas where the data are very intensely dense in contrast to areas of lesser density, then the class width can vary according to significant changes in value density. In certain cases, most of the data are relatively evenly scattered within some range while there are extreme values that are located in isolated areas on either end of the data array. Then, it is sometimes advisable to specify no lower bound to the lowest class and no upper bound to the uppermost class. Classes of this sort are called *open classes*. Moreover, one should consider the precision of the data as they are given. If values are rounded to the first decimal place but there is the chance that the exact value might vary within half a decimal about the value given, class bounds have to consider this lack of certainty by admitting half a decimal on either end of the class.

Cumulative Frequency Distributions

In contrast to the empirical cumulative frequency distributions, in this section we will introduce functions that convey basically the same information, that is, the frequency distribution, but rely on a few more assumptions. These cumulative frequency distributions introduced here, however, should not be confused with the theoretical definitions given in probability theory in the next appendix, even though one will clearly notice that the notion is akin to both.

The *absolute cumulative frequency* at each class bound states how many observations have been counted up to this particular class bound. However, we do not exactly know how the data are distributed within the classes. On the other hand, when relative frequencies are used, the cumulative relative frequency distribution states the overall proportion of all values up to a certain lower or upper bound of some class.

So far, things are not much different from the definition of the empirical cumulative frequency distribution and empirical cumulative relative frequency distribution. At each bound, the empirical cumulative frequency distribution and cumulative frequency coincide. However, an additional assumption is made regarding the distribution of the values between bounds of each class when computing the cumulative frequency distribution. The data are thought of as being continuously distributed and equally spread between the particular bounds. Hence, both forms of the cumulative frequency distributions increase in a linear fashion between the two class bounds. So for both forms of cumulative distribution functions, one can compute the accumulated frequencies at values inside of classes.

For a more thorough analysis of this, let's use a more formal presentation. Let I denote the set of all class indexes i with i being some integer value between 1 and $n_I = |I|$ (i.e., the number of classes). Moreover, let a_j and f_j denote the (absolute) frequency and relative frequency of some class j, respectively. The cumulative frequency distribution at some upper bound, x_u^i, of a given class i is computed as

$$F(x_u^i) = \sum_{j:x_u^j \leq x_u^i} a_j = \sum_{j:x_u^j \leq x_l^i} a_j + a_i \qquad (A.1)$$

In words, this means that we sum up the frequencies of all classes in which the upper bound is less than x_u^i plus the frequency of class i itself. The corresponding cumulative relative frequency distribution at the same value is then,

$$F^f(x_u^i) = \sum_{j:x_u^j \leq x_u^i} f_j = \sum_{j:x_u^j \leq x_l^i} f_j + f_i \qquad (A.2)$$

This describes the same procedure as in equation (A.1) using relative frequencies instead of frequencies. For any value x in between the boundaries of, say, class i, x_l^i and x_u^i, the cumulative relative frequency distribution is defined by

$$F^f(x) = F^f(x_l^i) + \frac{x - x_l^i}{x_u^i - x_l^i} f_i \qquad (A.3)$$

In words, this means that we compute the cumulative relative frequency distribution at value x as the sum of two things. First, we take the cumulative relative frequency distribution at the lower bound of class i. Second, we add that share of the relative frequency of class i that is determined by the part of the whole interval of class i that is covered by x.

MEASURES OF LOCATION AND SPREAD

Once we have the data at our disposal, we now want to retrieve key numbers conveying specific information about the data. As key numbers we will introduce measures for the center and location of the data as well as measures for the spread of the data.

Parameters versus Statistics

Before we go further, we have to introduce a distinction that is valid for any type of data. We have to be aware of whether we are analyzing the entire population or just a sample from that population. The key numbers when dealing with populations are called *parameters*, while we refer to *statistics* when we observe only a sample. Parameters are commonly denoted by Greek letters while statistics are usually assigned Roman letters.

The difference between these two measures is that parameters are valid values for the entire population or universe of data and, hence, remain constant throughout whereas statistics may vary with every different sample even though they each are selected from the very same population. This is easily understood using the following example. Consider the average return of all stocks listed in the S&P 500 index during a particular year. This quantity is a parameter μ, for example, since it represents all these stocks. If one randomly selects 10 stocks included in the S&P 500, however, one may end up with an average return for this sample that deviates from the population average, μ. The reason would be that by chance one has picked stocks that do not represent the population very well. For example, one might by chance select the top 10 performing stocks included in the S&P 500. Their returns will yield an average (statistic) that is above the average of all 500 stocks (parameter). The opposite analog arises if one had picked the 10 worst performers. In general, deviations of the statistics from the parameters are the result of one selecting the sample.

Center and Location

The measures we present first are those revealing the center and the location of the data. The center and location are expressed by three different measures: mean, mode, and median.

The *mean* is the quantity given by the sum of all values divided by the *size* of the data set. The size is the number of values or observations. The *mode* is the value that occurs most often in a data set. If the distribution of some population or the empirical distribution of some sample are known, the mode can be determined to be the value corresponding to the highest frequency. Roughly speaking, the *median* divides data by value into a lower half and an upper half. A more rigorous definition for the median is that we require that at least half of the data are no greater and at least half of the data are no smaller than the median itself.

The interpretation of the mean is as follows: the mean gives an indication as to which value the data are scattered about. Moreover, on average, one has to expect a data value equal to the mean when selecting an observation at random. However, one incurs some loss of information that is not insignificant. Given a certain data size, a particular mean can be obtained from different values. One extreme would be that all values are equal to the mean. The other extreme could be that half of the observations are extremely to the left and half of the observations are extremely to the right of the mean, thus, leveling out, on average.

Of the three measures of central tendency, the mode is the measure with the greatest loss of information. It simply states which value occurs most often and reveals no further insight. This is the reason why the mean and median enjoy greater use in descriptive statistics. While the mean is sensitive to changes in the data set, the mode is absolutely invariant as long as the maximum frequency is obtained by the same value. The mode, however, is of importance, as will be seen, in the context of the shape of the distribution of data. A positive feature of the mode is that it is applicable to all data levels.

Variation

Rather than measures of the center or one single location, we now discuss measures that capture the way the data are spread either in absolute terms or relative terms to some reference value such as, for example, a measure of location. Hence, the measures introduced here are *measures of variation*. We may be given the average return, for example, of a selection of stocks during some period. However, the average value alone is incapable of providing us with information about the variation in returns. Hence, it is insufficient for a more profound insight into the data. Like almost everything in real life, the individual returns will most likely deviate from this reference value, at least to some extent. This is due to the fact that the driving force behind each individual object will cause it to assume a value for some respective attribute that is inclined more or less in some direction away from the standard.

While there are a great number of measures of variation that have been proposed in the finance literature, we limit our coverage to those that are more commonly used in financial econometrics—absolute deviation, standard deviation (variance), and skewness.

Absolute Deviation The *mean absolute deviation* (MAD) is the average deviation of all data from some reference value (which is usually a measure of the center). The deviation is usually measured from the mean. The MAD measure takes into consideration every data value.

Variance and Standard Deviation The *variance* is the measure of variation used most often. It is an extension of the MAD in that it averages not only the absolute but the squared deviations. The deviations are measured from the mean. The square has the effect that larger deviations contribute even more to the measure than smaller deviations as would be the case with the MAD.

This is of particular interest if deviations from the mean are more harmful the larger they are. In the conext of the variance, one often speaks of the averaged squared deviations as a risk measure.

The sample variance is defined by

$$s^2 = \frac{1}{n}\sum_{i=1}^{n}(x_i - \overline{x})^2 \tag{A.4}$$

using the sample mean. If, in equation (A.4) we use the divisor $n - 1$ rather than just n, we obtain the *corrected sample variance*.

Related to the variance is the even more commonly stated measure of variation, the *standard deviation*. The reason is that the units of the standard deviation correspond to the original units of the data whereas the units are squared in the case of the variance. The standard deviation is defined to be the positive square root of the variance. Formally, the sample standard deviation is

$$s = \sqrt{\frac{1}{n-1}\sum_{i=1}^{n}(x_i - \overline{x})^2} \tag{A.5}$$

Skewness The last measure of variation we describe is *skewness*. There exist several definitions for this measure. The *Pearson skewness* is defined as three times the difference between the median and the mean divided by the standard deviation.[4] Formally, the Pearson skewness for a sample is

$$s_P = \frac{3(m_d - \overline{x})}{s}$$

where m denotes the median.

As can be easily seen, for symmetrically distributed data, skewness is zero. For data with the mean being different from the median and, hence, located in either the left or the right half of the data, the data are skewed. If the mean is in the left half, the data are skewed to the left (or left skewe) since there are more extreme values on the left side compared to the right side. The opposite (i.e., skewed to the right, or right skewed), is true for data whose mean is further to the right than the median. In contrast to the MAD and variance, the skewness can obtain positive as well as negative values.

---

[4]To be more precise, this is only one of Pearson's skewness coefficients. Another one not presented here employs the mode instead of the mean.

This is because, not only is some absolute deviation of interest, but the direction is as well.

MULTIVARIATE VARIABLES AND DISTRIBUTIONS

Thus far in this appendix, we examined one variable only. However, for applications of financial econometrics, there is typically less of a need to analyze one variable in isolation. Instead, a typical problem is to investigate the common behavior of several variables and joint occurrences of events. In other words, there is the need to establish joint frequency distributions and introduce measures determining the extent of dependence between variables.

Frequencies

As in the single variable case, we first gather all joint observations of our variables of interest. For a better overview of occurrences of the variables, it might be helpful to set up a table with rows indicating observations and columns representing the different variables. This table is called the *table of observations*. Thus, the cell of, say, row i and column j contains the value that observation i has with respect to variable j. Let us express this relationship between observations and variables a little more formally by some functional representation.

In the following, we will restrict ourselves to observations of pairs, that is, $k = 2$. In this case, the observations are *bivariate variables* of the form $x = (x_1, x_2)$. The first component x_1 assumes values in the set V of possible values while the second component x_2 takes values in W, that is, the set of possible values for the second component.

Consider the Dow Jones Industrial Average over some period, say one month (roughly 22 trading days). The index includes the stock of 30 companies. The corresponding table of observations could then, for example, list the roughly 22 observation dates in the columns and the individual company names row-wise. So, in each column, we have the stock prices of all constituent stocks at a specific date. If we single out a particular row, we have narrowed the observation down to one component of the joint observation at that specific day.

Since we are not so much interested in each particular observation's value with respect to the different variables, we condense the information to the degree where we can just tell how often certain variables have occurred.[5] In other words, we are interested in the frequencies of all possible pairs with

---

[5]This is reasonable whenever the components assume certain values more than once.

all possible combinations of first and second components. The task is to set up the so-called *joint frequency distribution*. The *absolute joint frequency* of the components x and y is the number of occurrences counted of the pair (v,w). The *relative joint frequency distribution* is obtained by dividing the absolute frequency by the number of observations.

While joint frequency distributions exist for all data levels, one distinguishes between qualitative data, on the one hand, and rank and quantitative data, on the other hand, when referring to the table displaying the joint frequency distribution. For qualitative (nominal scale) data, the corresponding table is called a *contingency table* whereas the table for rank (ordinal) scale and quantitative data is called a *correlation table*.

Marginal Distributions

Observing bivariate data, one might be interested in only one particular component. In this case, the joint frequency in the contingency or correlation table can be aggregated to produce the univariate distribution of the one variable of interest. In other words, the joint frequencies are projected into the frequency dimension of that particular component. This distribution so obtained is called the *marginal distribution*. The marginal distribution treats the data as if only the one component was observed while a detailed joint distribution in connection with the other component is of no interest.

The frequency of certain values of the component of interest is measured by the *marginal frequency*. For example, to obtain the marginal frequency of the first component whose values v are represented by the rows of the contingency or correlation table, we add up all joint frequencies in that particular row, say i. Thus, we obtain the row sum as the marginal frequency of this component v_i. That is, for each value v_i, we sum the joint frequencies over all pairs (v_i, w_j) where v_i is held fixed.

To obtain the marginal frequency of the second component whose values w are represented by the columns, for each value w_j, we add up the joint frequencies of that particular column j to obtain the column sum. This time we sum over all pairs (v_i, w_j) keeping w_j fixed.

Graphical Representation

A common graphical tool used with bivariate data arrays is given by the so-called *scatter diagram* or *scatter plot*. In this diagram, the values of each pair are displayed. Along the horizontal axis, usually the values of the first component are displayed while along the vertical axis, the values of the second component are displayed. The scatter plot is helpful in visualizing

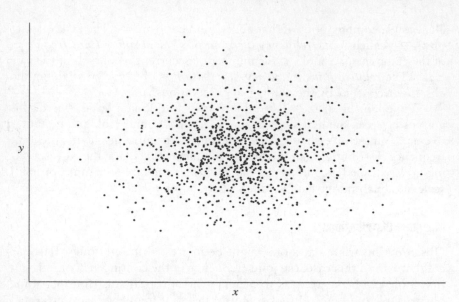

FIGURE A.1 Scatter Plot: Extreme 1—No Relationship of Component Variables x and y

whether the variation of one component variable somehow affects the variation of the other. If, for example, the points in the scatter plot are dispersed all over in no discernible pattern, the variability of each component may be unaffected by the other. This is visualized in Figure A.1.

The other extreme is given if there is a functional relationship between the two variables. Here, two cases are depicted. In Figure A.2, the relationship is linear whereas in Figure A.3, the relationship is of some higher order.[6] When two (or more) variables are observed at a certain point in time, one speaks of *cross-sectional analysis*. In contrast, analyzing one and the same variable at different points in time, one refers to it as *time series analysis*. We will come back to the analysis of various aspects of joint behavior in more detail later.

Figure A.4 shows bivariate monthly return data of the S&P 500 stock index and the GE stock for the period January 1996 to December 2003 (96 observation pairs). We plot the pairs of returns such that the GE returns are the horizontal components while the index returns are the vertical components. By observing the plot, we can roughly assess, at first, that there

---

[6] As a matter of fact, in Figure A.2, we have $y = 0.3 + 1.2x$. In Figure A.3, we have $y = 0.2 + x3$.

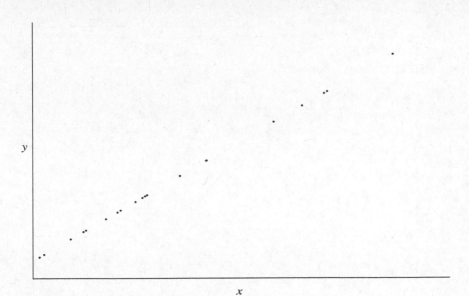

FIGURE A.2 Scatter Plot: Extreme 2—Perfect Linear Relationship between Component Variables x and y

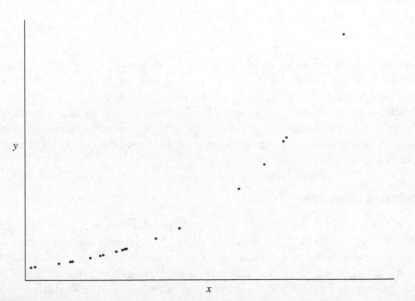

FIGURE A.3 Scatter Plot: Extreme 3—Perfect Cubic Functional Relationship between Component Variables x and y

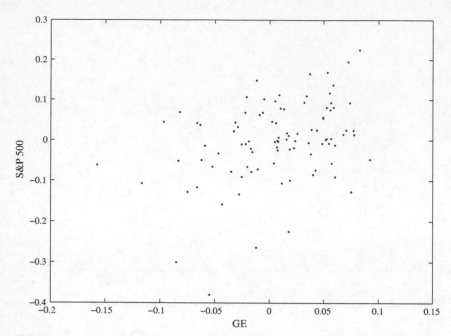

FIGURE A.4   Scatter Plot of Monthly S&P 500 Stock Index Returns versus Monthly GE Stock Returns

appears to be no distinct structure in the joint behavior of the data. However, by looking a little bit more thoroughly, one might detect a slight linear relationship underlying the two returns series. That is, the observations appear to move around some invisible line starting from the bottom left corner and advancing to the top right corner. This would appear quite reasonable since one might expect some link between the GE stock and the overall index.

Conditional Distribution

With the marginal distribution as previously defined, we obtain the frequency of component x at a certain value v, for example. We treat variable x as if variable y did not exist and we only observed x. Hence, the sum of the marginal frequencies of x has to be equal to one. The same is true in the converse case for variable y. Looking at the contingency or correlation table, the joint frequency at the fixed value v of the component x may vary in the values w of component y. Then, there appears to be some kind of influence of component y on the occurrence of value v of component x. The influence, as will be shown later, is mutual. Hence, one is interested in the distribution of one component given a certain value for the other component. This distribution is called the *conditional frequency distribution*. The conditional relative frequency *of* x conditional on w is defined by

$$f_{x|w}(v) = f(x|w) = \frac{f_{x,y}(v,w)}{f_y(w)} \tag{A.6}$$

The conditional relative frequency of y on v is defined analogously. In equation (A.6), both commonly used versions of the notations for the conditional frequency are given on the left side. The right side, that is, the definition of the conditional relative frequency, uses the joint frequency at v and w divided by the marginal frequency of y at w. The use of conditional distributions reduces the original space to a subset determined by the value of the conditioning variable. If in equation (A.6) we sum over all possible values v, we obtain the marginal distribution of y at the value w, $f_y(w)$, in the numerator of the expression on the right side. This is equal to the denominator. Thus, the sum over all conditional relative frequencies of x conditional on w is one. Hence, the cumulative relative frequency of x at the largest value x can obtain, conditional on some value w of y, has to be equal to one. The equivalence for values of y conditional on some value of x is true as well.

Analogous to univariate distributions, it is possible to compute measures of center and location for conditional distributions.

Independence

The previous discussion raised the issue that a component may have influence on the occurrence of values of the other component. This can be analyzed by comparing the joint frequencies of x and y with the value in one component fixed, say $x = v$. If these frequencies vary for different values of y, then the occurrence of values x is not independent of the value of y. It is equivalent to check whether a certain value of x occurs more frequently given a certain value of y, that is, check the conditional frequency of x conditional on y, and compare this conditional frequency with the marginal frequency at this particular value of x.

The formal definition of *independence* is if for all v,w

$$f_{x,y}(v,w) = f_x(v) \cdot f_y(w) \tag{A.7}$$

That is, for any pair (v, w), the joint frequency is the mathematical product of their respective marginals. By the definition of the conditional frequencies, we can state an equivalent definition as in the following:

$$f_x(v) = f(v \mid w) = \frac{f_{x,y}(v, w)}{f_y(w)} \tag{A.8}$$

which, in the case of independence of x and y, has to hold for all values v and w. Conversely, an equation equivalent to (A.8) has to be true for the marginal frequency of y, $f_y(w)$, at any value w. In general, if one can find one pair (v, w) where either equations (A.7) or (A.8) and, hence, both do not hold, then x and y are *dependent*. So, it is fairly easy to show that x and y are dependent by simply finding a pair violating equations (A.7) and (A.8).

Now we show that the concept of influence of x on values of y is analogous. Thus, the feature of statistical dependence of two variables is mutual. This will be shown in a brief formal way by the following. Suppose that the frequency of the values of x depends on the values of y, in particular,[7]

$$f_x(v) \neq \frac{f_{x,y}(v, w)}{f_y(w)} = f(v \mid w) \tag{A.9}$$

Multiplying each side of equation (A.9) by $f_y(w)$ yields

$$f_{x,y}(v, w) \neq f_x(v) \cdot f_y(w) \tag{A.10}$$

which is just the definition of dependence. Dividing each side of equation (A.10) by $f_x(v) > 0$ gives

$$\frac{f_{x,y}(v, w)}{f_x(v)} = f(w \mid v) \neq f_y(w)$$

showing that the values of y depend on x. Conversely, one can demonstrate the mutuality of the dependence of the components.

Covariance

In this bivariate context, there is a measure of joint variation for quantitative data. It is the (sample) *covariance* defined by

$$s_{x,y} = \mathrm{cov}(x, y) = \frac{1}{n} \sum_{i=1}^{n} (x_i - \bar{x})(y_i - \bar{y}) \tag{A.11}$$

---

[7] This holds provided that $f_y(w) > 0$.

In equation (A.11), for each observation, the deviation of the first component from its mean is multiplied by the deviation of the second component from its mean. The sample covariance is then the average of all joint deviations. Some tedious calculations lead to an equivalent representation of equation (A.11)

$$s_{x,y} = \text{cov}(x, y) = \frac{1}{n}\sum_{i=1}^{n} v_i w_i - \overline{x}\,\overline{y}$$

which is a transformation analogous to the one already presented for variances.

The covariance of independent variables is equal to zero. The converse, however, is not generally true; that is, one cannot automatically conclude independence from zero covariance. This statement is one of the most important results in statistics and probability theory. Technically, if the covariance of x and y is zero, the two variables are said to be uncorrelated. For any value of $\text{cov}(x,y)$ different from zero, the variables are correlated. Since two variables with zero covariance are uncorrelated but not automatically independent, it is obvious that independence is a stricter criterion than no correlation.[8]

This concept is exhibited in Figure A.5. In the plot, the two sets representing correlated and uncorrelated variables are separated by the dashed line. Inside of the dashed line, we have uncorrelated variables while the correlated variables are outside. Now, as we can see by the dotted line, the set of independent variables is completely contained within the dashed oval of uncorrelated variables. The complementary set outside the dotted circle (i.e., the dependent variables) contains all of the correlated as well as part of the uncorrelated variables. Since the dotted circle is completely inside of the dashed oval, we see that independence is a stricter requirement than uncorrelatedness.

The concept behind Figure A.5 of zero covariance with dependence can be demonstrated by a simple example. Consider two hypothetical securities, x and y, with the payoff pattern given in Table A.2. In the left column below y, we have the payoff values of security y while in the top row we have the payoff values of security x. Inside of the table are the joint frequencies of the pairs (x,y). As we can see, each particular value of x occurs in combination with only one particular value of y. Thus, the two variables (i.e., the payoffs of x and y) are dependent. We compute the means of the two variables to be

---

[8]The reason is founded in the fact that the terms in the sum of the covariance can cancel out each other even though the variables are not independent.

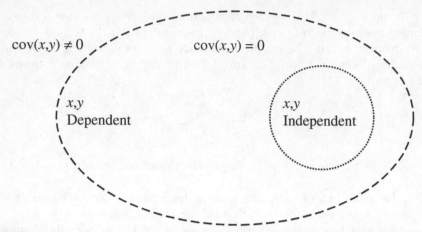

FIGURE A.5 Relationship between Correlation and Dependence of Bivariate Variables

$\bar{x} = 0$ and $\bar{y} = 0$, respectively. The resulting sample covariance according to equation (A.11) is then

$$s_{X,Y} = \frac{1}{3} \cdot \left(\frac{7}{6} - 0 \right) \cdot (1 - 0) + \ldots + \frac{1}{3} \left(-\frac{11}{6} - 0 \right) (1 - 0) = 0$$

which indicates zero correlation. Note that despite the fact that the two variables are obviously dependent, the joint occurrence of the individual values is such that, according to the covariance, there is no relationship apparent.

Correlation

If the covariance of two variables is non-zero we know that, formally, the variables are dependent. However, the degree of correlation is not uniquely determined.

TABLE A.2 Payoff Table of the Hypothetical Variables x and y with Joint Frequencies

y	x			
	7/6	13/6	–5/6	–11/6
1	1/3			
–2		1/6		
2			1/6	
–1				1/3

This problem is apparent from the following illustration. Suppose we have two variables, x and y, with a $\text{cov}(x, y)$ of a certain value. A linear transformation of, at least, one variable, say $ax + b$, will generally lead to a change in value of the covariance due to the following property of the covariance:

$$\text{cov}(ax + b, y) = a\,\text{cov}(x, y)$$

This does not mean, however, that the transformed variable is more or less correlated with y than x was. Since the covariance is obviously sensitive to transformation, it is not a reasonable measure to express the degree of correlation.

This shortcoming of the covariance can be circumvented by dividing the joint variation as defined by equation (A.11) by the product of the respective variations of the component variables. The resulting measure is the *Pearson correlation coefficient* or simply the *correlation coefficient* defined by

$$r_{x,y} = \frac{\text{cov}(x, y)}{s_x \cdot s_y} \tag{A.12}$$

where the covariance is divided by the product of the standard deviations of x and y. By definition, $r_{x,y}$ can take on any value from -1 to 1 for any bivariate quantitative data. Hence, we can compare different data with respect to the correlation coefficient equation (A.12). Generally, we make the distinction $r_{x,y} < 0$, negative correlation; $r_{x,y} = 0$, no correlation; and $r_{x,y} > 0$, positive correlation to indicate the possible direction of joint behavior.

In contrast to the covariance, the correlation coefficient is invariant with respect to linear transformation. That is, it is said to be *scaling invariant*. For example, if we translate x to $ax + b$, we still have

$$r_{ax+b,y} = \text{cov}(ax + b, y) / (s_{ax+b} \cdot s_y) = a\,\text{cov}(x, y) / as_x \cdot s_y = r_{x,y}$$

Contingency Coefficient

So far, we could only determine the correlation of quantitative data. To extend this analysis to any type of data, we introduce another measure, the so-called *chi-square test statistic* denoted by χ^2. Using relative frequencies, the chi-square test statistic is defined by

$$\chi^2 = n \sum_{i=1}^{r} \sum_{j=1}^{s} \frac{(f_{x,y}(v_i, w_j) - f_x(v_i)f_y(w_j))^2}{f_x(v_i)f_y(w_j)} \tag{A.13}$$

An analogous formula can be used for absolute frequencies.

The intuition behind equation (A.13) is to measure the average squared deviations of the joint frequencies from what they would be in case of independence. When the components are, in fact, independent, then the chi-square test statistic is zero. However, in any other case, we have the problem that, again, we cannot make an unambiguous statement to compare different data sets. The values of the chi-square test statistic depend on the data size n. For increasing n, the statistic can grow beyond any bound such that there is no theoretical maximum. The solution to this problem is given by the *Pearson contingency coefficient* or simply *contingency coefficient* defined by

$$C = \sqrt{\frac{\chi^2}{n + \chi^2}} \qquad (A.14)$$

The contingency coefficient by the definition given in equation (A.14) is such that $0 \leq C < 1$. Consequently, it assumes values that are strictly less than one but may become arbitrarily close to one. This is still not satisfactory for our purpose to design a measure that can uniquely determine the respective degrees of dependence of different data sets.

There is another coefficient that can be used based on the following. Suppose we have bivariate data in which the value set of the first component variable contains r different values and the value set of the second component variable contains s different values. In the extreme case of total dependence of x and y, each variable will assume a certain value if and only if the other variable assumes a particular corresponding value. Hence, we have $k = \min\{r,s\}$ unique pairs that occur with positive frequency whereas any other combination does not occur at all (i.e., has zero frequency). Then one can show that

$$C = \sqrt{\frac{k-1}{k}}$$

such that, generally, $0 \leq C \leq \sqrt{(k-1)/k} < 1$. Now, the standardized coefficient can be given by

$$C_{corr} = \sqrt{\frac{k}{k-1}} C \qquad (A.15)$$

which is called the *corrected contingency coefficient* with $0 \leq C \leq 1$. With the measures given in equations (A.13), (A.14), and (A.15), and the corrected contingency coefficient, we can determine the degree of dependence for any type of data.

Continuous Probability Distributions Commonly Used in Financial Econometrics

In this appendix, we discuss the more commonly used continuous probability distributions are used in financial econometrics. The four distributions discussed are the normal distribution, the chi-square distribution, the Student's t-distribution, the Fisher's F-distribution. It should be emphasized that although many of these distributions enjoy widespread attention in financial econometrics as well as financial theory (e.g., the normal distribution), due to their well-known characteristics or mathematical simplicity, the use of some of them might be ill-suited to replicate the real-world behavior of financial returns. In particular, the four distributions just mentioned are appealing in nature because of their mathematical simplicity, due to the observed behavior of many quantities in finance, there is a need for more flexible distributions compared to keeping models mathematically simple. For example, although the Student's t-distribution that will be discussed in this appendix is able to mimic some behavior inherent in financial data such as so-called *fat tails* or *heavy tails* (which means that a lot of the probability mass is attributed to extreme values),[1] it fails to capture other observed behavior such as skewness. For this reason, there has been increased interest in a continuous probability distribution in finance and financial econometrics known as the α-stable distribution. We will describe this distribution at the end of this appendix.

---

[1] There are various characterizations of fat tails in the literature. In finance, typically the tails that are heavier than those of the exponential distribution are considered "heavy."

NORMAL DISTRIBUTION

The first distribution we discuss is the *normal distribution*. It is the distribution most commonly used in finance despite its many limitations. This distribution, also referred to as the *Gaussian distribution*, is characterized by the two parameters: mean (μ) and standard deviation (σ). The distribution is denoted by $N(\mu, \sigma^2)$. When $\mu = 0$ and $\sigma^2 = 1$, then we obtain the *standard normal distribution*.

The density function for the normal distribution is given by

$$f(x) = \frac{1}{\sqrt{2\pi}\sigma} \cdot e^{-\frac{(x-\mu)^2}{2\sigma^2}} \qquad (B.1)$$

The density function is symmetric about μ. A plot of the density function for several parameter values is given in Figure B.1. As can be seen, the value of μ results in a horizontal shift from 0 while σ inflates or deflates the graph. A characteristic of the normal distribution is that the densities are bell shaped.

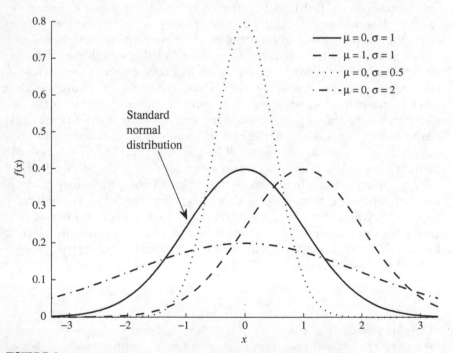

FIGURE B.1 Normal Density Function for Various Parameter Values

A problem is that the distribution function cannot be solved for analytically and therefore has to be approximated numerically. In the particular case of the standard normal distribution, the values are tabulated. Standard statistical software provides the values for the standard normal distribution as well as most of the distributions presented in this chapter. The standard normal distribution is commonly denoted by the Greek letter Φ such that we have $\Phi(x) = F(x) = P(X \leq x)$, for some standard normal random variable X. In Figure B.2, graphs of the distribution function are given for three different sets of parameters.

Properties of the Normal Distribution

The normal distribution provides one of the most important classes of probability distributions due to two appealing properties:

> *Property 1.* The distribution is *location-scale invariant*. That is, if X has a normal distribution, then for every constant a and b, $aX + b$ is again a normal random variable.

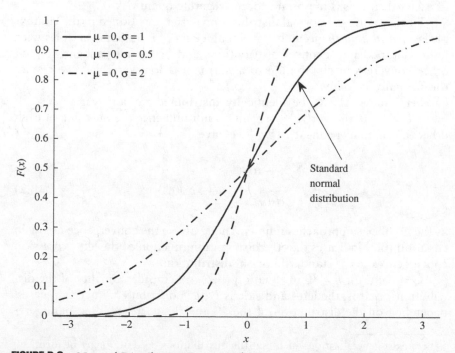

FIGURE B.2 Normal Distribution Function for Various Parameter Values

Property 2. The distribution is *stable under summation.* That is, if X has a normal distribution F, and $X_1, \ldots, X_n$ are n independent random variables with distribution F, then $X_1 + \ldots + X_n$ is again a normal distributed random variable.

In fact, if a random variable X has a distribution satisfying Properties 1 and 2 and X has a finite variance, then X has a normal distribution.

Property 1, the location-scale invariance property, guarantees that we may multiply X by b and add a where a and b are any real numbers. Then, the resulting $a + b \cdot X$ is, again, normally distributed, more precisely, $N(a + \mu, b\sigma)$. Consequently, a normal random variable will still be normally distributed if we change the units of measurement. The change into $a + b \cdot X$ can be interpreted as observing the same X, however, measured in a different scale. In particular, if a and b are such that the mean and variance of the resulting $a + b \cdot X$ are 0 and 1, respectively, then $a + b \cdot X$ is called the *standardization of X.*

Property 2, stability under summation, ensures that the sum of an arbitrary number n of normal random variables, $X_1, X_2, \ldots, X_n$ is, again, normally distributed provided that the random variables behave independently of each other. This is important for aggregating quantities.

Furthermore, the normal distribution is often mentioned in the context of the *central limit theorem.* It states that a sum of n random variables with finite variance and identical distributions and being independent of each other, converges in distribution to a normal random variable.[2] We restate this formally as follows:

Let $X_1, X_2, \ldots, X_n$ be identically distributed random variables with mean $E(X_i) = \mu$ and $var(X_i) = \sigma^2$ and do not influence the outcome of each other (i.e., are independent). Then, we have

$$\frac{\sum_{i=1}^{n} X_i - n \cdot \mu}{\sigma \sqrt{n}} \xrightarrow{D} N(0,1) \tag{B.2}$$

as the number n approaches infinity. The D above the convergence arrow in equation (B.2) indicates that the distribution function of the left expression convergences to the standard normal distribution.

Generally, for $n = 30$ in equation (B.2), we consider equality of the distributions; that is, the left-hand side is $N(0,1)$ distributed. In certain cases, depending on the distribution of the X_i and the corresponding parameter

---

[2]There exist generalizations such that the distributions need no longer be identical. However, this is beyond the scope of this appendix.

values, $n < 30$ justifies the use of the standard normal distribution for the left-hand side of equation (B.2).

These properties make the normal distribution the most popular distribution in finance. This popularity is somewhat contentious, however, for reasons that will be given when we describe the α-stable distribution.

The last property we will discuss of the normal distribution that is shared with some other distributions is the bell shape of the density function. This particular shape helps in roughly assessing the dispersion of the distribution due to a rule of thumb commonly referred to as the *empirical rule*. Due to this rule, we have

$$P(X \in [\mu \pm \sigma]) = F(\mu + \sigma) - F(\mu - \sigma) \approx 68\%$$

$$P(X \in [\mu \pm 2\sigma]) = F(\mu + 2\sigma) - F(\mu - 2\sigma) \approx 95\%$$

$$P(X \in [\mu \pm 3\sigma]) = F(\mu + 3\sigma) - F(\mu - 3\sigma) \approx 100\%$$

The above states that approximately 68% of the probability is given to values that lie in an interval one standard deviation σ about the mean μ. About 95% probability is given to values within 2σ to the mean, while nearly all probability is assigned to values within 3σ from the mean.

CHI-SQUARE DISTRIBUTION

Our next distribution is the *chi-square distribution*. Let Z be a standard normal random variable, in brief $Z \sim N(0,1)$, and let $X = Z^2$. Then X is distributed chi-square with one degree of freedom. We denote this as $X \sim \chi^2(1)$. The *degrees of freedom* indicate how many independently behaving standard normal random variables the resulting variable is composed of. Here X is just composed of one, namely Z, and therefore has one degree of freedom.

Because Z is squared, the chi-square distributed random variable assumes only nonnegative values; that is, the support is on the nonnegative real numbers. It has mean $E(X) = 1$ and variance $\text{var}(X) = 2$.

In general, the chi-square distribution is characterized by the degrees of freedom n, which assume the values $1, 2, \ldots$, and so on. Let $X_1, X_2, \ldots, X_n$ be n $\chi^2(1)$ distributed random variables that are all independent of each other. Then their sum, S, is

$$S = \sum_{i=1}^{n} X_i \sim \chi^2(n) \tag{B.3}$$

In words, the sum is again distributed chi-square but this time with n degrees of freedom. The corresponding mean is $E(X) = n$, and the variance equals $\text{var}(X) = 2 \cdot n$. So, the mean and variance are directly related to the degrees of freedom.

From the relationship in equation (B.3), we see that the degrees of freedom equal the number of independent $\chi^2(1)$ distributed X_i in the sum. If we have two independent random variables $X_1 \sim \chi^2(n_1)$ and $X_2 \sim \chi^2(n_2)$, it follows that

$$X_1 + X_2 \sim \chi^2(n_1 + n_2) \tag{B.4}$$

From equation (B.4), we have that chi-square distributions have Property 2; that is, they are stable under summation in the sense that the sum of any two independent chi-squared distributed random variables is itself chi-square distributed.

We won't present the chi-squared distribution's density function here. However, Figure B.3 shows a few examples of the plot of the chi-square density function with varying degrees of freedom. As can be observed, the chi-square distribution is skewed to the right.

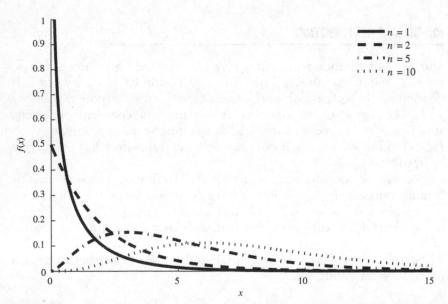

FIGURE B.3 Density Functions of Chi-Square Distributions for Various Degrees of Freedom n

STUDENT'S *t*-DISTRIBUTION

An important continuous probability distribution when the population variance of a distribution is unknown is the *Student's t-distribution* (also referred to as the *t-distribution* and *Student's distribution*).

To derive the distribution, let X be distributed standard normal, that is, $X \sim N(0,1)$, and S be chi-square distributed with n degrees of freedom, that is, $S \sim \chi^2(n)$. Furthermore, if X and S are independent of each other, then

$$Z = \frac{X}{\sqrt{S/n}} \sim t(n)$$

(B.5)

In words, equation (B.5) states that the resulting random variable Z is Student's *t*-distributed with n degrees of freedom. The degrees of freedom are inherited from the chi-square distribution of S.

Here is how we can interpret equation (B.5). Suppose we have a population of normally distributed values with zero mean. The corresponding normal random variable may be denoted as X. If one also knows the standard deviation of X,

$$\sigma = \sqrt{\text{var}(X)}$$

with X/σ, we obtain a standard normal random variable.

However, if σ is not known, we instead have to use, for example,

$$\sqrt{S/n} = \sqrt{1/n \cdot (X_1^2 + \ldots + X_n^2)}$$

where $X_1^2, \ldots, X_n^2$ are n random variables identically distributed as X. Moreover, $X_1, \ldots, X_n$ have to assume values independently of each other. Then, the distribution of

$$X/\sqrt{S/n}$$

is the *t*-distribution with n degrees of freedom, that is,

$$X/\sqrt{S/n} \sim t(n)$$

By dividing by σ or S/n, we generate rescaled random variables that follow a standardized distribution. Quantities similar to $X/\sqrt{S/n}$ play an important role in parameter estimation.

It is unnecessary to provide the complicated formula for the Student's *t*-distribution's density function here. Basically, the density function of the

Student's t-distribution has a similar shape to the normal distribution, but with thicker tails. For large degrees of freedom n, the Student's t-distribution does not significantly differ from the standard normal distribution. As a matter of fact, for $n \geq 50$, it is practically indistinguishable from $N(0,1)$.

Figure B.4 shows the Student's t-density function for various degrees of freedom plotted against the standard normal density function. The same is done for the distribution function in Figure B.5.

In general, the lower the degrees of freedom, the heavier the tails of the distribution, making extreme outcomes much more likely than for greater degrees of freedom or, in the limit, the normal distribution. This can be seen by the distribution function that we depicted in Figure B.5 for $n = 1$ and $n = 5$ against the standard normal cumulative distribution function (cdf). For lower degrees of freedom such as $n = 1$, the solid curve starts to rise earlier and approach 1 later than for higher degrees of freedom such as $n = 5$ or the $N(0,1)$ case.

This can be understood as follows. When we rescale X by dividing by $\sqrt{S/n}$ as in equation (B.5), the resulting $X/\sqrt{S/n}$ obviously inherits randomness from both X and S. Now, when S is composed of few X_i, only, say $n = 3$, such that $X/\sqrt{S/n}$ has three degrees of freedom, there is a lot of

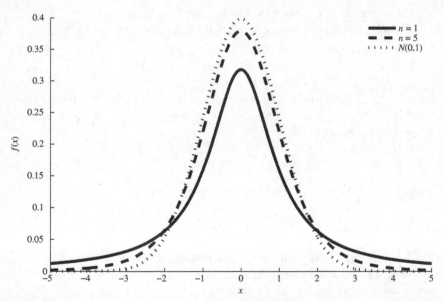

FIGURE B.4 Density Function of the t-Distribution for Various Degrees of Freedom n Compared to the Standard Normal Density Function $N(0,1)$

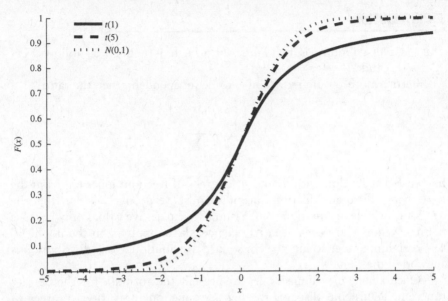

FIGURE B.5   Distribution Function of the *t*-Distribution for Various Degrees of Freedom *n* Compared to the Standard Normal Density Function $N(0,1)$

dispersion from S relative to the standard normal distribution. By including more independent $N(0,1)$ random variables X_i such that the degrees of freedom increase, S becomes less dispersed. Thus, much uncertainty relative to the standard normal distribution stemming from the denominator in $X / \sqrt{S/n}$ vanishes. The share of randomness in $X / \sqrt{S/n}$ originating from X alone prevails such that the normal characteristics preponderate. Finally, as n goes to infinity, we have something that is nearly standard normally distributed.

The mean of the Student's t random variable is zero, that is $E(X) = 0$, while the variance is a function of the degrees of freedom n as follows

$$\sigma^2 = \text{var}(X) = \frac{n}{n-2}$$

For $n = 1$ and 2, there is no finite variance. Distributions with such small degrees of freedom generate extreme movements quite frequently relative to higher degrees of freedom. Precisely for this reason, stock price returns are often found to be modeled quite well using distributions with small degrees of freedom, or alternatively, distributions with heavy tails with power decay, with power parameter less than 6.

F-DISTRIBUTION

Our next distribution is the *F-distribution*. It is defined as follows. Let $X \sim \chi^2(n_1)$ and $Y \sim \chi^2(n_2)$.

Furthermore, assuming X and Y to be independent, then the ratio

$$F(n_1, n_2) = \frac{\dfrac{X}{n_1}}{\dfrac{Y}{n_2}} \tag{B.6}$$

has an *F*-distribution with n_1 and n_2 degrees of freedom inherited from the underlying chi-square distributions of X and Y, respectively. We see that the random variable in equation (B.6) assumes nonnegative values only because neither X nor Y are ever negative. Hence, the support is on the nonnegative real numbers. Also like the chi-square distribution, the *F*-distribution is skewed to the right.

Once again, it is unnecessary to present the formula for the density function. Figure B.6 displays the density function for various degrees of freedom. As the degrees of freedom n_1 and n_2 increase, the function graph becomes more peaked and less asymmetric while the tails lose mass.

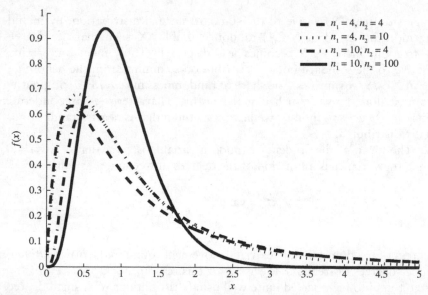

FIGURE B.6 Density Function of the *F*-Distribution for Various Degrees of Freedom n_1 and n_2

The mean is given by

$$E(X) = \frac{n_2}{n_2 - 2} \text{ for } n_2 > 2 \tag{B.7}$$

while the variance equals

$$\sigma^2 = \text{var}(X) = \frac{2n_2^2(n_1 + n_2 - 2)}{n_1(n_2 - 2)^2(n_2 - 4)} \text{ for } n_2 > 4 \tag{B.8}$$

Note that according to equation (B.7), the mean is not affected by the degrees of freedom n_1 of the first chi-square random variable, while the variance in equation (B.8) is influenced by the degrees of freedom of both random variables.

α-STABLE DISTRIBUTION

While many models in finance have been modeled historically using the normal distribution based on its pleasant tractability, concerns have been raised that this distribution underestimates the danger of downturns of extreme magnitude in stock markets that have been observed in financial markets. Many distributional alternatives providing more realistic chances to severe price movements have been presented earlier, such as the Student's *t*. In the early 1960s, Benoit Mandelbrot suggested as a distribution for commodity price changes the class of Lévy *stable distributions* (simply referred to as the *stable distributions*).[3] The reason is that, through their particular parameterization, they are capable of modeling moderate scenarios, as supported by the normal distribution, as well as extreme ones.

The stable distribution is characterized by the four parameters α, β, σ, and μ. In brief, we denote the stable distribution by $S(\alpha, \beta, \sigma, \mu)$. Parameter α is the so called *tail index* or *characteristic exponent*. It determines how much probability is assigned around the center and the tails of the distribution. The lower the value α, the more pointed about the center is the density and the heavier are the tails. These two features are referred to as *excess kurtosis* relative to the normal distribution. This can be visualized graphically as we have done in Figure B.7 where we compare the normal density to an α-stable

---

[3] Benoit B. Mandelbrot, "The Variation of Certain Speculative Prices," *Journal of Business* 36 (1963): 394–419.

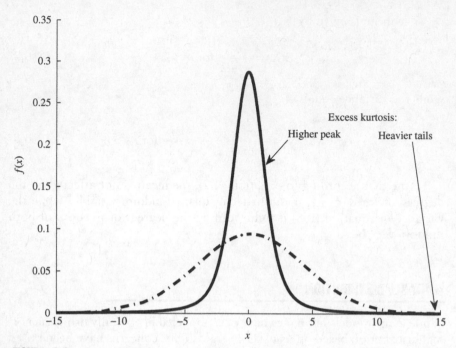

FIGURE B.7 Comparison of the Normal (Dash-Dotted) and α-Stable (Solid) Density Functions

density with a low $\alpha = 1.5$.[4] The density graphs are obtained by fitting the distributions to the same sample data of arbitrarily generated numbers. The parameter α is related to the parameter ξ of the Pareto distribution resulting in the tails of the density functions of α-stable random variables to vanish at a rate proportional to the Pareto tail.

The tails of the Pareto as well as the α-stable distribution decay at a rate with fixed power α, $Cx^{-\alpha}$ (i.e., *power law*) where C is a positive constant, which is in contrast to the normal distribution whose tails decay at an exponential rate (i.e., roughly $x^{-1}e^{-x^2/2}$).

The parameter β indicates *skewness* where negative values represent left skewness while positive values indicate right skewness. The *scale* parameter σ has a similar interpretation to the standard deviation. Finally, the parameter μ indicates *location* of the distribution. Its interpretability depends on the parameter α. If the latter is between 1 and 2, then μ is equal to the mean.

---

[4]In the figure, the parameters for the normal distribution are $\mu = 0.14$ and $\sigma = 4.23$. The parameters for the stable distribution are $\alpha = 1.5$, $\beta = 0$, $\sigma = 1$, and $\mu = 0$. Note that symbols common to both distributions have different meanings.

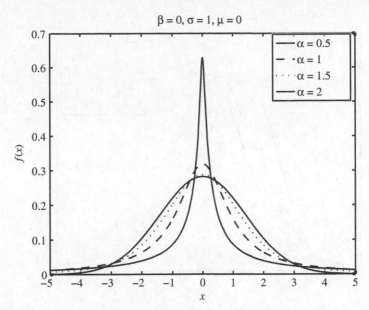

FIGURE B.8   Influence of α on the Resulting Stable Distribution

Possible values of the parameters are listed below:

α (0,2]

β [−1,1]

σ (0,∞)

μ any real number

Depending on the parameters α and β, the distribution has either support on the entire real line or only the part extending to the right of some location.

In general, the density function is not explicitly presentable. Instead, the distribution of the α-stable random variable is given by its characteristic function which we do not present here.[5]

Figure B.8 shows the effect of α on tail thickness of the density as well as peakedness at the origin relative to the normal distribution (collectively

---

[5]There are three possible ways to uniquely define a probability distribution: the cumulative distribution function, the probability density function, and the characteristic function. The precise definition of a characteristics function needs some advanced mathematical concepts and is not of major interest for this book. At this point, we just state the fact that knowing the characteristic function is mathematically equivalent to knowing the probability density or the cumulative distribution function. In only three cases does the density of a stable distribution have a closed-form expression.

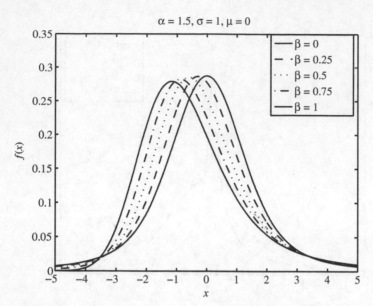

FIGURE B.9 Influence of β on the Resulting Stable Distribution

the "kurtosis"of the density), for the case of β = 0, μ = 0, and σ = 1. As the values of α decrease, the distribution exhibits fatter tails and more peakedness at the origin. Figure B.9 illustrates the influence of β on the skewness of the density function for α = 1.5, μ = 0, and σ = 1. Increasing (decreasing) values of β result in skewness to the right (left).

Only in the case of an α of 0.5, 1, or 2 can the functional form of the density be stated. For our purpose here, only the case α = 2 is of interest because, for this special case, the stable distribution represents the normal distribution. Then, the parameter β ceases to have any meaning since the normal distribution is not asymmetric.

A feature of the stable distributions is that moments such as the mean, for example, exist only up to the power α. So, except for the normal case (where α = 2), there exists no finite variance. It becomes even more extreme when α is equal to 1 or less such that not even the mean exists any more. The non existence of the variance is a major drawback when applying stable distributions to financial data. This is one reason that the use of this family of distribution in finance is still disputed.

This class of distributions owes its name to the *stability property* that we described earlier for the normal distribution (Property 2): The weighted sum of an arbitrary number of independent α-stable random variables with the same parameters is, again, α-stable distributed. More formally, let $X_1, \ldots,$

X_n be identically distributed and independent of each other. Then, assume that for large $n \in \mathbf{N}$, there exists a positive constant a_n and a real constant b_n such that the normalized sum $Y(n)$

$$Y(n) = a_n(X_1 + X_2 + \ldots + X_n) + b_n \sim S(\alpha, \beta, \sigma, \mu) \tag{B.9}$$

converges in distribution to a random variable X, then this random variable X must be stable with some parameters α, β, σ, and μ. The convergence in distribution means that the distribution function of $Y(n)$ in equation (B.9) converges to the distribution function on the right-hand side of equation (B.9).

In the context of financial returns, this means that α-stable monthly returns can be treated as the sum of weekly independent returns and, again, α-stable weekly returns themselves can be understood as the sum of daily independent returns. According to equation (B.9), they are equally distributed up to rescaling by the parameters a_n and b_n.

From the presentation of the normal distribution, we know that it serves as a limit distribution of a sum of identically distributed random variables that are independent and have finite variance. In particular, the sum converges in distribution to the standard normal distribution once the random variables have been summed and transformed appropriately. The prerequisite, however, was that the variance exists. Now, we can drop the requirement for finite variance and only ask for independent and identical distributions to arrive at the *generalized central limit theorem* expressed by equation (B.9). The data transformed in a similar fashion as on the left-hand side of equation (B.2) will have a distribution that follows a stable distribution law as the number n becomes very large. Thus, the class of α-stable distributions provides a greater set of limit distributions than the normal distribution containing the latter as a special case. Theoretically, this justifies the use of α-stable distributions as the choice for modeling asset returns when we consider the returns to be the resulting sum of many independent shocks with identical distributions.

Inferential Statistics

In Appendix A, we provided the basics of descriptive statistics. Our focus in this appendix is on inferential statistics, covering the three major topics of point estimators, confidence intervals, and hypothesis testing.

POINT ESTIMATORS

Since it is generally infeasible or simply too involved to analyze an entire population in order to obtain full certainty as to the true environment, we need to rely on a small sample to retrieve information about the population parameters. To obtain insight about the true but unknown parameter value, we draw a sample from which we compute statistics or estimates for the parameter.

In this section, we will learn about samples, statistics, and estimators. In particular, we present the linear estimator, explain quality criteria (such as the bias, mean squared error, and standard error) and the large-sample criteria. In the context of large-sample criteria, we present the idea behind consistency, for which we need the definition of convergence in probability and the law of large numbers. As another large-sample criterion, we introduce the unbiased efficiency, explaining the best linear unbiased estimator or, alternatively, the minimum-variance linear unbiased estimator.

Sample, Statistic, and Estimator

The probability distributions typically used in financial econometrics depend on one or more parameters. Here we will refer to simply the parameter θ, which will have one or several components, such as the parameters for the mean and variance. The set of parameters is given by Θ, which will be called the *parameter space*.

The general problem that we address is the process of gaining information on the true population parameter such as, for example, the mean of some portfolio returns. Since we do not actually know the true value of θ, we merely are aware of the fact that it has to be in Θ. For example, the normal distribution has the parameter $\theta = (\mu, \sigma^2)$ where the first component, the mean, denoted by μ, can technically be any real number between minus and plus infinity. The second component, the variance, denoted by σ^2, is any positive real number.

Sample Let Y be some random variable with a probability distribution that is characterized by parameter θ. To obtain the information about this population parameter, we draw a *sample* from the population of Y. A sample is the total of n drawings $X_1, X_2, \ldots, X_n$ from the entire population. Note that until the drawings from the population have been made, the X_i are still random. The actually observed values (i.e., realizations) of the n drawings are denoted by $x_1, x_2, \ldots, x_n$. Whenever no ambiguity will arise, we denote the vectors $(X_1, X_2, \ldots, X_n)$ and $(x_1, x_2, \ldots, x_n)$ by the short hand notation X and x, respectively.

To facilitate the reasoning behind this, let us consider the value of the Dow Jones Industrial Average (DJIA) as some random variable. To obtain a sample of the DJIA, we will "draw" two values. More specifically, we plan to observe its closing value on two days in the future, say June 12, 2009, and January 8, 2010. Prior to these two dates, say on January 2, 2009, we are still uncertain as to value of the DJIA on June 12, 2009, and January 8, 2010. So, the value on each of these two future dates is random. Then, on June 12, 2009, we observe that the DJIA's closing value is 8,799.26, while on January 8, 2010, it is 10,618.19. Now, after January 8, 2010, these two values are *realizations* of the DJIA and not random any more.

Let us return to the theory. Once we have realizations of the sample, any further decision will then be based solely on the sample. However, we have to bear in mind that a sample provides only incomplete information since it will be impractical or impossible to analyze the entire population. This process of deriving a conclusion concerning information about a population's parameters from a sample is referred to as *statistical inference* or, simply, *inference*.

Formally, we denote the set of all possible sample values for samples of given length n (which is also called the *sample size*) by $\mathbf{X}$.

Sampling Techniques There are two types of sampling methods: with replacement and without replacement. Sampling with replacement is preferred because this corresponds to independent draws such that the X_i are independent and identically distributed (i.i.d.).

In our discussion, we will assume that individual draws are performed independently and under identical conditions (i.e., the X_1, $X_2, \ldots$, X_n are i.i.d.).

We know that the joint probability distribution of independent random variables is obtained by multiplication of the marginal distributions.

Consider the daily stock returns of General Electric (GE) modeled by the continuous random variable X. The returns on 10 different days (X_1, $X_2, \ldots$, X_{10}) can be considered a sample of i.i.d. draws. In reality, however, stock returns are seldom independent. If, on the other hand, the observations are not made on 10 consecutive days but with larger gaps between them, it is fairly reasonable to assume independence. Furthermore, the stock returns are modeled as normal (or Gaussian) random variables.

Statistic What is the distinction between a *statistic* and a *population parameter*? In the context of estimation, the population parameter is inferred with the aid of the statistic. A statistic assumes some value that holds for a specific sample only, while the parameter prevails in the entire population.

The statistic, in most cases, provides a single number as an estimate of the population parameter generated from the sample. If the true but unknown parameter consists of, say, k components, the statistic will provide at least k numbers, that is at least one for each component. We need to be aware of the fact that the statistic will most likely not equal the population parameter due to the random nature of the sample from which its value originates.

Technically, the statistic is a function of the sample (X_1, $X_2, \ldots$, X_n). We denote this function by t. Since the sample is random, so is t and, consequently, any quantity that is derived from it.

We need to postulate measurability so that we can assign a probability to any values of the function $t(x_1, x_2, \ldots, x_n)$. Whenever it is necessary to express the dependence of statistic t on the outcome of the sample (x), we write the statistic as the function $t(x)$. Otherwise, we simply refer to the function t without explicit argument.

The statistic t as a random variable inherits its theoretical distribution from the underlying random variables (i.e., the random draws X_1, $X_2, \ldots$, X_n). If we vary the sample size n, the distribution of the statistics will, in most cases, change as well. This distribution expressing in particular the dependence on n is called the *sampling distribution* of t. Naturally, the sampling distribution exhibits features of the underlying population distribution of the random variable.

Estimator The easiest way to obtain a number for the population parameter would be to simply guess. But this method lacks any foundation since it is based on nothing but luck; in the best case, a guess might be justified by some experience. However, this approach is hardly analytical. Instead, we should use the information obtained from the sample, or better, the statistic.

When we are interested in the estimation of a particular parameter θ, we typically do not refer to the estimation function as a statistic but rather as an *estimator* and denote it by $\hat{\theta} : X \to \Theta$. This means that the estimator is a function from the sample space X mapping into the parameter space Θ. The estimator can be understood as some instruction of how to process the sample to obtain a valid representative of the parameter θ. The exact structure of the estimator is determined before the sample is realized. After the estimator has been defined, we simply need to enter the sample values accordingly.

Due to the estimator's dependence on the random sample, the estimator is itself random. A particular value of the estimator based on the realization of some sample is called an *estimate*. For example, if we realize 1,000 samples of given length n, we obtain 1,000 individual estimates $\hat{\theta}_i$, $i = 1, 2, \ldots, 1,000$. Sorting them by value, we can compute the distribution function of these realizations, which is similar to the empirical cumulative distribution function explained in Appendix A. Technically, this distribution function is not the same as the theoretical sampling distribution for this estimator for given sample length n introduced earlier. For increasing n, however, the distribution of the realized estimates will gradually become more and more similar in appearance to the sampling distribution.

Linear Estimators We turn to a special type of estimator, the *linear estimator*. Suppose we have a sample of size n such that $X = (X_1, X_2, \ldots, X_n)$. The linear estimator then has the following form:

$$\hat{\theta} = \sum_{i=1}^{n} a_i X_i$$

where each draw X_i is weighted by some real a_i, for $i = 1, 2, \ldots, n$. By construction, the linear estimator weights each draw X_i by some weight a_i. The usual constraints on the a_i is that they sum to 1, that is,

$$\sum_{i=1}^{n} a_i = 1$$

A particular version of the linear estimator is the sample mean where all $a_i = 1/n$.

Let's look at a particular distribution of the X_i, the normal distribution. As we know from Appendix B, this distribution can be expressed in closed form under linear affine transformation by Properties 1 and 2. That is, by adding several X_i and multiplying the resulting sum by some constant, we once again obtain a normal random variable. Thus, any linear estimator will be normal. This is an extremely attractive feature of the linear estimator.

Even if the underlying distribution is not the normal distribution, according to the central limit theorem as explained in Appendix B, the sample mean (i.e., when $a_i = 1/n$) will be approximately normally distributed as the sample size increases. This result facilitates parameter estimation for most distributions.

What sample size n is sufficient? If the population distribution is symmetric, it will not require a large sample size, often less than 10. If, however, the population distribution is not symmetric, we will need larger samples. In general, an n between 25 and 30 suffices. One is on the safe side when n exceeds 30.

The central limit theorem requires that certain conditions on the population distribution are met, such as finiteness of the variance. If the variance or even mean do not exist, another theorem, the so-called *generalized central limit theorem*, can be applied under certain conditions. However, these conditions are beyond the scope of this book. But we will give one example. The class of α-stable distributions provides such a *limiting distribution*, that is, one that certain estimators of the form

$$\sum_{i=1}^{n} a_i X_i$$

will approximately follow as n increases. We note this distribution because it is one that has been suggested by financial economists as a more general alternative to the Gaussian distribution to describe returns on financial assets.

Quality Criteria of Estimators

The question related to each estimation problem should be what estimator would be best suited for the problem at hand. Estimators suitable for the very same parameters can vary quite remarkably when it comes to quality of their estimation. Here we will explain some of the most commonly employed *quality criteria*.

Bias An important consideration in the selection of an estimator is the average behavior of that estimator over all possible scenarios. Depending on the sample outcome, the estimator may not equal the parameter value and, instead, be quite remote from it. This is a natural consequence of the variability of the underlying sample. However, the average value of the estimator is something we can control.

Let us begin by considering the *sampling error* that is the difference between the estimate and the population parameter. This distance is random due to the uncertainty associated with each individual draw. For the parameter θ and the estimator $\hat{\theta}$, we define the sample error as $(\hat{\theta} - \theta)$. Now, a most often preferred estimator should yield an expected sample error of zero. This expected value is defined as

$$E_\theta (\hat{\theta} - \theta) \tag{C.1}$$

and referred to as *bias*.[1] If the expression in equation (C.1) is different from zero, the estimator is said to be a *biased estimator* while it is an *unbiased estimator* if the expected value in equation (C.1) is zero.

The subscript θ in equation (C.1) indicates that the expected value is computed based on the distribution with parameter θ whose value is unknown. Technically, however, the computation of the expected value is feasible for a general θ.

Mean Squared Error Bias as a quality criterion tells us about the expected deviation of the estimator from the parameter. However, the bias fails to inform us about the variability or spread of the estimator. For a reliable inference for the parameter value, we should prefer an estimator with rather small variability or, in other words, high precision.

Assume that we repeatedly, say m times, draw samples of given size n. Using estimator $\hat{\theta}$ for each of these samples, we compute the respective estimate $\hat{\theta}_t$ of parameter θ, where $t = 1, 2, \ldots, m$. From these m estimates, we then obtain an empirical distribution of the estimates including an empirical spread given by the sample distribution of the estimates. We know that with increasing sample length n, the empirical distribution will eventually look like the normal distribution for most estimators. However, regardless of any empirical distribution of estimates, an estimator has a theoretical sampling distribution for each sample size n. So, the random estimator is, as a random variable, distributed by the law of the sampling distribution. The empirical and the sampling distribution will look more alike the larger is n. The sampling distribution provides us with a theoretical measure of spread of the estimator which is called the *standard error* (SE). This is a measure that can often be found listed together with the observed estimate.

To completely eliminate the variance, one could simply take a constant $\hat{\theta} = c$ as the estimator for some parameter. However, this not reasonable since it is insensitive to sample information and thus remains unchanged

---

[1] We assume in this chapter that the estimators and the elements of the sample have finite variance, and in particular the expression in equation (C.1) is well-defined.

for whatever the true parameter value θ may be. Hence, we stated the bias as an ultimately preferable quality criterion. Yet, a bias of zero may be too restrictive a criterion if an estimator $\hat{\theta}$ is only slightly biased but has a favorably small variance compared to all possible alternatives, biased or unbiased. So, we need some quality criterion accounting for both bias and variance.

That criterion can be satisfied by using the *mean squared error* (MSE). Taking squares rather than the loss itself incurred by the deviation, the MSE is defined as the expected square loss

$$\text{MSE}(\hat{\theta}) = E_\theta[(\hat{\theta} - \theta)]^2$$

where the subscript θ indicates that the mean depends on the true but unknown parameter value. The mean squared error can be decomposed into the variance of the estimator and a transform (i.e., square) of the bias. If the transform is zero (i.e., the estimator is unbiased), the mean squared error equals the estimator variance.

It is interesting to note that MSE-minimal estimators are not available for all parameters. That is, we may have to face a trade-off between reducing either the bias or the variance over a set of possible estimators. As a consequence, we simply try to find a minimum-variance estimator of all unbiased estimators, which is called the *minimum-variance unbiased estimator*. We do this because in many applications, unbiasedness has priority over precision.

Large-Sample Criteria

The treatment of the estimators thus far has not included their possible change in behavior as the sample size *n* varies. This is an important aspect of estimation, however. For example, it is possible that an estimator that is biased for any given finite *n* gradually loses its bias as *n* increases. Here we will analyze the estimators as the sample size approaches infinity. In technical terms, we focus on the so-called *large-sample* or *asymptotic properties of estimators*.

Consistency   Some estimators display stochastic behavior that changes as we increase the sample size. It may be that their exact distribution including parameters is unknown as long as the number of draws *n* is small or, to be precise, finite. This renders the evaluation of the quality of certain estimators difficult. For example, it may be impossible to give the exact bias of some estimator for finite *n*, in contrast to when *n* approaches infinity.

If we are concerned about some estimator's properties, we may reasonably have to remain undecided about the selection of the most suitable estimator for the estimation problem we are facing. In the fortunate cases, the uncertainty regarding an estimator's quality may vanish as n goes to infinity, so that we can base conclusions concerning its applicability for certain estimation tasks on its large-sample properties.

The central limit theorem plays a crucial role in assessing the properties of estimators. This is because normalized sums turn into standard normal random variables, which provide us with tractable quantities. The asymptotic properties of normalized sums may facilitate deriving the large-sample behavior of more complicated estimators.

At this point, we need to think about a rather technical concept that involves controlling the behavior of estimators in the limit. Here we will analyze an estimator's *convergence* characteristics. That means we consider whether the distribution of an estimator approaches some particular probability distribution as the sample sizes increase. To do so, we state the following definition:

> *Convergence in probability.* We say that a random variable such as an estimator built on a sample of size n, $\hat{\theta}_n$, *is a convergence in probability* to some constant c if

$$\lim_{n \to \infty} P(|\hat{\theta}_n - c| > \varepsilon) = 0 \qquad (C.2)$$

holds for any $\varepsilon > 0$.

Equation (C.2) states that as the sample size becomes arbitrarily large, the probability that our estimator will assume a value that is more than ε away from c will become increasingly negligible, even as ε becomes smaller. Instead of the rather lengthy form of equation (C.2), we usually state that $\hat{\theta}_n$ converges in probability to c more briefly as

$$\text{plim}\hat{\theta}_n = c \qquad (C.3)$$

Here, we introduce the index n to the estimator $\hat{\theta}_n$ to indicate that it depends on the sample size n. Convergence in probability does not mean that an estimator will eventually be equal to c, and hence constant itself, but the chance of a deviation from it will become increasingly unlikely.

Suppose now that we draw several samples of size n. Let the number of these different samples be N. Consequently, we obtain N estimates $\hat{\theta}_n^{(1)}, \hat{\theta}_n^{(2)}, \ldots, \hat{\theta}_n^{(N)}$ where $\hat{\theta}_n^{(1)}$ is estimated on the first sample, $\hat{\theta}_n^{(2)}$ on the second, and so on. Utilizing the prior definition, we formulate the following law.

Law of large numbers. Let $X^{(1)} = (X_1^{(1)}, X_2^{(1)}, \ldots, X_n^{(1)})$, $X^{(2)} = (X_1^{(2)}$ $X_2^{(2)}, \ldots, X_n^{(2)})$, and $X^{(N)} = (X_1^{(N)}, X_2^N, \ldots, X_n^N)$ be a series of N independent samples of size n. For each of these samples, we apply the estimator $\hat{\theta}_n$ such that we obtain N independent and identically distributed as $\hat{\theta}_n$ random variables $\hat{\theta}_n^{(1)}, \hat{\theta}_n^{(2)}, \ldots, \hat{\theta}_n^{(N)}$. Further, let $E(\hat{\theta}_n)$ denote the expected value of $\hat{\theta}_n$ and $\hat{\theta}_n^{(1)}, \hat{\theta}_n^{(2)}, \ldots, \hat{\theta}_n^{(N)}$. Because they are identically distributed, it holds that[2]

$$\text{plim} \frac{1}{N} \sum_{k=1}^{N} \hat{\theta}_n^{(k)} = E(\hat{\theta}_n) \tag{C.4}$$

The law of large numbers given by equation (C.4) states that the average over all estimates obtained from the different samples (i.e., their sample mean) will eventually approach their expected value or population mean. According to equation (C.2), large deviations from $E(\hat{\theta}_n)$ will become ever less likely the more samples we draw. So, we can say with a high probability that if N is large, the sample mean

$$1/N \sum_{k=1}^{N} \hat{\theta}_n^{(k)}$$

will be near its expected value. This is a valuable property since when we have drawn many samples, we can assert that it will be highly unlikely that the average of the observed estimates such as

$$1/N \sum_{k=1}^{N} \bar{x}_k$$

for example, will be a realization of some distribution with very remote parameter $E(\bar{X}) = \mu$.

An important aspect of the convergence in probability becomes obvious now. Even if the expected value of $\hat{\theta}_n$ is not equal to θ (i.e., $\hat{\theta}_n$ is biased for finite sample lengths n), it can still be that $\text{plim}\, \hat{\theta}_n = \theta$. That is, the expected value $E(\hat{\theta}_n)$ may gradually become closer to and eventually indistinguishable from θ, as the sample size n increases. To account for these and all unbiased estimators, we introduce the next definition.

---

[2]Formally, equation (C.4) is referred to as the *weak law of large numbers*. Moreover, for the law to hold, we need to assure that the $\hat{\theta}_n^{(k)}$ have identical finite variance. Then by virtue of the Chebychev inequality we can derive equation (C.4). Chebyshev's inequality states that at least a certain amount of data should fall within a stated number of standard deviations from the mean.

Consistency. An estimator $\hat{\theta}_n$ is a *consistent estimator* for θ if it converges in probability to θ, as given by equation (C.3), that is, $\text{plim}\hat{\theta}_n = \theta$. The consistency of an estimator is an important property since we can rely on the consistent estimator to systematically give sound results with respect to the true parameter. This means that if we increase the sample size n, we will obtain estimates that will deviate from the parameter θ only in rare cases.

Unbiased Efficiency   In the previous discussions, we tried to determine where the estimator tends to. This analysis, however, left unanswered the question of how fast the estimator gets there. For this purpose, we introduce the notion of *unbiased efficiency.*

Let us suppose that two estimators $\hat{\theta}$ and $\hat{\theta}^*$ are unbiased for some parameter θ. Then, we say that $\hat{\theta}$ is a more *efficient estimator* than $\hat{\theta}^*$ if it has a smaller variance; that is,

$$\text{var}_\theta(\hat{\theta}) < \text{var}_\theta(\hat{\theta}^*) \tag{C.5}$$

for any value of the parameter θ. Consequently, no matter what the true parameter value is, the standard error of $\hat{\theta}$ is always smaller than that of $\hat{\theta}^*$. Since they are assumed to be both unbiased, the first should be preferred.[3]

Linear Unbiased Estimators   A particular sort of estimators are *linear unbiased estimators*. We introduce them separately from the linear estimators here because they often display appealing statistical features.

In general, linear unbiased estimators are of the form

$$\hat{\theta} = \sum_{i=1}^{n} a_i X_i$$

To meet the condition of zero bias, the weights a_i have to add to one. Due to their lack of bias, the MSE will only consist of the variance part. With sample size n, their variances can be easily computed as

$$\text{var}_\theta(\hat{\theta}) = \sum_{i=1}^{n} a_i^2 \sigma_X^2$$

---

[3] If the parameter consists of more than one component, then the definition of efficiency in equation (C.5) needs to be extended to an expression that uses the covariance matrix of the estimators rather than only the variances.

where $\sigma_{\bar{X}}^2$ denotes the common variance of each drawing. This variance can be minimized with respect to the coefficients a_i and we obtain the *best linear unbiased estimator* (BLUE) or *minimum-variance linear unbiased estimator* (MVLUE). We have to be aware, however, that we are not always able to find such an estimator for each parameter.

An example of a BLUE is given by the sample mean $\bar{x}$. We know that $a_i = 1/n$. This not only guarantees that the sample mean is unbiased for the population mean μ, but it also provides for the smallest variance of all unbiased linear estimators. Therefore, the sample mean is efficient among all linear estimators. By comparison, the first draw is also unbiased. However, its variance is n times greater than that of the sample mean.

CONFIDENCE INTERVALS

In making financial decisions, the population parameters characterizing the respective random variable's probability distribution needs to be known. However, in most realistic situations, this information will not be available. In this section, we deal with this problem by estimating the unknown parameter with a point estimator to obtain a single number from the information provided by a sample. It will be highly unlikely, however, that this estimate—obtained from a finite sample—will be exactly equal to the population parameter value even if the estimator is consistent—a notion introduced in the previous section. The reason is that estimates most likely vary from sample to sample. However, for any realization, we do not know by how much the estimate will be off.

To overcome this uncertainty, one might think of computing an interval or, depending on the dimensionality of the parameter, an area that contains the true parameter with high probability. That is, we concentrate in this section on the construction of confidence intervals. We begin with the presentation of the confidence level. This will be essential in order to understand the confidence interval that will be introduced subsequently. We then present the probability of error in the context of confidence intervals, which is related to the confidence level.

Confidence Level and Confidence interval

In the previous section, we inferred the unknown parameter with a single estimate. The likelihood of the estimate exactly reproducing the true parameter value may be negligible. Instead, by estimating an interval, which we may denote by I_θ, we use a greater portion of the parameter space and not just a single number. This may increase the likelihood that the true parameter is one of the many values included in the interval.

If, in one extreme case, we select as an interval the entire parameter space, the true parameter will definitely lie inside of it. Instead, if we choose our interval to consist of one value only, the probability of this interval containing the true value approaches zero and we end up with the same situation as with the point estimator. So, there is a trade-off between a high probability of the interval I_θ containing the true parameter value, achieved through increasing the interval's width, and the precision gained by a very narrow interval.

As in our discussion of point estimates in the previous section, we should use the information provided by the sample. Hence, it should be reasonable that the interval bounds depend on the sample in some way. Then technically each interval bound is a function that maps the sample space, denoted by **X**, into the parameter space since the sample is some outcome in the sample space and the interval bound transforms the sample into a value in the parameter space representing the minimum or maximum parameter value suggested by the interval. Because the interval depends on the sample $X = (X_1, X_2, \ldots, X_n)$, and since the sample is random, the interval $[l(X),$ $u(X)]$ is also random. We can derive the probability of the interval lying beyond the true parameter (i.e., either completely below or above) from the sample distribution. These two possible errors occur exactly if either $u(x) < \theta$ or $\theta < l(x)$.

Our objective is then to construct an interval so as to minimize the probability of these errors occurring. Suppose we want this probability of error to be equal to α. For example, we may select $\alpha = 0.05$ such that in 5% of all outcomes, the true parameter will not be covered by the interval. Let

$$p_l = P(\theta < l(X)) \text{ and } p_u = P(u(X) < \theta)$$

Then, it must be that

$$P(\theta \notin [l(X), u(X)]) = p_l + p_u = \alpha$$

Now let's provide two important definitions: a confidence level and confidence interval.

Definition of a Confidence Level   For some parameter θ, let the probability of the interval not containing the true parameter value be given by the probability of error α. Then, with probability $1 - \alpha$, the true parameter is covered by the interval $[l(X), u(X)]$. The probability

$$P(\theta \in [l(X), u(X)]) = 1 - \alpha$$

is called *confidence level*.

It may not be possible to find bounds to obtain a confidence level exactly. We, then, simply postulate for the confidence level $1 - \alpha$ that

$$P(\theta \in [l(X), u(X)]) = 1 - \alpha$$

is satisfied, no matter what the value θ may be.

Definition and Interpretation of a Confidence Interval   Given the definition of the confidence level, we can refer to an interval $[l(X), u(X)]$ as $1 - \alpha$ *confidence interval* if

$$P(\theta \in [l(X), u(X)]) = 1 - \alpha$$

holds no matter what is the true but unknown parameter value θ.[4]

The interpretation of the confidence interval is that if we draw an increasing number of samples of constant size n and compute an interval, from each sample, $1 - \alpha$ of all intervals will eventually contain the true parameter value θ.

The bounds of the confidence interval are often determined by some standardized random variable composed of both the parameter and point estimator, and whose distribution is known. Furthermore, for a symmetric density function such as that of the normal distribution, it can be shown that with given α, the confidence interval is the tightest if we have $p_l = \alpha/2$ and $p_u = \alpha/2$ with p_l and p_u as defined before. That corresponds to bounds l and u with distributions that are symmetric to each other with respect to the the true parameter θ. This is an important property of a confidence interval since we seek to obtain the maximum precision possible for a particular confidence level.

Often in discussions of confidence intervals the statement is made that with probability $1 - \alpha$, the parameter falls inside of the confidence interval and is outside with probability α. This interpretation can be misleading in that one may assume that the parameter is a random variable. Recall that only the confidence interval bounds are random. The position of the

---

[4]Note that if equality cannot be exactly achieved, we take the smallest interval for which the probability is greater than $1 - \alpha$.

confidence interval depends on the outcome x. By design, as we have just shown, the interval is such that in $(1 - \alpha) \times 100\%$ of all outcomes, the interval contains the true parameter and in $\alpha \times 100\%$, it does not cover the true parameter value.

Note that the parameter is invariant, only the interval is random.

HYPOTHESIS TESTING

Thus far in this appendix, inference on some unknown parameter meant that we had no knowledge of its value and therefore we had to obtain an estimate. This could either be a single point estimate or an entire confidence interval. However, sometimes, one already has some idea of the value a parameter might have or used to have. Thus, it might not be important to obtain a particular single value or range of values for the parameter, but instead to gain sufficient information to conclude that the parameter more likely either belongs to a particular part of the parameter space or not. So, instead we need to obtain information to verify whether some assumption concerning the parameter can be supported or has to be rejected. This brings us to the field of *hypothesis testing*.

To perform hypothesis testing it is essential to express the competing statements about the value of a parameter as hypotheses. To test for these, we develop a *test statistic* for which we set up a *decision rule*. For a specific sample, this test statistic then either assumes a value in the acceptance region or the rejection region, regions that we describe in this chapter. Furthermore, we see the two error types one can incur when testing. We see that the hypothesis test structure allows one to control the probability of error through what we see to be the test size or significance level. We discover that each observation has a certain p-value expressing its significance. As a quality criterion of a test, we introduce the power from which the uniformly most powerful test can be defined. Furthermore, we explain what is meant by an unbiased test—unbiasedness provides another important quality criterion—as well as whether a test is consistent.

Hypotheses

Before being able to test anything, we need to express clearly what we intend to achieve with the help of the test. For this task, it is essential that we unambiguously formulate the possible outcomes of the test. In the realm of hypothesis testing, we have two competing statements to decide upon. These statements are the *hypotheses* of the test.

Setting Up the Hypotheses Since in statistical inference we intend to gain information about some unknown parameter θ, the possible results of the test should refer to the parameter space Θ containing all possible values that θ can assume. More precisely, to form the hypotheses, we divide the parameter space into two disjoint sets Θ_0 and Θ_1 such that $\Theta = \Theta_0 \cup \Theta_1$. We assume that the unknown parameter is either in Θ_0 or Θ_1 since it cannot simultaneously be in both. Usually, the two alternative parameter sets either divide the parameter space into two disjoint intervals or regions (depending on the dimensionality of the parameter), or they contrast a single value with any other value from the parameter space.

Now, with each of the two subsets Θ_0 and Θ_1, we associate a hypothesis. In the following two definitions, we present the most commonly applied denominations for the hypotheses.

> *Null hypothesis.* The *null hypothesis*, denoted by H_0, states that the parameter θ is in Θ_0.

The null hypothesis may be interpreted as the assumption to be maintained if we do not find ample evidence against it.

> *Alternative hypothesis.* The *alternative hypothesis*, denoted by H_1, is the statement that the parameter θ is in Θ_1.

We have to be aware that only one hypothesis can hold and, hence, the outcome of our test should only support one.

When we test for a parameter or a single parameter component, we usually encounter the following two constructions of hypothesis tests. In the first construction, we split the parameter space Θ into a lower half up to some boundary value $\tilde{\theta}$ and an upper half extending beyond this boundary value. Then, we set the lower half either equal to Θ_0 or Θ_1. Consequently, the upper half becomes the counterpart Θ_1 or Θ_0, respectively. The boundary value $\tilde{\theta}$ is usually added to Θ_0; that is, it is the set valid under the null hypothesis. Such a test is referred to as a *one-tailed test*.

In the second construction, we test whether some parameter is equal to a particular value or not. Accordingly, the parameter space is once again divided into two sets Θ_0 and Θ_1. But this time, Θ_0 consists of only one value (i.e., $\Theta_0 = \tilde{\theta}$) while the set Θ_1, corresponding to the alternative hypothesis, is equal to the parameter space less the value belonging to the null hypothesis (i.e., $\Theta_1 = \Theta \backslash \tilde{\theta}$). This version of a hypothesis test is termed a *two-tailed test*.

Decision Rule   The object of hypothesis testing is to make a decision about these hypotheses. So, we either have to accept the null hypothesis and, consequently, must reject the alternative hypothesis, or we reject the null hypothesis and decide in favor of the alternative hypothesis.

A hypothesis test is designed such that the null hypothesis is maintained until evidence provided by the sample is so strong that we have to decide against it. This leads us to the two common ways of using the test.

With the first application, we simply want to find out whether a situation that we deemed correct actually is true. Thus, the situation under the null hypothesis is considered the status quo or the experience that is held on to until the support given by the sample in favor of the alternative hypothesis is too strong to sustain the null hypothesis any longer.

The alternative use of the hypothesis test is to try to promote a concept formulated by the alternative hypothesis by finding sufficient evidence in favor of it, rendering it the more credible of the two hypotheses. In this second approach, the aim of the tester is to reject the null hypothesis because the situation under the alternative hypothesis is more favorable.

In the realm of hypothesis testing, the decision is generally regarded as the process of following certain rules. We denote our decision rule by δ. The decision δ is designed to either assume value d_0 or value d_1. Depending on which way we are using the test, the meaning of these two values is as follows. In the first case, the value d_0 expresses that we hold on to H_0 while the contrarian value d_1 expresses that we reject H_0. In the second case, we interpret d_0 as being undecided with respect to H_0 and H_1 and that proof is not strong enough in favor of H_1. On the other hand, by d_1, we indicate that we reject H_0 in favor of H_1.

In general, d_1 can be interpreted as the result we obtain from the decision rule when the sample outcome is highly unreasonable under the null hypothesis.

So, what makes us come up with either d_0 or d_1? As discussed earlier in this chapter, we infer by first drawing a sample of some size n, $X = (X_1, X_2, \ldots, X_n)$. Our decision then should be based on this sample. That is, it would be wise to include in our decision rule the sample X such that the decision becomes a function of the sample, (i.e., $\delta(X)$). Then, $\delta(X)$ is a random variable due to the randomness of X. A reasonable step would be to link our test $\delta(X)$ to a statistic, denoted by $t(X)$, that itself is related or equal to an estimator $\hat{\theta}$ for the parameter of interest θ. Such estimators were introduced earlier in this chapter.

From now on, we will assume that our test rule δ is synonymous with checking whether the statistic $t(X)$ is assuming certain values or not from which we derive decision d_0 or d_1.

As we know from point estimates, by drawing a sample X, we select a particular value x from the sample space X. Depending on this realization x, the statistic $t(x)$ either leads to rejection of the null hypothesis (i.e., $\delta(x) = d_0$), or not (i.e., $\delta(x) = d_1$).

To determine when we have to make a decision d_0 or, alternatively, d_1, we split the state space Δ of $t(X)$ into two disjoint sets that we denote by Δ_A and Δ_C. The set Δ_A is referred to as the *acceptance region* while Δ_C is the *critical region* or *rejection region*.

When the outcome of the sample x is in Δ_A, we do not reject the null hypothesis (i.e., the result of the test is $\delta(x) = d_0$). If, on the other hand, x should be some value in Δ_C, the result of the test is now the contrary (i.e., $\delta(x) = d_1$), such that we decide in favor of the alternative hypothesis.

Error Types

We have to be aware that no matter how we design our test, we are at risk of committing an error by making the wrong decision. Given the two hypotheses, H_0 and H_1, and the two possible decisions, d_0 and d_1, we can commit two possible errors. These errors are discussed next.

Type I and Type II Error   The two possible errors we can incur are characterized by unintentionally deciding against the true hypothesis. Each error related to a particular hypothesis is referred to using the following standard terminology.

Type I error. The error resulting from rejection of the null hypothesis (H_0) (i.e., $\delta(X) = d_1$) given that it is actually true (i.e., $\theta \in \Theta_0$) is referred to as a *type I error*.

Type II error. The error resulting from not rejecting the null hypothesis (H_0) (i.e., $\delta(X) = d_0$) even though the alternative hypothesis (H_1) holds (i.e., $\theta \in \Theta_1$) is referred to as a *type II error*.

In the following table, we show all four possible outcomes from a hypothesis test depending on the respective hypothesis:

		H_0: θ in Θ_0	H_1: θ in Θ_1
	d_0	Correct	Type II error
Decision	d_1	Type I error	Correct

So, we see that in two cases, we make the correct decision. The first case occurs if we do not reject the null hypothesis (i.e., $\delta(X) = d_0$) when it actually holds. The second case occurs if we correctly decide against the null hypothesis (i.e., $\delta(X) = d_1$), when it is not true and, consequently, the alternative hypothesis holds. Unfortunately, however, we do not know whether we commit an error or not when we are testing. We do have some control, though, as to the probability of error given a certain hypothesis as we explain next.

Test Size

We just learned that, depending on which hypothesis is true, we can commit either a type I or a type II error. Now, we will concentrate on the corresponding probabilities of incurring these errors.

> *Test size.* The test size is the probability of committing a type I error. This probability is denoted by $P_I(\delta)$ for test δ.[5]

We illustrate this in Figure C.1, where we display the density function $f_{(t(X),\Theta_0)}$ of the test statistic $t(X)$ under the null hypothesis. The horizontal axis along which $t(X)$ assumes values is subdivided into the acceptance Δ_A and the

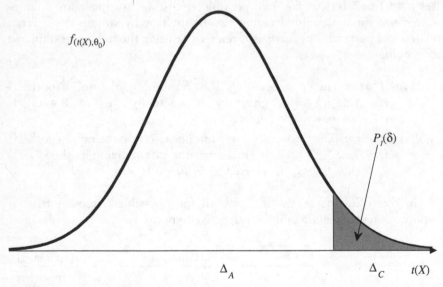

FIGURE C.1   Determining the Size $P_I(\delta)$ of Some Test δ via the Density Function of the Test Statistic $t(X)$

---

[5]The probability $P_I(\delta)$ could alternatively be written as $P_{\Theta_0}(d_1)$ to indicate that we erroneously reject the null hypothesis even though H_0 holds.

critical region Δ_C. The probability of this statistic having a value in the critical region is indicated by the shaded area.

Since, in general, the set Θ_0 belonging to the null hypothesis consists of several values (e.g., $\Theta_0 \subset \Theta$) the probability of committing a type I error, $P_I(\delta)$, may vary for each parameter value θ in Θ_0. By convention, we set the test size equal to the $P_I(\delta)$ computed at that value θ in Θ_0 for which this probability is maximal.[6] We illustrate this for some arbitrary test in Figure C.2, where we depict the graph of the probability of rejection of the null hypothesis depending on the parameter value θ. Over the set Θ_0, as indicated by the solid line in the figure, this is equal to the probability of a type I error while, over Θ_1, this is the probability of a correct decision (i.e., d_1). The latter is given by the dashed line.

Analogously to the probability $P_I(\delta)$, we denote the probability of committing a type II error as $P_{II}(\delta)$.

Deriving the wrong decision can lead to undesirable results. That is, the errors related to a test may come at some cost. To handle the problem, the hypotheses are generally chosen such that the type I error is more harmful

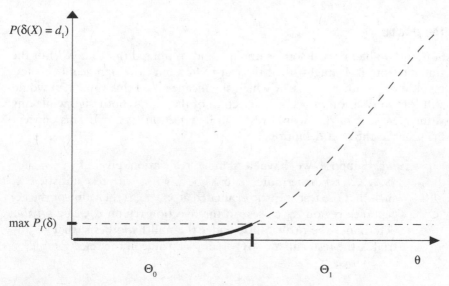

FIGURE C.2 Determining the Test Size α by Maximizing the Probability of a Type I Error over the Set Θ_0 of Possible Parameter Values under the Null Hypothesis

---

[6]Theoretically, this may not be possible for any test.

to us, no matter what we use the test for. Consequently, we attempt to avoid this type of error by trying to reduce the associated probability or, equivalently, the test size.

Fortunately, the test size is something we have control over. We can simply reduce $P_I(\delta)$ through selection of an arbitrarily large acceptance region Δ_A. In the most extreme case, we set Δ_A equal to the entire state space of δ so that, virtually, we never reject the null hypothesis. However, by inflating Δ_A, we have to reduce Δ_C, which generally results in an increase in the probability $P_{II}(d_0)$ of a type II error because now it becomes more likely for X to fall into Δ_A also when θ is in Θ_1 (i.e., under the alternative hypothesis). Thus, we are facing a trade-off between the probability of a type I error and a type II error. A common agreement is to limit the probability of occurrence of a type I error to some real number between zero and one. This α is referred to as the *significance level*. Frequently, values of $\alpha = 0.01$ or $\alpha = 0.05$ are found.

Formally, the postulate for the test is $P_I(\delta) \leq \alpha$. So, when the null hypothesis is true, in at most α of all outcomes, we will obtain a sample value x in Δ_C. Consequently, in at most α of the test runs, the test result will erroneously be d_1 (i.e., we decide against the null hypothesis).

The *p*-Value

Suppose we had drawn some sample x and computed the value $t(x)$ of the statistic from it. It might be of interest to find out how significant this test result is or, in other words, at which significance level this value $t(x)$ would still lead to decision d_0 (i.e., no rejection of the null hypothesis), while any value greater than $t(x)$ would result in its rejection (i.e., d_1). This concept brings us to the next definition.

> *p-value*. Suppose we have a sample realization given by $x = (x_1, x_2, \ldots, x_n)$. Furthermore, let $\delta(X)$ be any test with test statistic $t(X)$ such that the test statistic evaluated at x, $t(x)$, is the value of the acceptance region Δ_A closest to the rejection region Δ_C. The *p-value* determines the probability, under the null hypothesis, that in any trial X the test statistic $t(X)$ assumes a value in the rejection region Δ_C; that is,

$$p = P_{\theta_0}(t(X) \in \Delta_C) = P_{\theta_0}(\delta(X) = d_1)$$

We can interpret the *p*-value as follows. Suppose we obtained a sample outcome x such that the test statistics assumed the corresponding value $t(x)$. Now, we want to know the probability, given that the null hypothesis holds, that the test statistic might become even more extreme than $t(x)$. This probability is equal to the p-value.

If $t(x)$ is a value pretty close to the median of the distribution of $t(X)$, then the chance of obtaining a more extreme value, which refutes the null hypothesis more strongly, might be fairly feasible. Then, the p-value will be large. However, if, instead, the value $t(x)$ is so extreme that the chances will be minimal under the null hypothesis that, in some other test run we obtain a value $t(X)$ even more in favor of the alternative hypothesis, this will correspond to a very low p-value. If p is less than some given significance level α, we reject the null hypothesis and we say that the test result is *significant*.

We demonstrate the meaning of the p-value in Figure C.3. The horizontal axis provides the state space of possible values for the statistic $t(X)$. The figure displays the probability, given that the null hypothesis holds, of this $t(X)$ assuming a value greater than c, for each c of the state space, and in particular also at $t(x)$ (i.e., the statistic evaluated at the observation x). We can see that, by definition, the value $t(x)$ is the boundary between the acceptance region and the critical region, with $t(x)$ itself belonging to the acceptance region. In that particular instance, we happened to choose a test with $\Delta_A = (-\infty, t(x)]$ and $\Delta_C = (t(x), \infty)$.

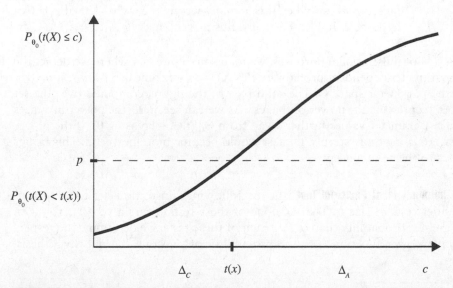

FIGURE C.3 Illustration of the p-Value for Some Test δ with Acceptance Region $\Delta_A = (-\infty, t(x)]$ and Critical Region $\Delta_C = (t(x), \infty)$

Quality Criteria of a Test

So far, we have learned how to construct a test for a given problem. In general, we formulate the two competing hypotheses and look for an appropriate test statistic to base our decision rule on and we are then done. However, in general, there is no unique test for any given pair of hypotheses. That is, we may find tests that are more suitable than others for our endeavor. How can we define what we mean by "suitable"? To answer this question, we will discuss the following quality criteria.

Power of a Test   Previously, we were introduced to the size of a test that may be equal to α. As we know, this value controls the probability of committing a type I error. So far, however, we may have several tests meeting a required test size α. The criterion selecting the most suitable ones among them involves the type II error. Recall that the type II error describes the failure of rejection of the null hypothesis when it actually is wrong. So, for parameter values $\theta \in \Theta_1$, our test should produce decision d_1 with as high a probability as possible in order to yield as small as possible a probability of a type II error, $P_{II}(d_0)$. In the following definition, we present a criterion that accounts for this ability of a test.

> *Power of a test.* The *power of a test* is the probability of rejecting the null hypothesis when it is actually wrong (i.e., when the alternative hypothesis holds). Formally, this is written as $P_{\theta_1}(\delta(X) = d_1)$.[7]

For illustrational purposes, we focus on Figure C.4 where we depict the parameter-dependent probability $P(\delta(X) = d_1)$ of some arbitrary test δ, over the parameter space Θ. The solid part of the figure, computed over the set Θ_1, represents the power of the test. As we can see, here, the power increases for parameter values further away from Θ_0 (i.e., increasing θ). If the power were rising more steeply, the test would become more powerful. This brings us to the next concept.

Uniformly Most Powerful Test   In the following illustration, let us only consider tests of size α. That is, none of these tests incurs a type I error with greater probability than α. For each of these tests, we determine the respective power function (i.e., the probability of rejecting the null hypothesis,

---

[7]The index θ_1 of the probability measure P indicates that the alternative hypothesis holds (i.e., the true parameter is a *value* in Θ_1).

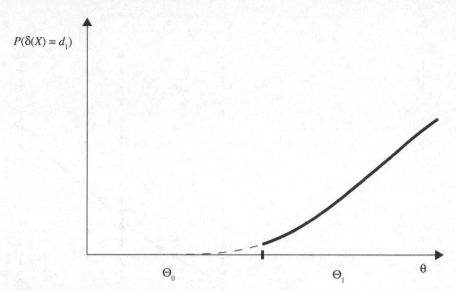

FIGURE C.4   The Solid Line of the Probability $P(\delta(X) = d_1)$, over the Set Θ_1, Indicates the Power of the Test δ

$P(\delta(X) = d_1)$, computed for all values θ in the set Θ_1 corresponding to the alternative hypothesis.

Recall that we can either obtain d_0 or d_1 as a test result, no matter what the value of the parameter may truly be. Since d_0 and d_1 are mutually exclusive, we have the relation

$$P(\delta(X) = d_0) + P(\delta(X) = d_1) = 1$$

Now, for any parameter value θ from Θ_1, this means that the power of the test and the probability of committing a type II error, $P_{II}(\delta(X))$, add up to one. We illustrate this in Figure C.5. The dashed lines indicate the probability $P_{II}(\delta(X))$, respectively, at the corresponding parameter values θ, while the dash-dotted lines represent the power for given $\theta \in \Theta_1$. As we can see, the power gradually takes over much of the probability mass from the type II error probability the greater the parameter values.

Suppose of all the tests with significance level α, we had one δ^*, which always had greater power than any of the others. Then it would be reasonable to prefer this test to all the others since we have the smallest chance of incurring a type II error. This leads to the following concept.

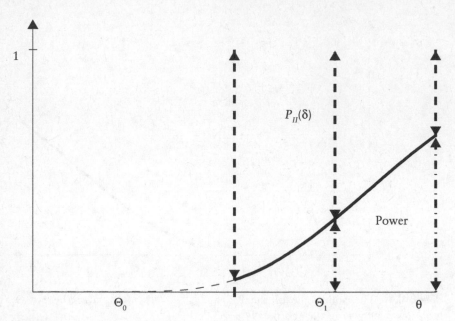

FIGURE C.5   Decomposition $1 = P_{II}(\delta) + P_{\theta_1}(\delta(X) = d_1)$, over Θ_1

> *Uniformly most powerful (UMP) test of size α.* A test δ^* of size α is *uniformly most powerful*, if of all the tests δ of size α, this test δ^* has greatest power for any $\theta \in \Theta_1$.

Unbiased Test   We know that when a test is of size α, the probability of it causing a type I error is never greater than α. And when the design of the test is reasonable, the power of the test should increase quickly once we are considering parameter values in Θ_1. In both cases (i.e., when we compute the probability of a type I error for $\theta \in \Theta_0$, as well as when we compute the power for $\theta \in \Theta_1$), we are dealing with the probability to reject the null hypothesis (i.e., $P(\delta(X) = d_1)$). In case $P(\delta(X) = d_1)$ should be smaller than α, then for certain parameter values $\theta \in \Theta_1$ it is more likely to accept the null hypothesis when it is wrong than when it holds. This certainly does not appear useful and we should try to avoid it when designing our test. This concept is treated in the following definition.

> *Unbiased test.* A test of size α is unbiased if the probability of a type II error is never greater than $1 - \alpha$; formally,

$$P_{II}(\delta(X)) \le 1 - \alpha \text{ for any } \theta \in \Theta_1$$

So if a test is unbiased, we reject the null hypothesis when it is in fact false in at least α of the cases. Consequently, the power of this test is at least α for all $\theta \in \Theta_1$. The probability of rejecting the null hypothesis falls below the significance level α for the highest parameter values.

Consistent Test Up to this point, the requirement of a good test is to produce as few errors as possible. We attempt to produce this ability by first limiting its test size by some level α and then looking for the highest power available given that significance level α.

By construction, each of our tests $\delta(X)$ is based on some test statistic $t(X)$. For this test statistic, we construct an acceptance as well as a critical region such that, given certain parameter values, the test statistic would fall into either one of these critical regions with limited probability. It may be possible that the behavior of these test statistics changes as we increase the sample size n. For example, it may be desirable to have a test of size α that has vanishing probability for a type II error.

From now on, we will consider certain tests that are based on test statistics that fall into their respective critical regions Δ_C with increasing probability, under the alternative hypothesis, as the number of sample drawings n tends to infinity. That is, these tests reject the null hypothesis more and more reliably when they actually should (i.e., $\theta \in \Theta_1$) for ever larger samples. In the optimal situation, these tests reject the null hypothesis (i.e., $\delta(X) = d_1$) with 100% certainty when the alternative hypothesis holds. This brings us to the next definition.

Consistent test. A test of size α is consistent if its power grows to one for increasing sample size.

Recall that in our coverage of point estimates we introduced the consistent estimator that had the positive feature that it varied about its expected value with vanishing probability. So, with increasing probability, it assumed values arbitrarily close to this expected value such that eventually it would become virtually indistinguishable from it. The use of such a statistic for the test leads to the following desirable characteristic: The test statistic will cease to assume values that are extreme under the respective hypothesis such that it will basically always end up in the acceptance region when the null hypothesis holds, and in the rejection region under the alternative hypothesis.

Fundamentals of Matrix Algebra

In financial econometrics, it is useful to consider operations performed on ordered *arrays* of numbers. Ordered arrays of numbers are called *vectors* and *matrices* while individual numbers are called *scalars*. In this appendix, we will discuss concepts, operations, and results of matrix algebra.

VECTORS AND MATRICES DEFINED

Let's now define precisely the concepts of vector and matrix. Though vectors can be thought of as particular matrices, in many cases it is useful to keep the two concepts—vectors and matrices—distinct. In particular, a number of important concepts and properties can be defined for vectors but do not generalize easily to matrices.[1]

Vectors

An *n-dimensional vector* is an ordered array of *n* numbers. Vectors are generally indicated with boldface lowercase letters, although we do not always follow that convention in the textbook. Thus a vector $\mathbf{x}$ is an array of the form:

$$\mathbf{x} = [x_1, \ldots, x_n]$$

The numbers a_i are called the *components* of the vector $\mathbf{x}$.

A vector is identified by the set of its components. Vectors can be *row vectors* or *column vectors*. If the vector components appear in a horizontal row, then the vector is called a row vector, as, for instance, the vector:

$$\mathbf{x} = [1, 2, 8, 7]$$

---

[1]Vectors can be thought as the elements of an abstract linear space while matrices are operators that operate on linear spaces.

Here are two examples. Suppose that we let w_n be a risky asset's weight in a portfolio. Assume that there are N risky assets. Then the following vector, **w**, is a row vector that represents a portfolio's holdings of the N risky assets:

$$\mathbf{w} = [w_1 \ w_2 \ldots w_N]$$

As a second example of a row vector, suppose that we let r_n be the *excess return* for a risky asset. (The excess return is the difference between the return on a risky asset and the risk-free rate.) Then the following row vector is the excess return vector:

$$\mathbf{r} = [r_1 \ r_2 \ldots r_N]$$

If the vector components are arranged in a column, then the vector is called a column vector.

For example, we know that a portfolio's excess return will be affected by what can be different *characteristics* or *attributes* that affect all asset prices. A few examples would be the price-earnings ratio, market capitalization, and industry. Let us denote for a particular attribute a column vector, **a**, that shows the exposure of each risky asset to that attribute, denoted a_i:

$$\mathbf{a} = \begin{bmatrix} a_1 \\ a_2 \\ \vdots \\ a_N \end{bmatrix}$$

Matrices

An $n \times m$ matrix is a bi-dimensional ordered array of $n \times m$ numbers. Matrices are usually indicated with boldface uppercase letters. Thus, the generic matrix **A** is an $n \times m$ array of the form

$$\mathbf{A} = \begin{bmatrix} a_{1,1} & \cdot & a_{1,j} & \cdot & a_{1,m} \\ \cdot & & \cdot & & \cdot \\ a_{i,1} & \cdot & a_{i,j} & \cdot & a_{i,m} \\ \cdot & & \cdot & & \cdot \\ a_{n,1} & \cdot & a_{n,j} & \cdot & a_{n,m} \end{bmatrix}$$

Note that the first subscript indicates rows while the second subscript indicates columns. The entries a_{ij}—called the *elements* of the matrix **A**—are the numbers at the crossing of the ith row and the jth column. The commas between the subscripts of the matrix entries are omitted when there is no risk of confusion: $a_{i,j} \equiv a_{ij}$. A matrix **A** is often indicated by its generic element between brackets:

$$\mathbf{A} = \{a_{ij}\}_{nm} \text{ or } \mathbf{A} = [a_{ij}]_{nm}$$

where the subscripts nm are the *dimensions* of the matrix.

There are several types of matrices. First there is a broad classification of square and rectangular matrices. A *rectangular matrix* can have different numbers of rows and columns; a *square matrix* is a rectangular matrix with the same number n of rows as of columns. Because of the important role that they play in applications, we focus on square matrices in the next section

SQUARE MATRICES

The $n \times n$ *identity matrix*, indicated as the matrix $\mathbf{I}_n$, is a square matrix in which diagonal elements (i.e., the entries with the same row and column suffix) are equal to one while all other entries are zero:

$$\mathbf{I}_n = \begin{bmatrix} 1 & 0 & \cdot & \cdot & \cdot & 0 \\ 0 & 1 & \cdot & \cdot & \cdot & 0 \\ \cdot & \cdot & \cdot & & & \cdot \\ \cdot & \cdot & & \cdot & & \\ \cdot & \cdot & & & \cdot & \\ 0 & 0 & \cdot & \cdot & \cdot & 1 \end{bmatrix}$$

A matrix in which entries are all zero is called a *zero matrix*.

A *diagonal matrix* is a square matrix in which elements are all zero except the ones on the diagonal:

$$\mathbf{A} = \begin{bmatrix} a_{11} & 0 & \cdot & \cdot & \cdot & 0 \\ 0 & a_{22} & \cdot & \cdot & \cdot & 0 \\ \cdot & \cdot & \cdot & & & \cdot \\ \cdot & \cdot & & \cdot & & \cdot \\ \cdot & \cdot & & & \cdot & \cdot \\ 0 & 0 & \cdot & \cdot & \cdot & a_{nn} \end{bmatrix}$$

Given a square $n \times n$ matrix $\mathbf{A}$, the matrix $\mathrm{dg}\mathbf{A}$ is the diagonal matrix extracted from $\mathbf{A}$. The diagonal matrix $\mathrm{dg}\mathbf{A}$ is a matrix whose elements are all zero except the elements on the diagonal which coincide with those of the matrix $\mathbf{A}$:

$$
\mathbf{A} = \begin{bmatrix}
a_{11} & a_{12} & \cdot & \cdot & a_{1n} \\
a_{21} & a_{22} & \cdot & \cdot & a_{2n} \\
\cdot & \cdot & & & \cdot \\
\cdot & \cdot & & & \cdot \\
\cdot & \cdot & & & \cdot \\
a_{n1} & a_{n2} & \cdot & \cdot & a_{nn}
\end{bmatrix} \Rightarrow \mathrm{dg}\mathbf{A} = \begin{bmatrix}
a_{11} & 0 & \cdot & \cdot & 0 \\
0 & a_{22} & \cdot & \cdot & 0 \\
\cdot & & & & \cdot \\
\cdot & & & & \cdot \\
\cdot & & & & \cdot \\
0 & 0 & \cdot & \cdot & a_{nn}
\end{bmatrix}
$$

The *trace* of a square matrix $\mathbf{A}$ is the sum of its diagonal elements:

$$
\mathrm{tr}\mathbf{A} = \sum_{i=1}^{n} a_{ii}
$$

A square matrix is called *symmetric* if the elements above the diagonal are equal to the corresponding elements below the diagonal: $a_{ij} = a_{ji}$. A matrix is said to be a *skew-symmetric* if the diagonal elements are zero and the elements above the diagonal are the opposite of the corresponding elements below the diagonal: $a_{ij} = -a_{ji}$.

The most commonly used symmetric matrix in financial econometrics and econometrics is the *covariance matrix*, also referred to as the *variance-covariance matrix*. For example, suppose that there are N risky assets and that the variance of the excess return for each risky asset and the covariances between each pair of risky assets are estimated. As the number of risky assets is N, there are N^2 elements, consisting of N variances (along the diagonal) and $N^2 - N$ covariances. Symmetry restrictions reduce the number of independent elements. In fact the covariance between risky asset i and risky asset j will be equal to the covariance between risky asset j and risky asset i. Hence, the variance-covariance matrix is a symmetric matrix.

DETERMINANTS

Consider a square, $n \times n$, matrix $\mathbf{A}$. The *determinant* of $\mathbf{A}$, denoted $|\mathbf{A}|$, is defined as follows:

$$
|\mathbf{A}| = \sum (-1)^{t(j_1, \dots, j_n)} \prod_{i=1}^{n} a_{ij}
$$

where the sum is extended over all permutations $(j_1, \ldots, j_n)$ of the set $(1, 2, \ldots, n)$ and $t(j_1, \ldots, j_n)$ is the number of transpositions (or inversions of positions) required to go from $(1, 2, \ldots, n)$ to $(j_1, \ldots, j_n)$. Otherwise stated, a determinant is the sum of all products formed taking exactly one element from each row with each product multiplied by $(-1)^{t(j_1, \ldots, j_n)}$. Consider, for instance, the case $n = 2$, where there is only one possible transposition: $1, 2 \Rightarrow 2, 1$. The determinant of a 2×2 matrix is therefore computed as follows:

$$|\mathbf{A}| = (-1)^0 a_{11}a_{22} + (-1)^1 a_{12}a_{21} = a_{11}a_{22} - a_{12}a_{21}$$

Consider a square matrix $\mathbf{A}$ of order n. Consider the matrix $\mathbf{M}_{ij}$ obtained by removing the ith row and the jth column. The matrix $\mathbf{M}_{ij}$ is a square matrix of order $(n-1)$. The determinant $|\mathbf{M}_{ij}|$ of the matrix $\mathbf{M}_{ij}$ is called the *minor* of a_{ij}. The signed minor $(-1)^{(i+j)} |\mathbf{M}_{ij}|$ is called the *cofactor* of a_{ij} and is generally denoted as α_{ij}.

A square matrix $\mathbf{A}$ is said to be *singular* if its determinant is equal to zero. A $n \times m$ matrix $\mathbf{A}$ is of *rank* r if at least one of its (square) r-minors is different from zero while all $(r + 1)$-minors, if any, are zero. A nonsingular square matrix is said to be of *full rank* if its rank r is equal to its order n.

SYSTEMS OF LINEAR EQUATIONS

A system of n linear equations in m unknown variables is a set of n simultaneous equations of the following form:

$$a_{11}x_1 + \ldots + a_{1m}x_m = b_1$$
$$\cdots\cdots\cdots\cdots\cdots\cdots\cdots\cdots\cdots$$
$$a_{n1}x_1 + \ldots + a_{1m}x_m = b_m$$

The $n \times m$ matrix:

$$\mathbf{A} = \begin{bmatrix} a_{1,1} & \cdot & a_{1,j} & \cdot & a_{1,m} \\ \cdot & & \cdot & & \cdot \\ a_{i,1} & \cdot & a_{i,j} & \cdot & a_{i,m} \\ \cdot & & \cdot & & \cdot \\ a_{n,1} & \cdot & a_{n,j} & \cdot & a_{n,m} \end{bmatrix}$$

formed with the coefficients of the variables is called the *coefficient matrix*. The terms b_i are called the *constant terms*. The *augmented matrix* $[\mathbf{A} \ \mathbf{b}]$—

formed by adding to the coefficient matrix a column formed with the constant term—is represented as follows:

$$[\mathbf{A} \ \mathbf{b}] = \begin{bmatrix} a_{1,1} & \cdot & a_{1,j} & \cdot & a_{1,m} & b_1 \\ \cdot & \cdot & \cdot & \cdot & \cdot & \cdot \\ a_{i,1} & \cdot & a_{i,j} & \cdot & a_{i,m} & b_i \\ \cdot & \cdot & \cdot & \cdot & \cdot & \cdot \\ a_{n,1} & \cdot & a_{n,j} & \cdot & a_{n,m} & b_n \end{bmatrix}$$

If the constant terms on the right side of the equations are all zero, the system is called *homogeneous*. If at least one of the constant terms is different from zero, the system is said to be *nonhomogeneous*. A system is said to be *consistent* if it admits a solution, that is, if there is a set of values of the variables that simultaneously satisfy all the equations. A system is referred to as *inconsistent* if there is no set of numbers that satisfy the system equations.

Let's first consider the case of nonhomogeneous linear systems. The fundamental theorems of linear systems are listed as follows:

Theorem 1. A system of n linear equations in m unknown is consistent (i.e., it admits a solution) if and only if the coefficient matrix and the augmented matrix have the same rank.

Theorem 2. If a consistent system of n equations in m variables is of rank $r < m$, it is possible to choose $n - r$ unknowns so that the coefficient matrix of the remaining r unknowns is of rank r. When these $m - r$ variables are assigned any arbitrary value, the value of the remaining variables is uniquely determined.

The immediate consequences of the two fundamental theorems are that (1) a system of n equations in n unknown variables admits a solution and (2) the solution is unique if and only if both the coefficient matrix and the augmented matrix are of rank n.

Let's now examine homogeneous systems. The coefficient matrix and the augmented matrix of a homogeneous system always have the same rank and thus a homogeneous system is always consistent. In fact, the trivial solution $x_1 = \ldots = x_m = 0$ always satisfies a homogeneous system.

Consider now a homogeneous system of n equations in n unknowns. If the rank of the coefficient matrix is n, the system has only the trivial solution. If the rank of the coefficient matrix is $r < n$, then Theorem 2 ensures that the system has a solution other than the trivial solution.

LINEAR INDEPENDENCE AND RANK

Consider an $n \times m$ matrix $\mathbf{A}$. A set of p columns extracted from the matrix $\mathbf{A}$

$$
\begin{bmatrix}
\cdot & a_{1,i_1} & \cdot & a_{1,i_p} & \cdot \\
\cdot & \cdot & \cdot & \cdot \\
\cdot & \cdot & \cdot & \cdot \\
\cdot & \cdot & \cdot & \cdot \\
\cdot & a_{n,i_1} & \cdot & a_{n,i_p} & \cdot
\end{bmatrix}
$$

are said to be linearly independent if it is not possible to find p constants $\beta_s, s = 1, \ldots, p$ such that the following n equations are simultaneously satisfied:

$$
\beta_1 a_{1,i_1} + \ldots + \beta_p a_{1,i_p} = 0
$$
$$
\cdots\cdots\cdots\cdots\cdots\cdots\cdots\cdots
$$
$$
\beta_1 a_{n,i_1} + \ldots + \beta_p a_{n,i_p} = 0
$$

Analogously, a set of q rows extracted from the matrix $\mathbf{A}$ are said to be linearly independent if it is not possible to find q constants $\lambda_s, \; s = 1, \ldots, q$ such that the following m equations are simultaneously satisfied:

$$
\lambda_1 a_{i_1,1} + \ldots + \lambda_q a_{i_q,1} = 0
$$
$$
\cdots\cdots\cdots\cdots\cdots\cdots\cdots\cdots
$$
$$
\lambda_1 a_{i_1,m} + \ldots + \lambda_q a_{i_q,m} = 0
$$

It can be demonstrated that in any matrix the number p of linearly independent columns is the same as the number q of linearly independent rows. This number is equal, in turn, to the rank r of the matrix. Recall that an $n \times m$ matrix $\mathbf{A}$ is said to be of rank r if at least one of its (square) r-minors is different from zero while all $(r + 1)$-minors, if any, are zero. The constant p, is the same for rows and for columns. We can now give an alternative definition of the rank of a matrix: Given a $n \times m$ matrix $\mathbf{A}$, its *rank*, denoted rank($\mathbf{A}$), is the number r of linearly independent rows or columns as the row rank is always equal to the column rank.

VECTOR AND MATRIX OPERATIONS

Let's now introduce the most common operations performed on vectors and matrices. An *operation* is a mapping that operates on scalars, vectors, and matrices to produce new scalars, vectors, or matrices. The notion of operations performed on a set of objects to produce another object of the same set is the key concept of algebra. Let's start with vector operations.

Vector Operations

The following three operations are usually defined on vectors: transpose, addition, and multiplication.

Transpose The *transpose* operation transforms a row vector into a column vector and vice versa. Given the row vector $\mathbf{x} = [x_1, \dots, x_n]$ its transpose, denoted as $\mathbf{x}^T$ or $\mathbf{x}'$, is the column vector:

$$\mathbf{x}^T = \begin{bmatrix} x_1 \\ \cdot \\ \cdot \\ \cdot \\ x_n \end{bmatrix}$$

Clearly the transpose of the transpose is the original vector: $\left(\mathbf{x}^T\right)^T = \mathbf{x}$.

Addition Two-row (or two-column) vectors $\mathbf{x} = [x_1, \dots, x_n]$, $\mathbf{y} = [y_1, \dots, y_n]$ with the same number n of components can be added. The *addition* of two vectors is a new vector whose components are the sums of the components:

$$\mathbf{x} + \mathbf{y} = [x_1 + y_1, \dots, x_n + y_n]$$

This definition can be generalized to any number N of summands:

$$\sum_{i=1}^{N} \mathbf{x}_i = \left[\sum_{i=1}^{N} x_{1i}, \dots, \sum_{i=1}^{N} y_{ni} \right]$$

The summands must be both column or row vectors; it is not possible to add row vectors to column vectors.

It is clear from the definition of addition that addition is a commutative operation in the sense that the order of the summands does not matter: $\mathbf{x} + \mathbf{y} = \mathbf{y} + \mathbf{x}$. Addition is also an associative operation in the sense that $\mathbf{x} + (\mathbf{y} + \mathbf{z}) = (\mathbf{x} + \mathbf{y}) + \mathbf{z}$.

Multiplication   We define two types of multiplication: (1) multiplication of a scalar and a vector and (2) scalar multiplication of two vectors (inner product).[2]

The multiplication of a scalar a and a row (or column) vector $\mathbf{x}$, denoted as $a\mathbf{x}$, is defined as the multiplication of each component of the vector by the scalar:

$$a\mathbf{x} = [ax_1, \ldots, ax_n]$$

A similar definition holds for column vectors. It is clear from this definition that multiplication by a scalar is associative as

$$a(\mathbf{x} + \mathbf{y}) = a\mathbf{x} + a\mathbf{y}$$

The *scalar product* (also called the *inner product*) of two vectors $\mathbf{x}$, $\mathbf{y}$, denoted as $\mathbf{x} \cdot \mathbf{y}$, is defined between a row vector and a column vector. The scalar product between two vectors produces a scalar according to the following rule:

$$\mathbf{x} \cdot \mathbf{y} = \sum_{i=1}^{n} x_i y_i$$

Two vectors $\mathbf{x}$, $\mathbf{y}$ are said to be *orthogonal* if their scalar product is zero.

Matrix Operations

Let's now define operations on matrices. The following five operations on matrices are usually defined: transpose, addition, multiplication, inverse, and adjoint.

Transpose   The definition of the *transpose* of a matrix is an extension of the transpose of a vector. The transpose operation consists in exchanging rows with columns. Consider the $n \times m$ matrix

$$\mathbf{A} = \{a_{ij}\}_{nm}$$

---

[2] A third type of product between vectors—the vector (or outer) product between vectors—produces a third vector. We do not define it here as it is not typically used in economics though widely used in the physical sciences.

The transpose of $\mathbf{A}$, denoted $\mathbf{A}^T$ or $\mathbf{A}'$ is the $m \times n$ matrix whose ith row is the ith column of $\mathbf{A}$:

$$\mathbf{A}^T = \left\{ a_{ji} \right\}_{mn}$$

The following should be clear from this definition:

$$\left(\mathbf{A}^T \right)^T = \mathbf{A}$$

and that a matrix is symmetric if and only if

$$\mathbf{A}^T = \mathbf{A}$$

Addition Consider two $n \times m$ matrices:

$$\mathbf{A} = \left\{ a_{ij} \right\}_{nm} \text{ and } \mathbf{B} = \left\{ b_{ij} \right\}_{nm}$$

The sum of the matrices $\mathbf{A}$ and $\mathbf{B}$ is defined as the $n \times m$ matrix obtained by adding the respective elements:

$$\mathbf{A} + \mathbf{B} = \left\{ a_{ij} + b_{ij} \right\}_{nm}$$

Note that it is essential for the definition of addition that the two matrices have the same order $n \times m$.

The operation of addition can be extended to any number N of summands as follows:

$$\sum_{s=1}^{N} \mathbf{A}_i = \left\{ \sum_{s=1}^{N} a_{s_{ij}} \right\}_{nm}$$

where $a_{s_{ij}}$ is the generic i,j element of the sth summand.

Multiplication Consider a scalar c and a matrix

$$\mathbf{A} = \left\{ a_{ij} \right\}_{nm}$$

The product $c\mathbf{A} = \mathbf{A}c$ is the $n \times m$ matrix obtained by multiplying each element of the matrix by c:

$$c\mathbf{A} = \mathbf{A}c = \left\{ ca_{ij} \right\}_{nm}$$

Multiplication of a matrix by a scalar is associative with respect to matrix addition:

$$c(A+B) = cA + cB$$

Let's now define the product of two matrices. Consider two matrices:

$$A = \{a_{it}\}_{np} \text{ and } B = \{b_{sj}\}_{pm}$$

The product $C = AB$ is defined as follows:

$$C = AB = \{c_{ij}\} = \left\{ \sum_{t=1}^{p} a_{it} b_{tj} \right\}$$

The product $C = AB$ is therefore a matrix whose generic element $\{c_{ij}\}$ is the scalar product of the ith row of the matrix A and the jth column of the matrix B. This definition generalizes the definition of scalar product of vectors: the scalar product of two n-dimensional vectors is the product of an $n \times 1$ matrix (a row vector) for a $1 \times n$ matrix (the column vector).

Inverse and Adjoint   Consider two square matrices of order n A and B. If AB = BA = I, then the matrix B is called the *inverse* of A and is denoted as A^{-1}. It can be demonstrated that the two following properties hold:

Property 1. A square matrix A admits an inverse A^{-1} if and only if it is nonsingular, that is, if and only if its determinant is different from zero. Otherwise stated, a matrix A admits an inverse if and only if it is of full rank.

Property 2. The inverse of a square matrix, if it exists, is unique. This property is a consequence of the property that, if A is nonsingular, then AB = AC implies B = C.

Consider now a square matrix of order n, $A = \{a_{ij}\}$ and consider its cofactors α_{ij}. Recall that the cofactors α_{ij} are the signed minors

$$(-1)^{(i+j)} |M_{ij}|$$

of the matrix **A**. The *adjoint* of the matrix **A**, denoted as Adj(**A**), is the following matrix:

$$
\text{Adj}(\mathbf{A}) =
\begin{bmatrix}
\alpha_{1,1} & \cdot & \alpha_{1,j} & \cdot & \alpha_{1,n} \\
\cdot & \cdot & \cdot & \cdot & \cdot \\
\alpha_{i,1} & \cdot & \alpha_{i,j} & \cdot & \alpha_{i,n} \\
\cdot & \cdot & \cdot & \cdot & \cdot \\
\alpha_{n,1} & \cdot & \alpha_{n,j} & \cdot & \alpha_{n,n}
\end{bmatrix}^{T}
=
\begin{bmatrix}
\alpha_{1,1} & \cdot & \alpha_{2,1} & \cdot & \alpha_{n,1} \\
\cdot & \cdot & \cdot & \cdot & \cdot \\
\alpha_{1,i} & \cdot & \alpha_{2,i} & \cdot & \alpha_{n,i} \\
\cdot & \cdot & \cdot & \cdot & \cdot \\
\alpha_{1,n} & \cdot & \alpha_{2,n} & \cdot & \alpha_{n,n}
\end{bmatrix}
$$

The adjoint of a matrix **A** is therefore the transpose of the matrix obtained by replacing the elements of **A** with their cofactors.

If the matrix **A** is nonsingular, and therefore admits an inverse, it can be demonstrated that

$$
\mathbf{A}^{-1} = \frac{\text{Adj}(\mathbf{A})}{|\mathbf{A}|}
$$

A square matrix of order n, **A**, is said to be *orthogonal* if the following property holds:

$$
\mathbf{A}\mathbf{A}' = \mathbf{A}'\mathbf{A} = \mathbf{I}_n
$$

Because in this case **A** must be of full rank, the transpose of an orthogonal matrix coincides with its inverse: $\mathbf{A}^{-1} = \mathbf{A}'$.

EIGENVALUES AND EIGENVECTORS

Consider a square matrix **A** of order n and the set of all n-dimensional vectors. The matrix **A** is a linear operator on the space of vectors. This means that **A** operates on each vector producing another vector subject to the following restriction:

$$
\mathbf{A}(a\mathbf{x} + b\mathbf{y}) = a\mathbf{A}\mathbf{x} + b\mathbf{A}\mathbf{y}
$$

Consider now the set of vectors **x** such that the following property holds:

$$
\mathbf{A}\mathbf{x} = \lambda\mathbf{x}
$$

Any vector such that the above property holds is called an *eigenvector* of the matrix **A** and the corresponding value of λ is called an *eigenvalue*.

To determine the eigenvectors of a matrix and the relative eigenvalues, consider that the equation $\mathbf{Ax} = \lambda\mathbf{x}$ can be written as

$$(\mathbf{A} - \lambda\mathbf{I})\mathbf{x} = 0$$

which can, in turn, be written as a system of linear equations:

$$(\mathbf{A} - \lambda\mathbf{I})\mathbf{x} = \begin{bmatrix} a_{1,1} - \lambda & \cdot & a_{1,j} & \cdot & a_{1,n} \\ \cdot & \cdot & \cdot & & \cdot \\ a_{i,1} & \cdot & a_{i,i} - \lambda & \cdot & a_{i,n} \\ \cdot & \cdot & \cdot & & \cdot \\ a_{n,1} & \cdot & a_{n,j} & \cdot & a_{n,n} - \lambda \end{bmatrix} \begin{bmatrix} x_1 \\ \cdot \\ x_i \\ \cdot \\ x_n \end{bmatrix} = 0$$

This system of equations has nontrivial solutions only if the matrix $\mathbf{A} - \lambda\mathbf{I}$ is singular. To determine the eigenvectors and the eigenvalues of the matrix $\mathbf{A}$ we must therefore solve the following equation:

$$|\mathbf{A} - \lambda\mathbf{I}| = \begin{vmatrix} a_{1,1} - \lambda & \cdot & a_{1,j} & \cdot & a_{1,n} \\ \cdot & \cdot & \cdot & & \cdot \\ a_{i,1} & \cdot & a_{i,i} - \lambda & \cdot & a_{i,n} \\ \cdot & \cdot & \cdot & & \cdot \\ a_{n,1} & \cdot & a_{n,j} & \cdot & a_{n,n} - \lambda \end{vmatrix} = 0$$

The expansion of this determinant yields a polynomial $\phi(\lambda)$ of degree n known as the *characteristic polynomial* of the matrix $\mathbf{A}$. The equation $\phi(\lambda) = 0$ is known as the *characteristic equation* of the matrix $\mathbf{A}$. In general, this equation will have n roots λ_s which are the eigenvalues of the matrix $\mathbf{A}$. To each of these eigenvalues corresponds a solution of the system of linear equations, illustrated as follows:

$$\begin{bmatrix} a_{1,1} - \lambda_s & \cdot & a_{1,j} & \cdot & a_{1,n} \\ \cdot & \cdot & \cdot & & \cdot \\ a_{i,1} & \cdot & a_{i,i} - \lambda_s & \cdot & a_{i,n} \\ \cdot & \cdot & \cdot & & \cdot \\ a_{n,1} & \cdot & a_{n,j} & \cdot & a_{n,n} - \lambda_s \end{bmatrix} \begin{bmatrix} x_{1_s} \\ \cdot \\ x_{i_s} \\ \cdot \\ x_{n_s} \end{bmatrix} = 0$$

Each solution represents the eigenvector $\mathbf{x}_s$ corresponding to the eigenvalue λ_s. As explained in Chapter 12, the determination of eigenvalues and eigenvectors is the basis for principal component analysis.

Model Selection Criterion: AIC and BIC

In several chapters we have discussed goodness-of-fit tests to assess the performance of a model with respect to how well it explains the data. However, suppose we want to select from among several candidate models. What criterion can be used to select the best model? In choosing a criterion for model selection, one accepts the fact that models only approximate reality. Given a set of data, the objective is to determine which of the candidate models best approximates the data. This involves trying to minimize the loss of information. Because the field of information theory is used to quantify or measure the expected value of information, the information-theoretic approach is used to derive the two most commonly used criteria in model selection—the Akaike information criterion and the Bayesian information criterion.[1] These two criteria, as described in this appendix, can be used for the selection of econometric models.[2]

---

[1] There are other approaches that have been developed. One approach is based on the theory of learning, the Vapnik-Chervonenkis (VC) theory of learning. This approach offers a complex theoretical framework for learning that, when applicable, is able to give precise theoretical bounds to the learning abilities of models. Though its theoretical foundation is solid, the practical applicability of the VC theory is complex. It has not yet found a broad following in financial econometrics. See Vladimir N. Vapnik, *Statistical Learning Theory* (New York: John Wiley & Sons, 1998).

[2] For a further discussion of these applications of AIC and BIC, see Herman J. Bierens, "Information Criteria and Model Selection," Pennsylvania State University, March 12, 2006, working paper. In addition to the AIC and BIC, Bierens discusses another criterion, the Hannan-Quinn criterion, in E. J. Hannan and B. G. Quinn, "The Determination of the Order of an Autoregression," *Journal of the Royal Statistical Society* B, no. 41 (1979): 190–195.

AKAIKE INFORMATION CRITERION

In 1951, Kullback and Leibler developed a measure to capture the information that is lost when approximating reality; that is, the Kullback and Leibler measure is a criterion for a good model that minimizes the loss of information.[3] Two decades later, Akaike established a relationship between the Kullback-Leibler measure and maximum likelihood estimation method—an estimation method used in many statistical analyses as described in Chapter 13—to derive a criterion (i.e., formula) for model selection.[4] This criterion, referred to as the *Akaike information criterion* (AIC), is generally considered the first model selection criterion that should be used in practice. The AIC is

$$\text{AIC} = -2\log L(\hat{\theta}) + 2k$$

where θ = the set (vector) of model parameters
  $L(\hat{\theta})$ = the likelihood of the candidate model given the data when evaluated at the maximum likelihood estimate of θ
  k = the number of estimated parameters in the candidate model

The AIC in isolation is meaningless. Rather, this value is calculated for every candidate model and the "best" model is the candidate model with the smallest AIC. Let's look at the two components of the AIC. The first component, $-2\log L(\hat{\theta})$, is the value of the likelihood function, $\log L(\hat{\theta})$, which is the probability of obtaining the data given the candidate model. Since the likelihood function's value is multiplied by -2, ignoring the second component, the model with the minimum AIC is the one with the highest value for the likelihood function. However, to this first component we add an adjustment based on the number of estimated parameters. The more parameters, the greater the amount added to the first component, increasing the value for the AIC and penalizing the model. Hence, there is a trade-off: the better fit, created by making a model more complex by requiring more parameters, must be considered in light of the penalty imposed by adding more parameters. This is why the second component of the AIC is thought of in terms of a penalty.

---

[3] S. Kullback and R. A. Leibler, "On Information and Sufficiency," *Annals of Mathematical Statistics* 22, no. 1 (1951): 79–86.

[4] Hirotugu Akaike, "Information Theory and an Extension of the Maximum Likelihood Principle," in *Second International Symposium on Information Theory*, ed. B. N. Petrov and F. Csake (Budapest: Akademiai Kiado, 1973), 267–281; and Hirotugu Akaike, "A New Look at the Statistical Model Identification," *I.E.E.E. Transactions on Automatic Control*, AC 19, (1974): 716–723.

For small sample sizes, the *second-order Akaike information criterion* (AIC_c) should be used in lieu of the AIC described earlier. The AIC_c is

$$AIC_c = -2 \log L(\hat{\theta}) + 2k + (2k+1) / (n-k-1)$$

where n is the number of observations.[5] A small sample size is when n/k is less than 40. Notice as the n increases, the third term in AIC_c approaches zero and will therefore give the same result as AIC. AIC_c has also been suggested to be used instead of AIC when n is small or k is large.[6] It has been suggested, for example, that in selecting the orders of an ARMA, as we described in Chapter 9, the AIC_c be used.[7]

Typically, to assess the strength of evidence for the each candidate model, two measures can be used:

1. The delta AIC
2. The Akaike weights

Consider first the *delta AIC* measure assuming there are M candidate models. An AIC can be calculated for each candidate model, denoted by AIC_m ($m = 1, \ldots, M$). The AIC with the minimum value, denoted by AIC^*, is then the best model. The delta AIC for the mth candidate model, denoted by Δ_m, is simply the difference between the AIC_m and AIC^*. This difference is then used as follows to determine the level of support for each candidate model. If the delta AIC is

- Less than 2, this indicates there is substantial evidence to support the candidate model (i.e., the candidate model is almost as good as the best model).
- Between 4 and 7, this indicates that the candidate model has considerably less support.
- Greater than 10, this indicates that there is essentially no support for the candidate model (i.e., it is unlikely to be the best model).[8]

The above values for the computed delta AICs are merely general rules of thumb.

Because the magnitude of the delta AIC is not meaningful in itself, to measure the strength of evidence for a candidate model we are interested

---

[5] Clifford M. Hurvich and Chih-Ling Tsai, "Regression and Time Series Model Selection in Small Samples," *Biometrika* 76, no. 2 (June 1989): 297–307.

[6] Kenneth P. Burnham and David R. Anderson, *Model Selection and Multimodel Inference: A Practical Information-Theoretic Approach,* 2nd ed. (New York: Springer-Verlag, 2002).

[7] Peter J. Brockwell and Richard A. Davis, *Time Series: Theory and Methods,* 2nd ed. (New York: Springer-Verlag, 2009), 273.

[8] Burnham and Anderson, *Model Selection and Multimodel Inference,* 70.

in the relative value of the delta AIC. The *Akaike weights*, denoted by w_m, are obtained by normalizing the relative likelihood values. That is, they are the ratios of a candidate model's delta AIC relative to the sum of the delta AICs for all candidate models, shown as follows:

$$w_m = \frac{\exp(-0.5\Delta_m)}{\sum_{j=1}^{M}\exp(-0.5\Delta_j)}$$

The interpretation of this measure of strength of each candidate model given the data is the following: the Akaike weights are the probability that the candidate model is the best among the set of candidate models. For example, if a candidate model has an Akaike weight of 0.60, this means that given the data, the candidate model has a 60% probability of being the best one.

Further information can be obtained by calculating the ratio of Akaike weights for different candidate models to determine to what extent one candidate model is better than another candidate model. These measures, called *evidence ratios*, can be used to compare, for example, the best model versus a candidate model. For example, if the evidence ratio computed as the ratio of the best model to some candidate model is 1.8, then this can be interpreted as the best model being 1.8 times more likely than that candidate model of being the best model.

What is the difference between the AIC and hypothesis tests in model selection described in Chapters 3 and 4 where we described statistical tests for various regression models and the use of stepwise regressions? The difference is that in those earlier chapters, the tests used for model selection are hypothesis tests where at a certain level of confidence an independent variable would be included or excluded from the model. In contrast, model selection applying AIC is based on the strength of the evidence and provides for each of the candidate models a measure of uncertainty. What is important to emphasize is that the AIC might identify which model is best among the candidate models but that does not mean that any of the candidate models do a good job of explaining the data.

BAYESIAN INFORMATION CRITERION

The *Bayesian information criterion* (BIC), proposed by Schwarz[9] and hence also referred to as the *Schwarz information criterion* and *Schwarz Bayesian*

---

[9] Gideon Schwarz, "Estimating the Dimension of a Model," *Annals of Statistics* 6 (1978): 461–464. The purpose of the BIC is to provide an asymptotic approximation to a transformation of the candidate model's Bayesian posterior probability.

information criterion, is another model selection criterion based on information theory but set within a Bayesian context. The difference between the BIC and the AIC is the greater penalty imposed for the number of parameters by the former than the latter. Burnham and Anderson provide theoretical arguments in favor of the AIC, particularly the AIC_c over the BIC.[10] Moreover, in the case of multivariate regression analysis, Yang explains why AIC is better than BIC in model selection.[11]

The BIC is computed as follows:

$$BIC = -2 \log L(\hat{\theta}) + k \log n$$

where the terms above are the same as described in our description of the AIC.

The best model is the one that provides the minimum BIC, denoted by BIC*. Like delta AIC for each candidate model, we can compute delta $BIC = BIC_m - BIC^*$. Given M models, the magnitude of the delta BIC can be interpreted as evidence *against a candidate model* being the best model. The rules of thumb are[12]

- Less than 2, it is not worth more than a bare mention.
- Between 2 and 6, the evidence against the candidate model is positive.
- Between 6 and 10, the evidence against the candidate model is strong.
- Greater than 10, the evidence is very strong.

---

[10] Burnham and Anderson, *Model Selection and Multimodel Inference*.

[11] Ying Yang, "Can the Strengths of AIC and BIC Be Shared?" *Biometrika* 92, no. 4 (December 2005): 937–950.

[12] Robert E. Kass and Adrian E. Raftery, "Bayes Factors," *Journal of the American Statistical Association* 90, no. 430 (June 1995): 773–795. The rules of thumb provided here are those modified in a presentation by Joseph E. Cavanaugh, "171:290 Model Selection: Lecture VI: The Bayesian Information Criterion" (PowerPoint presentation, The University of Iowa, September 29, 2009).

Robust Statistics

Robust statistics addresses the problem of making estimates that are insensitive to small changes in the basic assumptions of the statistical models employed. In this appendix we discuss the general concepts and methods of robust statistics. The reason for doing so is to provide background information for the discussion of robust estimation covered in Chapter 8.

ROBUST STATISTICS DEFINED

Statistical models are based on a set of assumptions; the most important include (1) the distribution of key variables, for example, the normal distribution of errors, and (2) the model specification, for example, model linearity or nonlinearity. Some of these assumptions are critical to the estimation process: if they are violated, the estimates become unreliable. Robust statistics (1) assesses the changes in estimates due to small changes in the basic assumptions and (2) creates new estimates that are insensitive to small changes in some of the assumptions. The focus of our exposition is to make estimates robust to small changes in the distribution of errors and, in particular, to the presence of outliers.

Robust statistics is also useful to separate the contribution of the tails from the contribution of the body of the data. We can say that robust statistics and classical nonrobust statistics are complementary. By conducting a robust analysis, one can better articulate important financial econometric findings.

As observed by Peter Huber, *robust*, *distribution-free*, and *nonparametrical* seem to be closely related properties but actually are not.[1] For example, the sample mean and the sample median are nonparametric estimates of the mean and the median but the mean is not robust to outliers. In fact, changes

---

[1] Huber's book is a standard reference on robust statistics: Peter J. Huber, *Robust Statistics* (New York: John Wiley & Sons, 1981). See also R. A. Maronna, R. D. Martin, and V. J. Yohai, *Robust Statistics: Theory and Methods* (Hoboken, NJ: John Wiley & Sons, 2006).

of one single observation might have unbounded effects on the mean, while the median is insensitive to changes of up to half the sample. Robust methods assume that there are indeed parameters in the distributions under study and attempt to minimize the effects of outliers as well as erroneous assumptions on the shape of the distribution.

A general definition of robustness is, by nature, quite technical. The reason is that we need to define robustness with respect to changes in distributions. That is, we need to make precise the concept that small changes in the distribution, which is a function, result in small changes in the estimate, which is a number. Therefore, we give only an intuitive, nontechnical overview of the modern concept of robustness and how to measure robustness.

QUALITATIVE AND QUANTITATIVE ROBUSTNESS

Let's begin by introducing the concepts of qualitative and quantitative robustness of estimators. Estimators are functions of the sample data. Given an N-sample of data $\mathbf{X} = (x_1, \ldots, x_N)'$ from a population with a cumulative distribution function (cdf) $F(x)$, depending on parameter θ_∞, an estimator for θ_∞ is a function of the data. Consider those estimators that can be written as functions of the empirical distribution defined as $F_N(x)$ = percentage of samples whose value is less than x.

For these estimators we can write

$$\hat{\vartheta} = \vartheta_N(F_N)$$

Most estimators can be written in this way with probability 1. In general, when $N \to \infty$ then $F_N(x) \to F(x)$ almost surely and $\hat{\vartheta}_N \to \vartheta_\infty$ in probability and almost surely. The estimator $\hat{\vartheta}_N$ is a random variable that depends on the sample. Under the distribution F, it will have a probability distribution $LF(\vartheta_N)$. Intuitively, statistics defined as functionals of a distribution are robust if they are continuous with respect to the distribution. This means that small changes in the statistics are associated with small changes in the cdf.

RESISTANT ESTIMATORS

An estimator is called *resistant* if it is insensitive to changes in one single observation.[2] Given an estimator $\hat{\vartheta} = \vartheta_N(F_N)$, we want to understand what happens if we add a new observation of value x to a large sample. To this

---

[2]For an application to the estimation of a stock's beta, see R. Douglas Martin and Timothy T. Simin, "Outlier Resistant Estimates of Beta," *Financial Analysts Journal* (September–October 2003): 56–58. We discuss this application in Chapter 8.

end we define the *influence curve* (IC), also called *influence function,* which measures the influence of a single observation x on a statistic ϑ for a given distribution F. In practice, the influence curve is generated by plotting the value of the computed statistic with a single point of X added to Y against that X value. For example, the *IC* of the mean is a straight line.

Several aspects of the influence curve are of particular interest:

- Is the curve "bounded" as the X-values become extreme? Robust statistics should be bounded. That is, a robust statistic should not be unduly influenced by a single extreme point.
- What is the general behavior as the X observation becomes extreme? For example, does it becomes smoothly down-weighted as the values become extreme?
- What is the influence if the X point is in the "center" of the Y points?

Let's now introduce concepts that are important in applied work, after which we introduce the robust estimators.

Breakdown Bound

The *breakdown* (BD) *bound* or *point* is the largest possible fraction of observations for which there is a bound on the change of the estimate when that fraction of the sample is altered without restrictions. For example, we can change up to 50% of the sample points without provoking unbounded changes of the median. On the contrary, changes of one single observation might have unbounded effects on the mean.

Rejection Point

The *rejection point* is defined as the point beyond which the IC becomes zero. Note that observations beyond the rejection point make no contribution to the final estimate except, possibly, through the auxiliary scale estimate. Estimators that have a finite rejection point are said to be redescending and are well protected against very large outliers. However, a finite rejection point usually results in the underestimation of scale. This is because when the samples near the tails of a distribution are ignored, an insufficient fraction of the observations may remain for the estimation process. This in turn adversely affects the efficiency of the estimator.

Gross Error Sensitivity

The *gross error sensitivity* expresses asymptotically the maximum effect that a contaminated observation can have on the estimator. It is the maximum absolute value of the IC.

Local Shift Sensitivity

The *local shift sensitivity* measures the effect of the removal of a mass at y and its reintroduction at x. For continuous and differentiable IC, the local shift sensitivity is given by the maximum absolute value of the slope of IC at any point.

Winsor's Principle

Winsor's principle states that all distributions are normal in the middle.

M-ESTIMATORS

M-estimators are those estimators that are obtained by minimizing a function of the sample data. As explained in Chapter 13, ordinary least squares estimators and maximum likelihood estimators are examples of *M*-estimators. Suppose that we are given an N-sample of data $X = (x_1, \ldots, x_N)'$. The estimator $T(x_1, \ldots, x_N)$ is called an M-estimator if it is obtained by

$$T = \mathrm{argmin}_t \left\{ J = \sum_{i=1}^{N} \rho(x_i, t) \right\}$$

where $\rho(x_i, t)$ is a function that depends on the estimator and "argmin_t" means to minimize the expression in the brackets with respect to the parameters t.

ML estimators are M-estimators with $\rho = -\log f$, where f is the probability density. (Actually, the name M-estimators means maximum likelihood-type estimators.) LS estimators are also M-estimators.

THE LEAST MEDIAN OF SQUARES ESTIMATOR

Instead of minimizing the sum of squared residuals, as in LS, to estimate the parameter vector, Rousseuw[3] proposed minimizing the median of squared residuals, referred to as the *least median of squares* (LMedS) *estimator*. This estimator effectively trims the $N/2$ observations having the largest residuals, and uses the maximal residual value in the remaining set as the criterion to be minimized. It is hence equivalent to *assuming* that the noise proportion is 50%.

---

[3] P. Rousseuw, "Least Median of Squares Regression," *Journal of the American Statistical Association* 79 (1984): 871–890.

LMedS is unwieldy from a computational point of view because of its nondifferentiable form. This means that a quasi-exhaustive search on all possible parameter values needs to be done to find the global minimum.

THE LEAST TRIMMED OF SQUARES ESTIMATOR

The *least trimmed of squares* (LTS) *estimator* offers an efficient way to find robust estimates by minimizing the objective function given by

$$\left\{ J = \sum_{i=1}^{h} r_{(i)}^2 \right\}$$

where $r_{(i)}^2$ is the ith smallest residual or distance when the residuals are ordered in ascending order, that is, $r_{(1)}^2 \leq r_{(2)}^2 \leq r_{(N)}^2$ and h is the number of data points the residuals of which we want to include in the sum. This estimator basically finds a robust estimate by identifying the $N - h$ points having the largest residuals as outliers, and discarding (trimming) them from the data set. The resulting estimates are essentially LS estimates of the trimmed data set. Note that h should be as close as possible to the number of points in the data set that we do not consider outliers.

ROBUST ESTIMATORS OF THE CENTER

The mean estimates the center of a distribution but it is not resistant. *Resistant estimators* of the center are the following:

- *Trimmed mean.* Suppose $x_{(1)} \leq x_{(2)} \leq \ldots \leq x_{(N)}$ are the sample order statistics (that is, the sample sorted). The trimmed mean $T_N(\delta, 1 - \gamma)$ is defined as follows:

$$T_N(\delta, 1 - \gamma) = \frac{1}{U_N - L_N} \sum_{j=L_N+1}^{U_N} x_j$$

$$\delta, \gamma \in (0, 0.5) \; L_N = \text{floor}[N\delta] \; U_N = \text{floor}[N\gamma]$$

- *Winsorized mean.* The Winsorized mean $\bar{X}_W$ is the mean of Winsorized data:

$$y_j = \begin{cases} x_{I_N+1} & j \leq L_N \\ x_j & L_N + 1 \leq j \leq U_N \\ x_j = x_{U_N+1} & j \geq U_N + 1 \end{cases}$$

$$\bar{X}_W = \bar{Y}$$

- *Median.* The median Med(X) is defined as that value that occupies a central position in sample order statistics:

$$\text{Med}(X) = \begin{cases} x_{((N+1)/2)} & \text{if } N \text{ is odd} \\ ((x_{(N/2)} + x_{(N/2+1)})/2) & \text{if } N \text{ is even} \end{cases}$$

ROBUST ESTIMATORS OF THE SPREAD

The variance is a classical estimator of the spread but it is not robust. Robust estimators of the spread are the following:

- *Median absolute deviation.* The median absolute deviation (MAD) is defined as the median of the absolute value of the difference between a variable and its median, that is,

$$\text{MAD} = \text{MED}|X - \text{MED}(X)|$$

- *Interquartile range.* The interquartile range (IQR) is defined as the difference between the highest and lowest quartile:

$$\text{IQR} = Q(0.75) - Q(0.25)$$

where $Q(0.75)$ and $Q(0.25)$ are the 75th and 25th percentiles of the data.

- *Mean absolute deviation.* The mean absolute deviation (MeanAD) is defined as follows:

$$\frac{1}{N} \sum_{j=1}^{N} |x_j - \text{MED}(X)|$$

- *Winsorized standard deviation.* The Winsorized standard deviation is the standard deviation of Winsorized data, that is,

$$\sigma_W = \frac{\sigma_N}{(U_N - L_N)/N}$$

ILLUSTRATION OF ROBUST STATISTICS

To illustrate the effect of robust statistics, consider the series of daily returns of Nippon Oil in the period 1986 through 2005 depicted in Figure F.1. If

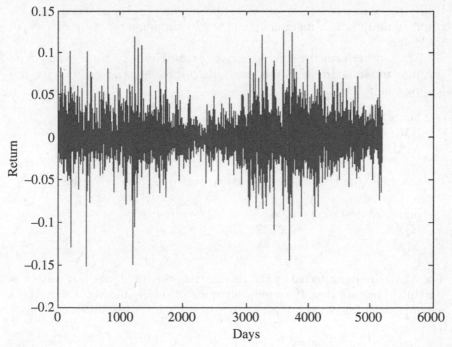

FIGURE F.1 Daily Returns Nippon Oil, 1986–2005

we compute the mean, the trimmed mean, and the median, we obtain the following results:

Mean $= 3.8396e{-}005$
Trimmed mean (20%)[4] $= -4.5636e{-}004$
Median $= 0$

In order to show the robustness properties of these estimators, let's multiply the 10% highest/lowest returns by 2. If we compute again the same quantities we obtain:

Mean $= 4.4756e{-}004$
Trimmed mean (20%) $= -4.4936e{-}004$
Median $= 0$

---

[4]Trimmed mean (20%) means that we exclude the 20%/2 = 10% highest and lowest observations.

While the mean is largely affected, the median is not affected and the trimmed mean is only marginally affected by doubling the value of 20% of the points.

We can perform the same exercise for measures of the spread. If we compute the standard deviation, the IQR, and the MAD, we obtain the following results:

    Standard deviation = 0.0229
    IQR   = 0.0237
    MAD   = 0.0164

Let's multiply the 10% highest/lowest returns by 2. The new values are:

    Standard deviation = 0.0415
    IQR   = 0.0237
    MAD   = 0.0248

The MAD are less affected by the change than the standard deviation while the IQR is not affected. If we multiply the 25% highest/lowest returns by 2 we obtain the following results:

    Standard deviation = 0.0450
    IQR   = 0.0237 (but suddenly changes if we add/subtract
                         one element)
    MAD   = 0.0299